Tom Dietz

# READINGS
## IN
## HUMAN
## POPULATION
## ECOLOGY

**Prentice-Hall**
**Biological Science Series**

*Carl P. Swanson, editor*

PRENTICE-HALL INTERNATIONAL, INC., *London*
PRENTICE-HALL OF AUSTRALIA, PTY. LTD., *Sydney*
PRENTICE-HALL OF CANADA, LTD., *Toronto*
PRENTICE-HALL OF INDIA PRIVATE LIMITED, *New Delhi*
PRENTICE-HALL OF JAPAN, INC., *Tokyo*

# READINGS
# IN
# HUMAN
# POPULATION
# ECOLOGY

WAYNE H. DAVIS
*University of Kentucky*

Editor

Prentice-Hall, Inc., Englewood Cliffs, New Jersey

Current printing (last digit):

10  9  8  7  6  5  4  3  2  1

P—13–757492–4
C—13–757500–9

Library of Congress Catalog Card Number 72–158837

Printed in the United States of America

# Contents

# SOCIAL PROBLEMS AND POPULATION GROWTH

# ECONOMICS AND POPULATION GROWTH

# IN SEARCH OF A SOLUTION

READINGS
IN
HUMAN
POPULATION
ECOLOGY

# Introduction

Man as a living creature is a part of nature with the requirements of food, water, oxygen, and a place to live. These needs he has in common with most of the other organisms which share his planet. As a large organism with a long life span, each man represents an enormous demand potential on the necessities of life. But in the affluent society of the United States, people demand much more than the necessities. The Rienows in their book *Moment in the Sun* say that in his lifetime the average American citizen will use 26,000,-000 gallons of water, 21,000 gallons of gasoline, 10,000 pounds of beef, and large quantities of other renewable and nonrenewable resources. He will produce enormous quantities of waste and make a demand upon society for services and increased physical facilities for schooling, health, housing, transportation, etc. He will also want a home and a piece of land in the suburbs. These demands face a finite land area which is being subdivided and covered with asphalt and ticky-tacky at a rate of 375 acres per day in California alone.

Although man is a rational being, it seems to be a natural characteristic for him to hesitate to believe facts which he finds unpleasant. Thus many smokers do not believe that cigarettes are harmful. Many people simply refuse to consider facts which would lead them to logical conclusions which are pessimistic. Nobody likes a pessimist. The tendency is to leave the problems to the politicians (that's their job) and to the scientists. But the politician, by the nature of his elective position, must present a façade of optimism. He must advance solutions, and they must be the kind of solutions the people want. The politician cannot change the basic thinking of the people.

The scientists are asked to provide technological solutions. In some cases they can, and in many others technology can help. But what today's students and tomorrow's leaders must realize is that for some of our most serious problems *there can be no technological solution*. For example, there can be no technical solution to the problem of an escalating arms race and, short of mass murder, there can be no technical solution to the human population problem. People want too many children. Because there is no technical solution is a major reason why such problems have not been solved.

This is not a pleasant book to read. It is blunt and realistic and paints a gloomy view of the likely future for mankind. Many scientists believe that we have already passed the point of no return and that man is an endangered species facing extinction. Perhaps this is so. This book was assembled in the hope that something can be done. The only hope is in education—making a large number of people aware of the urgency of our problems.

The younger the person, the more concerned he need be. Today's student cannot be apathetic. He hopes to survive on this planet longer than his teacher. He is sick and tired of the head-in-the-sand attitude of the older generation which has allowed the problems of human population and environmental degradation to develop unchallenged and even to be intentionally ignored (the Catholics and the job-providing industrialists would be offended, you know) until they threaten to overwhelm us.

The most relevant topics in biology are generally avoided in a college course because they are controversial. They are controversial because they are complex and sufficient data are not yet available upon which sound conclusions can be based. That is, they are not cut and dried. Most professors are hesitant when lecturing in their fields to give opinions which might be strongly disputed by other scientists. Thus they are more at ease describing cell division than the effects of pesticides on the ecosystem or of population growth upon our resources. Most professors will express opinions in personal discussions outside class, but hold closely to solid facts in the classroom. Perhaps this is as it should be.

But the controversial subjects are the dynamic ones, the most interesting to the students, and the most important to man today. In writing about these subjects, I and the other writers have taken stands with which many other people will disagree. We may be roundly condemned. The student may be shocked and angered at some things we have written. But he will also be provoked into thinking about modern environmental biology—about the most serious problems man has ever faced.

The problems presented in this book are not new. They have been treated extensively by many writers at various times in recent history. The first edition of Thomas Malthus' *Essay on the Principle of Population* appeared in 1798. In this and several later editions he developed the thesis that uncontrolled population growth in a finite world must lead to scarcity of natural resources, stifling of economic growth, and famine and misery among mankind. Unfortunately, however, Malthus' failure to foresee the industrial and agricultural revolutions, which brought increased affluence, caused many to ignore or ridicule his essentially sound thesis.

In 1865 *Man and Nature* by George Perkins Marsh appeared. This scholarly 500-page book described the destructive effects produced by man upon the earth and warned of the dire consequences of uncontrolled human behavior and population growth. It was highly influential for about 50 years and was probably in large part responsible for the development of the conservation movement in the United States under Theodore Roosevelt and Gifford Pinchot.

In 1948 the problems were treated once again, this time by William Vogt in *Road to Survival* and Fairfield Osborn in *Our Plundered Planet*. Although reviewers pleaded that these books had an important message that we should heed, they were nearly ignored by the American people for 20 years while we floated carefree upon a rapidly expanding economy carrying us to ever higher levels of temporary affluence. Now that the chickens are arriving at the roost, there has been a resurgence of interest in these books and a tremendous increase in the recent literature in the field. The present volume is a collection of the latter.

In making selections a special effort was made to present all sides of a controversial matter. Therefore the student should not be surprised to see that some authors directly contradict one another. I expect this to stimulate class discussion and encourage the student to investigate the subject further.

*Tom Dietz*

# THE PROBLEM

# The Population Crisis Is Here *Now*

## Walter E. Howard

The author is a professor of wildlife biology in the Department of Animal Physiology and a vertebrate ecologist in the Experiment Station, University of California, Davis.

### Preface

At the present world rate of population growth of 2% per year, a mere dozen people a thousand years ago could have produced the present world population, and in another thousand years each one of us could have 300 million living descendants. Obviously, that cannot be—something must be done. Either the birth rate must be significantly curtailed or the death rate drastically increased.

The world's overpopulation crisis is of a magnitude beyond human comprehension, yet the government and the public remain seemingly indifferent. Better awareness and a more forthright leadership are obviously needed, from biologists and politicians alike. Will you help? A vastly increased rate of involuntary premature deaths can be prevented only by an informed public, here and abroad, following dynamic leadership. No population can continue to increase indefinitely, no matter how much food there is. If civilization is to be viable, we must end the arrogant assumption that there are unlimited resources and infinite air and water. People must develop much greater voluntary restraint in reproduction—or conception itself will have to come under government control.

This earth does not have the resources necessary to provide even the present world population with the degree of affluence that the middle-class citizen enjoys. Even though the average birth rate in the United States has declined during the past decade from about seven children per family to fewer than three, the population density has been growing much more rapidly than before. The reason is the high population base level; there are now so many more women that their "small" families add a greater number of new people to the population each year than did their grandmothers, even with much larger families.

No population can continue to grow beyond certain limits; eventually, involuntary self-limitation—in the form of premature deaths from starvation, pestilence, and wars—will prevent any further increase in density. Since all finite space is limited, it is an indisputable fact that birth rates and death rates must someday be balanced. Already the rich are devouring the poor—the survival of the fittest.

### Introduction

The intent of this article is not to alarm the reader unnecessarily. But how is that possible? Alarm is called for; man should be alarmed. Man must be aware of his dilemma, for if he attempts to feed the world without effective control of the birth rate, he actually is only deferring the starvation of an even greater number of people to a later date.

The world is facing this acute overpopulation situation specifically because of advances in agriculture and health, through science and technology, and a lack of similar progress in the field of sensible birth control. Families are not having more babies, it is just that more now survive.

Passion between the sexes must, of course, remain a basic human right, but it cannot include the having of children at will. While intercourse remains an individual and private matter, procreation must become of public concern. Conception should not be a euphemism for sexual relations. The obvious goal for all societies wishing an abundant life and freedom from want should be a low-birth-rate, low-death-rate culture. Man's responsibility to the next generation includes a primary duty of limiting the size of that generation.

Our problem is uncontrolled human fertility—not underproduction and maldistribution—and corrective action is being dangerously delayed by wishful thinking that some miracle will solve the problem. There is a prodigious need for immediate public awareness of the current critical situation, since overpopulation is intimately involved with political, economic, and sociological problems—in fact, with everyone's peace, security, and general well-being. All of the world's desperate needs—ample food, permanent peace, good health, and high-quality living—are unattainable for all human beings both now and in the foreseeable future for one obvious reason: there are too many people. A soaring population means a shrinking of man's space on this earth.

Not only is population growth the most basic conservation problem of today, but its dominating influence will affect the ultimate survival of mankind. Man can no longer be indifferent to this basic population problem. Its severity behooves all to act now. Hunger and overpopulation will not go away if we do not discuss them, and the bringing of too many babies into this world is not just someone else's problem; it is everyone's concern. The destiny of overpopulation is erosion of civilized life.

### The World's Population

To appreciate the recent rapidity with which the world's population has grown—it took from the beginning of man until 1850 to reach a population of one billion people, only 80 years more (1930) to reach two billion, then only 30 years (1960) to reach the three billion mark, and in less than 15 years after 1960 we expect four billion. In the next 25 years after that, the population is expected to increase by another three and one-half billion people. If there have been about 77 billion births since the Stone Age, then about 1 out of every 22 persons born since then is alive today; but in only 30 or 40 years from now, if current rates of increase continue, 1 out of every 10 people ever born will be living at that time. The youth of today might see the United States with a population equal to what India has now.

Only a small proportion of the world's population has made the demographic

Reprinted by permission of the author and the publisher from *BioScience* 19:779–784, September 1969.

transition of attaining both a lower fertility and a lower mortality; most have decreased only the premature death rate. The population has continued to increase rapidly because reductions in fertility have not been sufficient to offset the effects of current reductions in mortality produced by technological sanitation, disease control, and pesticide use.

The reproductive potential of the world is grim, for 40 to 45% of the people alive today are under 15 years old. How can this tremendous number of babies soon be fed solid foods? And look how soon those who survive will be breeding.

Even though technology exists that could manufacture enough intrauterine devices for every woman, the problems of distribution and the shortage of doctors make it impossible for the devices to be inserted fast enough to control the world's population growth. Within a few years the number of people dying each year from causes related to poor nutrition will equal what is now the entire population of the United States.

In the United States if the fertility and mortality trends of 1950-60 should be re-established, replacing the 1968 low birth rate, in only 150 years our country alone could exceed the current world population of over 3.3 billion, and in 650 years there would be about one person per square foot. This will not happen, of course, because either the birth rate will decline, or more likely, the death rate will increase.

### Rate of Population Increase

The basic factor is the difference between birth and death rates, not what the levels of births and deaths happen to be. Continued doubling of a population soon leads to astronomical numbers. If the world population increase continued at the low rate of only 2%, the weight of human bodies would equal the weight of the earth in about 1500 years.

The world population is reported to be currently growing by 180,000 a day, more than a million a week, or about 65 million a year, and each year it increases in greater amounts. If current trends continue, the population will reach about 25 billion in only 100 years.

Prior to Christ, it took about 40,000 years to double the population, but the current growth rate of about 2% would require only 35 years to double the present population. Populations that grow by 3% per year double within a genera-

tion and increase eighteen-fold in 100 years.

### Population Dynamics

If 90% of a population survives long enough to reproduce, an average of 2.3 children per family will keep the population stable. Only a very slight increase to 2.5 children would produce an increase of 10% per generation, and 3.0 children per family would cause an increase of 31% per generation. If child-bearing families averaged 3.0 children, about one woman in four would need to be childless for the population to remain stable.

A sustained geometric increase in human beings is, of course, impossible; once the population's base level of density is high, as it now is, birth rates cannot continue much above the death rates for long without a truly impossible density being produced. As the base population density rises, even a lower birth rate can still mean that there will be a greater absolute increase in total numbers than was occurring before, when population was less and birth rates were higher.

Obviously, if input (natality) continues to exceed outgo (mortality), any finite space must eventually fill up and overflow. Populations increase geometrically, whereas food and subsistence increase arithmetically. The geometric ratio of population growth is also known as the ever-accelerating growth rate, the logistic curve, the well-known S-shaped or sigmoid growth curve, and compound interest.

When populations of people are exposed to stressing pressures, including those due to overpopulation, they may respond in a strange way of breeding earlier and more prolifically, further aggravating the situation. The principal way in which man differs from other animals is in his intellect, his ability to read and communicate, to learn, to use tools, and his society; and he also differs from other species in that he attempts to protect the unfit and all "surplus" births.

### Predisposition to Overpopulate

Nature has seen to it that all organisms are obsessed with a breeding urge and provided with the biological capacity to overproduce, thereby ensuring survival of the species. Since man now exercises considerable control over so many of the natural factors which once controlled his population, he must also learn to control his innate trait to reproduce excessively.

It is not a question of whether this earth has the resources for feeding a much greater population than is now present—of course, it has. The point is that the human population is now growing too fast for food production ever to catch up without stringent birth control.

### Carrying Capacity and Self-Limitation

No matter how far science and technology raise the carrying capacity of the earth for people, involuntary self-limiting forces will continue to determine man's upper population density. Surplus populations do not just quietly fade away—quite the contrary. Before surplus individuals die, they consume resources and contribute in general to other population stresses, all of which make the environment less suitable, thus lowering its carrying capacity. Man needs space to live as much as do plants and animals.

The balance of nature is governed primarily by the suitability of the habitat and species-specific self-limitation, where members of each species involuntarily prevent any further increase in their kind. This self-limitation consists of undesirable stresses which cause individual births in a family to be unwanted or cause a compensating increase in death rates. Members of the population become their own worst enemy in the sense that they are responsible for the increased rates of mortality and, perhaps, also some reduction in natality.

Nearly all organisms that are well-adapted to their environment have built-in mechanisms for checking population growth before the necessary food and cover are permanently destroyed. But nature's population control processes are unemotional, impartial, and truly ruthless, a set of conditions that educated men will surely wish to avoid.

Instead of man learning how to conquer nature, he may annihilate it, destroying himself in the process. In current times at least, there is no hope that man as a species will voluntarily limit his birth rate to the low level (zero or even minus replacement) that the overall population must have. Also, unfortunately, when a population level is below carrying capacity the innate desire to have larger families then becomes very strong, making human husbandry difficult to practice.

Nature does not practice good husbandry—all its components are predisposed to overpopulate and, in fact, attempt to do so, thus causing a high rate of premature deaths. If food supply alone were the principal factor limiting the number of people, man would long ago have increased to a density where all of the food would have been consumed and he would have become an extinct species.

When other organisms follow a population growth curve similar to what man is currently experiencing—and they do this only in disturbed (usually man-modified) environments—they can then become so destructive to their habitat that the subsequent carrying capacity may be dramatically reduced if not completely destroyed, thus causing not only mass individual suffering and a high rate of premature deaths but also a permanent destruction of the ecosystem.

Whenever man's population density has been markedly reduced through some catastrophe, or his technology has appreciably increased the carrying capacity of his habitat (environment), the growth rate of his population increases. The population then tends to overcompensate, temporarily growing beyond the upper limits of the carrying capacity of the environment. The excess growth is eventually checked, however, by the interaction of a number of different kinds of self-limiting population stress factors. These include such forces as inadequate food and shelter, social stress factors, competition for space, wars, an increase in pestilence, or any of many other subtle vicissitudes of life that either increase the death rate, reduce successful births, or cause individuals to move elsewhere. Unfortunately, in the developed countries, science and technology are developing at an exponential rate, so the population growth may not again be sufficiently halted by self-limitation until the earth's resources are largely exploited or a world famine or other drastic mortality factor appears.

Although nature practices survival of the fittest, man believes that all who are born should be given every opportunity to live to an old age. If this is to be our objective, and I am sure it will, then we have only one other alternative, i.e., to restrict the number of births. And to accomplish this, it seems better to reduce conception rather than to rely on abortions. Abortions are a solution, however, when other means of preventing conceptions have broken down. Surprising to most people, abortions induced by a doctor are safer than childbearing.

There is a need too for man to establish a stable relationship with the environment. Man must recognize that he also

responds to many, in fact, most of the laws of nature. And his population checks are largely famine, pestilence, and war. Man has transferred himself from being just a member of the ecosystem to a dominant position, where he now mistakenly assumes that the ecosystem is his to control at will. He forgets that he is part of nature. To see his true place in the world he must not attempt to transcend too much over nature, but to discover and assimilate all he can about the truth of nature and his own role in nature.

Only self-limitation can stem the population tide, and the only voice man has in the matter is whether it will be done involuntarily by nature's undesirable stresses, as witnessed by the history of civilization, or will be done consciously by not allowing his kind to exceed an optimum carrying capacity.

## Socio-Economic Situations

It is incongruous that student unrest is so great and race problems so much in the front, yet almost everyone seems unaware that the basic cause of most of these socio-economic stresses is overpopulation, about which almost nothing is said by all of these energetic and sometimes vociferous groups. The daily economic pressures of individuals attempting to provide a decent civilization, especially for themselves, may lead to the ultimate destruction of all ecosystems. Surplus individuals do not quietly fade away.

In spite of man's power of conscious thought, the only species so endowed, he seldom thinks beyond his lifetime or his own family's particular needs. The great desire of most people to provide their children and themselves with all of today's advantages is an important factor in reducing family size. That is not enough, however, for these families are still raising the population level.

At the same time that the world's population is increasing, both the number and the percentage of the "have-nots" increase and, in addition, the gap widens between the "haves" and "have-nots." As tragic as it may sound, when an underdeveloped country's population density is growing rapidly, both health and agricultural aid from the United States may not only be wasted but may severely aggravate the already deplorable social and economic situation in that country.

In industrially developed countries, middle-class couples often have fewer children than they would like (if they only

had more money, domestic help, etc.), whereas in underdeveloped countries and ghettos the reverse is too frequently true. High birth rates tend to nullify national efforts to raise average per capita income since there is less money for savings and developmental investments. Neither families nor a nation can escape when life is held close to the margin of subsistence.

Overpopulation inevitably commits too many people to poverty and despair. With perpetual pregnancies the bonds of welfare become inescapable, for unskilled parents cannot feed a large family from the wages they can earn. No matter how you look at it, families of more than two or three children intensify the problem of national development, and this happens whether the parents are poor, middle class, or wealthy.

A complete reorientation of social values and attitudes regarding births is urgently needed now. We need new baby ethics, an awareness of the tragedies associated with too many babies. Bringing births and deaths into balance will demand great social, economic, and political changes.

With reference to our affluence, we cannot turn back—if for no other reason than the fact that there are now too many people to permit going back—to a less materialistic existence without cars, pesticides, diesel exhaust, sewage and garbage disposal, etc. The stork has passed the plow. Food prices in developing nations are rising faster than the purchasing power.

## Economic Interests

Man seems to be governed by economic self-interest. Societies become conditioned to the tenets of the economists—that money can buy anything. Without the basic resources there can be no wealth and affluence; but, unfortunately, the exploitation of resources seems to be considered the very foundation of all "progress."

"Progress" is the magic word. It means to increase property values and returns on one's investment; it is the deity of modern civilization. Yet, do any of us really know what we are progressing toward? Too often, the chamber-of-commerce form of "progress" is the next man's destruction.

Man seems to be more concerned with the quality of his goals than with the quantity of his goods. The more slowly a population increases the more rapid is the growth of both its gross and per capita income.

The harmful consequences of overpopulation are blindly overlooked by those who favor an expanding population for reasons of military strength, economic progress, scientific and agricultural development, and eugenics.

Man's economic dreams, his selfishness, and his materialism interfere with his awareness of the fate of the unborn. He is too busy in the United States in covering two acres per minute with houses, factories, and stores. His highways are now equivalent to paving the entire state of Indiana. Every day, California loses 300 acres of agricultural land.

Unfortunately, little planning has been done on how the socio-economic problems can be handled once the population growth is stopped. If the rush of today's living and industrial development or defense spending just slows down, a painful recession is upon us. We have no government study on how the nation could exist without a growing population.

### Resource Management

Insidious economic pressures seem to prevent any effective management of resources in a manner that would provide for their utilization in perpetuity. Concrete and pavement surely are not the epitome of the human species' fulfillment. An ecological appreciation of resource management is needed, and ecological ethics must replace ecological atrocities.

Man is rapidly depleting the nonreplenishable resources. Half of the energy used by man during the past 2000 years was used in the last century. Man is reported to have mined more in the past 100 years than during all previous time. But, every barrel has a bottom; unbridled technology promises to speed us faster toward that bottom. Our planet's resources diminish faster as society's affluence is increased. Our qualitative sense of appreciation of our environment seems to be replaced by mere quantitative values. Why cannot civilization fulfill its obligation of being a competent steward of all resources?

It is inevitable that the limited legacy of natural resources must steadily yield in the face of the current explosion in the world population. As the population swells, open spaces are inundated by a flood of housing, and resources shrink faster. The United States and other developed nations are consuming a disproportionately large share of the world's

nonrenewable and other resources at an ever-accelerating rate, perhaps 20 to 30 times as much on a per capita basis as are individuals in undeveloped countries. In 1954, the United States was reported to be using about 50% of the raw-material resources consumed in the world each year, and by 1980 it might be 80%. But we do not have an endless earth of boundless bounty. Any finite resource is subject to eventual exhaustion.

### Effect of Science and Technology

The world may have sufficient resources, but it has never provided enough food and other necessities of life for all people at any one time. As technology improved, enabling better utilization of resources, the population similarly increased, so that there have always been many who died prematurely, as Malthus predicted.

No one anticipated the scope and rapidity of the technological changes that have occurred in Western society. About one-third of the people now consume about two-thirds of the world's food production, while the other two-thirds go undernourished. But, unfortunately, these starving people reproduce at a high rate. As individual aspirations rise and per capita resources fall, the widening gap between the haves and the have-nots could well generate some serious social and political pressures.

In recent times spectacular gains have been made in controlling mass killers such as typhus, malaria, yellow fever, small pox, cholera, plague, and influenza; but no corresponding checks have been made on birth rates. It is ironic that the root of our overpopulation problem is technical advances brought about by our increasing intellect (the knowledge explosion of the last hundred years).

Technology can produce almost anything, but only at the usually recognized high price of resource consumption and waste accumulation. As our technology advances, the amount of resources utilized per person also increases, and the supply is not endless.

Technology and science can and do progress at an ever-increasing rate, but can social, political, and religious views change rapidly enough to cope with this "progress"? The fruits of all our scientific and technological advances will be ephemeral if the world's population continues to explode. Our intelligence is so powerful that it may destroy us because we lack the wisdom and insight to recog-

nize and correct what we are doing to ourselves and, especially, to future generations. We are passing on an enormous population problem to the next generation.

### Pollution and Waste Disposal

Affluent societies have also been labeled "effluent" societies. That man is a highly adaptable species that can live in polluted environments, in extremely crowded conditions, in situations of acute malnutrition, and in some of the most depressing of environments is well exemplified today. But why should he? And how much lower can he sink and still survive as a "successful" species?

Mushrooming with the population are pollution and litter. We produce 70% of the world's solid wastes but have only 10% of the world's population. There is a need to make the reuse and disposal of rubbish more economical.

### Popular Solutions and Misconceptions

Hopeful but inadequate panaceas include synthetic foods (proteins and vitamins), hydroponics, desalinization of seawater, food from the ocean, more agricultural research, fertilizers, irrigation, the vast unused lands, land reforms, government regulation, price support, migrations, redistribution of food and wealth, and private enterprise.

Science and technology may find a way to produce more food and to accommodate more people, but in the end this, of course, will only make matters that much worse if birth control is not effective. It should be obvious that the only solution is a drastically reduced birth rate or a greatly increased death rate. The one inescapable fact about a country's population—about the world's population—is that the death rate must someday equal the birth rate, regardless of how plentiful food may be.

Unfortunately, a basic American philosophy is the belief that our free-enterprise system can produce anything that is necessary, a false cornucopian faith that our population growth is not a real threat. Our overpopulation-underdevelopment dilemma is not a matter of increasing production to meet the demand for more food; rather, the only solution is to limit demand for food so that production may someday catch up to the population's needs.

## Role of Family Planning

There is no question that family planning has made great progress. But today's society and religious groups must recognize the urgency for adopting the pill, IUD, other chemical and mechanical devices (both undependable), sterilization, abortion—in fact, any means of limiting childbirth. The promotion of some form of effective means of artificial birth control is the only moral, human, and political approach available to prevent the misery and suffering which will result if people are permitted to have as many "planned" children as they want.

Despite the great benefits of family planning programs, especially the benefits to the families concerned, family planning is not a euphemism for birth control. We need to develop a social and cultural philosophy that even a family of three children is too large and to overcome the fear of some ethic and religious sects that other groups may multiply faster, becoming more dominant. Family planning per se has little relevance to the underdeveloped countries of the world or to poverty groups in the more advanced countries. Therefore anything other than government control of conception may be self-defeating.

## Sexual Desire and Love of Children

The basic conflict with the overpopulation problem is that of desires—actually drives—and the fact that most young women are fecund; without either the strong drives or the ability of women to conceive, there would be no problem. As with all organisms, man's potential fecundity and predisposition to overproduce are the basic causes for his excess fertility over deaths. Most babies are the consequence of passion, not love. But children are loved.

Motherhood must become a less significant role for women. We must forego some of our love for children and learn to be content with fewer numbers. What is needed in the way of governmental control of births is not control of an individual's behavior but control of the consequence of such behavior, the prevention of intemperate breeding.

There is no question that children make family ties more intimate, but man has already done too well toward "fathering" the country. Compassionate relations between spouses, not the having of children, must become the primary goal of marriages in the future. There is no need to

find drugs that destroy sexual desire; the objective is to control the conception rate, not frequency of intercourse.

## Is Having Children a Basic Right?

One price that society must be willing to pay for sustained world peace is a stringent universal birth-control program, which will require revolutionary revisions of modes of thought about our basic human rights with regard to family planning.

The increasing disparity between population density and food supply, by itself, justifies effective birth control regardless of the "morality" associated with depriving parents of the right to have as many planned children as they choose.

Having too many children can no longer be dismissed as an act of God, for it is now truly the consequence of a complacent society that is unwilling to take any of many steps available for preventing surplus births. Our primitive reproductive instincts cannot be condoned in the the face of modern survival rates. The two are no longer in balance.

To say that the opportunity to decide the number and spacing of children is a basic human right is to say that man may do whatever he wants with nature without thought of its inevitable consequence to future generations. Our legal and ethical right should be to have only enough children to replace ourselves.

No longer can we consider procreation an individual and private matter. Intercourse, yes, but not unregulated numbers of conceptions since they affect the welfare of all other individuals living at that time plus those to be born in the future.

## Religious Complications

It needs to be said over and over again that the bringing of surplus children into this world, whether from personal desire or from religious edicts, destines not only some of these children but many others to a premature death. Overproduction actually lowers the maximum density that can be sustained for normal life spans, thereby increasing the number of souls in need of salvation.

The "morality" of birth control in today's burgeoning human population has taken on an entirely new aspect. God clearly never meant for man to overpopulate this earth to the point where he would destroy many other forms of life and perhaps even himself. The religious doctrines we lean on today were estab-

lished before science and technology had dramatically raised the carrying capacity for man.

The question of complete abstinence as the only acceptable means of family regulation is as ludicrous as compulsory euthanasia. The mortal sin, if there is one, in God's eyes surely would be associated with those who do *not* practice birth control, for to let babies come "as they naturally do" will prove to be a form of murder—through starvation, pestilence, and wars resulting from excess babies. It must be recognized that the number of children can no longer be left to "the will of God" or to our own desires and family plans, and if population controls are to be successful, they may have to be determined by government regulations.

Religious views that do not condone rigorous birth control must realize that every surplus birth their philosophy promotes will guarantee, on the average, a horrible death some day to more than one individual.

Although the Christian attitude implies that everything on this earth was created for man's use, in reality man is inescapably also part of nature.

Some form of compulsory control of birth rates is essential, although I see no reason why various religious groups cannot be permitted to achieve birth limitations in whatever manner they choose. If a woman or a couple exceeds the limit set by society, however, then they must be dealt with by law compelling them to be sterilized, to have an abortion, or by some other repayment to society.

Birth control is not murder, as some claim, but lack of it in today's overpopulated world most surely will be. For those who strongly oppose the setting of any limit on the number of children a family can have, I ask them to tell the rest of us just how they think the premature death rate should be increased to offset their extra births.

## Wealth vs. Number of Children

Civilization can no longer endure a way of life in which people believe they have the right to have as many children as they can afford. This is hypocritical, for those who can "afford" luxurious living are already utilizing many times their share of the limited food and other resources, and also they are contributing much more pollution to the environment than are the have-nots. The affluent population needs to be made aware of the overpopulation problems, for they often desire to have more children per family than those who are in poverty.

Too much of today's religious climate makes birth control a politically sensitive area, thus constraining public officials. But, as citizens, are we not justified in asking why our governmental officials have not done more to make us aware of the urgency of population control—political sensitivities notwithstanding?

Governments should be guiding the development of a better life and world to live in, but if it does not recognize the need for human husbandry, then it will be fostering the ultimate destruction of the earth rather than the goals it seeks.

Man, in spite of his intellect, is so concerned with the present that he too often turns a deaf ear to alarming sounds of the future. Another difficulty in stabilizing the population is that our standard of living and our economy cannot survive in a static state.

### Limiting Size of Families

We can no longer be prophets and philosophers; we must act. The biomagnification of births must be brought to an abrupt halt. Procreation must come under governmental control if no other way can be found. Perhaps what is needed is a system of permits for the privilege of conceiving, or compulsory vasectomies of all men and sterilization of all women who have been responsible for two births.

Since the taboo against birth control is inviolable to some, regardless of the dire consequences of overpopulation, laws must be passed to regulate conceptions and births. Each individual needs to have the right to produce or adopt only a replacement for himself or herself.

The general public must be made to realize that from now on, for a married couple to have more than two children or three at most, is a very socially irresponsible act. We must advocate small families. When business is good and living has quality, marriages will naturally tend to be earlier and births more numerous; therefore, only through the development of new nonfamilial rewards can later marriages be made to appear attractive to people. Taxes now subsidize children, whereas we should be taxed for the privilege of having children.

A rising age at marriage is an effective way of reducing births, and, sociologically and economically, it gives women more time to become better educated, acquire nonfamily sorts of interests, and develop greater cautions toward pregnancy.

Up to now, only death has been of public concern; procreation has remained an individual and highly cherished private matter. But this privilege cannot continue, and regulation of the number of conceptions, or at least births, must also become a government function.

### Population Control or Premature Deaths

Man must decide whether the future growth of populations will be governed by famine, pestilence, and war, on whether he will use his intellect to control birth rates artificially. If the population growth is not controlled by lower birth rates, hundreds of millions of people must soon die prematurely each year.

Man must use his intellect to counteract his excessive fertility, for all species have been endowed by nature to be overfecund. If he does not, the extra individuals will be eliminated by the natural process of "struggle for existence—survival of the fittest," which causes all surplus individuals to die prematurely as a result of nature's ruthless laws of involuntary "self-limitation" whenever the carrying capacity has been exceeded. That territoriality and aggression are life-preserving functions of the social order of animals is frightening when man applies these same principles to his own species.

There have always been hungry people in the world, but both the total number of individuals and the percentage of the total population that are destined to go hungry in the future will be dramatically increased if birth rates are not drastically checked. Many like to think that nature will somehow take care of things. They fail to remember how nature has taken care of many species that were no longer adaptable to existence on this earth—they are now preserved as fossils.

Modern public-health methods and medical technology have lessened the chronic hunger, general economic misery, and other vicissitudes that once caused high mortality rates. But, sooner or later, any increase in births over deaths will be balanced by an increase in the rate of premature deaths.

### Human Husbandry and Quality Living

Human husbandry implies that we regulate the population density before the natural self-limiting demographic and societal stress factors do it for us. But human motivation will always work against good human husbandry, because to each individual who has quality living, a large family will seem desirable.

The population of the world is so great that what used to be a ripple when it doubled now means catastrophic effects because of the great numbers involved and the lack of this earth's ability to support them. Man is not practicing good husbandy when he lets his population density expand beyond the carrying capacity.

The most important thesis regarding the need for human husbandry is that human beings will not voluntarily restrict their number of children to just two when economic, social, and political conditions appear to be personally favorable. A quality society with quality existence is now unattainable in many parts of the world, and may soon be unattainable any place in the world. The "economic" struggle of overpopulation is the world's greatest threat to quality living, enriched leisure, and even man's ultimate existence.

### Conclusion

The ultimate goal must be a zero population growth. To achieve "quality living" instead of nature's "survival of the fittest," as has persisted throughout the history of mankind, the birth rate must not continue to exceed the death rate. If the birth rate of nations and the world are not greatly reduced, an ever-increasing amount of starvation and other types of premature deaths are inevitable. There is a prodigious need for mankind to practice human husbandry (Human Husbandry, a guest editorial in *BioScience*, **18**: 372-373, 1968, by Walter E. Howard).

A conscientious regulation of fertility is needed, or a calamitous rise in premature mortality rates is inevitable. Without this tremendous voluntary restraint or the development of a strong social stigma against bearing more than two or three children, the rate of conceptions must come under some form of governmental control. It can no longer be a basic human right to have as many children as one wants, especially if such action dooms others to a premature death.

Even though the above picture is bleak, the world is not going to come to an end. In fact, none of the people who read this article are going to starve, but their very existence is going to cause others who are less well off to perish. As overpopulation becomes worse, the percentage of the people who will fall into this nonsurviving unfit category must obviously increase. If babies of the future are to live, there must be fewer of them now.

# PREVALENCE OF PEOPLE*

ROY O. GREEP†

It is a principle of nature that no species can multiply indefinitely without hindrance, and *Homo sapiens* is on a collision course with disaster.

That man is becoming more numerous is common knowledge. Population pressure is felt in many aspects of our daily lives. We feel it in morning traffic, in housing, in pollution of our air and water, in the destruction of natural beauty, and in the gradual erosion of individual freedom and loss of privacy. From the air, likewise, one sees the ugly, cancerous growth of urban sprawl with metastases extending into fresh cuts of the bulldozer.

Our large metropolitan areas are overcrowded and rotting at the core with festering slums and ghettos. Yet, population growth is one of the most ignored of the major problems facing the peoples of the world, including the United States, today. We may occasionally glance at an article in the Sunday paper about the population explosion and what the future has in store. The figures are astronomical, impersonal, and not readily translated into reality. Never before in all the vast range of man's history have excessive numbers been a serious threat to his species. In earlier days when the famous Four Horsemen of the Apocalypse—war, pestilence, famine, and death—strode the land, man was not troubled by an undue increase in numbers. Unhappily, the prospects, even for our time, are beyond the powers of the imagination to conceive.

Man is a creature of nature, and nature has her own harsh system of keeping the population of animal species in check. Most wild species are held in check by food supply, disease, and predation, and also, as recently discovered, by loss of fertility when overcrowding occurs. Some species, such as the jackrabbit, muskrat, deer, and lemming, go through cyclic changes in population density. They die off in great numbers at regular

* This is a modified version of a paper which appeared in the *Harvard Alumni Bulletin*. Publication costs were kindly contributed to *Perspectives* by E. R Squibb & Sons.

† Department of Anatomy, Harvard Medical School, 25 Shattuck Street, Boston, Massachusetts 02115.

intervals and then proceed to replenish their stock. Lemmings relieve their population pressure every four years, and, contrary to popular belief, they do not migrate to the sea but simply move into an unfavorable climate and die. These population crashes are now known to be due to the psycho-physiological trauma of overcrowding—sometimes referred to as "pathological togetherness."

Not only is the present pace of human population growth unprecedented, but, more alarmingly, it is accelerating. In order to get a better appreciation of what is afoot, it will be helpful to glance quickly at how the human species has faired in absolute numbers over the long reaches of history. At the beginning of the Christian era, or some 10,000 years from the dawn of human civilization, man had reached a total population of 250,000,000; 1,500 years later he had only reached the half-billion mark. But from there on he has been doing better. He made it to 1 billion in 1840, 2 billion in 1930, and 3 billion in 1961. We are now working on the fourth billion at the rate of 70,000,000 per year, or a city of 190,000 persons every day, seven days a week. The early figures are informed estimates and may be off by a considerable margin, but that makes little difference. The important point is that for the modern era—or from about 1800, when census taking became a common practice—the figures involve very little, if any, guesswork as to what has been happening.

There are two favorite means of measuring the rate of population growth and of determining trends: one is by the *annual percentage increase*, and the other is by the number of years required for a *doubling* of the population. They are, of course, related. The annual percentage increase expresses the difference between the number of births and the number of deaths. For example, if the birth rate were thirty-five per thousand and the death rate twenty-five, then the difference is ten per thousand or, as generally expressed, 1 per cent annual increase. At a yearly growth rate of 1 per cent it will take not 100 years to double the population but seventy years, because population grows by the principle of compound interest (i.e., each year the base is increased). The number of years that it will take to double the population at any given annual rate of increase can be had by simply dividing the annual rate into seventy—with a growth rate of 2 per cent the population will double in approximately thirty-five years. It has been truthfully said that man and his money each breeds its own kind, and they happen to do so by the same mathematical principles.

The *annual rate of increase* in the 1920's and 1930's was 1.1 per cent. It began to climb after World War II, reaching 2 per cent in 1963, and will almost certainly continue to climb for some time because the most populated areas are expanding at rates of 2.5–3.5 per cent. Glancing now at the *doubling rate* and starting at the beginning of the Christian era, the first doubling took 1,650 years; the second, 200 years; the third, 90 years; and the one now in the making may not take more than 35 years. The world population stands now at 3.3 billion and is virtually certain to reach 6–7 billion by the end of this century. The tragic and sobering fact is that 85 per cent of this growth will take place in the underdeveloped and over-populated areas of the world. Growth of the human population is determined not by absolute birth rate or absolute death rate but by the existing relation of one to the other. When the rate of population growth was very slow, the birth rates and death rates were nearly equal, and both were stabilized around thirty-five to forty per thousand. Birth rates and death rates began to separate around 1800, due in part to the gradual decline in death rates brought about by mass vaccination, better food distribution, improved sanitation, and cultural changes accompanying the industrial revolution. Later came the golden age of medical science, with its inoculations, sulfa drugs, antibiotics, insecticides, pesticides, hormones, and wonder drugs. These, along with food aid programs, brought a further dramatic fall in the death rate, reaching levels of fifteen to twenty in the less developed countries and ten or below in the more advanced countries. Much later the birth rate was also to decline somewhat in advanced areas, but not nearly so dramatically as the death rates. The situation now is that the advanced, industrial nations have death rates of around ten and birth rates of fifteen to twenty, whereas the low-income areas of Asia, Africa, and Latin America have death rates of fifteen to twenty but unchanged birth rates of forty to forty-five.

In a nutshell, the reason for the present unprecedented increase in population growth is the introduction of death control without birth control. In the emerging nations it is now possible to cut the death rate in half within a period of five to ten years but with no reduction or even an increase in the birth rate. The result of these changes is that the advanced countries constituting one-third of the world's population are growing at a modest rate, whereas the less developed and heavily populated areas of the world are showing fantastic population increments.

It is commonly assumed that death control means more old people, and to a minor degree it does. But the predominant effect on the age structure of society is to expand the younger age groups. That portion of the population under fifteen years of age is usually about 20–25 per cent in advanced countries, whereas the figure is 40–45 per cent in areas of rapid population growth. Under the latter circumstances, the dependency burden on the productive age groups becomes an enormous handicap.

The population of the United States at midcentury stood at 152,000,000. Recently the 200,000,000 bench mark was submerged, and the flood tide is yet to come. Our death rates have reached eight per thousand, but our birth rates fluctuate in somewhat cyclic and unpredictable fashion, much like the hemline. There was a decline in births during the years of economic depression between the two world wars, but a similar decline has occurred since 1957 and during a period of great affluence. Our present birth rate is 17.9 per thousand, which leaves us with an annual growth rate of just a fraction under 1 per cent. Our present growth rate would provide some encouragement were it not that the baby-boom generation is just now coming into its period of greatest fertility. The number of births will skyrocket over the next few years. Consider what this means in respect to college enrollment, and add the fact that an ever-increasing percentage of our young people are seeking a college education. Our college enrolment stands now at slightly over 6,000,000, but the children who will bring this total to 12,000,000 in 1980 are already born. Reflect for a moment that we have just twelve years in which to build as many college facilities as have been accumulated over the past 300 years and that the end is not in sight. Obviously, we are not prepared to meet this crisis in terms either of construction or of teaching personnel. The dimensions of our own population problems are staggering, and we are not, ourselves, setting a particularly good example for the world to follow.

It will be of interest to compare the population statistics of the two great powers, the United States and the U.S.S.R. Their death rates are identical, and their birth rates are very similar. The U.S.S.R. has a population of 224,000,000 and a growth rate of 1.3 per cent against our population of 200,000,000 and a growth rate of 1 per cent. The Russians take less official notice of population matters, but they are, obviously, not unmindful of the importance of keeping the birth rate consistent with their own resources and economic development.

India is an example of a country in which population pressure is especially threatening. Her population is officially placed at 516,000,000, but an actual count might run to 550,000,000. With a birth rate of 41 per cent and a death rate of 17 per cent she is growing at 24 per cent or in excess of 13,000,000 per year. It will provide perspective to note that in the short span of twenty years since India gained her independence she has added more people than currently exist in the whole of the North American continent. Here is a country whose population has already outstripped its food-producing resources, whose economic development is being swamped by massive problems of keeping multitudes alive, to say nothing of their housing or education, and whose considerable national efforts over the past fifteen years toward reducing the birth rate are, as yet, almost totally ineffectual. The educational and socioeconomic problems which must precede a successful program of birth control are of such magnitude as to make a hopeful outcome seem rather remote.

Latin America is another area to watch. Here the population growth is more truly explosive than anywhere else on the face of the globe. Some of the less developed Latin American countries have growth rates in excess of 3 per cent, and a few have reached a phenomenal 4 per cent or higher. Their total population is now only 250,000,000, but if the present rates continue, this figure will grow to 650,000,000 by the year 2000. Moreover, poverty and malnutrition are already extremely serious in some of these countries.

Let us turn now to a consideration of the dangers of this rapid, excessive, and unlimited population growth. Here I can touch only on the cardinal consequences of overpopulation:

1. *Marginal subsistence.*—The world is replete with examples of overcrowded peoples suffering from chronic malnutrition and high infant mortality. These millions endure with passive resignation the frustrations of grinding poverty, hopelessness, and despair. Under such circumstances there can be no planning for the future, no human aspiration, only concern for day-to-day existence and degradation of the human spirit.

2. *Failure of economic growth and development in the emerging nations.*— Capital is a requisite for industrialization, and industrialization is essential to both economic development and productive labor. Where excess population exists, it has proved difficult and usually impossible to accumulate enough capital to achieve an economic breakthrough. In terms of economic development, the gap between the developing and industrialized nations of the world is not closing but growing steadily wider.

*3. Illiteracy.*—Illiterate, impoverished, and hungry people cannot be expected to place much emphasis on education. In areas of severe overpopulation 70 to 80 per cent of the children never see the inside of a school. In these same areas the problem is magnified because the illiteracy rate among women (the mothers) is extremely high, reaching 95 per cent in some instances. Such shocking propagation of ignorance in this age of enlightenment is one of the greatest anachronisms of the twentieth century. Beyond food for subsistence, education is the *sine qua non* of all that we refer to as progress in human welfare.

*4. Erosion of human rights and individual freedom.*—Probably the most dangerous consequence of overpopulation is the threat that it poses to the rights and dignity of the individual. The concept of what constitutes human rights changes as population pressure rises. Beyond a certain point in density the public interest becomes paramount. Mounting crime rates and group violence make greater regimentation necessary. Privacy becomes more and more difficult to assure.

*5. Social unrest and political tensions.*—People enduring privation and with little to lose are easily stirred to action against neighbors or brothers by the prospect or promise of bettering their lot. Civil strife becomes commonplace. Political ideologies compete for the seizure of power, which, in any event, tends to become centralized. The socioeconomic problems reach such magnitude that no instrument of society other than the central government is capable of coping with them.

*6. Threat to world peace.*—Local population pressures have many times in the past served as an excuse for war. Bertrand Russell concedes that "nothing is more likely to lead to an H-bomb war than the threat of universal destitution through overpopulation." In December, 1967, thirty world leaders at the United Nations signed a *Declaration on Population* stating, among other convictions, that "lasting and meaningful peace will depend upon how the challenge of population growth is met."

*7. Destruction or depletion of natural resources and pollution of the environment.*—Here I refer to the shameful sacrifice of our fields, forests, and wildlife, the conversion of our lakes and streams into virtual cesspools, and the contamination of the air we must breathe with dangerous pollutants. These bitter fruits of our folly are too well known to justify further comment.

*8. Impairment of the quality of life and living.*—Man's priceless and ever novel experience of living is determined in large part by the forces which impinge upon him from the environment and by his fellow beings. The detrimental effects of crowding on *Homo sapiens* are not as well known as they are for many laboratory or wild animal species, but they most surely exist. Man is a complex being. He is both gregarious and individualistic. He congregates in cities and at the same time longs for the peace and seclusion of the countryside. Nevertheless, beyond a critical point in density man clearly suffers irritations, frustrations, and a serious decline in human dignity. We are even experiencing an alarming increase in the use of drugs: tranquilizers, pep pills, and the more dangerous varieties. More people are suffering from emotional anxieties, and our mental institutions are overflowing. Crowding unquestionably nurtures man's baser instincts and predisposes him not only to violence and criminal behavior but to a callous inhumaneness. The shocking example of pedestrian indifference to murder on the streets of New York is a case in point. In India, starving beggars lie on the streets near death, but the throngs pass by or step over them with total lack of concern. Life cheapens in its own abundance.

We now come to a consideration of population growth in relation to food supply. The situation now is that two-thirds of the human population are living on marginal subsistence with no food reserves and an increasingly heavy reliance on importation of grain, mostly on a concessional or gift basis. A factor of critical importance to the world situation is that the food reserves in countries with heavy agricultural production, such as the United States, Canada, Australia, and Argentina, are rapidly being depleted. It has come as something of a shock to the people of the United States to discover that quite suddenly their enormous agricultural surpluses of five years ago have vanished. Among those who study this problem, some hold that science and technology will come to the rescue. They speak of indefinitely increasing crop yields, of harvesting algae from the sea, herding fish with dolphins, and using yeast to synthesize protein from petroleum. The realists are questioning how long the world can continue to feed itself. The answer, on a short-term basis, boils down to how long the underdeveloped and already overpopulated areas of the world can continue to feed themselves. These are the areas where the need to increase agricultural production is greatest and its achievement most difficult. Ignorance, reluctance to change established farming practices, inability to pay the high costs of modern farming machinery, fertilizers, and improved seeds, and lack of water for irrigation are some of the hindrances that are enormously difficult to overcome. In the advanced nations of the world the prospects are good that for the remainder of this century food production will, by and large, keep pace with the expansion of the consuming public. On a longer term basis, and assuming that growth of the population will not be brought under effective control, then it is, of course, inevitable that the crisis in food supply will become worldwide and of appalling nature. A recent report by the Panel on World Food Supply of the President's Science Advisory Committee states that "maximum effort will be required if the pangs of hunger are to be alleviated, if the irreparable damages of infant and childhood malnutrition are to be prevented, and if the growing threat of outright mass starvation is to be turned aside." There is no question that increasing the world's food resources is an urgent and humanitarian effort, but it is also true this can never be more than a temporary and palliative measure unless growth of the population is brought under control.

Obviously, to those who are in a position to sense the future situation, there is mounting apprehension. They disagree not on whether famines will occur in the less developed areas, only on how soon. Some, like the Paddock brothers, predict such famines in 1975; and many fear that we shall not get past 1985 without a major disaster.

The problem will be particularly acute for the United States, since we are looked upon as the principal supplier of grain on a cash-free basis for the hungry throughout the world, even in politically hostile areas. When famine strikes and the food source no longer suffices, then we shall have to face the awful question of who shall survive.

The only actual solution to the population problem is birth control, whether practiced with contraceptive aids or by voluntary restraint. Such birth control practices have played a prominent role in keeping the population growth rate within reasonable limits in many of the European countries over the past century and are continually operative in all advanced nations today. It is estimated that among the educated women of reproductive age about 85 per cent use some form of birth control at least for family planning purposes. On the other side of the coin, among the uneducated poor, less than 10 per cent of the women of childbearing age practice any form of birth control. Among the total population the number of women presently using contraceptive aids is too small to have any noticeable effect on the rate of world population growth.

Why is birth control so hard to effect? The public attitude toward birth control is very different from that toward death control. Death control has a very special meaning for the individual and is something that he accepts readily. Birth control has less obvious advantages and often conflicts with religious convictions, cultural traditions, and established patterns of sexual behavior. The family is the fundamental unit of human societies, and with it goes an incentive for childbearing that is universal and one of life's basic biological fulfilments. The poor have more children than they desire, and the better-off have less. But in either case the actual number is far in excess of the replacement level.

Among the very poor there is another and even more impelling reason for not adopting birth control. Children are, in a very real sense, the only security available. They are the sole means of support for the aged and for others unable to engage in productive work.

Obviously, impoverished nations cannot afford social security; and until such can be guaranteed by the state, the poor are not going to forego the protection of having productive members of the family at all times. In underdeveloped countries large segments of the population are tied to the land, where children tend to be an economic asset, whereas in an urbanized society such as ours children are in reality a great economic liability. The average cost of raising one child to the age of eighteen in the United States is $23,000.

Up to this point all birth control programs have been on a strictly voluntary basis, and, while we have some evidence that such control may be effective under the most favorable circumstances, the fact still remains that birth control has not yet had the slightest decelerating effect on the rates of worldwide population growth. Moralists recoil from the thought of involuntary fertility control, but such may become necessary purely as a humanitarian measure. The decision to add another citizen affects the welfare of the community, state, and nation and cannot forever be left to the will of individuals who abuse the privilege.

Birth control is new only in the sense that it has suddenly come to public attention. In practice, it is very old. Egyptian papyri dating to 5000 B.C. advocate contraception. Innumerable methods have been tried by ancient peoples, including vaginal barriers made of all manner of natural products such as wool or other fibers in combination with honey, vinegar, oils, alligator dung, etc. Animal membranes, especially bladders, have been used as condoms by males and females for centuries. Vile potions concocted from weeds, barks, and animal parts and often fortified with harmful ingredients were swallowed in the belief that they would prevent conception. It is clear that for thousands of years women in desperation from excessive childbearing have sought relief at any cost, including that of their own lives.

Medical scientists and practitioners, in their noble efforts to save lives, have paid small heed to the legitimate need for birth control. Weighty clerical and legal issues have been raised, especially in regard to abortion and infanticide. Nonetheless, birth control has been practiced successfully in many European countries over the past 150 years, wholly outside of medical, legal, or religious considerations. These people have, by intent, kept their population growth in check by late marriages, failure to marry, self-restraint, the condom, *coitus interruptus*, abortion, and, to varying extent, infanticide.

One of the greatest obstacles to family planning stems from the fact that well over 90 per cent of all human births are the by-product of a moment of passion rather than of family planning per se. Mating among animals is invariably for the purpose of procreation; among *Homo sapiens* the same act seldom involves anything other than sexual fulfilment. Fortunately or unfortunately, depending on circumstances, the risk of pregnancy, like the risk in Russian roulette, is generally present.

Science has the means now to stop the female biological rhythm on a mass basis. It is a sobering thought, but it is important to realize that if feasibility and know-how were the only considerations, total impotence could be imposed on virtually the whole human race in a matter of months.

It is not at all inconceivable that in the twenty-first century women will have to take a pill in order to make pregnancy possible. As in adoption procedures, some demonstration of qualification for responsible parenthood may be required in order to secure the pill.

It is an absolute certainty that the world population will not contract automatically, and involuntary control is not likely to come until the possibilities of voluntary control have been exhausted—probably too late. What, then, can be done on a voluntary basis?

Persuasion has not yet been tried on an all-out grass-roots propaganda basis in an underdeveloped country. Contraceptive information and supplies can be made available on a much expanded and worldwide basis. There are several contraceptive methods available which are highly effective *if* they are used and *if* they are used properly. These are big "ifs."

Here at home we unwittingly lend all manner of encouragement to motherhood through our established customs and our attitude toward the role of women in our society. We operate on the popular notion that marriage at an early age is the prime objective of a woman's life. The social pressure to marry has all but eliminated spinsters and bachelors. Of today's youth 97 per cent will marry, but at a later age than the current average. The teen-age marriage is giving way to the experience of a college education. Our colleges and universities are caught in a flood of students, but the avalanche is yet to come.

Our national attitude toward the role of women in society has advanced little since frontier days. The upbringing and education of women centers on their functions in the home and family setting. Our paperbacks, theater, music, and dances all extol the qualifications of women for a nesting role. Women have not been encouraged, as they should be, to enter the professions on an equal basis with men. The health field, the whole matter of caring for people, is a natural field for women.

Our system of personal income tax puts another premium on childbearing and penalizes the non-married person. A reversal of the basic philosophy would not only be more just; it could also be expected to have a salutary effect on the birth rate practically overnight. In this regard, it is of great interest to note that the Indian state of Maharashtra has just recently taken the first positive step toward compulsory family planning by imposing a tax and other penalties on parents who produce more than three children.

The military's dependency allowance provides incentive for close spacing of children, and our welfare system has done a notable job of spawning illegitimate children. The poverty program and the war on hunger are doomed to continued failure as long as they ignore the propensity of the poverty-stricken to reproduce.

The need for expanded research in the field of reproduction and fertility control must be obvious. Governmental support of such research has been senselessly minor. Only a few years ago the National Institute of Health was spending $800,000,000 on death control and $1,000,000 on birth control. Federal support of family planning activities has skyrocketed in the past year, but it still remains minuscule in comparison with the magnitude of the problem.

Although the size of the population ought to be a concern of every nation, the idea of having a population policy has seldom been seriously considered. The United States—with Massachusetts as its leading example of puritanical absurdity—is among the most backward nations in terms of defining what its population policy ought to be. Our own conglomerate society and fear of differential fertility patterns makes the prospect of developing a population policy for the United States remote indeed. The prospects are no more encouraging at the level of the United Nations, for the same reason. I feel that one of the most important steps that should be taken immediately is for enlightened groups to undertake discussions aimed at framing a sane population policy. Every nation should know not just what population it can tolerate but what sized population is in its own best interests. The population goal of every nation should, in general, be consonant both with its own resources and with the welfare of mankind at large.

I would leave with you the thought that man, the inheritor of the earth, is a rational being and capable of determining his fate. In flesh and blood, however, he is akin to the beasts and possessed of inborn survival attributes. Among these is the urge to perpetuate the species through propagation. The survival issue now is between man's use of his intellectual powers and his sexual proclivities. It is time that he inquire what it is that he would ask of life and to consider whether a doubling of the population over the the next thirty-odd years will benefit the quality of life for himself and his children. With the population bomb in one hand and the atomic bomb in the other, man is now the king of his planet and guardian not just of himself but of every living species on earth. The fruits of untold millions of years of evolutionary development are at stake. His stewardship rests now on his ability to stay both bombs. Man is a mighty being. He is now tinkering with the universe.

Without prejudice as to the powers that shape our ends, and in the words of my favorite spiritual, I surmise that it is man who "holds the whole world in his hands."

# The Tragedy of the Commons

The population problem has no technical solution;
it requires a fundamental extension in morality.

Garrett Hardin

At the end of a thoughtful article on the future of nuclear war, Wiesner and York (1) concluded that: "Both sides in the arms race are . . . confronted by the dilemma of steadily increasing military power and steadily decreasing national security. *It is our considered professional judgment that this dilemma has no technical solution.* If the great powers continue to look for solutions in the area of science and technology only, the result will be to worsen the situation."

I would like to focus your attention not on the subject of the article (national security in a nuclear world) but on the kind of conclusion they reached, namely that there is no technical solution to the problem. An implicit and almost universal assumption of discussions published in professional and semipopular scientific journals is that the problem under discussion has a technical solution. A technical solution may be defined as one that requires a change only in the techniques of the natural sciences, demanding little or nothing in the way of change in human values or ideas of morality.

In our day (though not in earlier times) technical solutions are always welcome. Because of previous failures in prophecy, it takes courage to assert that a desired technical solution is not possible. Wiesner and York exhibited this courage; publishing in a science journal, they insisted that the solution to the problem was not to be found in the natural sciences. They cautiously qualified their statement with the phrase, "It is our considered profes-

The author is professor of biology, University of California, Santa Barbara. This article is based on a presidential address presented before the meeting of the Pacific Division of the American Association for the Advancement of Science at Utah State University, Logan, 25 June 1968.

sional judgment. . . ." Whether they were right or not is not the concern of the present article. Rather, the concern here is with the important concept of a class of human problems which can be called "no technical solution problems," and, more specifically, with the identification and discussion of one of these.

It is easy to show that the class is not a null class. Recall the game of tick-tack-toe. Consider the problem, "How can I win the game of tick-tack-toe?" It is well known that I cannot, if I assume (in keeping with the conventions of game theory) that my opponent understands the game perfectly. Put another way, there is no "technical solution" to the problem. I can win only by giving a radical meaning to the word "win." I can hit my opponent over the head; or I can drug him; or I can falsify the records. Every way in which I "win" involves, in some sense, an abandonment of the game, as we intuitively understand it. (I can also, of course, openly abandon the game—refuse to play it. This is what most adults do.)

The class of "No technical solution problems" has members. My thesis is that the "population problem," as conventionally conceived, is a member of this class. How it is conventionally conceived needs some comment. It is fair to say that most people who anguish over the population problem are trying to find a way to avoid the evils of overpopulation without relinquishing any of the privileges they now enjoy. They think that farming the seas or developing new strains of wheat will solve the problem—technologically. I try to show here that the solution they seek cannot be found. The population problem cannot be solved in a technical way, any more than can the problem of winning the game of tick-tack-toe.

## What Shall We Maximize?

Population, as Malthus said, naturally tends to grow "geometrically," or, as we would now say, exponentially. In a finite world this means that the per capita share of the world's goods must steadily decrease. Is ours a finite world?

A fair defense can be put forward for the view that the world is infinite; or that we do not know that it is not. But, in terms of the practical problems that we must face in the next few generations with the foreseeable technology, it is clear that we will greatly increase human misery if we do not, during the immediate future, assume that the world available to the terrestrial human population is finite. "Space" is no escape (2).

A finite world can support only a finite population; therefore, population growth must eventually equal zero. (The case of perpetual wide fluctuations above and below zero is a trivial variant that need not be discussed.) When this condition is met, what will be the situation of mankind? Specifically, can Bentham's goal of "the greatest good for the greatest number" be realized?

*No*—for two reasons, each sufficient by itself. The first is a theoretical one. It is not mathematically possible to maximize for two (or more) variables at the same time. This was clearly stated by von Neumann and Morgenstern (3), but the principle is implicit in the theory of partial differential equations, dating back at least to D'Alembert (1717–1783).

The second reason springs directly from biological facts. To live, any organism must have a source of energy (for example, food). This energy is utilized for two purposes: mere maintenance and work. For man, maintenance of life requires about 1600 kilocalories a day ("maintenance calories"). Anything that he does over and above merely staying alive will be defined as work, and is supported by "work calories" which he takes in. Work calories are used not only for what we call work in common speech; they are also required for all forms of enjoyment, from swimming and automobile racing to playing music and writing poetry. If our goal is to maximize population it is obvious what we must do: We must make the work calories per person approach as close to zero as possible. No gourmet meals, no vacations, no sports, no music, no literature, no art . . . . I think that everyone will grant, without argument or proof, that maximizing population does not maximize goods. Bentham's goal is impossible.

In reaching this conclusion I have made the usual assumption that it is the acquisition of energy that is the problem. The appearance of atomic energy has led some to question this assumption. However, given an infinite source of energy, population growth still produces an inescapable problem. The problem of the acquisition of energy is replaced by the problem of its dissipation, as J. H. Fremlin has so wittily shown (4). The arithmetic signs in the analysis are, as it were, reversed; but Bentham's goal is still unobtainable.

The optimum population is, then, less than the maximum. The difficulty of defining the optimum is enormous; so far as I know, no one has seriously tackled this problem. Reaching an acceptable and stable solution will surely require more than one generation of hard analytical work—and much persuasion.

We want the maximum good per person; but what is good? To one person it is wilderness, to another it is ski lodges for thousands. To one it is estuaries to nourish ducks for hunters to shoot; to another it is factory land. Comparing one good with another is, we usually say, impossible because goods are incommensurable. Incommensurables cannot be compared.

Theoretically this may be true; but in real life incommensurables *are* commensurable. Only a criterion of judgment and a system of weighting are needed. In nature the criterion is survival. Is it better for a species to be small and hideable, or large and powerful? Natural selection commensurates the incommensurables. The compromise achieved depends on a natural weighting of the values of the variables.

Man must imitate this process. There is no doubt that in fact he already does, but unconsciously. It is when the hidden decisions are made explicit that the arguments begin. The problem for the years ahead is to work out an acceptable theory of weighting. Synergistic effects, nonlinear variation, and difficulties in discounting the future make the intellectual problem difficult, but not (in principle) insoluble.

Has any cultural group solved this practical problem at the present time, even on an intuitive level? One simple fact proves that none has: there is no prosperous population in the world today that has, and has had for some

time, a growth rate of zero. Any people that has intuitively identified its optimum point will soon reach it, after which its growth rate becomes and remains zero.

Of course, a positive growth rate might be taken as evidence that a population is below its optimum. However, by any reasonable standards, the most rapidly growing populations on earth today are (in general) the most miserable. This association (which need not be invariable) casts doubt on the optimistic assumption that the positive growth rate of a population is evidence that it has yet to reach its optimum.

We can make little progress in working toward optimum poulation size until we explicitly exorcize the spirit of Adam Smith in the field of practical demography. In economic affairs, *The Wealth of Nations* (1776) popularized the "invisible hand," the idea that an individual who "intends only his own gain," is, as it were, "led by an invisible hand to promote . . . the public interest" (5). Adam Smith did not assert that this was invariably true, and perhaps neither did any of his followers. But he contributed to a dominant tendency of thought that has ever since interfered with positive action based on rational analysis, namely, the tendency to assume that decisions reached individually will, in fact, be the best decisions for an entire society. If this assumption is correct it justifies the continuance of our present policy of laissez-faire in reproduction. If it is correct we can assume that men will control their individual fecundity so as to produce the optimum population. If the assumption is not correct, we need to reexamine our individual freedoms to see which ones are defensible.

## Tragedy of Freedom in a Commons

The rebuttal to the invisible hand in population control is to be found in a scenario first sketched in a little-known pamphlet (6) in 1833 by a mathematical amateur named William Forster Lloyd (1794–1852). We may well call it "the tragedy of the commons," using the word "tragedy" as the philosopher Whitehead used it (7): "The essence of dramatic tragedy is not unhappiness. It resides in the solemnity of the remorseless working of things." He then goes on to say, "This inevitableness of destiny can only be illustrated in terms of human life by incidents which in fact in-

volve unhappiness. For it is only by them that the futility of escape can be made evident in the drama."

The tragedy of the commons develops in this way. Picture a pasture open to all. It is to be expected that each herdsman will try to keep as many cattle as possible on the commons. Such an arrangement may work reasonably satisfactorily for centuries because tribal wars, poaching, and disease keep the numbers of both man and beast well below the carrying capacity of the land. Finally, however, comes the day of reckoning, that is, the day when the long-desired goal of social stability becomes a reality. At this point, the inherent logic of the commons remorselessly generates tragedy.

As a rational being, each herdsman seeks to maximize his gain. Explicitly or implicitly, more or less consciously, he asks, "What is the utility *to me* of adding one more animal to my herd?" This utility has one negative and one positive component.

1) The positive component is a function of the increment of one animal. Since the herdsman receives all the proceeds from the sale of the additional animal, the positive utility is nearly $+1$.

2) The negative component is a function of the additional overgrazing created by one more animal. Since, however, the effects of overgrazing are shared by all the herdsmen, the negative utility for any particular decision-making herdsman is only a fraction of $-1$.

Adding together the component partial utilities, the rational herdsman concludes that the only sensible course for him to pursue is to add another animal to his herd. And another; and another. . . . But this is the conclusion reached by each and every rational herdsman sharing a commons. Therein is the tragedy. Each man is locked into a system that compels him to increase his herd without limit—in a world that is limited. Ruin is the destination toward which all men rush, each pursuing his own best interest in a society that believes in the freedom of the commons. Freedom in a commons brings ruin to all.

Some would say that this is a platitude. Would that it were! In a sense, it was learned thousands of years ago, but natural selection favors the forces of psychological denial (8). The individual benefits as an individual from his ability to deny the truth even though society as a whole, of which he is a part, suffers.

Education can counteract the natural tendency to do the wrong thing, but the inexorable succession of generations requires that the basis for this knowledge be constantly refreshed.

A simple incident that occurred a few years ago in Leominster, Massachusetts, shows how perishable the knowledge is. During the Christmas shopping season the parking meters downtown were covered with plastic bags that bore tags reading: "Do not open until after Christmas. Free parking courtesy of the mayor and city council." In other words, facing the prospect of an increased demand for already scarce space, the city fathers reinstituted the system of the commons. (Cynically, we suspect that they gained more votes than they lost by this retrogressive act.)

In an approximate way, the logic of the commons has been understood for a long time, perhaps since the discovery of agriculture or the invention of private property in real estate. But it is understood mostly only in special cases which are not sufficiently generalized. Even at this late date, cattlemen leasing national land on the western ranges demonstrate no more than an ambivalent understanding, in constantly pressuring federal authorities to increase the head count to the point where overgrazing produces erosion and weed-dominance. Likewise, the oceans of the world continue to suffer from the survival of the philosophy of the commons. Maritime nations still respond automatically to the shibboleth of the "freedom of the seas." Professing to believe in the "inexhaustible resources of the oceans," they bring species after species of fish and whales closer to extinction (9).

The National Parks present another instance of the working out of the tragedy of the commons. At present, they are open to all, without limit. The parks themselves are limited in extent—there is only one Yosemite Valley—whereas population seems to grow without limit. The values that visitors seek in the parks are steadily eroded. Plainly, we must soon cease to treat the parks as commons or they will be of no value to anyone.

What shall we do? We have several options. We might sell them off as private property. We might keep them as public property, but allocate the right to enter them. The allocation might be on the basis of wealth, by the use of an auction system. It might be on the basis of merit, as defined by some agreed-upon standards. It might be by lottery. Or it might be on a first-come, first-served basis, administered to long queues. These, I think, are all the reasonable possibilities. They are all objectionable. But we must choose—or acquiesce in the destruction of the commons that we call our National Parks.

## Pollution

In a reverse way, the tragedy of the commons reappears in problems of pollution. Here it is not a question of taking something out of the commons, but of putting something in—sewage, or chemical, radioactive, and heat wastes into water; noxious and dangerous fumes into the air; and distracting and unpleasant advertising signs into the line of sight. The calculations of utility are much the same as before. The rational man finds that his share of the cost of the wastes he discharges into the commons is less than the cost of purifying his wastes before releasing them. Since this is true for everyone, we are locked into a system of "fouling our own nest," so long as we behave only as independent, rational, free-enterprisers.

The tragedy of the commons as a food basket is averted by private property, or something formally like it. But the air and waters surrounding us cannot readily be fenced, and so the tragedy of the commons as a cesspool must be prevented by different means, by coercive laws or taxing devices that make it cheaper for the polluter to treat his pollutants than to discharge them untreated. We have not progressed as far with the solution of this problem as we have with the first. Indeed, our particular concept of private property, which deters us from exhausting the positive resources of the earth, favors pollution. The owner of a factory on the bank of a stream—whose property extends to the middle of the stream—often has difficulty seeing why it is not his natural right to muddy the waters flowing past his door. The law, always behind the times, requires elaborate stitching and fitting to adapt it to this newly perceived aspect of the commons.

The pollution problem is a consequence of population. It did not much matter how a lonely American frontiersman disposed of his waste. "Flowing water purifies itself every 10 miles," my grandfather used to say, and the myth was near enough to the truth when he was a boy, for there were not too many people. But as population became denser, the natural chemical and biological recycling processes became overloaded, calling for a redefinition of property rights.

## How To Legislate Temperance?

Analysis of the pollution problem as a function of population density uncovers a not generally recognized principle of morality, namely: *the morality of an act is a function of the state of the system at the time it is performed* (10). Using the commons as a cesspool does not harm the general public under frontier conditions, because there is no public; the same behavior in a metropolis is unbearable. A hundred and fifty years ago a plainsman could kill an American bison, cut out only the tongue for his dinner, and discard the rest of the animal. He was not in any important sense being wasteful. Today, with only a few thousand bison left, we would be appalled at such behavior.

In passing, it is worth noting that the morality of an act cannot be determined from a photograph. One does not know whether a man killing an elephant or setting fire to the grassland is harming others until one knows the total system in which his act appears. "One picture is worth a thousand words," said an ancient Chinese; but it may take 10,000 words to validate it. It is as tempting to ecologists as it is to reformers in general to try to persuade others by way of the photographic shortcut. But the essence of an argument cannot be photographed: it must be presented rationally—in words.

That morality is system-sensitive escaped the attention of most codifiers of ethics in the past. "Thou shalt not . . ." is the form of traditional ethical directives which make no allowance for particular circumstances. The laws of our society follow the pattern of ancient ethics, and therefore are poorly suited to governing a complex, crowded, changeable world. Our epicyclic solution is to augment statutory law with administrative law. Since it is practically impossible to spell out all the conditions under which it is safe to burn trash in the back yard or to run an automobile without smog-control, by law we delegate the details to bureaus. The result is administrative law, which is rightly feared for an ancient reason—*Quis custodiet ipsos custodes?*—"Who shall watch the watchers themselves?" John Adams said that we must have "a government of laws and not men." Bureau administrators, trying to evaluate the morality of acts in the total system, are singularly liable to corruption, producing a government by men, not laws.

Prohibition is easy to legislate (though not necessarily to enforce); but how do we legislate temperance? Experience indicates that it can be accomplished best through the mediation of administrative law. We limit possibilities unnecessarily if we suppose that the sentiment of *Quis custodiet* denies us the use of administrative law. We should rather retain the phrase as a perpetual reminder of fearful dangers we cannot avoid. The great challenge facing us now is to invent the corrective feedbacks that are needed to keep custodians honest. We must find ways to legitimate the needed authority of both the custodians and the corrective feedbacks.

## Freedom To Breed Is Intolerable

The tragedy of the commons is involved in population problems in another way. In a world governed solely by the principle of "dog eat dog"—if indeed there ever was such a world—how many children a family had would not be a matter of public concern. Parents who bred too exuberantly would leave fewer descendants, not more, because they would be unable to care adequately for their children. David Lack and others have found that such a negative feedback demonstrably controls the fecundity of birds (*11*). But men are not birds, and have not acted like them for millenniums, at least.

*If* each human family were dependent only on its own resources; *if* the children of improvident parents starved to death; *if,* thus, overbreeding brought its own "punishment" to the germ line— *then* there would be no public interest in controlling the breeding of families. But our society is deeply committed to the welfare state (*12*), and hence is confronted with another aspect of the tragedy of the commons.

In a welfare state, how shall we deal with the family, the religion, the race, or the class (or indeed any distinguishable and cohesive group) that adopts overbreeding as a policy to secure its own aggrandizement (*13*)? To couple the concept of freedom to breed with the belief that everyone born has an

equal right to the commons is to lock the world into a tragic course of action.

Unfortunately this is just the course of action that is being pursued by the United Nations. In late 1967, some 30 nations agreed to the following (*14*):

The Universal Declaration of Human Rights describes the family as the natural and fundamental unit of society. It follows that any choice and decision with regard to the size of the family must irrevocably rest with the family itself, and cannot be made by anyone else.

It is painful to have to deny categorically the validity of this right; denying it, one feels as uncomfortable as a resident of Salem, Massachusetts, who denied the reality of witches in the 17th century. At the present time, in liberal quarters, something like a taboo acts to inhibit criticism of the United Nations. There is a feeling that the United Nations is "our last and best hope," that we shouldn't find fault with it; we shouldn't play into the hands of the archconservatives. However, let us not forget what Robert Louis Stevenson said: "The truth that is suppressed by friends is the readiest weapon of the enemy." If we love the truth we must openly deny the validity of the Universal Declaration of Human Rights, even though it is promoted by the United Nations. We should also join with Kingsley Davis (*15*) in attempting to get Planned Parenthood-World Population to see the error of its ways in embracing the same tragic ideal.

## Conscience Is Self-Eliminating

It is a mistake to think that we can control the breeding of mankind in the long run by an appeal to conscience. Charles Galton Darwin made this point when he spoke on the centennial of the publication of his grandfather's great book. The argument is straightforward and Darwinian.

People vary. Confronted with appeals to limit breeding, some people will undoubtedly respond to the plea more than others. Those who have more children will produce a larger fraction of the next generation than those with more susceptible consciences. The difference will be accentuated, generation by generation.

In C. G. Darwin's words: "It may well be that it would take hundreds of generations for the progenitive instinct to develop in this way, but if it should do so, nature would have taken her revenge, and the variety *Homo contra-*

*cipiens* would become extinct and would be replaced by the variety *Homo progenitivus*" (*16*).

The argument assumes that conscience or the desire for children (no matter which) is hereditary—but hereditary only in the most general formal sense. The result will be the same whether the attitude is transmitted through germ cells, or exosomatically, to use A. J. Lotka's term. (If one denies the latter possibility as well as the former, then what's the point of education?) The argument has here been stated in the context of the population problem, but it applies equally well to any instance in which society appeals to an individual exploiting a commons to restrain himself for the general good—by means of his conscience. To make such an appeal is to set up a selective system that works toward the elimination of conscience from the race.

## Pathogenic Effects of Conscience

The long-term disadvantage of an appeal to conscience should be enough to condemn it; but has serious short-term disadvantages as well. If we ask a man who is exploiting a commons to desist "in the name of conscience," what are we saying to him? What does he hear?—not only at the moment but also in the wee small hours of the night when, half asleep, he remembers not merely the words we used but also the nonverbal communication cues we gave him unawares? Sooner or later, consciously or subconsciously, he senses that he has received two communications, and that they are contradictory: (i) (intended communication) "If you don't do as we ask, we will openly condemn you for not acting like a responsible citizen"; (ii) (the unintended communication) "If you *do* behave as we ask, we will secretly condemn you for a simpleton who can be shamed into standing aside while the rest of us exploit the commons."

Everyman then is caught in what Bateson has called a "double bind." Bateson and his co-workers have made a plausible case for viewing the double bind as an important causative factor in the genesis of schizophrenia (*17*). The double bind may not always be so damaging, but it always endangers the mental health of anyone to whom it is applied. "A bad conscience," said Nietzsche, "is a kind of illness."

To conjure up a conscience in others

is tempting to anyone who wishes to extend his control beyond the legal limits. Leaders at the highest level succumb to this temptation. Has any President during the past generation failed to call on labor unions to moderate voluntarily their demands for higher wages, or to steel companies to honor voluntary guidelines on prices? I can recall none. The rhetoric used on such occasions is designed to produce feelings of guilt in noncooperators.

For centuries it was assumed without proof that guilt was a valuable, perhaps even an indispensable, ingredient of the civilized life. Now, in this post-Freudian world, we doubt it.

Paul Goodman speaks from the modern point of view when he says: "No good has ever come from feeling guilty, neither intelligence, policy, nor compassion. The guilty do not pay attention to the object but only to themselves, and not even to their own interests, which might make sense, but to their anxieties" (18).

One does not have to be a professional psychiatrist to see the consequences of anxiety. We in the Western world are just emerging from a dreadful two-centuries-long Dark Ages of Eros that was sustained partly by prohibition laws, but perhaps more effectively by the anxiety-generating mechanisms of education. Alex Comfort has told the story well in The Anxiety Makers (19); it is not a pretty one.

Since proof is difficult, we may even concede that the results of anxiety may sometimes, from certain points of view, be desirable. The larger question we should ask is whether, as a matter of policy, we should ever encourage the use of a technique the tendency (if not the intention) of which is psychologically pathogenic. We hear much talk these days of responsible parenthood; the coupled words are incorporated into the titles of some organizations devoted to birth control. Some people have proposed massive propaganda campaigns to instill responsibility into the nation's (or the world's) breeders. But what is the meaning of the word responsibility in this context? Is it not merely a synonym for the word conscience? When we use the word responsibility in the absence of substantial sanctions are we not trying to browbeat a free man in a commons into acting against his own interest? Responsibility is a verbal counterfeit for a substantial quid pro quo. It is an attempt to get something for nothing.

If the word responsibility is to be used at all, I suggest that it be in the sense Charles Frankel uses it (20). "Responsibility," says this philosopher, "is the product of definite social arrangements." Notice that Frankel calls for social arrangements—not propaganda.

## Mutual Coercion
### Mutually Agreed upon

The social arrangements that produce responsibility are arrangements that create coercion, of some sort. Consider bank-robbing. The man who takes money from a bank acts as if the bank were a commons. How do we prevent such action? Certainly not by trying to control his behavior solely by a verbal appeal to his sense of responsibility. Rather than rely on propaganda we follow Frankel's lead and insist that a bank is not a commons; we seek the definite social arrangements that will keep it from becoming a commons. That we thereby infringe on the freedom of would-be robbers we neither deny nor regret.

The morality of bank-robbing is particularly easy to understand because we accept complete prohibition of this activity. We are willing to say "Thou shalt not rob banks," without providing for exceptions. But temperance also can be created by coercion. Taxing is a good coercive device. To keep downtown shoppers temperate in their use of parking space we introduce parking meters for short periods, and traffic fines for longer ones. We need not actually forbid a citizen to park as long as he wants to; we need merely make it increasingly expensive for him to do so. Not prohibition, but carefully biased options are what we offer him. A Madison Avenue man might call this persuasion; I prefer the greater candor of the word coercion.

Coercion is a dirty word to most liberals now, but it need not forever be so. As with the four-letter words, its dirtiness can be cleansed away by exposure to the light, by saying it over and over without apology or embarrassment. To many, the word coercion implies arbitrary decisions of distant and irresponsible bureaucrats; but this is not a necessary part of its meaning. The only kind of coercion I recommend is mutual coercion, mutually agreed upon by the majority of the people affected.

To say that we mutually agree to coercion is not to say that we are required to enjoy it, or even to pretend we enjoy it. Who enjoys taxes? We all grumble about them. But we accept compulsory taxes because we recognize that voluntary taxes would favor the conscienceless. We institute and (grumblingly) support taxes and other coercive devices to escape the horror of the commons.

An alternative to the commons need not be perfectly just to be preferable. With real estate and other material goods, the alternative we have chosen is the institution of private property coupled with legal inheritance. Is this system perfectly just? As a genetically trained biologist I deny that it is. It seems to me that, if there are to be differences in individual inheritance, legal possession should be perfectly correlated with biological inheritance—that those who are biologically more fit to be the custodians of property and power should legally inherit more. But genetic recombination continually makes a mockery of the doctrine of "like father, like son" implicit in our laws of legal inheritance. An idiot can inherit millions, and a trust fund can keep his estate intact. We must admit that our legal system of private property plus inheritance is unjust—but we put up with it because we are not convinced, at the moment, that anyone has invented a better system. The alternative of the commons is too horrifying to contemplate. Injustice is preferable to total ruin.

It is one of the peculiarities of the warfare between reform and the status quo that it is thoughtlessly governed by a double standard. Whenever a reform measure is proposed it is often defeated when its opponents triumphantly discover a flaw in it. As Kingsley Davis has pointed out (21), worshippers of the status quo sometimes imply that no reform is possible without unanimous agreement, an implication contrary to historical fact. As nearly as I can make out, automatic rejection of proposed reforms is based on one of two unconscious assumptions: (i) that the status quo is perfect; or (ii) that the choice we face is between reform and no action; if the proposed reform is imperfect, we presumably should take no action at all, while we wait for a perfect proposal.

But we can never do nothing. That which we have done for thousands of years is also action. It also produces evils. Once we are aware that the status quo is action, we can then compare its discoverable advantages and disadvantages with the predicted advantages and disadvantages of the proposed reform, discounting as best we can for our lack of experience. On the basis of such a comparison, we can make a rational decision which will not involve the unworkable assumption that only perfect systems are tolerable.

**Recognition of Necessity**

Perhaps the simplest summary of this analysis of man's population problems is this: the commons, if justifiable at all, is justifiable only under conditions of low-population density. As the human population has increased, the commons has had to be abandoned in one aspect after another.

First we abandoned the commons in food gathering, enclosing farm land and restricting pastures and hunting and fishing areas. These restrictions are still not complete throughout the world.

Somewhat later we saw that the commons as a place for waste disposal would also have to be abandoned. Restrictions on the disposal of domestic sewage are widely accepted in the Western world; we are still struggling to close the commons to pollution by automobiles, factories, insecticide sprayers, fertilizing operations, and atomic energy installations.

In a still more embryonic state is our recognition of the evils of the commons in matters of pleasure. There is almost no restriction on the propagation of sound waves in the public medium. The shopping public is assaulted with mindless music, without its consent. Our

government is paying out billions of dollars to create supersonic transport which will disturb 50,000 people for every one person who is whisked from coast to coast 3 hours faster. Advertisers muddy the airwaves of radio and television and pollute the view of travelers. We are a long way from outlawing the commons in matters of pleasure. Is this because our Puritan inheritance makes us view pleasure as something of a sin, and pain (that is, the pollution of advertising) as the sign of virtue?

Every new enclosure of the commons involves the infringement of somebody's personal liberty. Infringements made in the distant past are accepted because no contemporary complains of a loss. It is the newly proposed infringements that we vigorously oppose; cries of "rights" and "freedom" fill the air. But what does "freedom" mean? When men mutually agreed to pass laws against robbing, mankind became more free, not less so. Individuals locked into the logic of the commons are free only to bring on universal ruin; once they see the necessity of mutual coercion, they become free to pursue other goals. I believe it was Hegel who said, "Freedom is the recognition of necessity."

The most important aspect of necessity that we must now recognize, is the necessity of abandoning the commons in breeding. No technical solution can rescue us from the misery of overpopulation. Freedom to breed will bring ruin to all. At the moment, to avoid hard decisions many of us are tempted to propagandize for conscience and responsible parenthood. The temptation must be resisted, because an appeal to independently acting con-

sciences selects for the disappearance of all conscience in the long run, and an increase in anxiety in the short.

The only way we can preserve and nurture other and more precious freedoms is by relinquishing the freedom to breed, and that very soon. "Freedom is the recognition of necessity"—and it is the role of education to reveal to all the necessity of abandoning the freedom to breed. Only so, can we put an end to this aspect of the tragedy of the commons.

**References**

1. J. B. Wiesner and H. F. York, *Sci. Amer.* **211** (No. 4), 27 (1964).
2. G. Hardin, *J. Hered.* **50**, 68 (1959); S. von Hoernor, *Science* **137**, 18 (1962).
3. J. von Neumann and O. Morgenstern, *Theory of Games and Economic Behavior* (Princeton Univ. Press, Princeton, N.J., 1947), p. 11.
4. J. H. Fremlin, *New Sci.*, No. 415 (1964), p. 285.
5. A. Smith, *The Wealth of Nations* (Modern Library, New York, 1937), p. 423.
6. W. F. Lloyd, *Two Lectures on the Checks to Population* (Oxford Univ. Press, Oxford, England, 1833), reprinted (in part) in *Population, Evolution, and Birth Control*, G. Hardin, Ed. (Freeman, San Francisco, 1964), p. 37.
7. A. N. Whitehead, *Science and the Modern World* (Mentor, New York, 1948), p. 17.
8. G. Hardin, Ed. *Population, Evolution, and Birth Control* (Freeman, San Francisco, 1964), p. 56.
9. S. McVay, *Sci. Amer.* **216** (No. 8), 13 (1966).
10. J. Fletcher, *Situation Ethics* (Westminster, Philadelphia, 1966).
11. D. Lack, *The Natural Regulation of Animal Numbers* (Clarendon Press, Oxford, 1954).
12. H. Girvetz, *From Wealth to Welfare* (Stanford Univ. Press, Stanford, Calif., 1950).
13. G. Hardin, *Perspec. Biol. Med.* **6**, 366 (1963).
14. U. Thant, *Int. Planned Parenthood News*, No. 168 (February 1968), p. 3.
15. K. Davis, *Science* **158**, 730 (1967).
16. S. Tax, Ed., *Evolution after Darwin* (Univ. of Chicago Press, Chicago, 1960), vol. 2, p. 469.
17. G. Hardin, D. D. Jackson, J. Haley, J. Weakland, *Behav. Sci.* **1**, 251 (1956).
18. P. Goodman, *New York Rev. Books* **10**(8), 22 (23 May 1968).
19. A. Comfort, *The Anxiety Makers* (Nelson, London, 1967).
20. C. Frankel, *The Case for Modern Man* (Harper, New York, 1955), p. 203.
21. J. D. Roslansky, *Genetics and the Future of Man* (Appleton-Century-Crofts, New York, 1966), p. 177.

# Population Policy:
# Will Current Programs Succeed?

Grounds for skepticism concerning the demographic
effectiveness of family planning are considered.

Kingsley Davis

Throughout history the growth of
population has been identified with
prosperity and strength. If today an
increasing number of nations are seeking to curb rapid population growth by
reducing their birth rates, they must
be driven to do so by an urgent crisis.
My purpose here is not to discuss the
crisis itself but rather to assess the present and prospective measures used to

meet it. Most observers are surprised
by the swiftness with which concern
over the population problem has turned
from intellectual analysis and debate to
policy and action. Such action is a
welcome relief from the long opposition, or timidity, which seemed to block
forever any governmental attempt to
restrain population growth, but relief
that "at last something is being done"

is no guarantee that what is being done
is adequate. On the face of it, one could
hardly expect such a fundamental reorientation to be quickly and successfully implemented. I therefore propose
to review the nature and (as I see them)
limitations of the present policies and
to suggest lines of possible improvement.

## The Nature of Current Policies

With more than 30 nations now trying or planning to reduce population
growth and with numerous private and
international organizations helping, the
degree of unanimity as to the kind of
measures needed is impressive. The
consensus can be summed up in the
phrase "family planning." President
Johnson declared in 1965 that the
United States will "assist family planning programs in nations which request
such help." The Prime Minister of India

The author is professor of sociology and director of International Population and Urban
Research, University of California, Berkeley. This
article is abridged from a paper presented at the
annual meeting of the National Research Council,
14 March 1967.

said a year later, "We must press forward with family planning. This is a programme of the highest importance." The Republic of Singapore created in 1966 the Singapore Family Planning and Population Board "to initiate and undertake population control programmes" (*1*).

As is well known, "family planning" is a euphemism for contraception. The family-planning approach to population limitation, therefore, concentrates on providing new and efficient contraceptives on a national basis through mass programs under public health auspices. The nature of these programs is shown by the following enthusiastic report from the Population Council (*2*):

No single year has seen so many forward steps in population control as 1965. Effective national programs have at last emerged, international organizations have decided to become engaged, a new contraceptive has proved its value in mass application, . . . and surveys have confirmed a popular desire for family limitation . . .

An accounting of notable events must begin with Korea and Taiwan . . . Taiwan's program is not yet two years old, and already it has inserted one IUD [intrauterine device] for every 4-6 target women (those who are not pregnant, lactating, already sterile, already using contraceptives effectively, or desirous of more children). Korea has done almost as well . . . has put 2,200 full-time workers into the field, . . . has reached operational levels for a network of IUD quotas, supply lines, local manufacture of contraceptives, training of hundreds of M.D.'s and nurses, and mass propaganda . . .

Here one can see the implication that "population control" is being achieved through the dissemination of new contraceptives, and the fact that the "target women" exclude those who want more children. One can also note the technological emphasis and the medical orientation.

What is wrong with such programs? The answer is, "Nothing at all, if they work." Whether or not they work depends on what they are expected to do as well as on how they try to do it. Let us discuss the goal first, then the means.

## Goals

Curiously, it is hard to find in the population-policy movement any explicit discussion of long-range goals. By implication the policies seem to promise a great deal. This is shown by the use of expressions like *population control* and *population planning* (as in the passages quoted above). It is also shown by the characteristic style of reasoning. Expositions of current policy usually start off by lamenting the speed and the consequences of runaway population growth. This growth, it is then stated, must be curbed—by pursuing a vigorous family-planning program. That family planning can solve the problem of population growth seems to be taken as self-evident.

For instance, the much-heralded statement by 12 heads of state, issued by Secretary-General U Thant on 10 December 1966 (a statement initiated by John D. Rockefeller III, Chairman of the Board of the Population Council), devotes half its space to discussing the harmfulness of population growth and the other half to recommending family planning (*3*). A more succinct example of the typical reasoning is given in the Provisional Scheme for a Nationwide Family Planning Programme in Ceylon (*4*):

The population of Ceylon is fast increasing. . . . [The] figures reveal that a serious situation will be created within a few years. In order to cope with it a Family Planning programme on a nationwide scale should be launched by the Government.

The promised goal—to limit population growth so as to solve population problems—is a large order. One would expect it to be carefully analyzed, but it is left imprecise and taken for granted, as is the way in which family planning will achieve it.

When the terms *population control* and *population planning* are used, as they frequently are, as synonyms for current family-planning programs, they are misleading. Technically, they would mean deliberate influence over all attributes of a population, including its age-sex structure, geographical distribution, racial composition, genetic quality, and total size. No government attempts such full control. By tacit understanding, current population policies are concerned with only the *growth* and *size* of populations. These attributes, however, result from the death rate and migration as well as from the birth rate; their control would require deliberate influence over the factors giving rise to all three determinants. Actually, current policies labeled population control do not deal with mortality and migration, but deal only with the birth input. This is why another term, *fertility control,* is frequently used to describe current policies. But, as I show below, family planning (and hence current policy) does not undertake to influence most of the determinants of human reproduction. Thus the programs should not be referred to as population control or planning, because they do not attempt to influence the factors responsible for the attributes of human populations, taken generally; nor should they be called fertility control, because they do not try to affect most of the determinants of reproductive performance.

The ambiguity does not stop here, however. When one speaks of controlling population size, any inquiring person naturally asks, What is "control"? Who is to control whom? Precisely what population size, or what rate of population growth, is to be achieved? Do the policies aim to produce a growth rate that is nil, one that is very slight, or one that is like that of the industrial nations? Unless such questions are dealt with and clarified, it is impossible to evaluate current population policies.

The actual programs seem to be aiming simply to achieve a reduction in the birth rate. Success is therefore interpreted as the accomplishment of such a reduction, on the assumption that the reduction will lessen population growth. In those rare cases where a specific demographic aim is stated, the goal is said to be a short-run decline within a given period. The Pakistan plan adopted in 1966 (*5*, p. 889) aims to reduce the birth rate from 50 to 40 per thousand by 1970; the Indian plan (*6*) aims to reduce the rate from 40 to 25 "as soon as possible"; and the Korean aim (*7*) is to cut population growth from 2.9 to 1.2 percent by 1980. A significant feature of such stated aims is the rapid population growth they would permit. Under conditions of modern mortality, a crude birth rate of 25 to 30 per thousand will represent such a multiplication of people as to make use of the term *population control* ironic. A rate of increase of 1.2 percent per year would allow South Korea's already dense population to double in less than 60 years.

One can of course defend the programs by saying that the present goals and measures are merely interim ones. A start must be made somewhere. But we do not find this answer in the population-policy literature. Such a defense, if convincing, would require a presentation of the *next* steps, and these are not considered. One suspects that the entire question of goals is instinctively left vague because thorough limitation of population growth would run counter to national and group aspirations. A consideration of hypothetical goals throws further light on the matter.

*Industrialized nations as the model.* Since current policies are confined to family planning, their maximum demographic effect would be to give the underdeveloped countries the same level of reproductive performance that the industrial nations now have. The latter, long oriented toward family planning, provide a good yardstick for determining what the availability of contraceptives can do to population growth. Indeed, they provide more than a yardstick; they are actually the model which inspired the present population policies.

What does this goal mean in practice? Among the advanced nations there is considerable diversity in the level of fertility (*8*). At one extreme are countries such as New Zealand, with an average gross reproduction rate (GRR) of 1.91 during the period 1960–64; at the other extreme are countries such as Hungary, with a rate of 0.91 during the same period. To a considerable extent, however, such divergencies are matters of timing. The birth rates of most industrial nations have shown, since about 1940, a wave-like movement, with no secular trend. The average level of reproduction during this long period has been high enough to give these countries, with their low mortality, an extremely rapid population growth. If this level is maintained, their population will double in just over 50 years—a rate higher than that of world population growth at any time prior to 1950, at which time the growth in numbers of human beings was already considered fantastic. The advanced nations are suffering acutely from the effects of rapid population growth in combination with the production of ever more goods per person (*9*). A rising share of their supposedly high per capita income, which itself draws increasingly upon the resources of the underdeveloped countries (who fall farther behind in relative economic position), is spent simply to meet the costs, and alleviate the nuisances, of the unrelenting production of more and more goods by more people. Such facts indicate that the industrial nations provide neither a suitable demographic model for the nonindustrial peoples to follow nor the leadership to plan and organize effective population-control policies for them.

*Zero population growth as a goal.* Most discussions of the population crisis

lead logically to zero population growth as the ultimate goal, because *any* growth rate, if continued, will eventually use up the earth. Yet hardly ever do arguments for population policy consider such a goal, and current policies do not dream of it. Why not? The answer is evidently that zero population growth is unacceptable to most nations and to most religious and ethnic communities. To argue for this goal would be to alienate possible support for action programs.

*Goal peculiarities inherent in family planning.* Turning to the actual measures taken, we see that the very use of family planning as the means for implementing population policy poses serious but unacknowledged limits on the intended reduction in fertility. The family-planning movement, clearly devoted to the improvement and dissemination of contraceptive devices, states again and again that its purpose is that of enabling couples to have the number of children they want. "The opportunity to decide the number and spacing of children is a basic human right," say the 12 heads of state in the United Nations declaration. The 1965 Turkish Law Concerning Population Planning declares (*10*):

*Article 1.* Population Planning means that individuals can have as many children as they wish, whenever they want to. This can be ensured through preventive measures taken against pregnancy. . . .

Logically, it does not make sense to use *family* planning to provide *national* population control or planning. The "planning" in family planning is that of each separate couple. The only control they exercise is control over the size of *their* family. Obviously, couples do not plan the size of the nation's population, any more than they plan the growth of the national income or the form of the highway network. There is no reason to expect that the millions of decisions about family size made by couples in their own interest will automatically control population for the benefit of society. On the contrary, there are good reasons to think they will not do so. At most, family planning can reduce reproduction to the extent that unwanted births exceed wanted births. In industrial countries the balance is often negative—that is, people have fewer children as a rule than they would like to have. In underdeveloped countries the reverse is normally true, but the elimination of unwanted births would still leave an ex-

tremely high rate of multiplication.

Actually, the family-planning movement does not pursue even the limited goals it professes. It does not fully empower couples to have only the number of offspring they want because it either condemns or disregards certain tabooed but nevertheless effective means to this goal. One of its tenets is that "there shall be freedom of choice of method so that individuals can choose in accordance with the dictates of their consciences" (*11*), but in practice this amounts to limiting the individual's choice, because the "conscience" dictating the method is usually not his but that of religious and governmental officials. Moreover, not every individual may choose: even the so-called recommended methods are ordinarily not offered to single women, or not all offered to women professing a given religious faith.

Thus, despite its emphasis on technology, current policy does not utilize all available means of contraception, much less all birth-control measures. The Indian government wasted valuable years in the early stages of its population-control program by experimenting exclusively with the "rhythm" method, long after this technique had been demonstrated to be one of the least effective. A greater limitation on means is the exclusive emphasis on contraception itself. Induced abortion, for example, is one of the surest means of controlling reproduction, and one that has been proved capable of reducing birth rates rapidly. It seems peculiarly suited to the threshold stage of a population-control program—the stage when new conditions of life first make large families disadvantageous. It was the principal factor in the halving of the Japanese birth rate, a major factor in the declines in birth rate of East-European satellite countries after legalization of abortions in the early 1950's, and an important factor in the reduction of fertility in industrializing nations from 1870 to the 1930's (*12*). Today, according to *Studies in Family Planning (13)*, "abortion is probably the foremost method of birth control throughout Latin America." Yet this method is rejected in nearly all national and international population-control programs. American foreign aid is used to help *stop* abortion (*14*). The United Nations excludes abortion from family planning, and in fact justifies the latter by presenting it as a means of combating abortion (*15*).

Studies of abortion are being made in Latin America under the presumed auspices of population-control groups, not with the intention of legalizing it and thus making it safe, cheap, available, and hence more effective for population control, but with the avowed purpose of reducing it (*16*).

Although few would prefer abortion to efficient contraception (other things being equal), the fact is that both permit a woman to control the size of her family. The main drawbacks to abortion arise from its illegality. When performed, as a legal procedure, by a skilled physician, it is safer than childbirth. It does not compete with contraception but serves as a backstop when the latter fails or when contraceptive devices or information are not available. As contraception becomes customary, the incidence of abortion recedes even without its being banned. If, therefore, abortions enable women to have only the number of children they want, and if family planners do not advocate—in fact decry—legalization of abortion, they are to that extent denying the central tenet of their own movement. The irony of anti-abortionism in family-planning circles is seen particularly in hair-splitting arguments over whether or not some contraceptive agent (for example, the IUD) is in reality an abortifacient. A Mexican leader in family planning writes (*17*):

One of the chief objectives of our program in Mexico is to prevent abortions. If we could be sure that the mode of action [of the IUD] was not interference with nidation, we could easily use the method in Mexico.

The questions of sterilization and unnatural forms of sexual intercourse usually meet with similar silent treatment or disapproval, although nobody doubts the effectiveness of these measures in avoiding conception. Sterilization has proved popular in Puerto Rico and has had some vogue in India (where the new health minister hopes to make it compulsory for those with a certain number of children), but in both these areas it has been for the most part ignored or condemned by the family-planning movement.

On the side of goals, then, we see that a family-planning orientation limits the aims of current population policy. Despite reference to "population control" and "fertility control," which presumably mean determination of demographic results by and for the nation

as a whole, the movement gives control only to couples, and does this only if they use "respectable" contraceptives.

## The Neglect of Motivation

By sanctifying the doctrine that each woman should have the number of children she wants, and by assuming that if she has only that number this will automatically curb population growth to the necessary degree, the leaders of current policies escape the necessity of asking why women desire so many children and how this desire can be influenced (*18*, p. 41; *19*). Instead, they claim that satisfactory motivation is shown by the popular desire (shown by opinion surveys in all countries) to have the means of family limitation, and that therefore the problem is one of inventing and distributing the best possible contraceptive devices. Overlooked is the fact that a desire for availability of contraceptives is compatible with *high* fertility.

Given the best of means, there remain the questions of how many children couples want and of whether this is the requisite number from the standpoint of population size. That it is not is indicated by continued rapid population growth in industrial countries, and by the very surveys showing that people want contraception—for these show, too, that people also want numerous children.

The family planners do not ignore motivation. They are forever talking about "attitudes" and "needs." But they pose the issue in terms of the "acceptance" of birth control devices. At the most naive level, they assume that lack of acceptance is a function of the contraceptive device itself. This reduces the motive problem to a technological question. The task of population control then becomes simply the invention of a device that *will* be acceptable (*20*). The plastic IUD is acclaimed because, once in place, it does not depend on repeated *acceptance* by the woman, and thus it "solves" the problem of motivation (*21*).

But suppose a woman does not want to use *any* contraceptive until after she has had four children. This is the type of question that is seldom raised in the family-planning literature. In that literature, wanting a specific number of children is taken as complete motivation, for it implies a wish to control the size of one's family. The problem

woman, from the standpoint of family planners, is the one who wants "as many as come," or "as many as God sends." Her attitude is construed as due to ignorance and "cultural values," and the policy deemed necessary to change it is "education." No compulsion can be used, because the movement is committed to free choice, but movie strips, posters, comic books, public lectures, interviews, and discussions are in order. These supply information and supposedly change values by discounting superstitions and showing that unrestrained procreation is harmful to both mother and children. The effort is considered successful when the woman decides she wants only a certain number of children and uses an effective contraceptive.

In viewing negative attitudes toward birth control as due to ignorance, apathy, and outworn tradition, and "mass-communication" as the solution to the motivation problem (*22*), family planners tend to ignore the power and complexity of social life. If it were admitted that the creation and care of new human beings is socially motivated, like other forms of behavior, by being a part of the system of rewards and punishments that is built into human relationships, and thus is bound up with the individual's economic and personal interests, it would be apparent that the social structure and economy must be changed before a deliberate reduction in the birth rate can be achieved. As it is, reliance on family planning allows people to feel that "something is being done about the population problem" without the need for painful social changes.

Designation of population control as a medical or public health task leads to a similar evasion. This categorization assures popular support because it puts population policy in the hands of respected medical personnel, but, by the same token, it gives responsibility for leadership to people who think in terms of clinics and patients, of pills and IUD's, and who bring to the handling of economic and social phenomena a self-confident naiveté. The study of social organization is a technical field; an action program based on intuition is no more apt to succeed in the control of human beings than it is in the area of bacterial or viral control. Moreover, to alter a social system, by deliberate policy, so as to regulate births in accord with the demands of the collective welfare would require political power, and this is not likely to inhere in public health officials, nurses, midwives, and social workers. To entrust population policy to them is "to take action," but not dangerous "effective action."

Similarly, the Janus-faced position on birth-control technology represents an escape from the necessity, and onus, of grappling with the social and economic determinants of reproductive behavior. On the one side, the rejection or avoidance of religiously tabooed but otherwise effective means of birth prevention enables the family-planning movement to avoid official condemnation. On the other side, an intense preoccupation with contraceptive technology (apart from the tabooed means) also helps the family planners to avoid censure. By implying that the only need is the invention and distribution of effective contraceptive devices, they allay fears, on the part of religious and governmental officials, that fundamental changes in social organization are contemplated. Changes basic enough to affect motivation for having children would be changes in the structure of the family, in the position of women, and in the sexual mores. Far from proposing such radicalism, spokesmen for family planning frequently state their purpose as "protection" of the family—that is, closer observance of family norms. In addition, by concentrating on *new* and *scientific* contraceptives, the movement escapes taboos attached to old ones (the Pope will hardly authorize the condom, but may sanction the pill) and allows family planning to be regarded as a branch of medicine: overpopulation becomes a disease, to be treated by a pill or a coil.

We thus see that the inadequacy of current population policies with respect to motivation is inherent in their overwhelmingly family-planning character. Since family planning is by definition private planning, it eschews any societal control over motivation. It merely furnishes the means, and, among possible means, only the most respectable. Its leaders, in avoiding social complexities and seeking official favor, are obviously activated not solely by expediency but also by their own sentiments as members of society and by their background as persons attracted to the family-planning movement. Unacquainted for the most part with technical economics, sociology, and demography, they tend honestly and instinctively to believe that something they vaguely call population control can be achieved by making better contraceptives available.

### The Evidence of Ineffectiveness

If this characterization is accurate, we can conclude that current programs will not enable a government to control population size. In countries where couples have numerous offspring that they do not want, such programs may possibly accelerate a birth-rate decline that would occur anyway, but the conditions that cause births to be wanted or unwanted are beyond the control of family planning, hence beyond the control of any nation which relies on family planning alone as its population policy.

This conclusion is confirmed by demographic facts. As I have noted above, the widespread use of family planning in industrial countries has not given their governments control over the birth rate. In backward countries today, taken as a whole, birth rates are rising, not falling; in those with population policies, there is no indication that the government is controlling the rate of reproduction. The main "successes" cited in the well-publicized policy literature are cases where a large number of contraceptives have been distributed or where the program has been accompanied by some decline in the birth rate. Popular enthusiasm for family planning is found mainly in the cities, or in advanced countries such as Japan and Taiwan, where the people would adopt contraception in any case, program or no program. It is difficult to prove that present population policies have even speeded up a lowering of the birth rate (the least that could have been expected), much less that they have provided national "fertility control."

Let us next briefly review the facts concerning the level and trend of population in underdeveloped nations generally, in order to understand the magnitude of the task of genuine control.

### Rising Birth Rates
### in Underdeveloped Countries

In ten Latin-American countries, between 1940 and 1959 (*23*), the average birth rates (age-standardized), as estimated by our research office at the University of California, rose as follows: 1940–44, 43.4 annual births per 1000 population; 1945–49, 44.6; 1950–54, 46.4; 1955–59, 47.7.

In another study made in our office, in which estimating methods derived from the theory of quasi-stable popula-

tions were used, the recent trend was found to be upward in 27 underdeveloped countries, downward in six, and unchanged in one (*24*). Some of the rises have been substantial, and most have occurred where the birth rate was already extremely high. For instance, the gross reproduction rate rose in Jamaica from 1.8 per thousand in 1947 to 2.7 in 1960; among the natives of Fiji, from 2.0 in 1951 to 2.4 in 1964; and in Albania from 3.0 in the period 1950–54 to 3.4 in 1960.

The general rise in fertility in backward regions is evidently not due to failure of population-control efforts, because most of the countries either have no such effort or have programs too new to show much effect. Instead, the rise is due, ironically, to the very circumstance that brought on the population crisis in the first place—to improved health and lowered mortality. Better health increases the probability that a woman will conceive and retain the fetus to term; lowered mortality raises the proportion of babies who survive to the age of reproduction and reduces the probability of widowhood during that age (*25*). The significance of the general rise in fertility, in the context of this discussion, is that it is giving would-be population planners a harder task than many of them realize. Some of the upward pressure on birth rates is independent of what couples do about family planning, for it arises from the fact that, with lowered mortality, there are simply more couples.

### Underdeveloped Countries
### with Population Policies

In discussions of population policy there is often confusion as to which cases are relevant. Japan, for instance, has been widely praised for the effectiveness of its measures, but it is a very advanced industrial nation and, besides, its government policy had little or nothing to do with the decline in the birth rate, except unintentionally. It therefore offers no test of population policy under peasant-agrarian conditions. Another case of questionable relevance is that of Taiwan, because Taiwan is sufficiently developed to be placed in the urban-industrial class of nations. However, since Taiwan is offered as the main showpiece by the sponsors of current policies in underdeveloped areas, and since the data are excellent, it merits examination.

Taiwan is acclaimed as a showpiece

Table 1. Decline in Taiwan's fertility rate, 1951 through 1966.

| Year | Registered births per 1000 women aged 15–49 | Change in rate (percent)* |
|------|------|------|
| 1951 | 211 | |
| 1952 | 198 | −5.6 |
| 1953 | 194 | −2.2 |
| 1954 | 193 | −0.5 |
| 1955 | 197 | +2.1 |
| 1956 | 196 | −0.4 |
| 1957 | 182 | −7.1 |
| 1958 | 185 | +1.3 |
| 1959 | 184 | −0.1 |
| 1960 | 180 | −2.5 |
| 1961 | 177 | −1.5 |
| 1962 | 174 | −1.5 |
| 1963 | 170 | −2.6 |
| 1964 | 162 | −4.9 |
| 1965 | 152 | −6.0 |
| 1966 | 149 | −2.1 |

* The percentages were calculated on unrounded figures. Source of data through 1965, *Taiwan Demographic Fact Book* (1964, 1965); for 1966, *Monthly Bulletin of Population Registration Statistics of Taiwan* (1966, 1967).

because it has responded favorably to a highly organized program for distributing up-to-date contraceptives and has also had a rapidly dropping birth rate. Some observers have carelessly attributed the decline in the birth rate —from 50.0 in 1951 to 32.7 in 1965— to the family-planning campaign (*26*), but the campaign began only in 1963 and could have affected only the end of the trend. Rather, the decline represents a response to modernization similar to that made by all countries that have become industrialized (*27*). By 1950 over half of Taiwan's population was urban, and by 1964 nearly two-thirds were urban, with 29 percent of the population living in cities of 100,000 or more. The pace of economic development has been extremely rapid. Between 1951 and 1963, per capita income increased by 4.05 percent per year. Yet the island is closely packed, having 870 persons per square mile (a population density higher than that of Belgium). The combination of fast economic growth and rapid population increase in limited space has put parents of large families at a relative disadvantage and has created a brisk demand for abortions and contraceptives. Thus the favorable response to the current campaign to encourage use of the IUD is not a good example of what birth-control technology can do for a genuinely backward country. In fact, when the program was started, one reason for expecting receptivity was that the island was already on its way to modernization and family planning (*28*).

At most, the recent family-planning campaign—which reached significant proportions only in 1964, when some 46,000 IUD's were inserted (in 1965 the number was 99,253, and in 1966, 111,242) (*29*; *30*, p. 45)—could have caused the increase observable after 1963 in the rate of decline. Between 1951 and 1963 the average drop in the birth rate per 1000 women (see Table 1) was 1.73 percent per year; in the period 1964–66 it was 4.35 percent. But one hesitates to assign all of the acceleration in decline since 1963 to the family-planning campaign. The rapid economic development has been precisely of a type likely to accelerate a drop in reproduction. The rise in manufacturing has been much greater than the rise in either agriculture or construction. The agricultural labor force has thus been squeezed, and migration to the cities has skyrocketed (*31*). Since housing has not kept pace, urban families have had to restrict reproduction in order to take advantage of career opportunities and avoid domestic inconvenience. Such conditions have historically tended to accelerate a decline in birth rate. The most rapid decline came late in the United States (1921–33) and in Japan (1947–55). A plot of the Japanese and Taiwanese birth rates (Fig. 1) shows marked similarity of the two curves, despite a difference in level. All told, one should not attribute all of the post-1963 acceleration in the decline of Taiwan's birth rate to the family-planning campaign.

The main evidence that *some* of this acceleration is due to the campaign comes from the fact that Taichung, the city in which the family-planning effort was first concentrated, showed subsequently a much faster drop in fertility than other cities (*30*, p. 69; *32*). But the campaign has not reached throughout the island. By the end of 1966, only 260,745 women had been fitted with an IUD under auspices of the campaign, whereas the women of reproductive age on the island numbered 2.86 million. Most of the reduction in fertility has therefore been a matter of individual initiative. To some extent the campaign may be simply substituting sponsored (and cheaper) services for those that would otherwise come through private and commercial channels. An island-wide survey in 1964 showed that over 150,000 women were already using the traditional Ota ring (a metallic intrauterine device popular in Japan); almost as many had been sterilized; about 40,000 were using foam tablets; some 50,000 admitted to having had at least one abortion; and

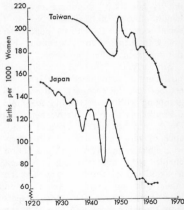

Fig. 1. Births per 1000 women aged 15 through 49 in Japan and Taiwan.

many were using other methods of birth control (*30*, pp. 18, 31).

The important question, however, is not whether the present campaign is somewhat hastening the downward trend in the birth rate but whether, even if it is, it will provide population control for the nation. Actually, the campaign is not designed to provide such control and shows no sign of doing so. It takes for granted existing reproductive goals. Its aim is "to integrate, through education and information, the idea of family limitation *within the existing attitudes, values, and goals* of the people" [*30*, p. 8 (italics mine)]. Its target is *married* women who do not want any more children; it ignores girls not yet married, and women married and wanting more children.

With such an approach, what is the maximum impact possible? It is the difference between the number of children women have been having and the number they want to have. A study in 1957 found a median figure of 3.75 for the number of children wanted by women aged 15 to 29 in Taipei, Taiwan's largest city; the corresponding figure for women from a satellite town was 3.93; for women from a fishing village, 4.90; and for women from a farming village, 5.03. Over 60 percent of the women in Taipei and over 90 percent of those in the farming village wanted 4 or more children (*33*). In a sample of wives aged 25 to 29 in Taichung, a city of over 300,000, Freedman and his co-workers found the average number of children wanted was 4; only 9 percent wanted less than 3, 20 percent wanted 5 or more (*34*). If, therefore, Taiwanese women used contraceptives that were 100-percent effective and had the number of children they desire, they would have about 4.5 each. The goal of the family-planning effort would be achieved. In the past the Taiwanese woman who married and lived through the reproductive period had, on the average, approximately 6.5 children; thus a figure of 4.5 would represent a substantial decline in fertility. Since mortality would continue to decline, the population growth rate would decline somewhat less than individual reproduction would. With 4.5 births per woman and a life expectancy of 70 years, the rate of natural increase would be close to 3 percent per year (35).

In the future, Taiwanese views concerning reproduction will doubtless change, in response to social change and economic modernization. But how far will they change? A good indication is the number of children desired by couples in an already modernized country long oriented toward family planning. In the United States in 1966, an average of 3.4 children was considered ideal by white women aged 21 or over (36). This average number of births would give Taiwan, with only a slight decrease in mortality, a long-run rate of natural increase of 1.7 percent per year and a doubling of population in 41 years.

Detailed data confirm the interpretation that Taiwanese women are in the process of shifting from a "peasant-agrarian" to an "industrial" level of reproduction. They are, in typical fashion, cutting off higher-order births at age 30 and beyond (37). Among young wives, fertility has risen, not fallen. In sum, the widely acclaimed family-planning program in Taiwan may, at most, have somewhat speeded the later phase of fertility decline which would have occurred anyway because of modernization.

Moving down the scale of modernization, to countries most in need of population control, one finds the family-planning approach even more inadequate. In South Korea, second only to Taiwan in the frequency with which it is cited as a model of current policy, a recent birth-rate decline of unknown extent is assumed by leaders to be due overwhelmingly to the government's family-planning program. However, it is just as plausible to say that the net effect of government involvement in population control has been, so far, to delay rather than hasten a decline in reproduction made inevitable by social

and economic changes. Although the government is advocating vasectomies and providing IUD's and pills, it refuses to legalize abortions, despite the rapid rise in the rate of illegal abortions and despite the fact that, in a recent survey, 72 percent of the people who stated an opinion favored legalization. Also, the program is presented in the context of maternal and child health; it thus emphasizes motherhood and the family rather than alternative roles for women. Much is made of the fact that opinion surveys show an overwhelming majority of Koreans (89 percent in 1965) favoring contraception (38, p. 27), but this means only that Koreans are like other people in wishing to have the means to get what they want. Unfortunately, they want sizable families: "The records indicate that the program appeals mainly to women in the 30–39 year age bracket who have four or more children, including at least two sons . . ." (38, p. 25).

In areas less developed than Korea the degree of acceptance of contraception tends to be disappointing, especially among the rural majority. Faced with this discouragement, the leaders of current policy, instead of reexamining their assumptions, tend to redouble their effort to find a contraceptive that will appeal to the most illiterate peasant, forgetting that he wants a good-sized family. In the rural Punjab, for example, "a disturbing feature . . . is that the females start to seek advice and adopt family planning techniques at the fag end of their reproductive period" (39). Among 5196 women coming to rural Punjabi family-planning centers, 38 percent were over 35 years old, 67 percent over 30. These women had married early, nearly a third of them before the age of 15 (40); some 14 percent had eight or more living children when they reached the clinic, 51 percent six or more.

A survey in Tunisia showed that 68 percent of the married couples were willing to use birth-control measures, but the average number of children they considered ideal was 4.3 (41). The corresponding averages for a village in eastern Java, a village near New Delhi, and a village in Mysore were 4.3, 4.0, and 4.2, respectively (42, 43). In the cities of these regions women are more ready to accept birth control and they want fewer children than village women do, but the number they consider desirable is still wholly unsatisfactory from the standpoint of population control. In an urban family-plan-

ning center in Tunisia, more than 600 of 900 women accepting contraceptives had four living children already (44). In Bangalore, a city of nearly a million at the time (1952), the number of offspring desired by married women was 3.7 on the average; by married men, 4.1 (43). In the metropolitan area of San Salvador (350,000 inhabitants) a 1964 survey (45) showed the number desired by women of reproductive age to be 3.9, and in seven other capital cities of Latin America the number ranged from 2.7 to 4.2. If women in the cities of underdeveloped countries used birth-control measures with 100-percent efficiency, they still would have enough babies to expand city populations senselessly, quite apart from the added contribution of rural-urban migration. In many of the cities the difference between actual and ideal number of children is not great; for instance, in the seven Latin-American capitals mentioned above, the ideal was 3.4 whereas the actual births per women in the age range 35 to 39 was 3.7 (46). Bombay City has had birth-control clinics for many years, yet its birth rate (standardized for age, sex, and marital distribution) is still 34 per 1000 inhabitants and is tending to rise rather than fall. Although this rate is about 13 percent lower than that for India generally, it has been about that much lower since at least 1951 (47).

## Is Family Planning the "First Step" in Population Control?

To acknowledge that family planning does not achieve population control is not to impugn its value for other purposes. Freeing women from the need to have more children than they want is of great benefit to them and their children and to society at large. My argument is therefore directed not against family-planning programs as such but against the assumption that they are an effective means of controlling population growth.

But what difference does it make? Why not go along for awhile with family planning as an initial approach to the problem of population control? The answer is that any policy on which millions of dollars are being spent should be designed to achieve the goal it purports to achieve. If it is only a first step, it should be so labeled, and its connection with the next step (and the nature of that next step) should be carefully examined. In the present case, since no "next step" seems ever to be mentioned, the question arises, Is reliance on family planning in fact a basis for dangerous postponement of effective steps? To continue to offer a remedy as a cure long after it has been shown merely to ameliorate the disease is either quackery or wishful thinking, and it thrives most where the need is greatest. Today the desire to solve the population problem is so intense that we are all ready to embrace any "action program" that promises relief. But postponement of effective measures allows the situation to worsen.

Unfortunately, the issue is confused by a matter of semantics. "Family *planning*" and "fertility *control*" suggest that reproduction is being regulated according to some rational plan. And so it is, but only from the standpoint of the individual couple, not from that of the community. What is rational in the light of a couple's situation may be totally irrational from the standpoint of society's welfare.

The need for societal regulation of individual behavior is readily recognized in other spheres—those of explosives, dangerous drugs, public property, natural resources. But in the sphere of reproduction, complete individual initiative is generally favored even by those liberal intellectuals who, in other spheres, most favor economic and social planning. Social reformers who would not hesitate to force all owners of rental property to rent to anyone who can pay, or to force all workers in an industry to join a union, balk at any suggestion that couples be permitted to have only a certain number of offspring. Invariably they interpret societal control of reproduction as meaning direct police supervision of individual behavior. Put the word *compulsory* in front of any term describing a means of limiting births—*compulsory sterilization, compulsory abortion, compulsory contraception*—and you guarantee violent opposition. Fortunately, such direct controls need not be invoked, but conservatives and radicals alike overlook this in their blind opposition to the idea of collective determination of a society's birth rate.

That the exclusive emphasis on family planning in current population policies is not a "first step" but an escape from the real issues is suggested by two facts. (i) No country has taken the "next step." The industrialized countries have had family planning for half a century without acquiring control over either the birth rate or population

increase. (ii) Support and encouragement of research on population policy other than family planning is negligible. It is precisely this blocking of alternative thinking and experimentation that makes the emphasis on family planning a major obstacle to population control. The need is not to abandon family-planning programs but to put equal or greater resources into other approaches.

## New Directions in Population Policy

In thinking about other approaches, one can start with known facts. In the past, all surviving societies had institutional incentives for marriage, procreation, and child care which were powerful enough to keep the birth rate equal to or in excess of a high death rate. Despite the drop in death rates during the last century and a half, the incentives tended to remain intact because the social structure (especially in regard to the family) changed little. At most, particularly in industrial societies, children became less productive and more expensive (48). In present-day agrarian societies, where the drop in death rate has been more recent, precipitate, and independent of social change (49), motivation for having children has changed little. Here, even more than in industrialized nations, the family has kept on producing abundant offspring, even though only a fraction of these children are now needed.

If excessive population growth is to be prevented, the obvious requirement is somehow to impose restraints on the family. However, because family roles are reinforced by society's system of rewards, punishments, sentiments, and norms, any proposal to demote the family is viewed as a threat by conservatives and liberals alike, and certainly by people with enough social responsibility to work for population control. One is charged with trying to "abolish" the family, but what is required is selective restructuring of the family in relation to the rest of society.

The lines of such restructuring are suggested by two existing limitations on fertility. (i) Nearly all societies succeed in drastically discouraging reproduction among unmarried women. (ii) Advanced societies unintentionally reduce reproduction among married women when conditions worsen in such a way as to penalize childbearing more severely than it was penalized before. In both cases the causes are motivational and economic rather than technological.

It follows that population-control policy can de-emphasize the family in two ways: (i) by keeping present controls over illegitimate childbirth yet making the most of factors that lead people to postpone or avoid marriage, and (ii) by instituting conditions that motivate those who do marry to keep their families small.

## Postponement of Marriage

Since the female reproductive span is short and generally more fecund in its first than in its second half, postponement of marriage to ages beyond 20 tends biologically to reduce births. Sociologically, it gives women time to get a better education, acquire interests unrelated to the family, and develop a cautious attitude toward pregnancy (50). Individuals who have not married by the time they are in their late twenties often do not marry at all. For these reasons, for the world as a whole, the average age at marriage for women is negatively associated with the birth rate: a rising age at marriage is a frequent cause of declining fertility during the middle phase of the demographic transition; and, in the late phase, the "baby boom" is usually associated with a return to younger marriages.

Any suggestion that age at marriage be raised as a part of population policy is usually met with the argument that "even if a law were passed, it would not be obeyed." Interestingly, this objection implies that the only way to control the age at marriage is by direct legislation, but other factors govern the actual age. Roman Catholic countries generally follow canon law in stipulating 12 years as the minimum *legal* age at which girls may marry, but the actual average age at marriage in these countries (at least in Europe) is characteristically more like 25 to 28 years. The actual age is determined, not by law, but by social and economic conditions. In agrarian societies, postponement of marriage (when postponement occurs) is apparently caused by difficulties in meeting the economic prerequisites for matrimony, as stipulated by custom and opinion. In industrial societies it is caused by housing shortages, unemployment, the requirement for overseas military service, high costs of education, and inadequacy of consumer services. Since almost no research has been devoted to the subject, it is difficult to assess the relative weight of the factors that govern the age at marriage.

## Encouraging Limitation of
## Births within Marriage

As a means of encouraging the limitation of reproduction within marriage, as well as postponement of marriage, a greater rewarding of nonfamilial than of familial roles would probably help. A simple way of accomplishing this would be to allow economic advantages to accrue to the single as opposed to the married individual, and to the small as opposed to the large family. For instance, the government could pay people to permit themselves to be sterilized (51); all costs of abortion could be paid by the government; a substantial fee could be charged for a marriage license; a "child-tax" (52) could be levied; and there could be a requirement that illegitimate pregnancies be aborted. Less sensationally, governments could simply reverse some existing policies that encourage childbearing. They could, for example, cease taxing single persons more than married ones; stop giving parents special tax exemptions; abandon income-tax policy that discriminates against couples when the wife works; reduce paid maternity leaves; reduce family allowances (53); stop awarding public housing on the basis of family size; stop granting fellowships and other educational aids (including special allowances for wives and children) to married students; cease outlawing abortions and sterilizations; and relax rules that allow use of harmless contraceptives only with medical permission. Some of these policy reversals would be beneficial in other than demographic respects and some would be harmful unless special precautions were taken. The aim would be to reduce the number, not the quality, of the next generation.

A closely related method of de-emphasizing the family would be modification of the complementarity of the roles of men and women. Men are now able to participate in the wider world yet enjoy the satisfaction of having several children because the housework and childcare fall mainly on their wives. Women are impelled to seek this role by their idealized view of marriage and motherhood and by either the scarcity of alternative roles or the difficulty of combining them with family roles. To change this situation women could be required to work outside the home, or compelled by circumstances to do so. If, at the same time, women were paid as well as men and given

equal educational and occupational opportunities, and if social life were organized around the place of work rather than around the home or neighborhood, many women would develop interests that would compete with family interests. Approximately this policy is now followed in several Communist countries, and even the less developed of these currently have extremely low birth rates (54).

That inclusion of women in the labor force has a negative effect on reproduction is indicated by regional comparisons (18, p. 1195; 55). But in most countries the wife's employment is subordinate, economically and emotionally, to her family role, and is readily sacrificed for the latter. No society has restructured both the occupational system and the domestic establishment to the point of permanently modifying the old division of labor by sex.

In any deliberate effort to control the birth rate along these lines, a government has two powerful instruments—its command over economic planning and its authority (real or potential) over education. The first determines (as far as policy can) the economic conditions and circumstances affecting the lives of all citizens; the second provides the knowledge and attitudes necessary to implement the plans. The economic system largely determines who shall work, what can be bought, what rearing children will cost, how much individuals can spend. The schools define family roles and develop vocational and recreational interests; they could, if it were desired, redefine the sex roles, develop interests that transcend the home, and transmit realistic (as opposed to moralistic) knowledge concerning marriage, sexual behavior, and population problems. When the problem is viewed in this light, it is clear that the ministries of economics and education, not the ministry of health, should be the source of population policy.

## The Dilemma of Population Policy

It should now be apparent why, despite strong anxiety over runaway population growth, the actual programs purporting to control it are limited to family planning and are therefore ineffective. (i) The goal of zero, or even slight, population growth is one that nations and groups find difficult to accept. (ii) The measures that would be required to implement such a goal,

though not so revolutionary as a Brave New World or a Communist Utopia, nevertheless tend to offend most people reared in existing societies. As a consequence, the goal of so-called population control is implicit and vague; the method is only family planning. This method, far from de-emphasizing the family, is familistic. One of its stated goals is that of helping sterile couples to *have* children. It stresses parental aspirations and responsibilities. It goes along with most aspects of conventional morality, such as condemnation of abortion, disapproval of premarital intercourse, respect for religious teachings and cultural taboos, and obeisance to medical and clerical authority. It deflects hostility by refusing to recommend any change other than the one it stands for: availability of contraceptives.

The things that make family planning acceptable are the very things that make it ineffective for population control. By stressing the right of parents to have the number of children they want, it evades the basic question of population policy, which is how now to give societies the number of children they need. By offering only the means for *couples* to control fertility, it neglects the means for societies to do so.

Because of the predominantly pro-family character of existing societies, individual interest ordinarily leads to the production of enough offspring to constitute rapid population growth under conditions of low mortality. Childless or single-child homes are considered indicative of personal failure, whereas having three to five living children gives a family a sense of continuity and substantiality (56).

Given the existing desire to have moderate-sized rather then small families, the only countries in which fertility has been reduced to match reduction in mortality are advanced ones temporarily experiencing worsened economic conditions. In Sweden, for instance, the net reproduction rate (NRR) has been below replacement for 34 years (1930–63), if the period is taken as a whole, but this is because of the economic depression. The average replacement rate was below unity (NRR = 0.81) for the period 1930–42, but from 1942 through 1963 it was above unity (NRR = 1.08). Hardships that seem particularly conducive to deliberate lowering of the birth rate are (in managed economies) scarcity of housing and other consumer goods despite full employment, and required high participation of women in the labor force, or (in freer economies) a great deal of unemployment and economic insecurity. When conditions are good, any nation tends to have a growing population.

It follows that, in countries where contraception is used, a realistic proposal for a government policy of lowering the birth rate reads like a catalogue of horrors: squeeze consumers through taxation and inflation; make housing very scarce by limiting construction; force wives and mothers to work outside the home to offset the inadequacy of male wages, yet provide few child-care facilities; encourage migration to the city by paying low wages in the country and providing few rural jobs; increase congestion in cities by starving the transit system; increase personal insecurity by encouraging conditions that produce unemployment and by haphazard political arrests. No government will institute such hardships simply for the purpose of controlling population growth. Clearly, therefore, the task of contemporary population policy is to develop attractive substitutes for family interests, so as to avoid having to turn to hardship as a corrective. The specific measures required for developing such substitutes are not easy to determine in the absence of research on the question.

In short, the world's population problem cannot be solved by pretense and wishful thinking. The unthinking identification of family planning with population control is an ostrich-like approach in that it permits people to hide from themselves the enormity and unconventionality of the task. There is no reason to abandon family-planning programs; contraception is a valuable technological instrument. But such programs must be supplemented with equal or greater investments in research and experimentation to determine the required socioeconomic measures.

### References and Notes

1. *Studies in Family Planning, No. 16* (1967).
2. *Ibid., No. 9* (1966), p. 1.
3. The statement is given in *Studies in Family Planning* (*1*, p. 1), and in *Population Bull. 23*, 6 (1967).
4. The statement is quoted in *Studies in Family Planning* (*1*, p. 2).
5. *Hearings on S. 1676, U.S. Senate, Subcommittee on Foreign Aid Expenditures, 89th Congress, Second Session, April 7, 8, 11* (1966), pt. 4.
6. B. L. Raina, in *Family Planning and Population Programs*, B. Berelson, R. K. Anderson, O. Harkavy, G. Maier, W. P. Mauldin, S. G. Segal, Eds. (Univ. of Chicago Press, Chicago, 1966).
7. D. Kirk, *Ann. Amer. Acad. Polit. Soc. Sci. 369*, 53 (1967).
8. As used by English-speaking demographers, the word *fertility* designates actual reproductive performance, not a theoretical capacity.
9. K. Davis, *Rotarian 94*, 10 (1959); *Health Educ. Monographs 9*, 2 (1960); L. Day and A. Day, *Too Many Americans* (Houghton Mifflin, Boston, 1964); R. A. Piddington, *Limits of Mankind* (Wright, Bristol, England, 1956).
10. *Official Gazette* (15 Apr. 1965); quoted in *Studies in Family Planning* (*1*, p. 7).
11. J. W. Gardner, Secretary of Health, Education, and Welfare, "Memorandum to Heads of Operating Agencies" (Jan. 1966), reproduced in *Hearings on S. 1676* (*5*), p. 783.
12. C. Tietze, *Demography 1*, 119 (1964); J. *Chronic Diseases 18*, 1161 (1964); M. Muramatsu, *Milbank Mem. Fund Quart. 38*, 153 (1960); K. Davis, *Population Index 29*, 345 (1963); R. Armijo and T. Monreal, *J. Sex Res. 1964*, 143 (1964); Proceedings World Population Conference, Belgrade, 1965; Proceedings International Planned Parenthood Federation.
13. *Studies in Family Planning, No. 4* (1964), p. 3.
14. D. Bell (then administrator for Agency for International Development), in *Hearings on S. 1676* (*5*), p. 862.
15. *Asian Population Conference* (United Nations, New York, 1964), p. 30.
16. R. Armijo and T. Monreal, in *Components of Population Change in Latin America* (Milbank Fund, New York, 1965), p. 272; E. Rice-Wray, *Amer. J. Public Health 54*, 313 (1964).
17. E. Rice-Wray, in "Intra-Uterine Contraceptive Devices," *Excerpta Med. Intern. Congr. Ser. No. 54* (1962), p. 135.
18. J. Blake, in *Public Health and Population Change*, M. C. Sheps and J. C. Ridley, Eds. (Univ. of Pittsburgh Press, Pittsburgh, 1965).
19. J. Blake and K. Davis, *Amer. Behavioral Scientist, 5*, 24 (1963).
20. See "Panel discussion on comparative acceptability of different methods of contraception," in *Research in Family Planning*, C. V. Kiser, Ed. (Princeton Univ. Press, Princeton, 1962), pp. 373–86.
21. "From the point of view of the woman concerned, the whole problem of controlling motivation disappears, . . ." [D. Kirk, in *Population Dynamics*, M. Muramatsu and P. A. Harper, Eds. (Johns Hopkins Press, Baltimore, 1965)].
22. "For influencing family size norms, certainly the examples and statements of public figures are of great significance . . . also . . . use of mass-communication methods which help to legitimize the small-family style, to provoke conversation, and to establish a vocabulary for discussion of family planning." [M. W. Freymann, in *Population Dynamics*, M. Muramatsu and P. A. Harper, Eds. (Johns Hopkins Press, Baltimore, 1965)].
23. O. A. Collver, *Birth Rates in Latin America* (International Population and Urban Research, Berkeley, Calif., 1965), pp. 27–28; the ten countries were Colombia, Costa Rica, El Salvador, Ecuador, Guatemala, Honduras, Mexico, Panamá, Peru, and Venezuela.
24. J. R. Rele, *Fertility Analysis through Extension of Stable Population Concepts*. (International Population and Urban Research, Berkeley, Calif., 1967).
25. J. C. Ridley, M. C. Sheps, J. W. Lingner, J. A. Menken, *Milbank Mem. Fund Quart. 45*, 77 (1967); E. Arriaga, unpublished paper.
26. "South Korea and Taiwan appear successfully to have checked population growth by the use of intrauterine contraceptive devices" [U. Borell, *Hearings on S. 1676* (*5*), p. 556].
27. K. Davis, *Population Index 29*, 345 (1963).
28. R. Freedman, *ibid. 31*, 421 (1965).
29. Before 1964 the Family Planning Association had given advice to fewer than 60,000 wives in 10 years and a Pre-Pregnancy Health Program had reached some 10,000, and, in the current campaign, 3650 IUD's were inserted in 1965, in a total population of 2½ million women of reproductive age. See *Studies in Family Planning, No. 19* (1967), p. 4, and R. Freedman et al., *Population Studies 16*, 231 (1963).
30. R. W. Gillespie, *Family Planning on Taiwan* (Population Council, Taichung, 1965).
31. During the period 1950–60 the ratio of growth of the city to growth of the noncity population was 5:3; during the period 1960–64 the ratio was 5:2; these ratios are based on data of Shaohsing Chen, *J. Sociol. Taiwan 1*, 74 (1963) and data in the United Nations *Demographic Yearbooks*.
32. R. Freedman, *Population Index 31*, 434 (1965). Taichung's rate of decline in 1963–64 was roughly double the average in four other cities, whereas just prior to the campaign its rate of decline had been much less than theirs.
33. S. H. Chen, *J. Soc. Sci. Taipei 13*, 72 (1963).
34. R. Freedman *et al.*, *Population Studies 16*, 227 (1963); *ibid.*, p. 232.
35. In 1964 the life expectancy at birth was already 66 years in Taiwan, as compared to 70 for the United States.
36. J. Blake, *Eugenics Quart. 14*, 68 (1967).
37. Women accepting IUD's in the family-planning program are typically 30 to 34 years old and have already had four children. [*Studies in Family Planning No. 19* (1967), p. 5].
38. Y. K. Cha, in *Family Planning and Population Programs*, B. Berelson *et al.*, Eds. (Univ. of Chicago Press, Chicago, 1966).
39. H. S. Ayalvi and S. S. Johl, *J. Family Welfare 12*, 60 1965).
40. Sixty percent of the women had borne their first child before age 19. Early marriage is strongly supported by public opinion. Of couples polled in the Punjab, 48 percent said that girls *should* marry before age 16, and 94 percent said they should marry before age 20 (H. S. Ayalvi and S. S. Johl, *ibid.*, p. 57). A study of 2380 couples in 60 villages of Uttar Pradesh found that the women had consummated their marriage at an average age of 14.6 years [J. R. Rele, *Population Studies 15*, 268 (1962)].
41. J. Morsa, in *Family Planning and Population Programs*, B. Berelson *et al.*, Eds. (Univ. of Chicago Press, Chicago, 1966).
42. H. Gille and R. J. Pardoko, *ibid.*, p. 515; S. N. Agarwala, *Med. Dig. Bombay 4*, 653 (1961).
43. *Mysore Population Study* (United Nations, New York, 1961), p. 140.
44. A. Daly, in *Family Planning and Population Programs*, B. Berelson *et al.*, Eds. (Univ. of Chicago Press, Chicago, 1966).
45. C. J. Goméz, paper presented at the World Population Conference, Belgrade, 1965.
46. C. Miro, in *Family Planning and Population Programs*, B. Berelson *et al.*, Eds. (Univ. of Chicago Press, Chicago, 1966).
47. *Demographic Training and Research Centre (India) Newsletter 20*, 4 (Aug. 1966).
48. K. Davis, *Population Index 29*, 345 (1963). For economic and sociological theory of motivation for having children, see J. Blake [Univ. of California (Berkeley)], in preparation.
49. K. Davis, *Amer. Economic Rev. 46*, 305 (1956); *Sci. Amer. 209*, 68 (1963).
50. J. Blake, *World Population Conference [Belgrade, 1965]* (United Nations, New York, 1967), vol. 2, pp. 132–36.
51. S. Enke, *Rev. Economics Statistics 42*, 175 (1960); ———, *Econ. Develop. Cult. Change 8*, 339 (1960); ———, *ibid. 10*, 427 (1962); A. O. Krueger and L. A. Sjaastad, *ibid.*, p. 423.
52. T. J. Samuel, *J. Family Welfare India 13*, 12 (1966).
53. Sixty-two countries, including 27 in Europe, give cash payments to people for having children [U.S. Social Security Administration, *Social Security Programs Throughout the World, 1967* (Government Printing Office, Washington, D.C., 1967), pp. xxvii–xxviii].
54. Average gross reproduction rates in the early 1960's were as follows: Hungary, 0.91; Bulgaria, 1.09; Romania, 1.15; Yugoslavia, 1.32.
55. O. A. Collver and E. Langlois, *Econ. Develop. Cult. Change 10*, 367 (1962); J. Weeks, [Univ. of California (Berkeley)], unpublished paper.
56. Roman Catholic textbooks condemn the "small" family (one with fewer than four children) as being abnormal [J. Blake, *Population Studies 20*, 27 (1966)].
57. Judith Blake's critical readings and discussions have greatly helped in the preparation of this article.

# The "Perfect Contraceptive" Population

The extent and implications of unwanted fertility in the United States are considered.

Larry Bumpass and Charles F. Westoff

Recent discussions of population policy have raised and sharpened the question of unwanted fertility in the United States (1). The issue is whether the elimination of unwanted fertility would have a significant effect on our rate of population growth, and the discussion has revolved in part around what might be called the demographic implications of "perfect contraception." We are not suggesting that such a technological development is in sight, or that, if it were,

we would not have to be concerned about problems of distribution and use. The "perfect contraceptive" population is simply a model in which couples can avoid having more children than they want and do not have children before they want them. In the broader sense we are visualizing the "complete fertility controlling population" rather than the "perfectly contraceptive population." The achievement of such a state of affairs might well require social policies for the development of more effective contraceptive techniques and more efficient distribution systems as well as the legalization of abortion on request. However, this article is focused on *implications* of the elimination of unwanted fertility rather than on specific policies necessary to realize this goal.

We make no artificial assumptions about fecundity; we assume that the current incidence of subfecundity (less than normal capacity to reproduce) in the United States will continue. Also, we are *not* assuming that every couple will practice contraception or that all couples will begin using contraception at the same stage of their marriage. The system is completely voluntary. The only condition we are imposing is that couples can control their fertility completely in the sense that they can, within the limits of physiological capacity and variability, have the number of children they want, when they want them. If a husband and wife prefer to have chil-

Dr. Bumpass is assistant professor of sociology at the University of Wisconsin, Madison. Dr. Westoff is professor of sociology at Princeton University, Princeton, New Jersey, and executive director of the National Commission on Population Growth and the American Future, Washington, D.C.

Table 1. Percentages of births occurring between 1960 and 1965 reported to have been unwanted, by birth order and race. The values in parentheses are numbers of births.*

| Race | All | Birth order | | | | | |
|------|-----|---|---|---|---|---|---|
| | | 1 | 2 | 3 | 4 | 5 | 6+ |
| | | *1) Unwanted by both spouses* | | | | | |
| Total | 17 | 4 | 6 | 18 | 25 | 39 | 45 |
| White | 14 | 3 | 5 | 17 | 23 | 36 | 39 |
| Negro | 31 | 9 | 17 | 24 | 37 | 51 | 61 |
| | | *2) Unwanted by at least one spouse* | | | | | |
| Total | 22 | 5 | 10 | 24 | 35 | 49 | 55 |
| White | 19 | 4 | 7 | 23 | 32 | 46 | 48 |
| Negro | 41 | 15 | 24 | 37 | 51 | 61 | 72 |
| | | *3) Medium estimate, average of categories 1 and 2* | | | | | |
| Total | 19 (4,264) | 5 (1,090) | 8 (1,020) | 21 (792) | 30 (532) | 44 (328) | 50 (502) |
| White | 17 (3,091) | 4 (839) | 6 (779) | 20 (602) | 28 (397) | 41 (215) | 43 (259) |
| Negro | 36 (1,108) | 12 (234) | 20 (229) | 30 (180) | 44 (131) | 56 (107) | 66 (227) |

* The 1965 NFS double-sampled Negroes. Consequently, for measures computed for the total sample, the data for non-Negroes are weighted by a factor of 2. In this and all subsequent tables based on the NFS, the number of cases reported for the total are unweighted and represent the actual number of sample cases on which the statistics are based. Non-whites other than Negroes are included in the total.

dren right away or want a large family, they may use no contraception at all. On the other hand, if they wish to control their fertility (a virtually universal wish in the sense that practically all exposed couples in the United States use contraception sooner or later) (2), they shall be able to practice completely effective and completely acceptable contraception continuously. "Completely effective" means that the failure rate is zero; "completely acceptable" means that the use of contraception carries no costs of any kind—economic, social, or psychological—and that its use would be interrupted only for the purpose of conceiving. While such conditions are Utopian, the model provides a useful framework for assessing the implications of current levels of unwanted fertility in the United States for the rate of population growth.

Radically different policy implications flow from (i) the position that achieving a zero or near-zero rate of population growth requires changing the number of children couples want, and (ii) the position that eliminating unwanted births is sufficient. Consequently, it is important that we evaluate the number of unwanted births in the United States on the basis of the most recent detailed data available. Our estimates are based on the 1965 National Fertility Study (NFS), an interview survey of a probability sample of 5600 married women throughout the nation (3).

## Measurement of Unwanted Fertility

Reliable reports on unwanted births are difficult to obtain, since the admission that a birth was unwanted reflects on the respondent's ability to control fertility and perhaps also on the status of the child. Unwanted fertility was measured in the 1965 NFS on the basis of questions about the circumstances of each pregnancy. Women who reported the use of some contraceptive method preceding a pregnancy were asked, "Under which of these circumstances did this pregnancy occur?" A card listing the following categories was shown to the respondent:

1) While using a method and did not want to become pregnant at that time.
2) While not using a method but did not want to become pregnant at that time.
3) When stopped using a method in order to have a child.

Women who reported circumstances 1 or 2 were then asked, "Before you became pregnant this time, did you want to have a child (or another child) sometime?" and "Did your husband want to have a child (or another child) sometime?"

Women who reported not having practiced contraception prior to pregnancy were asked: "Was the *only* reason you did not use any method then because you wanted to have a baby as soon as possible?" Those who answered "No" were asked the same questions as the other group about whether they had wanted another child sometime.

Since couples are not always in agreement on the desirability of having additional children, alternative definitions of "unwanted" fertility are possible. A minimal definition would require that both spouses had been reported not to have wanted another child before pregnancy occurred. A broader definition would require only that one spouse had been reported not to have wanted an additional child. When husband and wife disagree on this question, some couples will intentionally have another child, others will not. It seems reasonable to assume that the proportion of unwanted births lies somewhere between estimates resulting from these two definitions, and that the average of the two constitutes a best estimate. We use this estimate throughout the text, although the consequences of alternative definitions are reported in several tables for the reader's evaluation.

To what extent are these measures of unwanted fertility reliable and valid? As part of the 1965 NFS, a subsample of the original sample of women was re-interviewed 3 to 5 months later, to assess the reliability of survey data on fertility and family planning. The percentage of births classified as unwanted differs by 0.3 percent in the two interviews. Checks for internal consistency reveal that none of the women who reported that their last child was unwanted replied (to a different question) that they intended to have additional children. In addition, the NFS estimate is consistent with reports of other fertility surveys based on differing measurement techniques (4).

An indirect check on the validity of our estimates can be made in terms of contraceptive efficacy. When we consider women who are near the end of the childbearing stage (40 to 44 years of age), the percentage classified as having experienced at least one unwanted birth implies, even when allowance is made for underreporting, an average contraceptive efficacy that is improbably high (5). Realistic assumptions about the level of contraceptive efficacy of this population would very likely lead to a figure for the proportion who had experienced at least one unwanted birth that is higher than the estimate obtained by the measures used here (6). This is independent evidence that there is considerable rationalization in the report of unwanted births and that our estimates of unwanted fertility are not likely to be too high.

## Incidence and Characteristics of Unwanted Fertility

In order to focus on the most recent picture for which data are available, we have limited the analysis in this section to births which occurred between the beginning of 1960 and the time of interview, the autumn of 1965.

It is evident from the data of Table 1 that unwanted births comprised a substantial proportion of total births during these years. Our estimates indicate that one-fifth of all births and more than one-third of Negro births between 1960 and 1965 were unwanted. As one would expect, the proportion of unwanted births increases rapidly with birth order. Almost one-third of all fourth-order births and one-half of all sixth- or higher-order births were unwanted; for Negroes the corresponding proportions are nearly one-half and two-thirds. This high level of unwanted births among Negroes indicates the magnitude of the burden of unwanted dependents that is borne by this population, but the problems of unwanted births are substantial among whites as well.

The incidence of unwanted births is negatively related to both education and income (Tables 2 and 3). In general, the proportion of unwanted births is approximately twice as high among wives with less than a high school education as among wives who have attended college. By income, the proportion of births reported as unwanted varies little for families whose 1964 income was over $5000, but it is more than twice as high for families with

incomes of less than $3000 as for those with incomes of over $10,000. This differential is particularly marked among Negroes.

We have approximated the Social Security Administration's definition of poverty (7), and the results are presented in Table 4. Since family size is one component of that definition, many couples would not have been classified as poor were it not for their having had unwanted children. Consequently, the results indicate the coincidence of poverty and unwanted births rather than a propensity of the "poor" to have unwanted children. Among the "poor" in 1965, unwanted births constituted almost two-fifths of all births and three-fifths of all sixth- and higher-order births; among the "non-poor" one out of every seven births was unwanted among whites and one out of every five among Negroes (8).

### Estimates for All Women

The foregoing analysis is based on a sample of married women living with their husbands in 1965; consequently, births to women not living with their

husbands and most illegitimate births are not represented (9). In the absence of reliable data on the subject, our procedures are based on the assumption that the incidence and birth-order distribution of unwanted births are the same for such births as for births reported by wives now living with their husbands. This undoubtedly is a bias in the direction of underestimating the extent of unwanted fertility.

We prepared our estimates separately by race and birth order and then summed them to obtain the total. We estimate that in the period 1960 to 1965 there were 4.7 million births that would have been prevented by "perfect contraception." These births represent one-fifth of all births during the period. Approximately 2 million of these unwanted births occurred among the poor and the near-poor, and half of these among the Negro poor and near-poor (Table 5).

### Timing Failures

While the level of unwanted births is high, the data of Table 6 make it clear that many desired births are tim-

Table 2. Percentages of unwanted births (medium estimate) occurring between 1960 and 1965, by wife's education, by race, and by birth order. The values in parentheses are numbers of births.*

| Wife's education | Total | White | Negro | Birth order for total | | | | | |
|---|---|---|---|---|---|---|---|---|---|
| | | | | 1 | 2 | 3 | 4 | 5 | 6+ |
| Less than 12 years | 26 (1,842) | 21 (1,153) | 42 (653) | 5 (341) | 11 (380) | 26 (339) | 31 (249) | 42 (188) | 54 (335) |
| 12 years | 16 (1,742) | 14 (1,361) | 28 (358) | 4 (525) | 6 (437) | 20 (232) | 32 (207) | 48 (102) | 44 (139) |
| College | 13 (688) | 11 (577) | 25 (95) | 4 (223) | 8 (202) | 16 (121) | 22 (76) | 42 (38) | 45 (28) |

* See footnote to Table 1.

Table 3. Percentages of unwanted births (medium estimate) occurring between 1960 and 1965, by 1964 family income, birth order, and race. The values in parentheses are numbers of births.*

| Income (dollars) | Total | White | Negro | Birth order for total | | | | |
|---|---|---|---|---|---|---|---|---|
| | | | | 1 | 2 | 3 | 4 | 5+ |
| Less than 3,000 | 34 (436) | 27 (178) | 42 (244) | 10 (95) | 14 (79) | 38 (62) | 42 (48) | 57 (152) |
| 3,000–4,999 | 24 (1,032) | 18 (562) | 39 (446) | 7 (282) | 12 (224) | 23 (170) | 30 (122) | 56 (234) |
| 5,000–6,999 | 16 (1,289) | 14 (977) | 30 (298) | 3 (358) | 6 (335) | 22 (248) | 30 (144) | 44 (204) |
| 7,000–9,999 | 16 (867) | 16 (772) | 28 (84) | 4 (214) | 4 (226) | 20 (174) | 29 (121) | 42 (132) |
| 10,000 and over | 15 (561) | 15 (541) | 16 (19) | 3 (123) | 9 (143) | 14 (120) | 26 (88) | 34 (87) |

* See footnote to Table 1.

Table 4. Percentages of unwanted births (medium estimate) occurring between 1960 and 1965, by poverty status, race, and birth order. The values in parentheses are numbers of births.*

| Poverty status | Total | White | Negro | Birth order for total | | | | | |
|---|---|---|---|---|---|---|---|---|---|
| | | | | 1 | 2 | 3 | 4 | 5 | 6+ |
| Poor and near-poor | 32 | 25 | 46 | 7 | 14 | 28 | 34 | 46 | 56 |
| Poor | 37 (861) | 31 (346) | 47 (494) | 9 (135) | 16 (179) | 30 (213) | 35 (186) | 47 (178) | 61 (337) |
| Near-poor | 23 (424) | 16 (253) | 40 (170) | 5 (137) | 10 (151) | 22 (130) | 32 (77) | 43 (63) | 42 (120) |
| Non-poor | 15 (2,979) | 15 (2,492) | 22 (444) | 4 (1,674) | 6 (1,481) | 20 (1,061) | 28 (670) | 42 (308) | 42 (320) |

* See footnote to Table 1.

Table 5. Estimated numbers (in thousands) of unwanted births in the United States between 1960 and 1965,* by birth order, race, and poverty status.

| Race | All birth orders | Poor and near-poor | Non-poor | Birth order for total | | | | | |
|---|---|---|---|---|---|---|---|---|---|
| | | | | 1 | 2 | 3 | 4 | 5 | 6+ |
| | | | *1) Unwanted by both spouses* | | | | | | |
| Total | 4,050 | 1,738 | 2,312 | 261 | 369 | 831 | 742 | 669 | 1,178 |
| White | 2,828 | 838 | 1,990 | 176 | 236 | 677 | 576 | 499 | 664 |
| Negro | 1,103 | 836 | 267 | 82 | 116 | 126 | 151 | 157 | 471 |
| | | | *2) Unwanted by at least one spouse* | | | | | | |
| Total | 5,321 | 2,214 | 3,107 | 376 | 553 | 1,102 | 1,031 | 841 | 1,418 |
| White | 3,736 | 1,062 | 2,674 | 234 | 375 | 879 | 800 | 632 | 816 |
| Negro | 1,432 | 1,067 | 365 | 132 | 163 | 193 | 206 | 186 | 552 |
| | | | *3) Medium estimate, average of categories 1 and 2* | | | | | | |
| Total | 4,685 | 1,976 | 2,709 | 319 | 461 | 966 | 886 | 755 | 1,298 |
| White | 3,282 | 950 | 2,332 | 205 | 306 | 778 | 688 | 566 | 740 |
| Negro | 1,267 | 951 | 316 | 107 | 139 | 159 | 178 | 172 | 512 |

* Proportions of unwanted births in the NFS sample are applied to vital statistics data for the United States (see Appendix for technical details). In the absence of official data on births by poverty status, we have estimated the number of unwanted births to the poor and near-poor on the basis of the distribution by poverty status of unwanted births in the NFS sample.

ing failures. A birth was classified as a timing failure when it was reported as wanted but not the result of the deliberate interruption of contraception.

Of wanted births occurring between 1960 and 1965, two-fifths would have occurred later if their timing had been controlled. The short-run demographic effects of the prevention of timing failures depend upon the length of time considered and the assumed time required for the transition to perfect contraception (contraception enabling every couple to avoid failures in regulating family size and in timing births). For example, if perfect contraception had been universally employed at the beginning of 1960, perhaps 7 percent of the wanted births that occurred between 1960 and 1965 would have been delayed until after 1965. This estimate is based on the assumption that the average length of a successfully planned interval is 1 year longer than that of an interval in which timing was not controlled. If births are delayed, total fertility for each cohort (women born in the same year) being kept constant, there is a dip in births while the change occurs and no subsequent "makeup" of the lost births until the mean age of childbearing falls. When the transition is complete, a certain number of births will have been deferred to subsequent

years, and this number will remain fixed so long as the new spacing pattern persists.

After the transitory dip is over, the number of births may be affected by increased spacing (total fertility for each cohort being kept constant) because fertility is centered on a lower portion of the stable age distribution. This effect is negligible in a low-mortality population reproducing at a rate near replacement.

There is, however, one possible indirect consequence of such timing changes that has potential long-run significance. It has been suggested that the longer a birth is delayed, the less likely a woman is to have that birth or a subsequent birth (10). The longer a couple puts off having a "wanted" child, the more opportunity the wife has to acquire role patterns at variance with early child-care responsibility. At some point that birth, or a desired subsequent birth, may no longer seem so desirable. In addition, the delay of a desired birth increases the possibility that the birth will be prevented by subfecundity. In any event, the major demographic effect of the universal use of contraception would be the prevention of unwanted births. In the next section we will discuss the long-run implications of this effect.

## Long-Run Implications for U.S. Growth Rate

Since nearly 20 percent of all recent births were unwanted, the elimination of unwanted births could substantially reduce our future growth rate. However, the size of this reduction would depend upon the number of children that women now entering the childbearing years will ultimately want to have.

Viewed from a cohort perspective, for women who were near the end of their childbearing years in 1965 (ages 35 to 44), the elimination of births reported to have been unwanted would have reduced their fertility from 3.0 to 2.5 births per woman. Since an eventual zero rate of population growth would require cohort fertility of about 2.25 births per woman, the elimination of unwanted births would not have been sufficient to establish exact replacement for this cohort, but it would have resulted in considerable progress toward that objective. The proportion of unwanted births (16 percent) reported by this cohort—the figure used to calculate the above estimate of 2.5 births—is lower than the proportion reported for all women in the period 1960–1965, probably due to additional underreporting of unwanted births resulting from the longer period of time that had elapsed since the events in question in the case of the women aged 35 to 44. The demographic effect of eliminating unwanted births is probably greater than we infer because of this underreporting by older women and the probable underreporting of unwanted births in general, and also because the additional children born to these older women before they reach menopause will undoubtedly be mostly unwanted.

The above estimate is based on the experience of married women whose childbearing took place in the high fertility period of the early 1950's. Under circumstances of perfect contraception, women now entering the childbearing years might decide to have larger families than women who have preceded them would have had if they had complete control of fertility, but this does not seem likely. Rapid diffusion of use of the pill has continued since 1965, and one of the consequences of this diffusion may be reduction of the number of "desired" as well as of unwanted children. As women are able increasingly to postpone pregnancy and to enter into nonfamilial roles (particularly employment), many may prefer to have

Table 6. Percentages of wanted births classified as timing failures,* by birth order and race. The values in parentheses are numbers of births.†

| Race | All birth orders | Birth order | | | | | |
|---|---|---|---|---|---|---|---|
| | | 1 | 2 | 3 | 4 | 5 | 6+ |
| Total | 43 (3,217) | 38 (1,020) | 42 (906) | 50 (587) | 50 (335) | 44 (162) | 47 (207) |
| White | 42 (2,513) | 36 (805) | 40 (722) | 48 (466) | 48 (269) | 42 (116) | 46 (135) |
| Negro | 56 (657) | 50 (199) | 61 (174) | 59 (114) | 62 (64) | 57 (42) | 50 (64) |

* A birth was classified as a timing failure when reported as wanted but not the result of deliberate interruption of contraception.   † See footnote to Table 1.

smaller families than they would otherwise have chosen. If, in addition, there is a trend toward nonfamilial female roles, there may be strong pressures against any upsurge in the average family size that would be achieved by American women with complete fertility control.

In fact there are already indications that the ultimate family size of the most recent cohorts may be lower than that of preceding cohorts (11). This decline may be the result of some reduction in unwanted births, in some reduction in the number of children women want to have, or in some combination of these factors. Predicting the fertility of young women is always precarious, but it seems likely to us that, under the assumption of perfect contraception, the ultimate number of children today's young women would bear would be below the number inferred, under the same assumption, for women who were between the ages of 35 and 44 in 1965. There is some evidence from longitudinal studies that success in the control of fertility results in smaller families than were originally desired (12).

However, it is very important that we keep in mind the legacy of past fertility when considering the potential implications, for the U.S. growth rate, of the elimination of unwanted births. Even if exact cohort replacement could be achieved, the population would not immediately cease to grow. The time required for cohort fertility to reach the replacement rate would depend upon the speed with which universal perfect contraception was achieved. After the replacement rate had been attained, it would be some time before the effects of past fertility on the age structure would level off. Frejka has prepared estimates directly relevant to this question (13). He demonstrates that if the cohort comprised of women entering their childbearing years between 1965 and 1970 and all subsequent cohorts were to achieve a cohort fertility of exact replacement, the population would continue to grow at least until the year 2035, with a resultant increase in size of 40 to 50 percent.

In summary, the elimination of unwanted births would lead to a reduced growth rate for the United States, barring a marked increase in the average number of children desired. However, even if cohort replacement were achieved (perhaps as a consequence of other developments as well), a zero growth rate for the United States could

not be achieved for over 60 years, by which time the population would number over 280 million. The longer it takes to achieve universal perfect contraception, the longer it will take to reduce our growth rate, and the larger, of course, will be the eventual size of our population.

In terms of the implications for a population policy goal of zero growth, our findings do not imply that the task of influencing people to want fewer children should be ignored, especially since this number could shift upward again. However, the elimination of unwanted births would have considerable demographic effect, it would be desirable in human terms, and it would probably be a more readily attainable objective.

## Appendix: Comparison with Other Measures

Since the conclusions reached by the use of more conventional measures of "desired" or "ideal" family size (14) differ radically from those reached by our procedure of inferring the desired number of children, a word on the differences in the two approaches is necessary. The first is used typically in surveys with married women of all ages within the reproductive span and with varying numbers of children; in this approach the woman is simply asked how many children she would like to have or how many she would consider ideal for herself, or, in some instances, for the average American family. Our approach has been to infer the desired number of children by subtracting the number of unwanted births from the total number of births. The latter procedure results in considerably lower estimates of the number desired. For example, married women aged 35 to 44 in 1965 reported, through the direct approach, a "desired family size" of 3.4 children, as compared with 2.5 children as estimated by our procedure.

In general, the difference is probably attributable to real differences reflected by the two types of measurement. In the direct approach, desired family size relates to the time of the survey and is based on the respondent's fertility history and on her and her husband's adjustment to it. It is not at all inconsistent for a couple that has had a child that had been unwanted to state later, on the basis of a satisfactory (even beneficial) adjustment to the unwanted

birth, that the size of their family is what they desire. To infer that this is the number of children such couples would have wanted under the conditions of perfect fertility control would be erroneous. For couples early in their life cycle, the measure of "desired family size" may be highly invalid as a predictor of the number of children they would have if they could control their fertility. The average family size desired by young couples corresponds closely with the eventual average family size for these couples, regardless of the number of unwanted births; this suggests that the number of children young couples desire before the experience of childrearing may be largely a reflection of the observed sizes of the families of other couples of similar social status.

On the other hand, when desired family size is measured by subtracting (for women past the childbearing years) the number of unwanted births from the number of children borne, the time focus is on evaluation of the event at the time of pregnancy. Although the responses may still be influenced by intervening experience, this bias should be much less than the bias when the reference is to the present, or to the future conditioned by the present.

The two types of variables can be measured independently, since about half of the women who reported an unwanted birth also said they would not have preferred to have fewer children than they had. Both measures are useful, but it seems to us that the approach we have defined in this article is the more suited to the task of assessing the demographic implications of perfect contraception.

### References and Notes

1. J. Blake, *Science* 164, 522 (1969); O. Harkavy, F. S. Jaffe, S. Wishik, *ibid.* 165, 367 (1969).
2. C. F. Westoff and N. B. Ryder, in *Fertility and Family Planning: A World View*, S. J. Behrman, L. Corsa, R. Freedman, Eds. (Univ. of Michigan Press, Ann Arbor, 1969), p. 394.
3. For a description of this sample see N. B. Ryder and C. F. Westoff, *Science* 153, 1199 (1966). A high level of unwanted fertility in the United States has been reported on the basis of national fertility studies; in this article we draw attention to the implications of the current patterns of unwanted births. For the earlier reports see R. Freedman, P. K. Whelpton, A. A. Campbell, *Family Planning, Sterility and Population Growth* (McGraw-Hill, New York, 1959), pp. 100–153; P. K. Whelpton, A. A. Campbell, J. E. Patterson, *Fertility and Family Planning in the U.S.* (Princeton Univ. Press, Princeton, N.J., 1966), pp. 221–275, 361–370; N. B. Ryder and C. F. Westoff, *Demography* 6, 435 (1969).
4. N. B. Ryder and C. F. Westoff, *Reproduction in the United States: 1965* (Princeton Univ. Press, Princeton, N.J., in press), chap. 14, table 5.
5. Ryder notes that these levels of unwanted fertility are consistent with a regulatory pro-

cedure that is 99 percent perfect. See N. B. Ryder, "The time series of fertility in the United States," paper presented before the International Union for the Scientific Study of Population, London, 1969.
6. R. G. Potter and J. M. Sakoda, *Demography* **3**, 450 (1966).
7. M. Orshansky, *Soc. Secur. Bull.* (March 1968).
8. These estimates of the percentages of unwanted births among poor and non-poor, and the estimates of the gross number of unwanted births in the period 1960 to 1965, discussed in the next section, are of the same order of magnitude as values presented in a preliminary approximation by F. S. Jaffe and A. F. Guttmacher, *Demography* **5**, 910 (1968).
9. Our sample design for a new national study in 1970 which calls for a sample of "ever married" women will provide a better basis for making these estimates.
10. R. Freedman, L. C. Coombs, L. Bumpass, *Demography* **2**, 267 (1965).
11. N. B. Ryder, in *Fertility and Family Planning: A World View*, S. J. Behrman, L. Corsa, R. Freedman, Eds. (Univ. of Michigan Press, Ann Arbor, 1969), pp. 99–123.
12. C. F. Westoff, E. G. Mishler, E. L. Kelly, *Amer. J. Sociol.* **62**, 494 (1957). Additional evidence pointing to the same hypothesis appears in the Princeton Fertility Study (unpublished tabulations).
13. T. Frejka, *Population Stud.* **22**, 394 (1968).
14. For discussion of the relationships between these variables see N. B. Ryder and C. F. Westoff, *Population Res.* (March 1969) and A. A. Campbell, *Fam. Planning Perspect.* **1**, No. 2, 33 (1969).
15. We thank Ansley J. Coale, Ronald Freedman, Fred Jaffe, Suzanne Keller, and Norman B. Ryder for critical appraisals of the manuscript. We also acknowledge the able computer programming assistance of Andrea Smith.

# Population and Panaceas: A Technological Perspective

*Paul R. Ehrlich and John P. Holdren*

Today more than one billion human beings are either undernourished or malnourished, and the human population is growing at a rate of 2% per year. The existing and impending crises in human nutrition and living conditions are well-documented but not widely understood. In particular, there is a tendency among the public, nurtured on Sunday-supplement conceptions of technology, to believe that science has the situation well in hand—that farming the sea and the tropics, irrigating the deserts, and generating cheap nuclear power in abundance hold the key to swift and certain solution of the problem. To espouse this belief is to misjudge the present severity of the situation, the disparate time scales on which technological progress and population growth operate, and the vast complexity of the problems beyond mere food production posed by population pressures. Unfortunately, scientists and engineers have themselves often added to the confusion by failing to distinguish between that which is merely theoretically feasible, and that which is economically and logistically practical.

As we will show here, man's present technology is inadequate to the task of maintaining the world's burgeoning billions, even under the most optimistic assumptions. Furthermore, technology is likely to remain inadequate until such time as the population growth rate is drastically reduced. This is not to assert that present efforts to "revolutionize" tropical agriculture, increase yields of fisheries, desalt water for irrigation, exploit new power sources, and implement related projects are not worthwhile. They may be. They could also easily produce the ultimate disaster for mankind if they are not applied with careful attention to their effects on the ecological systems necessary for our survival (Woodwell, 1967; Cole, 1968). And even if such projects are initiated with

The co-authors are affiliated, respectively, with the department of biological sciences, and with the Institute for Plasma Research and department of aeronautics and astronautics, Stanford University.

Reprinted by permission of the authors and the publisher from *BioScience* 19:1065–1071, December 1969.

unprecedented levels of staffing and expenditures, without population control they are doomed to fall far short. No effort to expand the carrying capacity of the Earth can keep pace with unbridled population growth.

To support these contentions, we summarize briefly the present lopsided balance sheet in the population/food accounting. We then examine the logistics, economics, and possible consequences of some technological schemes which have been proposed to help restore the balance, or, more ambitiously, to permit the maintenance of human populations much larger than today's. The most pertinent aspects of the balance are:

1) The world population reached 3.5 billion in mid-1968, with an annual increment of approximately 70 million people (itself increasing) and a doubling time on the order of 35 years (Population Reference Bureau, 1968).

2) Of this number of people, at least one-half billion are undernourished (deficient in calories or, more succinctly, slowly starving), and approximately an additional billion are malnourished (deficient in particular nutrients, mostly protein) (Borgstrom, 1965; Sukhatme, 1966). Estimates of the number actually perishing annually from starvation begin at 4 million and go up (Ehrlich, 1968) and depend in part on official definitions of starvation which conceal the true magnitude of hunger's contribution to the death rate (Lelyveld, 1968).

3) Merely to maintain present inadequate nutrition levels, the food requirements of Asia, Africa, and Latin America will, conservatively, increase by 26% in the 10-year period measured from 1965 to 1975 (Paddock and Paddock, 1967). World food production must double in the period 1965-2000 to stay even; it must triple if nutrition is to be brought up to minimum requirements.

## Food Production

That there is insufficient additional, good quality agricultural land available in the world to meet these needs is so well documented (Borgstrom, 1965) that we will not belabor the point here. What hope there is must rest with increasing yields on land presently cultivated, bringing marginal land into production, more efficiently exploiting the sea, and bringing less conventional methods of food production to fruition. In all these areas, science and technology play a dominant role. While space does not permit even a cursory look at all the proposals on these topics which have been advanced in recent years, a few representative examples illustrate our points.

*Conventional Agriculture.* Probably the most widely recommended means of increasing agricultural yields is through the more intensive use of fertilizers. Their production is straightforward, and a good deal is known about their effective application, although, as with many technologies we consider here, the environmental consequences of heavy fertilizer use are ill understood and potentially dangerous [1] (Wadleigh, 1968). But even ignoring such problems, we find staggering difficulties barring the implementation of fertilizer technology on the scale required. In this regard the accomplishments of countries such as Japan and the Netherlands are often cited as offering hope to the

[1] Barry Commoner, address to 135th Meeting of the AAAS, Dallas, Texas (28 December 1968).

underdeveloped world. Some perspective on this point is afforded by noting that if India were to apply fertilizer at the per capita level employed by the Netherlands, her fertilizer needs would be nearly half the present world output (United Nations, 1968).

On a more realistic plane, we note that although the goal for nitrogen fertilizer production in 1971 under India's fourth 5-year plan is 2.4 million metric tons (Anonymous, 1968a), Raymond Ewell (who has served as fertilizer production adviser to the Indian government for the past 12 years) suggests that less than 1.1 million metric tons is a more probable figure for that date.[2] Ewell cites poor plant maintenance, raw materials shortages, and power and transportation breakdowns as contributing to continued low production by existing Indian plants. Moreover, even when fertilizer is available, increases in productivity do not necessarily follow. In parts of the underdeveloped world lack of farm credit is limiting fertilizer distribution; elsewhere, internal transportation systems are inadequate to the task. Nor can the problem of educating farmers on the advantages and techniques of fertilizer use be ignored. A recent study (Parikh et al., 1968) of the Intensive Agriculture District Program in the Surat district of Gujarat, India (in which scientific fertilizer use was to have been a major ingredient) notes that "on the whole, the performance of adjoining districts which have similar climate but did not enjoy relative preference of input supply was as good as, if not better than, the programme district. . . . A particularly disheartening feature is that the farm production plans, as yet, do not carry any educative value and have largely failed to convince farmers to use improved practices in their proper combinations."

As a second example of a panacea in the realm of conventional agriculture, mention must be given to the development of new high-yield or high-protein strains of food crops. That such strains have the potential of making a major contribution to the food supply of the world is beyond doubt, but this potential is limited in contrast to the potential for population growth, and will be realized too slowly to have anything but a small impact on the immediate crisis. There are major difficulties impeding the widespread use of new high-yield grain varieties. Typically, the new grains require high fertilizer inputs to realize their full potential, and thus are subject to all the difficulties mentioned above. Some other problems were identified in a recent address by Lester R. Brown, administrator of the International Agricultural Development Service: the limited amount of irrigated land suitable for the new varieties, the fact that a farmer's willingness to innovate fluctuates with the market prices (which may be driven down by high-yield crops), and the possibility of tieups at market facilities inadequate for handling increased yields.[3]

Perhaps even more important, the new grain varieties are being rushed into production without adequate field testing, so that we are unsure of how resistant they will be to the attacks of insects and plant diseases. William Paddock has presented a plant pathologist's view of the crash programs to shift to new varieties (Paddock, 1967). He describes India's dramatic program of planting improved Mexican wheat, and continues: "Such a rapid switch to a new variety is clearly understandable in a country that tottered on the brink of famine. Yet with such limited testing, one wonders what unknown path-

---

[2] Raymond Ewell, private communication (1 December 1968).

[3] Lester R. Brown, address to the Second International Conference on the War on Hunger, Washington, D.C. (February 1968).

ogens await a climatic change which will give the environmental conditions needed for their growth." Introduction of the new varieties creates enlarged monocultures of plants with essentially unknown levels of resistance to disaster. Clearly, one of the prices that is paid for higher yield is a higher risk of widespread catastrophe. And the risks are far from local: since the new varieties require more "input" of pesticides (with all their deleterious ecological side effects), these crops may ultimately contribute to the defeat of other environment-related panaceas, such as extracting larger amounts of food from the sea.

A final problem must be mentioned in connection with these strains of food crops. In general, the hungriest people in the world are also those with the most conservative food habits. Even rather minor changes, such as that from a rice variety in which the cooked grains stick together to one in which the grains fall apart, may make new foods unacceptable. It seems to be an unhappy fact of human existence that people would rather starve than eat a nutritious substance which they do not recognize as food.[4]

Beyond the economic, ecological, and sociological problems already mentioned in connection with high-yield agriculture, there is the overall problem of time. We need time to breed the desired characteristics of yield and hardiness into a vast array of new strains (a tedious process indeed), time to convince farmers that it is necessary that they change their time-honored ways of cultivation, and time to convince hungry people to change the staples of their diet. The Paddocks give 20 years as the "rule of thumb" for a new technique or plant variety to progress from conception to substantial impact on farming (Paddock and Paddock, 1967). They write: "It is true that a *massive* research attack on the problem could bring some striking results in less than 20 years. But I do not find such an attack remotely contemplated in the thinking of those officials capable of initiating it." Promising as high-yield agriculture may be, the funds, the personnel, the ecological expertise, and the necessary years are unfortunately not at our disposal. Fulfillment of the promise will come too late for many of the world's starving millions, if it comes at all.

*Bringing More Land Under Cultivation.* The most frequently mentioned means of bringing new land into agricultural production are farming the tropics and irrigating arid and semiarid regions. The former, although widely discussed in optimistic terms, has been tried for years with incredibly poor results, and even recent experiments have not been encouraging. One essential difficulty is the unsuitability of tropical soils for supporting typical foodstuffs instead of jungles (McNeil, 1964; Paddock and Paddock, 1964). Also, "the tropics" are a biologically more diverse area than the temperate zones, so that farming technology developed for one area will all too often prove useless in others. We shall see that irrigating the deserts, while more promising, has serious limitations in terms of scale, cost, and lead time.

The feasible approaches to irrigation of arid lands appear to be limited to large-scale water projects involving dams and transport in canals, and desalination of ocean and brackish water. Supplies of usable ground water are already badly depleted in most areas where they are accessible, and natural recharge

---

[4] For a more detailed discussion of the psychological problems in persuading people to change their dietary habits, see McKenzie, 1968.

is low enough in most arid regions that such supplies do not offer a long-term solution in any case. Some recent statistics will give perspective to the discussion of water projects and desalting which follows. In 1966, the United States was using about 300 billion gal of water per day, of which 135 billion gal were consumed by agriculture and 165 billion gal by municipal and industrial users (Sporn, 1966). The bulk of the agricultural water cost the farmer from 5 to 10 cents/1000 gal; the highest price paid for agricultural water was 15 cents/1000 gal. For small industrial and municipal supplies, prices as high as 50 to 70 cents/1000 gal were prevalent in the U.S. arid regions, and some communities in the Southwest were paying on the order of $1.00/1000 gal for "project" water. The extremely high cost of the latter stems largely from transportation costs, which have been estimated at 5 to 15 cents/1000 gal per 100 miles (International Atomic Energy Agency, 1964).

We now examine briefly the implications of such numbers in considering the irrigation of the deserts. The most ambitious water project yet conceived in this country is the North American Water and Power Alliance, which proposes to distribute water from the great rivers of Canada to thirsty locations all over the United States. Formidable political problems aside (some based on the certainty that in the face of expanding populations, demands for water will eventually arise at the source), this project would involve the expenditure of $100 billion in construction costs over a 20-year completion period. At the end of this time, the yield to the United States would be 69 million acre feet of water annually (Kelly, 1966), or 63 billion gal per day. If past experience with massive water projects is any guide, these figures are overoptimistic; but if we assume they are not, it is instructive to note that this monumental undertaking would provide for an increase of only 21% in the water consumption of the United States, during a period in which the population is expected to increase by between 25 and 43% (U.S. Dept. of Commerce, 1966). To assess the possible contribution to the *world* food situation, we assume that all this water could be devoted to agriculture, although extrapolation of present consumption patterns indicates that only about one-half would be. Then using the rather optimistic figure of 500 gal per day to grow the food to feed one person, we find that this project could feed 126 million additional people. Since this is less than 8% of the projected world population growth during the construction period (say 1970 to 1990), it should be clear that even the most massive water projects can make but a token contribution to the solution of the world food problem in the long term. And in the crucial short term—the years preceding 1980—*no* additional people will be fed by projects still on the drawing board today.

In summary, the cost is staggering, the scale insufficient, and the lead time too long. Nor need we resort to such speculation about the future for proof of the failure of technological "solutions" in the absence of population control. The highly touted and very expensive Aswan Dam project, now nearing completion, will ultimately supply food (at the present miserable diet level) for less than Egypt's population growth during the time of construction (Borgstrom, 1965; Cole, 1968). Furthermore, its effect on the fertility of the Nile Delta may be disastrous, and, as with all water projects of this nature, silting of the reservoir will destroy the gains in the long term (perhaps in 100 years).

Desalting for irrigation suffers somewhat similar limitations. The desalting plants operational in the world today produce water at individual rates of 7.5 million gal/day and less, at a cost of 75 cents/1000 gal and up, the cost increasing as the plant size decreases (Bender, 1969). The most optimistic firm proposal which anyone seems to have made for desalting with present or soon-to-be available technology is a 150 million gal per day nuclear-powered installation studied by the Bechtel Corp. for the Los Angeles Metropolitan Water District. Bechtel's early figures indicated that water from this complex would be available at the site for 27–28 cents/1000 gal (Galstann and Currier, 1967). However, skepticism regarding the economic assumptions leading to these figures (Milliman, 1966) has since proven justified—the project was shelved after spiralling construction cost estimates indicated an actual water cost of 40–50 cents/1000 gal. Use of even the original figures, however, bears out our contention that the *most* optimistic assumptions do not alter the verdict that technology is losing the food/population battle. For 28 cents/1000 gal is still approximately twice the cost which farmers have hitherto been willing or able to pay for irrigation water. If the Bechtel plant had been intended to supply agricultural needs, which it was not, one would have had to add to an already unacceptable price the very substantial cost of transporting the water inland.

Significantly, studies have shown that the economies of scale in the distillation process are essentially exhausted by a 150 million gal per day plant (International Atomic Energy Agency, 1964). Hence, merely increasing desalting capacity further will not substantially lower the cost of the water. On purely economic grounds, then, it is unlikely that desalting will play a major role in food production by conventional agriculture in the short term.[5] Technological "break-throughs" will presumably improve this outlook with the passage of time, but world population growth will not wait.

Desalting becomes more promising if the high cost of the water can be offset by increased agricultural yields per gallon and, perhaps, use of a single nuclear installation to provide power for both the desalting and profitable on-site industrial processes. This prospect has been investigated in a thorough and well-documented study headed by E. A. Mason (Oak Ridge National Laboratory, 1968). The result is a set of preliminary figures and recommendations regarding nuclear-powered "agro-industrial complexes" for arid and semiarid regions, in which desalted water and fertilizer would be produced for use on an adjacent, highly efficient farm. In underdeveloped countries incapable of using the full excess power output of the reactor, this energy would be consumed in on-site production of industrial materials for sale on the world market. Both near-term (10 years hence) and far-term (20 years hence) technologies are considered, as are various mixes of farm and industrial products. The representative near-term case for which a detailed cost breakdown is given involves a seaside facility with a desalting capacity of 1 billion gal/day, a farm size of 320,000 acres, and an industrial electric power consumption of 1585 Mw. The initial investment for this complex is estimated at $1.8 billion, and annual operating costs at $236 million. If both the food and the industrial materials produced were sold (as opposed to giving the food, at

---

[5] An identical conclusion was reached in a recent study (Clawson et al., 1969) in which the foregoing points and numerous other aspects of desalting were treated in far more detail than was possible here.

least, to those in need who could not pay),[6] the estimated profit for such a complex, before subtracting financing costs, would be 14.6%.

The authors of the study are commendably cautious in outlining the assumptions and uncertainities upon which these figures rest. The key assumption is that 200 gal/day of water will grow the 2500 calories required to feed one person. Water/calorie ratios of this order or less have been achieved by the top 20% of farmers specializing in such crops as wheat, potatoes, and tomatoes; but more water is required for needed protein-rich crops such as peanuts and soybeans. The authors identify the uncertainty that crops usually raised separately can be grown together in tight rotation on the same piece of land. Problems of water storage between periods of peak irrigation demand, optimal patterns of crop rotation, and seasonal acreage variations are also mentioned. These "ifs" and assumptions, and those associated with the other technologies involved, are unfortunately often omitted when the results of such painstaking studies are summarized for more popular consumption (Anonymous, 1968b, 1968c). The result is the perpetuation of the public's tendency to confuse feasible and available, to see panaceas where scientists in the field concerned see only potential, realizable with massive infusions of time and money.

It is instructive, nevertheless, to examine the impact on the world food problem which the Oak Ridge complexes might have if construction were to begin today, and if all the assumptions about technology 10 years hence were valid *now*. At the industrial-agricultural mix pertinent to the sample case described above, the food produced would be adequate for just under 3 million people. This means that 23 such plants per year, at a cost of $41 billion, would have to be put in operation merely to keep pace with world population growth, to say nothing of improving the substandard diets of between one and two billion members of the present population. (Fertilizer production beyond that required for the on-site farm is of course a contribution in the latter regard, but the substantial additional costs of transporting it to where it is needed must then be accounted for.) Since approximately 5 years from the start of construction would be required to put such a complex into operation, we should commence work on at least 125 units post-haste, and begin at least 25 per year thereafter. If the technology *were* available now, the investment in construction over the next 5 years, prior to operation of the first plants, would be $315 billion—about 20 times the total U.S. foreign aid expenditure during the past 5 years. By the time the technology *is* available the bill will be much higher, if famine has not "solved" the problem for us.

This example again illustrates that scale, time, and cost are all working against technology in the short term. And if population growth is not decelerated, the increasing severity of population-related crises will surely neutralize the technological improvements of the middle and long terms.

*Other Food Panaceas.* "Food from the sea" is the most prevalent "answer" to the world food shortage in the view of the general public. This is not surprising, since estimates of the theoretical fisheries productivity of the sea run

---

[6] Confusing statements often are made about the possibility that food supply will outrun food demand in the future. In these statements, "demand" is used in the economic sense, and in this context many millions of starving people may generate no demand whatsoever. Indeed, one concern of those engaged in increasing food production is to find ways of increasing demand.

up to some 50-100 times current yields (Schmitt, 1965; Christy and Scott, 1965). Many practical and economic difficulties, however, make it clear that such a figure will never be reached, and that it will not even be approached in the foreseeable future. In 1966, the annual fisheries harvest was some 57 million metric tons (United Nations, 1968). A careful analysis (Meseck, 1961) indicates that this might be increased to a world production of 70 million metric tons by 1980. If this gain were realized, it would represent (assuming no violent change in population growth patterns) a small per capita *loss* in fisheries yield.

Both the short- and long-term outlooks for taking food from the sea are clouded by the problems of overexploitation, pollution (which is generally ignored by those calculating potential yields), and economics. Solving these problems will require more than technological legerdemain; it will also require unprecedented changes in human behavior, especially in the area of international cooperation. The unlikelihood that such cooperation will come about is reflected in the recent news (Anonymous, 1968d) that Norway has dropped out of the whaling industry because overfishing has depleted the stock below the level at which it may economically be harvested. In that industry, international controls were tried—and failed. The sea is, unfortunately, a "commons" (Hardin, 1968), and the resultant management problems exacerbate the biological and technical problems of greatly increasing our "take." One suspects that the return per dollar poured into the sea will be much less than the corresponding return from the land for many years, and the return from the land has already been found wanting.

Synthetic foods, protein culture with petroleum, saline agriculture, and weather modification all may hold promise for the future, but all are at present expensive and available only on an extremely limited scale. The research to improve this situation will also be expensive, and, of course, time-consuming. In the absence of funding, it will not occur at all, a fact which occasionally eludes the public and the Congress.

## Domestic and Industrial Water Supplies

The world has water problems, even exclusive of the situation in agriculture. Although total precipitation should in theory be adequate in quantity for several further doublings of population, serious shortages arising from problems of quality, irregularity, and distribution already plague much of the world. Underdeveloped countries will find the water needs of industrialization staggering: 240,000 gal of water are required to produce a ton of newsprint; 650,000 gal, to produce a ton of steel (International Atomic Energy Agency, 1964). Since maximum acceptable water costs for domestic and industrial use are higher than for agriculture, those who can afford it are or soon will be using desalination (40-100 + cents/1000 gal) and used-water renovation (54-57 cents/1000 gal [Ennis, 1967]). Those who cannot afford it are faced with allocating existing supplies between industry and agriculture, and as we have seen, they must choose the latter. In this circumstance, the standard of living remains pitifully low. Technology's only present answer is massive externally-financed complexes of the sort considered above, and we have already suggested there the improbability that we are prepared to pay the bill rung up by present population growth.

The widespread use of desalted water by those who *can* afford it brings up another problem only rarely mentioned to date, the disposal of the salts. The product of the distillation processes in present use is a hot brine with salt concentration several times that of seawater. Both the temperature and the salinity of this effluent will prove fatal to local marine life if it is simply exhausted to the ocean. The most optimistic statement we have seen on this problem is that "*smaller plants* (our emphasis) at seaside locations may return the concentrated brine to the ocean if proper attention is paid to the design of the outfall, and to the effect on the local marine ecology." (McIlhenny, 1966) The same writer identifies the major economic uncertainties connected with extracting the salts for sale (to do so is straightforward, but often not profitable). Nor can one simply evaporate the brine and leave the residue in a pile —the 150 million gal/day plant mentioned above would produce brine bearing 90 million lb. of salts daily (based on figures by Parker, 1966). This amount of salt would cover over 15 acres to a depth of one foot. Thus, every year a plant of the billion gallon per day, agro-industrial complex size would produce a pile of salt over 52 ft deep and covering a square mile. The high winds typical of coastal deserts would seriously aggravate the associated soil contamination problem.

## Energy

Man's problems with energy supply are more subtle than those with food and water: we are not yet running out of energy, but we are being forced to use it faster than is probably healthy. The rapacious depletion of our fossil fuels is already forcing us to consider more expensive mining techniques to gain access to lower-grade deposits, such as the oil shales, and even the status of our high-grade uranium ore reserves is not clear-cut (Anonymous, 1968e).

A widely held misconception in this connection is that nuclear power is "dirt cheap," and as such represents a panacea for developed and underdeveloped nations alike. To the contrary, the largest nuclear-generating stations now in operation are just competitive with or marginally superior to modern coal-fired plants of comparable size (where coal is not scarce); at best, both produce power for on the order of 4-5 mills (tenths of a cent) per kilowatt-hour. Smaller nuclear units remain less economical than their fossil-fueled counterparts. Underdeveloped countries can rarely use the power of the larger plants. Simply speaking, there are not enough industries, appliances, and light bulbs to absorb the output, and the cost of industrialization and modernization exceeds the cost of the power required to sustain it by orders of magnitude, regardless of the source of the power. (For example, one study noted that the capital requirement to consume the output of a 70,000 kilowatt plant— about $1.2 million worth of electricity per year at 40% utilization and 5 mills/ kwh—is $111 million per year if the power is consumed by metals industries, $270 million per year for petroleum product industries [E. S. Mason, 1957].) Hence, at least at present, only those underdeveloped countries which are short of fossil fuels or inexpensive means to transport them are in particular need of nuclear power.

Prospects for major reductions in the cost of nuclear power in the future hinge on the long-awaited breeder reactor and the still further distant thermonuclear reactor. In neither case is the time scale or the ultimate cost of energy a matter of any certainty. The breeder reactor, which converts more nonfissile uranium ($^{238}U$) or thorium to fissionable material than it consumes as fuel for itself, effectively extends our nuclear fuel supply by a factor of approximately 400 (Cloud, 1968). It is not expected to become competitive economically with conventional reactors until the 1980's (Bump, 1967). Reductions in the unit energy cost beyond this date are not guaranteed, due both to the probable continued high capital cost of breeder reactors and to increasing costs for the ore which the breeders will convert to fuel. In the latter regard, we mention that although crushing granite for its few parts per million of uranium and thorium is possible in theory, the problems and cost of doing so are far from resolved.[7] It is too soon to predict the costs associated with a fusion reactor (few who work in the field will predict whether such a device will work at all within the next 15-20 years). One guess puts the unit energy cost at something over half that for a coal or fission power station of comparable size (Mills, 1967), but this is pure speculation. Quite possibly the major benefit of controlled fusion will again be to extend the energy supply rather than to cheapen it.

A second misconception about nuclear power is that it can reduce our dependence on fossil fuels to zero as soon as that becomes necessary or desirable. In fact, nuclear power plants contribute only to the electrical portion of the energy budget; and in 1960 in the United States, for example, electrical energy comprised only 19% of the total energy consumed (Sporn, 1963). The degree to which nuclear fuels can postpone the exhaustion of our coal and oil depends on the extent to which that 19% is enlarged. The task is far from a trivial one, and will involve transitions to electric or fuel-cell powered transportation, electric heating, and electrically powered industries. It will be extremely expensive.

Nuclear energy, then, is a panacea neither for us nor for the underdeveloped world. It relieves, but does not remove, the pressure on fossil fuel supplies; it provides reasonably-priced power where these fuels are not abundant; it has substantial (but expensive) potential in intelligent applications such as that suggested in the Oak Ridge study discussed above; and it shares the propensity of fast-growing technology to unpleasant side effects (Novick, 1969). We mention in the last connection that, while nuclear power stations do not produce conventional air pollutants, their radioactive waste problems may in the long run prove a poor trade. Although the AEC seems to have made a good case for solidification and storage in salt mines of the bulk of the radioactive fission products (Blanko et al., 1967), a number of radioactive isotopes are released to the environment, and in some areas such isotopes have already turned up in potentially harmful concentrations (Curtis and Hogan, 1969). Projected order of magnitude increases in nuclear power generation will seriously aggravate this situation. Although it has frequently been stated that the eventual advent of fusion reactors will free us from such difficulties, at least one authority, F. L. Parker, takes a more cautious view. He contends that the large inventory of radioactive tritium in early fusion reactors will require new precautions to minimize emissions (Parker, 1968).

---

[7] A general discussion of extracting metals from common rock is given by Cloud, 1968.

A more easily evaluated problem is the tremendous quantity of waste heat generated at nuclear installations (to say nothing of the usable power output, which, as with power from whatever source, must also ultimately be dissipated as heat). Both have potentially disastrous effects on the local and world ecological and climatological balance. There is no simple solution to this problem, for, in general, "cooling" only moves heat; it does not *remove* it from the environment viewed as a whole. Moreover, the Second Law of Thermodynamics puts a ceiling on the efficiency with which we can do even this much, i.e., concentrate and transport heat. In effect, the Second Law condemns us to aggravate the total problem by generating still *more* heat in any machinery we devise for local cooling (consider, for example, refrigerators and air conditioners).

The only heat which actually leaves the whole system, the Earth, is that which can be radiated back into space. This amount steadily is being diminished as combustion of hydrocarbon fuels increases the atmospheric percentage of $CO_2$ which has strong absorption bands in the infrared spectrum of the outbound heat energy. (Hubbert, 1962, puts the increase in the $CO_2$ content of the atmosphere at 10% since 1900.) There is, of course, a competing effect in the Earth's energy balance, which is the increased reflectivity of the upper atmosphere to incoming sunlight due to other forms of air pollution. It has been estimated, ignoring both these effects, that man risks drastic (and perhaps catastrophic) climatological change if the amount of heat he dissipates in the environment on a global scale reaches 1% of the solar energy absorbed and reradiated at the Earth's surface (Rose and Clark, 1961). At the present 5% rate of increase in world energy consumption,[8] this level will be reached in less than a century, and in the immediate future the direct contribution of man's power consumption will create serious local problems. If we may safely rule out circumvention of the Second Law or the divorce of energy requirements from population size, this suggests that, whatever science and technology may accomplish, population growth must be stopped.

## Transportation

We would be remiss in our offer of a technological perspective on population problems without some mention of the difficulties associated with transporting large quantities of food, material, or people across the face of the Earth. While our grain exports have not begun to satisfy the hunger of the underdeveloped world, they already have taxed our ability to transport food in bulk over large distances. The total amount of goods of *all* kinds loaded at U.S. ports for external trade was 158 million metric tons in 1965 (United Nations, 1968). This is coincidentally the approximate amount of grain which would have been required to make up the dietary shortages of the underdeveloped world in the same year (Sukhatme, 1966). Thus, if the United States *had* such an amount of grain to ship, it could be handled only by displacing the entirety of our export trade. In a similar vein, the gross weight

[8] The rate of growth of world energy consumption fluctuates strongly about some mean on a time scale of only a few years, and the figures are not known with great accuracy in any case. A discussion of predicting the mean and a defense of the figure of 5% are given in Gúeron et al., 1957.

of the fertilizer, in excess of present consumption, required in the underdeveloped world to feed the additional population there in 1980 will amount to approximately the same figure—150 million metric tons (Sukhatme, 1966). Assuming that a substantial fraction of this fertilizer, should it be available at all, will have to be shipped about, we had best start building freighters! These problems, and the even more discouraging one of internal transportation in the hungry countries, coupled with the complexities of international finance and marketing which have hobbled even present aid programs, complete a dismal picture of the prospects for "external" solutions to ballooning food requirements in much of the world.

Those who envision migration as a solution to problems of food, land, and water distribution not only ignore the fact that the world has no promising place to put more people, they simply have not looked at the numbers of the transportation game. Neglecting the fact that migration and relocation costs would probably amount to a minimum of several thousand dollars per person, we find, for example, that the entire long-range jet transport fleet of the United States (about 600 planes [Molloy, 1968] with an average capacity of 150), averaging two round trips per week, could transport only about 9 million people per year from India to the United States. This amounts to about 75% of that country's annual population *growth* (Population Reference Bureau, 1968). Ocean liners and transports, while larger, are less numerous and much slower, and over long distances could not do as well. Does anyone believe, then, that we are going to compensate for the world's population growth by sending the excess to the planets? If there were a place to go on Earth, financially and logistically we could not send our surplus there.


## Conclusion

We have not attempted to be comprehensive in our treatment of population pressures and the prospects of coping with them technologically; rather, we hope simply to have given enough illustrations to make plausible our contention that technology, without population control, cannot meet the challenge. It may be argued that we have shown only that any one technological scheme taken individually is insufficient to the task at hand, whereas *all* such schemes applied in parallel might well be enough. We would reply that neither the commitment nor the resources to implement them all exists, and indeed that many may prove mutually exclusive (e.g., harvesting algae may diminish fish production).

Certainly, an optimum combination of efforts exists in theory, but we assert that no organized attempt to find it is being made, and that our examination of its probable eventual constituents permits little hope that even the optimum will suffice. Indeed, after a far more thorough survey of the prospects than we have attempted here, the President's Science Advisory Committee Panel on the world food supply concluded (PSAC, 1967): "The solution of the problem that will exist after about 1985 *demands* that programs of population control be initiated now." We most emphatically agree, noting that "now" was 2 years ago!

Of the problems arising out of population growth in the short, middle, and long terms, we have emphasized the first group. For mankind must pass the first hurdles—food and water for the next 20 years—to be granted the privilege of confronting such dilemmas as the exhaustion of mineral resources and physical space later.[9] Furthermore, we have not conveyed the extent of our concern for the environmental deterioration which has accompanied the population explosion, and for the catastrophic ecological consequences which would attend many of the proposed technological "solutions" to the population/food crisis. Nor have we treated the point that "development" of the rest of the world to the standards of the West probably would be lethal ecologically (Ehrlich and Ehrlich, 1970). For even if such grim prospects are ignored, it is abundantly clear that in terms of cost, lead time, and implementation on the scale required, technology without population control will be too little and too late.

What hope there is lies not, of course, in abandoning attempts at technological solutions; on the contrary, they must be pursued at unprecedented levels, with unprecedented judgment, and above all with unprecedented attention to their ecological consequences. We need dramatic programs now to find ways of ameliorating the food crisis—to buy time for humanity until the inevitable delay accompanying population control efforts has passed. But it cannot be emphasized enough that if the population control measures are *not* initiated immediately and effectively, all the technology man can bring to bear will not fend off the misery to come.[10] Therefore, confronted as we are with limited resources of time and money, we must consider carefully what fraction of our effort should be applied to the cure of the disease itself instead of to the temporary relief of the symptoms. We should ask, for example, how many vasectomies could be performed by a program funded with the 1.8 billion dollars required to build a single nuclear agro-industrial complex, and what the relative impact on the problem would be in both the short and long terms.

The decision for population control will be opposed by growth-minded economists and businessmen, by nationalistic statesmen, by zealous religious leaders, and by the myopic and well-fed of every description. It is therefore incumbent on all who sense the limitations of technology and the fragility of the environmental balance to make themselves heard above the hollow, optimistic chorus—to convince society and its leaders that there is no alternative but the cessation of our irresponsible, all-demanding, and all-consuming population growth.

[9] Since the first draft of this article was written, the authors have seen the manuscript of a timely and pertinent forthcoming book, *Resources and Man,* written under the auspices of the National Academy of Sciences and edited by Preston E. Cloud. The book reinforces many of our own conclusions in such areas as agriculture and fisheries and, in addition, treats both short- and long-term prospects in such areas as mineral resources and fossil fuels in great detail.

[10] This conclusion has also been reached within the specific context of aid to underdeveloped countries in a Ph.D. thesis by Douglas Daetz: "Energy Utilization and Aid Effectiveness in Nonmechanized Agriculture: A Computer Simulation of a Socioeconomic System" (University of California, Berkeley, May 1968).

## Acknowledgments

We thank the following individuals for reading and commenting on the manuscript: J. H. Brownell (Stanford University); P. A. Cantor (Aerojet General Corp.); P. E. Cloud (University of California, Santa Barbara); D. J. Eckstrom (Stanford University); R. Ewell (State University of New York at Buffalo); J. L. Fisher (Resources for the Future, Inc.); J. A. Hendrickson, Jr. (Stanford University); J. H. Hessel (Stanford University); R. W. Holm (Stanford University); S. C. McIntosh, Jr., (Stanford University); K. E. F. Watt (University of California, Davis). This work was supported in part by a grant from the Ford Foundation.

## References

Anonymous. 1968a. India aims to remedy fertilizer shortage. *Chem. Eng. News,* **46** (November 25): 29.

————. 1968b. Scientists Studying Nuclear-Powered Agro-Industrial Complexes to Give Food and Jobs to Millions. *New York Times.* March 10, p. 74.

————. 1968c. Food from the atom. *Technol. Rev.,* January, p. 55.

————. 1968d. Norway—The end of the big blubber. *Time,* November 29, p. 98.

————. 1968e. Nuclear fuel cycle. *Nucl. News,* January, p. 30.

Bender, R. J. 1969. Why water desalting will expand. *Power,* **113** (August): 171.

Blanko, R. E., J. O. Blomeke, and J. T. Roberts. 1967. Solving the waste disposal problem. *Nucleonics,* **25:** 58.

Borgstrom, Georg. 1965. *The Hungry Planet.* Collier-Macmillan, New York.

Bump, T. R. 1967. A third generation of breeder reactors. *Sci. Amer.,* May, p. 25.

Christy, F. C., Jr., and A. Scott. 1965. *The Commonwealth in Ocean Fisheries.* Johns Hopkins Press, Baltimore.

Clawson, M., H. L. Landsberg, and L. T. Alexander. 1969. Desalted seawater for agriculture: Is it economic? *Science,* **164:** 1141.

Cloud, P. R. 1968. Realities of mineral distribution. *Texas Quart.,* Summer, p. 103.

Cole, LaMont C. 1968. Can the world be saved? *BioScience,* **18:** 679.

Curtis, R., and E. Hogan. 1969. *Perils of the Peaceful Atom.* Doubleday, New York. p. 135, 150–152.

Ennis, C. E. 1967. Desalted water as a competitive commodity. *Chem. Eng. Progr.,* **63:** (1): 64.

Ehrlich, P. R. 1968. *The Population Bomb.* Sierra Club/Ballantine, New York.

Ehrlich, P. R., and Anne H. Ehrlich. 1970. *Population, Resources, and Environment.* W. H. Freeman, San Francisco (In press).

Galstann, L. S., and E. L. Currier. 1967. The Metropolitan Water District desalting project. *Chem. Eng. Progr.,* **63,** (1): 64.

Gúeron, J., J. A. Lane, I. R. Maxwell, and J. R. Menke. 1957. *The Eco-

*nomics of Nuclear Power. Progress in Nuclear Energy.* McGraw-Hill Book Co., New York. Series VIII. p. 23.

Hardin, G. 1968. The tragedy of the commons. *Science,* **162:** 1243.

Hubbert, M. K. 1962. Energy resources, A report to the Committee on Natural Resources. National Research Council Report 1000-D, National Academy of Sciences.

International Atomic Energy Agency. 1964. Desalination of water using conventional and nuclear energy. Technical Report 24, Vienna.

Kelly, R. P. 1966. North American water and power alliance. In: *Water Production Using Nuclear Energy,* R. G. Post and R. L. Seale (eds.). University of Arizona Press, Tucson, p. 29.

Lelyveld, D. 1968. Can India survive Calcutta? *New York Times Magazine,* October 13, p. 58.

Mason, E. S. 1957. Economic growth and energy consumption. In: *The Economics of Nuclear Power. Progress in Nuclear Energy,* Series VIII, J. Gúeron et al. (eds.). McGraw-Hill Book Co., New York, p. 56.

McIlhenny, W. F. 1966. Problems and potentials of concentrated brines. In: *Water Production Using Nuclear Energy,* R. G. Post and R. L. Seale (eds.). University of Arizona Press, Tucson, p. 187.

McKenzie, John. 1968. Nutrition and the soft sell. *New Sci.,* **40:** 423.

McNeil, Mary. 1964. Lateritic soils. *Sci. Amer.,* November, p. 99.

Meseck, G. 1961. Importance of fish production and utilization in the food economy. Paper R11.3, presented at FAO Conference on Fish in Nutrition, Rome.

Milliman, J. W. 1966. Economics of water production using nuclear energy. In: *Water Production Using Nuclear Energy.* R. G. Post and R. L. Seale (eds.). University of Arizona Press, Tucson, p. 49.

Mills, R. G. 1967. Some engineering problems of thermonuclear fusion. *Nucl. Fusion,* **7:** 223.

Molloy, J. F., Jr. 1968. The $12-billion financing problem of U.S. airlines. *Astronautics and Aeronautics,* October, p. 76.

Novick, S. 1969. *The Careless Atom.* Houghton Mifflin, Boston.

Oak Ridge National Laboratory. 1968. Nuclear energy centers, industrial and agro-industrial complexes, Summary Report. ORNL-4291, July.

Paddock, William. 1967. Phytopathology and a hungry world. *Ann. Rev. Phytopathol.,* **5:** 375.

Paddock, William, and Paul Paddock. 1964. *Hungry Nations.* Little, Brown & Co., Boston.

————. 1967. *Famine 1975!* Little, Brown & Co., Boston.

Parikh, G., S. Saxena, and M. Maharaja. 1968. Agricultural extension and IADP, a study of Surat. *Econ. Polit. Weekly,* August 24, p. 1307.

Parker, F. L. 1968. Radioactive wastes from fusion reactors. *Science,* **159:** 83. Parker, F. L., and D. J. Rose, *Science* **159:** 1376.

Parker, H. M. 1966. Environmental factors relating to large water plants. In: *Water Production Using Nuclear Energy,* R. G. Post and R. L. Seale (eds.). University of Arizona Press, Tucson, p. 209.

Population Reference Bureau. 1968. Population Reference Bureau Data Sheet. Pop. Ref. Bureau, Washington, D.C.

PSAC. 1967. *The World Food Problem.* Report of the President's Science

Advisory Committee. Vols. 1-3. U.S. Govt. Printing Office, Washington, D.C.

Rose, D. J., and M. Clark, Jr. 1961. *Plasma and Controlled Fusion.* M.I.T. Press, Cambridge, Mass., p. 3.

Schmitt, W. R. 1965. The planetary food potential. *Ann. N.Y. Acad. Sci.,* **118:** 645.

Sporn, Philip. 1963. *Energy for Man.* Macmillan, New York.

————. 1966. *Fresh Water from Saline Waters.* Pergamon Press, New York.

Sukhatme, P. V. 1966. The world's food supplies. *Roy. Stat. Soc. J.,* **129A:** 222.

United Nations. 1968. *United Nations Statistical Yearbook for 1967.* Statistical Office of the U.N., New York.

U.S. Dept. of Commerce. 1966. *Statistical Abstract of the U.S.* U.S. Govt. Printing Office, Washington, D.C.

Wadleigh, C. H. 1968. Wastes in relation to agriculture and industry. USDA Miscellaneous Publication No. 1065. March.

Woodwell, George M. 1967. Toxic substances and ecological cycles. *Sci. Amer.,* March, p. 24.

# CALIFORNIA:
## After 19 Million, What?

Human ingenuity is on trial in California. This geographic wonderland is reeling under the impact of an annual increase in population of over half a million. Mushrooming population is an old story in California. Between 1860 and 1960, the state's population increased fortyfold—while the nation's population increased 4½ times. And the trend continues: between 1950 and 1960, California's population increased by 48.5 percent in contrast to the national average of only 18.5 percent. Currently, the net daily gain for the state is about 1,500 souls.

Political, social, and economic problems are intensified by this fantastic proliferation of people. Natural resource management and provision of the essential services for exploding cities pose ever-increasing complexities. The byproducts of these pressures frequently receive national attention: smog-laden air over the cities and extending far afield; record breaking pile-ups on the frenzied free-

ways. Yet it is and must remain the conviction of responsible men that California's troubles are not beyond solution; that this solution must stem from intelligent planning today towards the solution of these unprecedented problems. Success would serve as an example of courageous creativity for the entire world.

California has always been part fantasy and proud of it. Where else is the range so broad between fairyland and nightmare? Since the early days, the state has amply justified her fairyland motto: the "Golden State." It began first with the hope of gold, then with the fact of it. In the early 1500's, a Spanish writer described this land, "on the right hand of the Indies," as peopled only by beautiful women who had no other metal than gold. While there are such creatures today in California—especially in Southern California—the real gold was not discovered in more than token quantity until 1848. When that played out, other golden vistas

Reprinted by permission of the author and the publisher from *Population Bulletin* 22(2):29–57, June 1966.

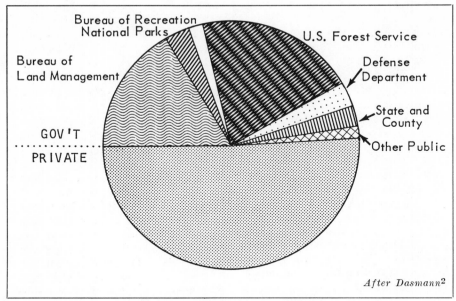

Bureau of Recreation
National Parks

U.S. Forest Service

Bureau of
Land Management

Defense
Department

GOV'T

State and
County

PRIVATE

Other Public

*After Dasmann*[2]

FIGURE 1. CALIFORNIA LANDOWNERSHIP

remained: a horizon of orange groves which led, in time, to the nation's richest and most varied agricultural production; the lure of black gold which is still pumped in millions of barrels from favored coastal regions (in 1964, California was exceeded only by Texas and Louisiana in the nation's oil production); the golden wings of a sky's-the-limit aerospace industry; and possibly the most irresistible gold of them all, that sun-gold which makes the flowers bloom very big, and which makes the middle-aged seem a little less so. In contrast, there are the nightmares: the heat of Death Valley; the tasteless-ness of Los Angeles; the stink of the microclimate which encom-passes California's freeways. The bad is everywhere with the good;

even the great redwood monuments to nature's majestic durability yield to increasing exploitation. Fertile valleys have been destroyed forever in the uncivilized convic-tion that every man is entitled to his own drab little box. In too many of the choicest coastal areas, California has become a vast un-kempt and unlovely bedroom.

Thus, a profound tension is cre-ated, a tension between land and people, between reality and hope, with the present drawn taut to the very breaking point between. Here is the challenge of the limits to which human ecology can become complex. Man and his environment interact in an explosive and per-plexing contest. It is an incompa-rable challenge for human wisdom, judgment, and restraint.

Within this context, let us look first at the land itself, the raw material for California's environment in the 1960's. How big is it? How fast and in what directions can it be stretched? How many mouths can it water and feed?

California trails only Alaska and Texas in size, boasting 158,693 square miles—almost exactly 100 million acres. Half of this vast land is owned by the state and federal governments. One third of this substantial domain is under the Bureau of Land Management in the Department of the Interior; and most of the balance is under the United States Forest Service in the Department of Agriculture. This leaves 50 million acres in private ownership. Much of this is better adapted for marginal use as range and scenery than for farms or for urban living. The lived-in and worked-in area of the state comprising much of the farm land, the cities and factories is centered on a tenth of the total area: 10 million acres.

The legendary Central Valley of the Sacramento and the San Joaquin, extending for about 400 miles from the Klamath Range close to Oregon to the Tehachapi Mountains behind Pasadena, is the state's principal bread and fruit basket. Its agricultural riches are supplemented only by the fabled Imperial Valley south of the Salton Sea and by rich parcels of land along the coastal plain. To the east and south of the Central Valley are snow-capped, rocky, saw-toothed mountains that split the sky, and southward and below are desert wastes of sage brush, chaparral, and sometimes, just sand. It is a man's country—and a no-man's country—in the 20,000 square miles of the sun-baked Colorado and Mojave Deserts. South of the Imperial Valley, there is nothing but the dry wilderness of Baja California, the Mexican peninsula which nature forgot.

In the coastal areas of the southwest, more than one half of California's cities are clogged in a narrow strip comprising not more than 10 percent of the state's total area, and much of its industry and agriculture. Competition for land is a free-for-all of short-term plans and local power. Although agriculture is a large money-maker for California, choice, close-in acreage is continually being smothered under the encroachment of urban sprawl —"slurbs" they have been called. Never was there a clearer example of a society's compulsion to bite the hand that feeds it than California's unplanned reckless consumption of its richest soil: some 375 acres going under the bulldozer each day.

Into this schizophrenic geography pour 1,460 new residents each day, expecting fulfillment in either escape or landscape — depending upon the viewpoint—and often bringing with them the barest of personal resources. This is the conspicuous side of California's "people problem." Less conspicuous, but far more serious, is not this astonishing growth itself, but the failure of the entire California society to plan, except superficially, beyond tomorrow.

## From Sutter's Mill to Hollywood

It all began scarcely more than a century ago with a few Indians, a few Spaniards, and a trickle of Yankees from over the mountains. Today, California is the largest, population-wise, of the 50 states— over 19 million by mid-1966. This is more people than are to be found in the twenty smallest of her sister states. California's gain for the six years 1960-1965 was greater than the 1960 population of six states: Alaska, Wyoming, Vermont, Nevada, Delaware, and New Hampshire.

In 1848, the year that gold was discovered, there were, according to the best of admittedly uncertain estimates, 14,000 non-Indians in the state. In 1850, the year that California became the nation's thirty-first state, this small company of 14,000 had grown to 170,-000, putting California twenty-eighth among the states. New York then ranked first, as it had since 1820 and continued to until 1963.

Granting that the 1848 figure was approximately accurate, California has enjoyed a 1,328-fold increase in 117 years. In the same interval, New York State had a five-fold increase. History has no record of a population that has multiplied at such a rate for so long a time. It is a fact that smashes head-on into the demographic principle that a rapid rate of increase cannot be maintained indefinitely. In a finite area, space is the ultimate irrefutable limitation. Before the standing-room-only point is reached, it is inevitable that social, economic, political, or "natural" factors will act to check the rate of growth— factors which might be called "demographic retro-factors."

At this point in California's evolution, it is easy to extrapolate a truly fantastic population for the Golden State in a remarkably short time. The Census Bureau's population projections for California in 1975 range from a low of 23 million to a high of 24.4 million— an increase of between 4.4 and 5.8 million above 1965. Unofficial and hopefully over-enthusiastic population projectors foresee even greater numbers. A report released by the California Department of Health in August 1965, projects a population for the state of 25 million by 1980 and 50 million by the end of the century.

Which, if any, of these forecasts come to pass depends on many developments very hard to foresee. Which retro-factors will begin to act to slow—perhaps ultimately to reverse—the current trend is an open guess. The one thing that is certain is that at some point the century-long pile-up of people will be checked, for the dynamics of growth are fundamentally altered by the interplay between man in increasing millions and a vulnerable environment.

Between 1955 and 1960, an average of 1,460 new residents crossed the state's borders each day. An additional 950 were left by the stork. On the other side of the ledger, the daily new arrivals were reduced by 610 who moved out of the state and by 340 who died. The net gain was about 1,460. Clearly,

California's century-long era of rapid population growth is not yet over.

What does it portend for the future? It means that the science of human ecology, as yet applied falteringly by fallible men, is facing its severest test. Human ecology embraces the analysis of the interplay between man and his total environment. It is housekeeping at the planetary level. To bring expanding human needs into a balanced accommodation with the limited natural resources of the planet must stand high on the agenda of the future.

The 19 million people now living in California are faced with major, specific, and now very urgent housekeeping problems. These center around the basic essentials of existence: pure air and pure water for residential, industrial, and agricultural use; sufficient land for living space; and the production of adequate energy to keep the whole complex operative. This is an unprecedented and incomparable challenge. It is a challenge which has been faced by some modern societies such as Sweden, but none was ever faced with so complex and rapidly expanding a culture.

## Who Are the Californians?

Exactly who are these 19 million people of whom the future necessarily expects so much? How can they be described?

The Spanish Colonial period, with strong overtones of Mexican nationalism in its last days, drew to an end in 1840. It is estimated that at that time there were approximately 5,000 non-Indian residents of the territory, which had become a Mexican province in 1822 after Mexico threw off the Spanish yoke in 1821.

The beginnings were in 1542, when Portuguese adventurer Juan Rodriguez Cabrillo sailed northward from Mexico exploring the coast. He dropped anchor in what is now San Diego Bay. Rodriguez Cabrillo died in the course of this voyage. His shipmates continued north for perhaps the full length of the present state.

Not until 1579, when Sir Francis Drake visited the coast of California, was there another flurry of exploration. Drake, of course, claimed the land for England. This infuriated the Spanish who sent other parties to defend their territory against Drake's claims.

There were 200 rough-and-ready years before Spanish culture confirmed its dominance through the inspired mission-building efforts of the redoubtable Franciscans. Twenty-one handsome missions and a network of forts to protect them were established between 1769 and 1823. In addition to these religious hostelries, there were a handful of small villages clinging to the coast. It was a fringe colony, a scattering of Spaniards and later of Mexicans who held the land by virtue of the benevolence of Indian tribes unaware of what the future held.

Prior to Mexican independence from Spain in 1821, there had been a thin filtering from the United States into the area. The first American sailing vessel to reach California anchored in Monterey in

1796. Following that, there were regular calls by New England ships —chiefly the famous California clippers—trading with the missions.

In 1841, the first substantial group of settlers came to California from the United States. These aggressive interlopers from across the mountains were not enthusiastically received by those already on the ground. In 1844, soldiers and naval vessels were sent by Washington to protect these newcomers and their property. In 1846, this expeditionary force under the command of John C. Fremont hoisted the American flag. The two ensuing years of war shaped the freedom of the West and in doing so shaped the entire national destiny as well. With the surrender of the Mexican army in 1848, Mexico yielded all claim to the territory. California was then prepared to move to statehood by 1850.

At the start, California became a state in which Indians outnumbered the white settlers by two or three to one. Most of this sprinkling of white settlers themselves were deeply immersed in a Spanish culture that had formed and sustained the modest communities of this coastal wilderness for two centuries. There was nothing of the eastern seaboard pioneer tradition in this environment.

With the discovery of gold at Sutter's Mill in 1848, a century of mushrooming population growth began. By 1850, the population had grown by 80,000—mainly adventurers from the United States whose backgrounds were English, Irish, or western European.

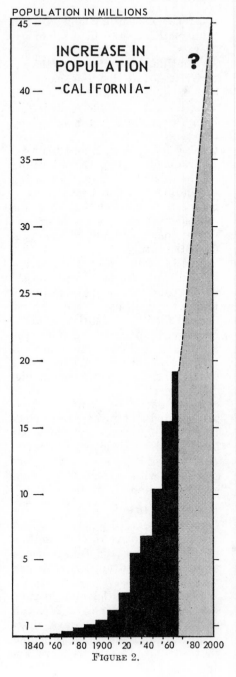

POPULATION IN MILLIONS

INCREASE IN
POPULATION

-CALIFORNIA-

?

FIGURE 2.

With the rising fever of speculation and enthusiasm at the outset of the railroad era, Chinese coolies were imported by the thousands to build the western leg of the first transcontinental railroad which was linked to the east coast in 1869.

The multi-national flood swept in in waves, decade after decade. By the turn of the century there were certain dominant groups. One half of the foreign born in California at that time was Mexican, English, German, Irish, or French.

Italians came to establish vineyards and orchards. They were followed by Germans. Swiss were attracted by shepherding in the pasture regions beyond the valleys.

It is axiomatic to say that in California, ethnic and minority groups found varied special appeals. It is a state attractive to many bloods and cultures. Some of these minorities had their day of ignominy and depression. Though the situation has improved, it is not yet completely resolved.

At the start, for example, the Chinese were received with open arms. They willingly did work no one else was prepared to do. This proved to be a mistake; they outworked their neighbors, and the competition was felt to be intolerable. Hence, a Chinese exclusion law was passed.

The story of tension short of outright exclusion was, with modifications, the story of the Irish, the Italians, and similar groups. After Pearl Harbor, for example, a double-action scapegoat was provided by a small contingent of disturbingly industrious Japanese. In 1942, all immigrants from Japan and native born citizens of Japanese ancestry were rounded up and herded into inland prison camps, their property confiscated. It was an unreasoning reaction against both the disaster of Pearl Harbor and the antagonism that was felt toward another alien group posing an economic threat. It was a dark, shameful incident for both California and the Union.

As the nation's population has grown and as the covered wagon has given place to the jet airliner, Horace Greeley's dictum, "Go west, young man," has increasingly been heeded by both men and women— by young and not-so-young alike. Between 1850 and 1900, migration added about 900,000 to California's population. From 1900 to 1930, migration contributed an additional 3.2 million people. In the 30 years between 1931 and 1960, the net civilian gain from migration was 6.5 million with an additional 300,000 contributed by the military.

The depressed decade of the 1930's sharply checked migration to California, but brought minority problems of its own. The decade's gain was only 21.7 percent compared with 65.7 percent in the 1920's. Much of this relatively modest increase was represented by escapees from the "dust bowl" tragedy, when hordes of destitute small farmers and sharecroppers fled the parched areas of the central and south central states. Many took refuge in the great valley of California, centering around Stockton, Fresno, Bakersfield, and the region to the south.

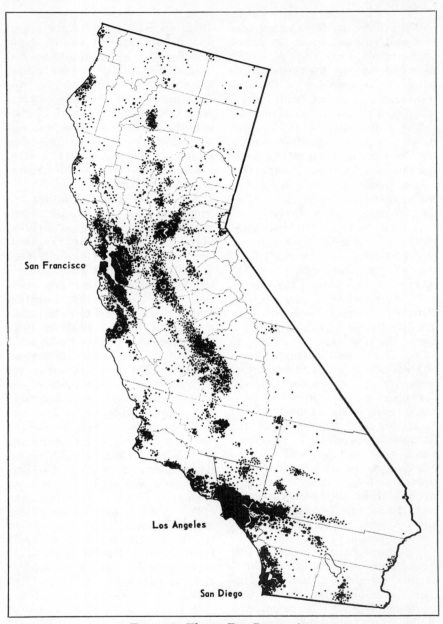

FIGURE 3. WHERE THE PEOPLE ARE.
Virtually all of the people, the industry, and much of the agriculture of California are found on less than 10 percent of the land area of the state.

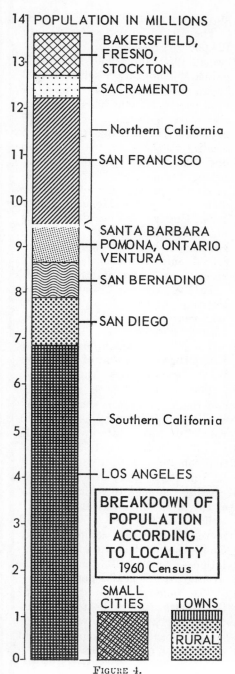

POPULATION IN MILLIONS

14
13 — BAKERSFIELD, FRESNO, STOCKTON
12 — SACRAMENTO
11 — Northern California
— SAN FRANCISCO
10
9 — SANTA BARBARA POMONA, ONTARIO VENTURA
— SAN BERNADINO
8 — SAN DIEGO
7
6
5 — Southern California
4 — LOS ANGELES
3
2 **BREAKDOWN OF POPULATION ACCORDING TO LOCALITY** 1960 Census
1 SMALL CITIES    TOWNS
0    RURAL

Figure 4.

The last half of this decade, 1935-1940, brought another distinct migration, this one from the west-north-central states. It was a time when Los Angeles came to be known to San Franciscans as "Iowa by the sea."

World War II brought a sharp upswing in the rate of population growth. A 53.3 percent population gain was recorded between 1940 and 1950, with 80 percent of it channeled into the metropolitan areas, unlike the predominantly rural trend of the 1930's. For the only time since the 1860's, San Francisco's growth was more rapid than that of Los Angeles—largely because of the huge shipyards that sprang up in the Bay area to meet the war emergency. Similarly, to the far south, wartime activities were responsible for a 92.4 percent increase in the population of the San Diego region.

The Census of 1950 showed significant changes from the pattern of the Thirties. The west-north-central and west-south-central states together furnished only 28 percent of California's interstate new arrivals in contrast to their large contribution during the previous decade. Instead, greater numbers arrived from the northeastern, mountain, and Pacific states.

Accompanying this decline in percentage from the agricultural midwest was a strong outmigration, particularly to the west-south-central states. Texas received more migrants from California in 1949 and 1950 than it sent west. Migration between California and the industrial, urban states of the northeast was predominantly westward, while that between California and the east-south-central states involved considerable movement in both directions.

By 1960, California had 2.3 million residents who had lived elsewhere five years earlier. The north-central region furnished one third of these residents; the Northeast supplied one sixth, and the South and Southwest each sent approximately one quarter of the total.

In the Los Angeles of 1960, the number coming from other states was almost twice as large as the total population of San Francisco at that time.

Thus, in a sense, the California of the mid-1960's affords a cross-section of the nation. It is composed of a larger foreign-born element than any other state of the Union except New York, and its native-born Americans spring literally from every corner of the country.

As has been a pattern of history, the least fortunate cultural groups tend to gravitate to minimal employment and subsistence living. Even today, California has disturbing vestiges of this pattern. While migrant farm labor is by no means a problem unique to California, it is perennial there, traditionally centered around a population mainly of Mexican origin or ancestry. The plight of the Mexican-American in California has thus far escaped solution and at times seems beyond remedy.

In the past decade, it has been joined by a second minority crisis with national implications: that of the Negro citizen caught in the slurb and sprawl of Los Angeles.

The 1940 Census counted only 124,000 Negroes in California. Between 1950 and 1960, California gained by migration some 220,400 Negro residents, who totaled in 1960 nearly 900,000. This migration represents a decrease of about 15 percent from the quarter million coming to the state between 1940 and 1950. These people are competing for jobs with other disadvantaged groups already in the state, mainly the Mexican-Americans. Under these conditions, it is not surprising that the Negro in California has an unemployment rate double that recorded for "all races" in recent tabulations.

In Los Angeles County, with a Negro population totaling 461,000 and centered in the Watts area, 25,000 Negroes are reportedly out of jobs—an unemployment rate two to three times that of the whites in the greater Los Angeles area.

The plight of both the Negro and the Mexican-American population is complicated by a high birth rate. The Negro rate in California was 33.3 births per 1,000 population compared with a white rate of 22.8 in 1960. There are no data regarding the definitely high fertility of the Mexican-Americans.

Even in the face of this rapid increase, Negroes comprise only 5.6 percent of the state's total population—about half the national average, which is 10.5 percent.

The violence and destruction of the Watts riots reflect the frustrated hopes of people who expected El Dorado and found instead deprivation and insecurity.

Movement of people is one side of the coin of population growth. It is rarely the predominant factor. The other side is natural increase —the excess of births over deaths. California, along with such extraordinary special cases as that of Israel, is the exception that proves this very general rule.

During the 19th century, migration played a dominant role in the growth of the nation. Between 1820 and 1900, 18.7 million immigrants came to these shores. In the decade 1881-1890, the U. S. population was increased by a net immigration of 4.5 million—the all-time record. This constituted only 35 percent of the nation's increase in that decade.

In California, between 1950 and 1960, 61 percent of the phenomenal population growth of 5.1 million was due to movement of people into the state and 39 percent to natural increase. In the United States between 1950 and 1960, the population grew by 28 million. Only 2.6 million of this increase, or 9.4 percent, was attributed to net immigration. The remaining 25.4 million was due to natural increase.

With respect to natural increase, the situation in California does not differ greatly from the rest of the nation. California's birth rate of 20.7 in 1964 was slightly lower than the U. S. rate of 21.0. Her death rate was 8.3, and her rate of natural increase was 12.4, by no means an explosive situation, and calculated to double the population in 56 years.

A more exact measure of fertility than the birth rate reveals the same pattern. At the time of the 1960 Census, the number of children born per 1,000 women ever married was 2,180 for California and 2,505 for the entire nation. The married women in the highly fertile ages, 15 to 24, had fertility rates approximating those of the married women in the rest of the country (1,289 vs. 1,304). Approximately 18.3 percent of all California married women had four or more children. This compares with 24 percent for the entire nation. The proportion of childless families has declined sharply in the past 15 years, from 24 percent in 1950 to 19 percent in 1960, following the national trend. More recent figures are not available, but it is interesting that the trends show minimal change. Thus, fertility rates and family size in California tend to be slightly below the U.S. average.

The relatively low fertility of the state suggests that the individual couples in California do not look upon the booster psychology of "the more the merrier" with rampant enthusiasm.

The fantastic growth of the population is clearly not due to a home-grown "baby boom."

If family size is below the national average, however, growing concern for education rides high above that found in all but the most privileged and progressive of American communities. Thus, in 1965, California's public school enrollment of over 4.2 million far outranked any other state, with New York's 3.2 million a poor second. In college enrollment, California distinguished herself even further, with 733,000 enrolled, as compared with 499,000 in New York in 1965. First-time college students in California outnumbered those in New York almost two to one: 191,000 to 99,000, respectively.

In California in 1965, 26.6 percent of the total population was in school; in New York, only 20.6 percent. Although she educates extensively, intensively, and tuition-free even at the college level, California ran a low second in number of earned college degrees conferred in 1964-65, a total of 52,390 compared with 68,680 in New York. However, in addition to these bachelor and graduate degrees, California conducts, through its remarkable free junior college system, a broad-based program of training. In this phase of education, California dominates the field with an enrollment of 489,000 in 1965. New York, the closest rival, counts only 117,000. California accounts for approximately two fifths of all junior college students in the nation.

The size of the California educational machine is impressive. Some 149,000 classrooms were in use in public elementary and high schools in California in 1965, as against only 116,000 in New York. Yet, to prevent overcrowding, California needed at that time 7,400 additional rooms, while New York needed many more—12,300. Surprisingly, 12,600 of California's classrooms were in temporary buildings, two fifths of all such rooms in the U. S. Moreover, in California 32,300 classrooms built after 1920 were in combustible buildings, about six times the number in any other

state and well over one third of this type in the entire country.

Expenditures for public elementary and secondary education in 1964-65 in California were $3.2 billion—half a billion more than New York. Another $1.0 billion went for higher education in California; $750 million in New York. California's public school teachers were the best paid in the nation, averaging $8,300 in 1964-65. But education apparently comes cheaper by the dozen, for in terms of expenditure per pupil, California spent $733, and New York $943. In California, expenditures for public elementary and secondary education amounted to 5.71 percent of personal per capita income. New York's 4.84 percent was close to the U.S. average of 4.74 percent.

What is the end product of all this time, money, and effort? The typical Californian can boast that he has attained better than a high school diploma, 12.1 years of schooling completed. Only Utah's 12.2 tops this. New York with 10.7 years is close to the national average of 10.6. California's nonwhites also rank high on the educational scale with 10.5 years completed. This is surpassed only by New Hampshire, 11.7; Colorado, 11.2; and Maine, 10.7. Nationally, nonwhites average 8.2 years of school completed. California bids fair to becoming an educational Utopia.

## "Go West" to the City

There is a paradox in that the state, which a century ago was chiefly a great open space, has from its beginnings accented the urban.

California's first big city was San Francisco. Between 1860 and 1880, 54 percent of the entire increase in the state was found in the Bay area. Until the present day, population gains have been concentrated in the cities. And this in spite of the fact that California leads the nation in the value of its agricultural production. It should be no surprise, therefore, that California leads all other states in the proportion of its population living in major urban areas. The farm population, comprising 2 percent of the total, contributes approximately 3.6 percent of the gross income.

In 1960, of the 16 million residents of the state, only about 4 million lived outside the ten major urbanized areas with populations of over 100,000. With the single exception of the Sacramento complex (about 500,000 people), the other urban areas lie to the south of the Bay region. Half the urban population of the entire state lives in the Los Angeles metropolitan area.

The pattern of urbanization in California differs from that of the heavily urbanized areas of the eastern seaboard. These contrasts are highlighted by comparing California and New York, which was for over a century our most populous state and which only in the past three years has taken second place to California.

New York has nearly as many people as California. Its area is about a third that of California, and its population density is 350 per square mile, as compared with California's 1960 density of 100 per square mile. The urbanized areas

1965

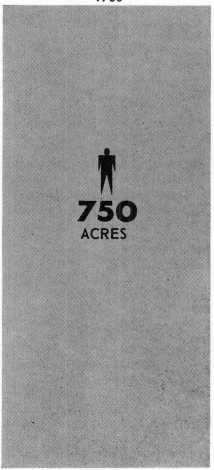

FIGURE 5. ACRES OF LAND PER PERSON—
CALIFORNIA, 1750-1965

in California total almost 3,000 square miles as compared with the New York total of about 2,500.

Of the 16 counties in the United States each having a population of over a million, six are in New York and two are in California. Of the six million-plus counties in New York, five are in the New York City complex with a total population of nearly 9 million. The area of these five counties is 554 square miles. The over-all population density is 15,933 per square mile.

The population of this urban complex is almost two million more than that of the two counties in California with a population of over a million each: Los Angeles (6,038,800) and San Diego (1,033,-000) with a combined population of 7,071,800. The area of these two counties is 8,315 square miles, 15 times that of the New York City complex. The density of Los Angeles, 1,487 per square mile for the county as a whole, 4,500 for the urbanized portions of the county, is about six times the density of San Diego, yet these are modest compared with eastern densities.

The urban density of New York in 1960 was 6,767 per square mile, and California was measurably less crowded with 4,006 per square mile. Los Angeles, where half of all California city dwellers live, has a density of 4,736 per square mile. This illustrates a vital difference. California's density sprawls horizontally, blanketing the coastal corridor. No wonder the word "slurb" has been coined to describe it.

In contrast, New Yorkers stack themselves into the sky in concrete cliffs, relying heavily on public transportation to get to work, to their recreation, etc. When the elevators and the subways stop, New Yorkers are in trouble. Californians avoid these occasional emergencies, but at a price paid each day as they build a permanent transportation crisis which makes the daily round of commuting an increasingly tedious and dangerous chore—and an ominous threat to the total health of the community. Not only is such super highway traffic increasingly dangerous to life and limb, but the automobiles are major contributors to the smog level which may prove California's greatest short-term hazard.

### Environmental Pollution

Human ecology, analyzing the interplay between man and his total environment, both physical and biological, derives from the Greek *oikos* meaning "house"—the basis for our earlier reference to ecology as "housekeeping." As people multiply, the ecological complications increase. Considering the complexities and the growing imbalance between people and the essentials for their subsistence, it is no exaggeration to say that man is not yet housebroken to the world in which his fate is cast.

The pressures and problems of human ecology are not limited to the state of California; they are universal. As man puts growing pressures on his environment, problems become increasingly acute. Because of its peculiar conditions, California affords a prime example of the challenge which ecology places upon man's ability to become master of his fate, rather than to fall victim to forces he generates and fails to control.

There is no state in the Union so richly and variously endowed with the beauty and abundance of the earth as the Golden State. This is not a wholly subjective judgment. It is a viewpoint subscribed to by a great many Americans, wherever they may live. Witness the multitude which, by the proof of continuing migration, still rate California a paradise.

Because of California's unique qualities and because of the astonishing increase in her population, the use that citizens of the state individually and collectively make of the resources available to them assumes unusual significance. It becomes, in fact, one of the prime issues before the nation. If Californians manage to resolve the acute ecological crises confronting them, states under less acute pressure can hopefully do as well. If California fails at her task and in the end is murked out in millions of acres of slurb, it would be a fateful warning to the nation.

Man has great power to despoil and soil his environment by profligate, wasteful, feckless exploitation of the resources at his disposal: by polluting the air, the land, and the waters upon which his very existence depends.

Unless he learns to keep the "House of Man" a mansion fit for the good life, he may bequeath to posterity only a wasteland surrounding a cesspool. Such a reckless exploitation of resources is an ugly and indisputable part of the ecological picture which cannot be ignored. But, under the pressure of California's 19 million people, the immediate threat is pollution.

The customs and practices which are bringing this about are not peculiar to that state, but are intensified by the originally pluperfect nature of the state's environment. In California south of San Francisco, where nearly three fourths of the people live, it is well known that water is a scarce commodity. Only recently has the startling truth been borne home that air also is in short supply because of the peculiar topography of the region. And air, unlike water, cannot be piped in from beyond the mountains. As we shall discuss more fully later, the little air that is available in the coastal plain and in some of the interior valleys is being ruthlessly exploited—smog being but one evidence.

In August 1965, a survey in depth of the overall problem of waste and pollution was released by the Department of Public Health of the State of California. This document, totaling 420 pages, was produced by the Aerojet-General Corporation. It explores in detail the enormous problems which center around the three major areas of pollution: the land, the water, and the air. We must be limited here to a brief quotation from the conclusion of the Aerojet-General report. This significant summary sketches the magnitude of the problem of waste, projects the threat of increased pollution during the next 15 to 30 years, and proposes a

comprehensive plan considered ade-  ting worse during this relatively
quate to prevent matters from get-  brief interval:

. . . Projected waste figures for California indicate that municipal
refuse in the next three decades will increase from 12 to 40 million tons
a year, agricultural solid waste from 13 million tons a year to 18 million
tons a year, gaseous hydrocarbons from 7345 to 9095 tons a day and
NOx from 2215 to 3975 tons a day.

\* \* \*

California is confronted with a serious problem in adequately dis-
posing of the wastes generated by a rapidly growing population. Open
dumps in Merced, burning agricultural wastes in the Sacramento Valley,
and degradation of land through mining in the Sacramento Valley and
Mother Lode Country are examples of blight produced through inadequate waste disposal. In 1965, there are industrial dumps and large
piles of waste from stockyards, dairies, and poultry farms in urban
and rural areas from Crescent City to Calexico. The South San Francisco Bay has become offensive to sight and smell through its use as a
cesspool. South coastal kelp beds have almost disappeared because of
increased sewage emission to the ocean. The transparency of Lake
Tahoe is endangered by liquid-borne wastes.

In addition to its impact on the environment, waste influences
the economic development of California. Many farms in the Central
Valley can now grow only salt-resistant plants, and the quality of aqui-
fers is steadily degrading because of inadequate drainage of irrigated
lands. Inland areas like the Santa Ana River basin are restricted in
their industrial growth because of limited waste-disposal capability. The
use of the Salton Sea as a disposal sink for agricultural and domestic
waste is already inhibiting the development of recreational industries in that area. Smog is responsible for crop and other damage in
various parts of the state.

There is also reason for concern from the standpoint of health. Eye
irritation caused by air pollution is a common complaint in the Los
Angeles area. In Riverside, contaminating organisms recently penetrated the water supply, causing a major epidemic of gastrointestinal
diseases.

Assuming that present practices are continued, the problems of waste
and its ultimate disposal are going to get worse. As the population doubles and automobiles more than double in California between now
and 1990, air pollution will spread over every major populated area of
the state. In the same time span, sewage wastes are expected to increase two and one-half times and municipal solid waste nearly fourfold.
Radioactive wastes are expected to become a major problem as nuclear
power generation in California approaches 100,000 megawatts by the
end of the century.

As the gap between the finite assimilative capacity of the environment and the amount of waste emission closes, it will take larger expenditures just to maintain the present pollution level. For example,
the City of San Francisco may have an acute problem within 18 months,
if it is unable to extend its sanitary landfill site contract with San Mateo
County and if dumping of solid wastes in San Francisco Bay is prohibited.

*   *   *

... The present study roughly estimates that between 1965 and 1990,
the total yearly cost of waste handling by government units is expected
to increase from $0.3 billion to almost $1 billion. Indirect costs to the
citizens of the state for damages from pollution are expected to increase
total costs to over $7 billion.[1]

*   *   *

The report notes that this vast problem is now being dealt with piecemeal. The obvious need for a state-wide waste authority is noted.

The Aerojet report interjects a further complication in that energy obtained from fusion and fusion reactions creates major and insidious pollutants in the "hot ashes" from atomic reactors. The heat released by these reactions, particularly in an "unknown" situation, could have profound effects. Only one ultimate escape from the dead-end of the energy-pollutants would be solar energy. The Southwest is ideally adapted to exploit this inexhaustible source.

An especially serious problem arises with air pollution in Southern California, from the Golden Gate to the Mexican border, not only in the coastal areas of Southern California but in the interior valleys as well. The reason for this is that a peculiar meteorological situation exists called an "inversion," which will be explained in detail below. The air above the inversion is, for practical purposes, nearly as unavailable to those urgently needing it as though the people were encased in a plastic bag.

Across the entire heavily urbanized areas of California air pollution is so severe as to cause frequent chronic eye irritation. The major agricultural areas suffer from chronic air pollution severe enough to damage crops. It is perhaps in this pollution of the atmosphere that California faces its most immediate ecological problem.

A searching analysis was published in 1964 by Dr. Philip A. Leighton, Professor of Physical Chemistry at Stanford University, and an authority on the chemistry of the atmosphere. Dr. Leighton presents his case so eloquently that to paraphrase his statement would be to weaken it. His main points are presented in the following extended excerpt:

... Man likes to take air for granted. Since earliest history he has
recognized that the land, food, and to a lesser extent the water resources
are limited, and has developed many systems for their ownership, protection and use. But throughout most of that history, air has been re-

garded as an unlimited resource. Just as it is traditional to respect rights of ownership in land, food, and water, so is it traditional to regard the air as free. Free to breathe, and free to be used for combustion, for industry, and for carrying off our wastes.

In terms of need, the use for breathing must of course come first, but in terms of volume, ever since Prometheus gave fire to mortals the other uses have been first by far. Now, as you drive along the highway in a modern American car, the engine of the car consumes well over a thousand times as much oxygen as do you. To carry off the exhaust gases, and dilute them to harmless concentrations requires from five to ten million times as much air as does the driver. In other words, just one automobile, moving along a Los Angeles County freeway, needs as much air to disperse its waste products as do all of the people in the County for breathing.* We are only too well aware of the consequences of this imbalance and have been aware for many years that the tradition of the free use of air is no longer tenable when other uses encroach on that for breathing.

One other contrast in man's interrelations with land, water, and air is in his ability to adapt them to his needs. Land, when he so wishes, he can improve, and water he can both improve and transport. But except on a small scale, as in homes and buildings, or the use of wind machines in orchards, he has not learned how to improve or transport air. The only large scale change man makes in outdoor air is to contaminate it.

There is, as yet, no indication that this situation will alter within the foreseeable future. In planning for that future, we must assume that it will continue to be necessary to make do with the natural supply of ambient air, and direct our attention toward keeping its contamination within acceptable limits. A discussion of man and air in California must, for this reason, be primarily a discussion of air pollution.

## Limitations on the Air Resource

The acceptable limits of air contamination have already been exceeded over most of the heavily populated areas in California. Indeed, I sometimes think that California now leads the nation in air pollution as well as in population. Yet our cities are not the most densely populated, our industry is not the most concentrated, we do not have the largest number of motor vehicles per square mile. Why, then, is our air pollution so severe? The answer is to be found in the limitations imposed by nature on the air resources in California.

---

*If the air over the Los Angeles Basin, up to 1000 feet above the surface, were divided into equal allotments for each person in the basin, a person electing to conserve his allotment for breathing would have enough to last 30 years. But the person electing to spend this allotment in dispersing the waste products of his "full size" automobile to harmless concentrations would run out of air in less than five minutes of average driving.

The three major areas of California which have been most favored, thus far, for development by man are the Coastal Valleys and basins, the Central Valley, and the Coachella-Imperial Valleys. In these areas are 97% of California's people, all of its major cities, most of its industries, and most of its agriculture. And in each of these areas, much of the time the amount of ventilation or replacement of surface air is limited.

In the coastal valleys and basins, this limitation is the result of a persistent overhead layer of warm air which originates by subsidence in the semi-permanent high pressure area over the Pacific ocean, and which moves onshore at a variable height above the surface. In the ocean along most of the California coast there is a cold upwelling which produces surface water temperatures lower than those further at sea. As the surface air moves landward in contact with this cold water, it also is cooled. One result of this is the familiar coastal fog. A more important result, from our immediate viewpoint, is that there is very little interchange, very little mixing, between this surface layer of cool air and the overhead layer of warm air. This phenomenon of warm air overlying cool air, known as an inversion, is chiefly responsible for limiting the supply of fresh air in California's coastal regions. The height to the base of the inversion may sometimes be as much as three thousand feet or more, sometimes as little as a hundred feet, and it is only the air beneath this inversion which man on the ground can use. There is in general some seaward motion of the air beneath the inversion at night and landward motion during the day, but in some regions, such as the Los Angeles basin and the San Francisco Bay Area, the air beneath the inversion sometimes tends to stagnate, another factor which limits the supply.

Only limited data are available on the extent to which the Pacific overhead inversion reaches into the interior valleys of California such as the Central Valley. It is known that it is modified as it extends inland and is often dissipated during periods of high temperature. In the interior valleys, therefore, it appears that the overhead inversion is not as important a factor as it is along the coast. But in these valleys there are other phenomena which limit the supply of fresh air.

\* \* \*

Fortunately, poor ventilation, produced by these conditions, does not exist all the time. Generally, as the surface inversion rises and the sea breeze picks up there is an improvement during the afternoons. On some days there is no overhead inversion and the pollution is reduced by upward mixing. On other days a mass of clean air moves in and there may be a period of almost no pollution at all. The sparkling clarity which we still enjoy on these good days, even in Los Angeles and the Bay Area, serves to emphasize the great effect of limited ventilation on the poor days, and the extent to which it increases our problems.

## Problems of Air Pollution in California

The contaminants which man introduces into this limited supply of surface air in California are of many forms. They range from wood smoke to peat dust, from automobile exhaust to chemical insecticides, from industrial fumes to fragments of turkey feathers. Each creates its problems, and to a large extent each problem is a case unto itself.

Perhaps the least complex of these problems arise in those cases in which the pollutants come from one or a few specific sources, which can be pinpointed and specifically controlled. The emission of sulfur dioxide from the Selby smelter and of stack dust from the Colton cement plant are examples of specific sources, control of which began about half a century ago. Steam locomotives are a case in which a specific pollution source was eliminated by change rather than by control. Another example is that of smoke from orchard heating in the citrus groves of Southern California. The finding that heat is more valuable than smoke gave the control officers an assist in this case, and it has become a diminishing problem as heaters are replaced by wind machines and orchards are replaced by subdivisions.

\* \* \*

The most complex, and the most difficult, problems occur in those cases in which the effects result from a general merging of pollutants from many diverse sources. General air pollution is, of course, most severe in the most densely populated areas, and in California this means the Los Angeles Basin and the San Francisco Bay area. Table 1 shows estimates, taken from various sources, . . . of the principal emissions which contribute to general air pollution in these two areas.

Table 1. GENERAL EMISSIONS TO THE ATMOSPHERE IN LOS ANGELES COUNTY AND THE SAN FRANCISCO BAY AREA

| Substances emitted | Amounts emitted, in tons per day | | | |
|---|---|---|---|---|
| | Los Angeles County | | | San Francisco Bay Area |
| | 1950 | —1963— | | 1959 |
| | | Winter | Summer . . . | |
| Particulates | 190 | 125 | 95 | 335 |
| Nitrogen oxides[a] | 430 | 850 | 710 | 460 |
| Sulfur dioxide | 610 | 545 | 130 | 550 |
| Carbon monoxide | 4800-7100 | 8600 | | 5000[b] |
| Hydrocarbons | 1690 | 2230 | | 1875 |
| Other organics (aldehydes, ketones, alcohols, ethers, etc.) | 200 | 190 | | 265-540[c] |

a. Mostly nitric oxide, but calculated as nitrogen dioxide
b. Estimate uncertain
c. During agricultural burning season

These estimates show several interesting features. For instance, consider the changes between 1950 and 1963 in Los Angeles County. The percentage increase in nitrogen oxide emissions during this period is the largest of any in the table because this pollutant was the least controlled. The smaller increases in carbon monoxide and hydrocarbon emissions and the actual decreases in particulate, sulfur dioxide, and non-hydrocarbon organic emissions reflect the control programs which were put into effect during the period. The present smaller emissions in summer as compared to winter in Los Angeles are due partly to the smaller use of fuel for heating, but mostly to the substitution of natural gas for fuel oil . . .

It has often been remarked that the Bay Area is not far behind Los Angeles in air pollution. In terms of emissions, as the table shows, in most cases the Bay Area in 1959 was about equal to or ahead of Los Angeles County in 1950. Currently, the time difference may be smaller, and in fact, due to the more advanced control program in Los Angeles, in particulate, sulfur dioxide, and non-hydrocarbon organic emissions San Francisco may now lead.

*  *  *

Other effects of general air pollution, less readily observed and more difficult to assess, include those on the economy, on property values, on agriculture, on where people and industries locate, and perhaps most important of all, on health. Possible health effects which are under study include mucosal irritation, decreased pulmonary function, interference with oxygen transport by the blood, interference with enzyme function, and contributions to emphysema, pneumonia, and lung cancer. One other effect which merits a place on the list is psychological depression. This, to some people, is very real, as those who live in badly contaminated areas know. . . .

### Aspects of the Attack on Air Pollution

The attack on the problems of air pollution shares at least three aspects in common with the attacks on problems of land and water. The first of these is in the lead time between recognition of a problem and the installation of measures for its abatement. For example, it has now been about twelve years since it was learned that hydrocarbons from automobile exhaust are a major contributor to air pollution, and it may be another twelve before present plans for the control of these hydrocarbons are fully in effect (twenty-four years in all). But we now have only sixteen years in which to recognize and prepare for the problems of the 1980's.

The second common aspect is that the problems are never static. As man's activities change with time, so do the problems change with time, and as population and industrialization increase, so do the problems become more critical and the steps required for a solution more severe.

84

These two aspects, the lead time and the changing nature and intensity of the problems, are to some extent antagonistic. Together, they are a formidable challenge to man's ability to foresee the future, and to his courage to take the steps that future demands.

The third aspect is the requirement of continued public support of the necessary steps. Here, I think all control officers will agree, the problems of air pollution are more insidious than those of land or water. Air pollution usually develops gradually, and people get used to it, adapt to it to some extent, and even refuse to recognize or admit it for what it is. Then a period of stagnant air comes along, causes a severe attack, the everlasting requirement for air to breathe suddenly becomes apparent, and people get excited. They demand that something be done immediately, and blame the control officers personally if it is not. Such a situation occurred in the Los Angeles Basin in the fall of 1953, and led not only to the virtual stoning of control officers in the streets and ostracizing of their children in the schools, but also to a request that the Governor declare Southern California an emergency area and to suggestions that parts of it be evacuated. Following such situations, the weather improves, the air clarifies, and interest sags. In a word, the problem is euphoria, and I do not know the solution, unless it be increased public education and understanding.

\* \* \*

In my opinion, the proper approach, and indeed the only approach short of population control which gives promise of a satisfactory and lasting solution to the problem of general air pollution in California, lies along a quite different line. In a sense, air pollution may be likened to a weed. Controls may clip back the weed, but they will not keep it from growing up again. To kill the weed we must get at the root, and the root of the whole problem of general air pollution is combustion. Combustion, in Los Angeles County, is responsible for virtually all of the oxides of nitrogen, and the preparation, handling and use of fuels for combustion is responsible for over five-sixths of the hydrocarbons which are emitted to the air. In addition, combustion is responsible for all or almost all of the smoke, the carbon monoxide, the carbon dioxide, the oxides of sulfur, the aldehydes, the carcinogens, and the lead compounds which are emitted.

I suggest, therefore, that the only proper approach to a lasting solution of these problems of man and air in California, the only way to kill the weed, is to attack, not the products of combustion, but combustion itself. To reduce by every possible means, the burning of fuels in favor of non-polluting sources of heat and power. To finally take action to limit this use of fire and air.

Such a change will occur eventually in any case as fossil fuels are exhausted. But by present indications this will not be for another century or more, and in California we cannot afford to wait that long.

Might it not be that the greatest reward, in terms of human gains versus money and effort expended, will come, not from controls, but from steps taken to accelerate this change?

* * *

Some of these changes, as Dr. Haagen-Smit has pointed out, would achieve gains beyond that of reducing the uses of combustion, they would also be permanent assets to better living. None is beyond our technical competence, it is a matter of how this may best be used, and here the burden falls on our social competence. All must be fought for, they will not come of themselves, and the fight will require both vision and courage.

Whether or not we find the courage, the path is clear. We may be sure that only by such steps will we escape an unending procession of ever increasing, ever more restrictive, ever unsatisfactory controls. Only by such steps will we make the air of California again an asset, instead of the liability to continued development it now is. Only by such steps will man here meet the challenge of his limited environment.[5]

* * *

In sum, pollution studies reveal that pollution—like the people who create it—tends to increase by compound interest. The rate of increase appears to be more rapid than that of human populations. This is one of the major reasons why a cutback in population growth is so essential to the continued welfare of the Golden State.

## The Time for Decision

Over 1.5 billion people would be living in California within 100 years if the state's population continues to grow at the rate of the last ten years. This would be nearly half of the population of the planet today.

Congestion of such magnitude would be both intolerable and impossible: there would be just one twentieth of an acre per person. Long before that the citizens of California would have fallen victim to a social and biological catastrophe; or they would have taken steps to prevent the disaster by drastic re-evaluation of current dogmas and by vigorous exercise of imaginative, effective, and humane controls over proliferation of people.

Not so long ago, men were chiefly occupied with providing their families, and sometimes the larger tribe or community, with the basic elements of subsistence: food, clothing, and shelter. Eventually, there emerged a second level of life in which the more acquisitive and gadget-oriented nations focused on material conveniences: central heat, electric refrigeration, the telephone, and television.

The affluent minority today, and this is not an insignificant part of the California menage, now looks beyond the smog and the polluted countryside to a third level: the quality of the human experience. Yet quality is a subjective judgment. For some, it means no more than an air-conditioned house, two air-conditioned automobiles, a private swimming pool, and winters in the Caribbean. "Quality," thus defined, is material comfort carried to the nth degree. These can be good and pleasant appurtenances. Then there are increasing numbers who look for quality of life in a more expansive, expressive use of leisure in which families can learn to live together again, in which a man can rediscover his vigor on empty beaches such as still exist in the Big Sur, or in wilderness isolation in the grand remoteness of the Sierra Nevada. Others find a satisfying quality of life in the magic of the theatre, the plastic arts, good music, in all those aesthetic and intellectual intangibles that are hopefully becoming an increasing part of the modern community.

Many ingredients contribute to a high quality of human experience. The essential elements exist in abundance in California. Blessed by great wealth and richly endowed with scientific and technological sophistication, these energetic California-Americans have a unique opportunity to realize the finest humanistic goals of Western civilization. What the European spirit produced through Leonardo, Rousseau, Locke, and other giants of the Renaissance and the Enlightenment could culminate in the potential pattern of life which is locked in the resources of the Golden State.

That California is presently moving toward the dawning of a Golden Age would hardly be conceded by a man from Mars, who presumably could appraise the situation objectively. The basis for his pessimism has been cited only in part in this report.

The related problems of pollution and congestion become increasingly acute. Resources are being ruthlessly exploited. Three fifths of the people in California are caught in the vast Los Angeles sprawl extending from Santa Barbara to San Diego; and another 6 million are squeezed into six other super cities of 100,000 or more.

The value systems of our society appear to give little reason to expect that existing patterns will change very rapidly. In the light of such considerations the prospects for a fulfilling human experience for many millions are very poor indeed. The crucial question is: will the wisdom to guide the managerial skills be forthcoming to change trends and to bring to birth the miracle of a Golden Age in California?

There is little indication that so fundamental a change is imminent. The dire and urgent warnings reviewed here, only in part, appear to have had no significant impact on the current booster-minded psychology at the policy level. One bit of arresting evidence that this is the case must suffice.

In February 1966, the press noted indications that an exodus from California might be in the making. The population office of the California Department of Finance felt it necessary to issue a statement countering this "alarming" prospect. The chief of the population staff of that department was quoted in this release as "still forecasting a net migration to California this year of 330,000. There is no solid evidence that would support [the] contention that a sharp decline in the rate of migration to the state is in prospect . . . nearly all of the migration indices indicate that the substantial net migration that California has experienced is continuing." Evidences from school enrollment and other statistics were cited in support of this position.

The warnings of trouble ahead, of which the two reports of pollution of the California environment cited above, appear to have elicited no change of heart. With time running short in which to alter the current demographic collision course, some very fundamental reevaluating of the ecological realities is urgently in order.

First must come the simple, clear, irrefutable recognition that the growth of California's population must be checked.

A reduction of approximately 50 percent in the birth rate would eventually stabilize growth attributable to natural increase. Fortunately, the birth rate is trending down both in California and the nation. If ingenuity can be brought to bear to accelerate this process, so much the better. It might even be posited that if the health hazards of smog are as serious as some medical authorities consider them to be, this may result in a reduction in the rate of growth through a rise in the death rate—which would hardly recommend itself as a way to reduce population growth.

The tactical problem is to find means to reduce sharply migration into the state, which now contributes two thirds of the population increase. This complex challenge deserves the highest priority.

A beginning is found in the frightening book, *The Destruction of California,* by native son Raymond F. Dasmann. The simplest of his suggestions is that the people stop building purposefully toward continuing population growth:

There are various answers to the problem of controlling population increase in California. One is relatively simple, and involves *not* planning for population growth. This means not encouraging new industries to move into an area. It means not developing our water resources to a maximum, and thus not providing the water that would make possible additional urban or industrial growth, or bring into production new farming areas. It means not building those new power stations or those new freeways. No real-estate development will be built in an area where electricity and water will not be provided. No industry will come where it will not receive space, power or water.

\* \* \*

The idea of controlling population increase by not providing for it, and indeed forbidding the development of new facilities, is not original. It has been used already, on a small scale. One of the most charming places in California is the city of Santa Barbara. It has maintained its quiet beauty by excluding the kind of industrial growth that other cities have welcomed. It has not allowed housing sprawl. It has fought the State Highway Commission and its monstrous freeway system to a halt, temporarily at least. The continuing charm of the Carmel region, farther north, has been maintained by a firm and definite stand against "progress" by its residents. But these are small places, inhabited by the wealthy. It is most unlikely that active discouragement of population increase on a statewide scale will be tried out. It goes against the entire philosophy of the expanding economy. Too many people look forward to population growth, even while they decry its effect, for them to accept a plan for its discouragement. Such a plan would mean that all those who had invested in land would find land values no longer increasing. It would say to those in business and industry that they could expect no further expansion of the California market. All of us are too used to being pushed to higher levels by people crowding in from below to accept the idea that growth and expansion have ended.

\* \* \*

Our very economic system prevents our doing the things needed to protect our environment from destruction, and we are sadly aware that other alternative economic systems in existence today work no better.[2]

\* \* \*

To check the rate of California's growth must inevitably take time; population trends do not change overnight. If the expansionist philosophy were to be abandoned, now is the time to begin to apply inspired ingenuity to the question of developing effective demographic retro-factors. Other means than those suggested by Dr. Dasmann might be brought to bear. The public facilities necessary to service a new family in the state have been variously estimated to range from $6,500 to $17,000. That these should be, at least in part, defrayed by a "come-in" tax levied on new arrivals has been suggested as a possible deterrent to the trek westward. The implementation of retro-factors of one kind or another would surely not be beyond the range of human ingenuity—once the need to take such actions is recognized.

Every available resource too must be applied in achieving a wise ecological management of the state's natural wealth. The two thrusts are inseparable. We must remember that the problem of numbers is not, in fact, merely numerical. Where the people are distributed is a major consideration.

For the state as a whole, the population density is a modest 120 per square mile. This is about twice the density of the continental United States, and not excessive. The difficulty is that nearly all of the people are crowded into less than 10 percent of the total land area. The Soil and Water Conservation Inventory locates perhaps 98 percent of the total population on some 8.7 million acres. Thus, density of this area is about 1,341 per square mile, which is comparable to that of the Island of Barbados in the West Indies with a record 1,400 people per square mile. If the existing trend of population concentration in California continues, the prospect in scarcely more than a generation is appalling. Yet, the Aerojet-General report appears to assume that this current trend toward concentration will continue.

A wiser, healthier distribution of a projected 50 million population throughout the state is essential and not impossible. Italy, with a land area three quarters that of California, has a population of 53 million, and with very slow population growth. Italy unquestionably has grave economic and social problems and a living level unacceptable in California today. Yet one might speculate that life in Italy as it is today might well be more favorable to man's individual needs than life for the average citizen would be a generation hence in California, with continuing ecological deterioration.

In the Aerojet-General report, we have a prime illustration of the strong tendency to ignore the need for ecological wisdom, and to depend on the computer for guidance when its role can only be that of analysis:

... The problem of waste management in an encapsulated environment has been the subject of intensive work by the aerospace industry. All factors affecting waste generation in the space cabin, its processing, reclamation and disposal were evaluated in approaching an optimized solution. The space waste disposal system as finally designed will represent the most advantageous compromise among the various significant features, such as performance, reliability, weight, volume, and cost. The tools used in this evaluation are system analysis and system engineering, with the selective application of a broad spectrum of technological capabilities. The possibility of using these tools to design an effective waste management system in an environment that is complicated by political, legal, and geographical considerations was studied by Aerojet-General in the scope of this contract. The criteria and environment are different from those of the space cabin, but the principles used in studying their interactions are the same and so is the end objective—to find the optimum solution to a highly complex problem.[1]

\*     \*     \*

That the computer's success in producing a viable encapsulated environment in the Gemini capsules can be taken as a safe guide to planning California's ecological future carries an analogy very far.

Applying the computer, the aerospace technicians hopefully blueprint a plan for 50 million Californians to hold the pollution of their water, their air, and their land to a point that will enable them at least to survive. This plan does not say anything about what might be done to assure an ever-enhanced *quality of life* for the people of the state. The late Norbert Wiener, pioneer in cybernetics and computer technology, in his posthumous book, *God and Golem, Inc.,* warned against the increasing tendency to cast our burdens on the computer and to hope for miracles. It requires only an abacus to establish that on a planet of finite size, no organism can continue to multiply indefinitely whether it be microbe, minnow, or man. The computer, which is an industrious slave when given exact directions, cannot "solve" any of the basic problems of ecology; it cannot apply *wisdom* to solving the burgeoning problems which confront modern man.

There, in these two necessities for population control and for pollution prevention, one sees the two dominant and determining issues which Californians, and the human race, must deal with effectively if any measure of the good life is to be possible on this hectic planet.

In the developing lands of Asia, Africa, and Latin America, the imbalance in population vs. resources appears to be reaching the gruesome end-point of famine on a scale never dreamed of before. This could check the runaway growth of human numbers. Perhaps after this awful cleansing, man will begin to see himself in his place on the planet in more rational perspective. Yet what is happening in California is different, and if current trends continue it may well prove more devastating in the long run than the impending tragedy some of the developing countries face. If human wisdom and

ingenuity fail in California, what hope will there be for breakthroughs elsewhere under less favorable circumstances?

Fortunately, the expansionist obsession is no longer universal. A number of ecology-oriented organizations exist in California. Among the pioneers is the Sierra Club of San Francisco, which has for a number of years carried on an increasingly effective campaign to conserve the resources of the region. The Save-the-Redwoods League has centered specifically on attempting to prevent the ruthless exploitation of one of California's unique resources. A number of other organizations are concerned with this problem.

There are a few hopeful indications that attitudes may be changing. A Gallup Poll released on April 24 indicates that the relentless tide of urban migration which has for so long gripped the United States may have passed its peak. The Poll found that "Of those persons who live in the biggest cities (500,-000 and over), nearly half would like to live somewhere else—in the suburbs, a small town, or on a farm. On the other hand, of those who live in these latter areas, few express any interest in moving to the big cities." If this report is substantiated by a definite change in migratory pattern, it will represent a profound change in attitude. Between 1950 and 1960, the large metropolitan centers grew by some 23 million people. A sharp slacking off in this trend could greatly modify population distribution in the United States.

Because California has come to embody the epitome of the American dream, it has drained millions from the rest of the nation. Because it has been the Mecca to which both young and old turned their eyes, its predicament has a national significance. If Californians take the essential steps to deal with the crisis which confronts them, it may well be a guidepost for the entire nation.

ROBERT C. COOK
*Editor*

## SOURCES

The reader is referred to the following sources for additional information:

1. Aerojet-General Corporation. *California Waste Management Study, A Report to the State of California Department of Public Health.* Report No. 3056, August 1965.
2. Dasmann, Raymond F. *The Destruction of California.* New York: Macmillan Company, 1965.
3. Gordon, Mitchell. *Sick Cities.* New York: Macmillan Company, 1963.
4. Higbee, Edward. *The Squeeze, Cities Without Space.* New York: William Morrow and Company, 1960.
5. Leighton, Philip A. *Man and Air in California.* Presented at the State-wide Conference on Man in California, 1980's, January 1964.
6. State of California, Documents Section. *California Statistical Abstract 1965.*
7. United States Bureau of the Census.
   a. *County and City Data Book, 1962.*
   b. *Population Estimates.* Series P 25, No. 324, January 20, 1966.
   c. *Historical Statistics of the United States: Colonial Times to 1957.*
   d. *U.S. Census of Population: 1960.* Final Report: PC(1) 1D; PC(1) 6A, 6B, 6D.
   e. ———. Final Report: PC(2) 2B.
8. United States Department of Agriculture.
   a. Economic Research Service. *Net Migration of the Population, 1950-60 by Age, Sex, and Color.* Vol. I, Part 6.
   b. Soil Conservation Service. *California Soil and Water Conservation Needs Inventory.* (California Conservation Needs Committee, November 1961).
9. United States Department of Health, Education, and Welfare.
   a. Office of Education. *Digest of Educational Statistics.* 1965.
   b. Public Health Service. *Monthly Vital Statistics Report.* Volume 14, No. 8, October 22, 1965.
10. Wiener, Norbert. *God and Golem, Inc.* Cambridge, Massachusetts: The M.I.T. Press, 1964.

\* \* \*

# The Age of Inverted Utopias

*"In the midst of old countries disappearing and new ones coming to birth, few men have paused to notice that a familiar and cherished nation, unique in offering honorary citizenship to all humanity, is in danger of quietly fading from the map. That country is Utopia . . . During this century there has been an unequaled production of imaginary societies . . . But the significant fact is this. A decreasing percentage of the imaginary worlds are utopias. An increasing percentage are nightmares. The 'dystopia' or 'inverted utopia' or 'anti-utopia' . . . was a minor satiric fringe of the utopian output in the 19th century. It promises to become the dominant type today. . . ."*—Chad Walsh, *From Utopia to Nightmare.*

Our Affluence Rests on a Crumbling Foundation

# Overpopulated America

## by Wayne H. Davis

I define as most seriously overpopulated that nation whose people by virtue of their numbers and activities are most rapidly decreasing the ability of the land to support human life. With our large population, our affluence and our technological monstrosities the United States wins first place by a substantial margin.

Let's compare the US to India, for example. We have 203 million people, whereas she has 540 million on much less land. But look at the impact of people on the land.

The average Indian eats his daily few cups of rice (or perhaps wheat, whose production on American farms contributed to our one percent per year drain in quality of our active farmland), draws his bucket of

WAYNE H. DAVIS *teaches in the school of biological sciences at the University of Kentucky.*

water from the communal well and sleeps in a mud hut. In his daily rounds to gather cow dung to burn to cook his rice and warm his feet, his footsteps, along with those of millions of his countrymen, help bring about a slow deterioration of the ability of the land to support people. His contribution to the destruction of the land is minimal.

An American, on the other hand, can be expected to destroy a piece of land on which he builds a home, garage and driveway. He will contribute his share to the 142 million tons of smoke and fumes, seven million junked cars, 20 million tons of paper, 48 billion cans, and 26 billion bottles the overburdened environment must absorb each year. To run his air conditioner we will strip-mine a Kentucky hillside, push the dirt and slate down into the stream, and burn coal in a power generator, whose smokestack contributes to a plume

Reprinted by permission of the author and the publisher from *The New Republic* 162(2):13–15, January 10, 1970. © 1970, Harrison-Blaine of New Jersey, Inc.

of smoke massive enough to cause cloud **seeding and** premature precipitation from Gulf winds which **should** be irrigating the wheat farms of Minnesota.

In his lifetime he will personally **pollute three mil**lion gallons of water, and industry and agriculture will use ten times this much water in his behalf. To provide these needs the US Army Corps of Engineers will build dams and flood farmland. He will also use 21,000 gallons of leaded gasoline containing boron, drink 28,000 pounds of milk and eat 10,000 pounds of meat. The latter is produced and squandered in a life pattern unknown to Asians. A steer on a Western range eats plants containing minerals necessary for plant life. Some of these are incorporated into the body of the steer which is later shipped for slaughter. After being eaten by man these nutrients are flushed down the toilet into the ocean or buried in the cemetery, the surface of which is cluttered with boulders called tombstones and has been removed from productivity. The result is a continual drain on the productivity of range land. Add to this the erosion of overgrazed lands, and the effects of the falling water table as we mine Pleistocene deposits of groundwater to irrigate to produce food for more people, and we can see why our land is dying far more rapidly than did the great civilizations of the Middle East, which experienced the same cycle. The average Indian citizen, whose fecal material goes back to the land, has but a minute fraction of the destructive effect on the land that the affluent American does.

Thus I want to introduce a new term, which I suggest be used in future discussions of human population and ecology. We should speak of our numbers in "Indian equivalents". An Indian equivalent I define as the average number of Indian citizens required to have the same detrimental effect on the land's ability to support human life as would the average American. This value is difficult to determine, but let's take an extremely conservative working figure of 25. To see how conservative this is, imagine the addition of 1000 citizens to your town and 25,000 to an Indian village. Not only would the Americans destroy much more land for homes, highways and a shopping center, but they would contribute far more to environmental deterioration in hundreds of other ways as well. For example, their demand for steel for new autos might increase the daily pollution equivalent of 130,000 junk autos which *Life* tells us that US Steel Corp. dumps into Lake Michigan. Their demand for textiles would help the cotton industry destroy the life in the Black Warrior River in Alabama with endrin. And they would contribute to the massive industrial pollution of our oceans (we provide one third to one half the world's share) which has caused the precipitous downward trend in our commercial fisheries landings during the past seven years.

The per capita gross national product of the United

States is 38 times that of India. Most of our goods and services contribute to the decline in the ability of the environment to support life. Thus it is clear that a figure of 25 for an Indian equivalent is conservative. It has been suggested to me that a more realistic figure would be 500.

In Indian equivalents, therefore, the population of the United States is at least four billion. And the rate of growth is even more alarming. We are growing at one percent per year, a rate which would double our numbers in 70 years. India is growing at 2.5 percent. Using the Indian equivalent of 25, our population growth becomes 10 times as serious as that of India. According to the Reinows[*] in their recent book *Moment in the Sun,* just one year's crop of American babies can be expected to use up 25 billion pounds of beef, 200 million pounds of steel and 9.1 billion gallons of gasoline during their collective lifetime. And the demands on water and land for our growing population are expected to be far greater than the supply available in the year 2000. We are destroying our land at a rate of over a million acres a year. We now have only 2.6 agricultural acres per person. By 1975 this will be cut to 2.2, the critical point for the maintenance of what we consider a decent diet, and by the year 2000 we might expect to have 1.2.

You might object that I am playing with statistics in using the Indian equivalent on the rate of growth. I am making the assumption that today's child will live 35 years (the average Indian life span) at today's level of affluence. If he lives an American 70 years, our rate of population growth would be 20 times as serious as India's.

But the assumption of continued affluence at today's level is unfounded. If our numbers continue to rise, our standard of living will fall so sharply that by the year 2000 any surviving Americans might consider today's average Asian to be well off. Our children's destructive effects on their environment will decline as they sink ever lower into poverty.

The United States is in serious economic trouble now. Nothing could be more misleading than today's affluence, which rests precariously on a crumbling foundation. Our productivity, which had been increasing steadily at about 3.2 percent a year since World War II, has been falling during 1969. Our export over import balance has been shrinking steadily from $7.1 billion in 1964 to $0.15 billion in the first half of 1969. Our balance of payments deficit for the second quarter was $3.7 billion, the largest in history. We are now importing iron ore, steel, oil, beef, textiles, cameras, radios and hundreds of other things.

Our economy is based upon the Keynesian concept of a continued growth in population and productivity. It worked in an underpopulated nation with excess resources. It could continue to work only if the earth

[*] Rienows

and its resources were expanding at an annual rate of 4 to 5 percent. Yet neither the number of cars, the economy, the human population, nor anything else can expand indefinitely at an exponential rate in a finite world. We must face this fact *now*. The crisis is here. When Walter Heller says that our economy will expand by 4 percent annually through the latter 1970s he is dreaming. He is in a theoretical world totally unaware of the realities of human ecology. If the economists do not wake up and devise a new system for us now somebody else will have to do it for them.

A civilization is comparable to a living organism. Its longevity is a function of its metabolism. The higher the metabolism (affluence), the shorter the life. Keynesian economics has allowed us an affluent but shortened life span. We have now run our course.

The tragedy facing the United States is even greater and more imminent than that descending upon the hungry nations. The Paddock brothers in their book, *Famine 1975!*, say that India "cannot be saved" no matter how much food we ship her. But India will be here after the United States is gone. Many millions will die in the most colossal famines India has ever known, but the land will survive and she will come back as she always has before. The United States, on the other hand, will be a desolate tangle of concrete and tickytacky, of strip-mined moonscape and silt-choked reservoirs. The land and water will be so contaminated with pesticides, herbicides, mercury fungicides, lead, boron, nickel, arsenic and hundreds of other toxic substances, which have been approaching critical levels of concentration in our environment as a result of our numbers and affluence, that it may be unable to sustain human life.

Thus as the curtain gets ready to fall on man's civilization let it come as no surprise that it shall first fall on the United States. And let no one make the mistake of thinking we can save ourselves by "cleaning up the environment." Banning DDT is the equivalent of the physician's treating syphilis by putting a bandaid over the first chancre to appear. In either case you can be sure that more serious and widespread trouble will soon appear unless the disease itself is treated. We cannot survive by planning to treat the symptoms such as air pollution, water pollution, soil erosion, etc.

What can we do to slow the rate of destruction of the United States as a land capable of supporting human life? There are two approaches. First, we must reverse the population growth. We have far more people now than we can continue to support at anything near today's level of affluence. American women average slightly over three children each. According to the *Population Bulletin* if we reduced this number to 2.5 there would still be 330 million people in the nation at the end of the century. And even if we re-

duced this to 1.5 we would have 57 million more people in the year 2000 than we have now. With our present longevity patterns it would take more than 30 years for the population to peak even when reproducing at this rate, which would eventually give us a net decrease in numbers.

Do not make the mistake of thinking that technology will solve our population problem by producing a better contraceptive. Our problem now is that people want too many children. Surveys show the average number of children wanted by the American family is 3.3. There is little difference between the poor and the wealthy, black and white, Catholic and Protestant. Production of children at this rate during the next 30 years would be so catastrophic in effect on our resources and the viability of the nation as to be beyond my ability to contemplate. To prevent this trend we must not only make contraceptives and abortion readily available to everyone, but we must establish a system to put severe economic pressure on those who produce children and reward those who do not. This can be done within our system of taxes and welfare.

The other thing we must do is to pare down our Indian equivalents. Individuals in American society vary tremendously in Indian equivalents. If we plot Indian equivalents versus their reciprocal, the percentage of land surviving a generation, we obtain a linear regression. We can then place individuals and occupation types on this graph. At one end would be the starving blacks of Mississippi; they would approach unity in Indian equivalents, and would have the least destructive effect on the land. At the other end of the graph would be the politicians slicing pork for the barrel, the highway contractors, strip-mine operators, real estate developers, and public enemy number one — the US Army Corps of Engineers.

We must halt land destruction. We must abandon the view of land and minerals as private property to be exploited in any way economically feasible for private financial gain. Land and minerals are resources upon which the very survival of the nation depends, and their use must be planned in the best interests of the people.

Rising expectations for the poor is a cruel joke foisted upon them by the Establishment. As our new economy of use-it-once-and-throw-it-away produces more and more products for the affluent, the share of our resources available for the poor declines. Blessed be the starving blacks of Mississippi with their outdoor privies, for they are ecologically sound, and they shall inherit a nation. Although I hope that we will help these unfortunate people attain a decent standard of living by diverting war efforts to fertility control and job training, our most urgent task to assure this nation's survival during the next decade is to stop the affluent destroyers.

Overpopulation as a Crisis Issue

# The Nonsense Explosion

## by Ben Wattenberg

As the concern about the environment has swept across
the nation, the ghost of the "population explosion" –
recently haunting only India and other ugly foreign
places – has suddenly been domestically resurrected
and we are again hearing how crowded it is in America.

*Life* magazine, for example, chose to launch the new
decade with the headline "Squeezing into the '70s,"
announcing that, because of the crowds, "the despair
of yesterday's soup line has been replaced by today's
ordeal of the steak line." Two months later *Life* fea-
tured a story about a young New Jersey mathematician
who had himself sterilized because he is "deeply worried by this country's wildly expanding population."

Crowded, crowded, crowded, we are told. Slums are
crowded, suburbs are crowded, megalopolis is crowded
and more and more and more people are eating up,

burning up and using up the beauty and wealth of
America – turning the land into a polluted, depleted
sprawl of scummy water and flickering neon, an ecological catastrophe stretching from the Everglades to
the Pacific Northwest. Crisis. Crisis. Crisis.

That so very much of this is preposterous, as we shall
see, should come as no real surprise to those who follow
the fads of crisis in America. There are no plain and
simple problems any more. From poverty to race to
crime to Vietnam all we face are crises which threaten
to bring down the world upon our heads. And now it is
ecology/environment – which is a perfectly good problem to be sure – but with its advent comes dragged in
by the heels our old friend the super-crisis of the population explosion, which is not nearly as real or immediate a problem in America, and ends up serving unfor-

Reprinted by permission of the author and the publisher from *The New Republic*
162(14–15):18–23, April 4–11, 1970. © 1970, Harrison-Blaine of New Jersey, Inc.

tunately as a political smokescreen that can obscure a host of legitimate concerns.

While the rhetoric rattles on about where will we ever put the next hundred million Americans, while the President tells us that the roots of so many of our current problems are to be found in the speed with which the last hundred million Americans came upon us, while the more apocalyptic demographers and biologists (like Dr. Paul Ehrlich) are talking about putting still nonexistent birth control chemicals in the water supply, and about federal licensing of babies – the critical facts in the argument remain generally unstated and the critical premises in the argument remain largely unchallenged.

—The critical facts are that America is not by any standard a crowded country and that the American birth rate has recently been at an all-time low,

—The critical premise is that population growth in America is harmful.

In not stating the facts and in not at least challenging the premises, politicians and planners alike seem to be leaving themselves open to both bad planning and bad politics. This happens by concentrating on what the problem is not, rather than on what the problem is. Let's, then, first look at the facts. The current population of the United States is 205 million. That population is distributed over 3,615,123 square miles of land, for a density of about 55 persons per square mile. In terms of density, this makes the United States one of the most sparsely populated nations in the world. As measured by density, Holland is about 18 times as "crowded" (at 975 persons per square mile), England is 10 times as dense (588 persons per square mile), scenic Switzerland seven times as dense (382), tropical Nigeria three times as dense (174) and even neighboring Mexico beats us out with 60 persons per square mile. The US, by international standards, is not a very "crowded" country.

But density in some cases can be very misleading in trying to judge "crowdedness." The Soviet Union, for example, is less dense than the US (29 per square mile), but has millions of square miles of uninhabitable land, just as does Brazil and Australia, two other nations also less densely populated than the US.

Of course, the US also has large areas of land that are equally uninhabitable: the Rockies, the Western deserts, parts of Alaska and so on.

But while it is of interest to know that America has some land that is uninhabitable, what is of far more importance is that we have in the United States vast unused areas of eminently habitable land, land that in fact was inhabited until very recently. In the last eight years one out of three counties in America actually *lost*

BEN WATTENBERG, *co-author of* This U.S.A., *a book on demography published by Doubleday in 1965, served on President Johnson's White House staff.*

population. Four states have lost population: North and South Dakota, West Virginia, and Wyoming; and another two states, Maine and Iowa, gained less than one percent in the eight years. Furthermore, three out of five counties had a net out-migration, that is, more people left the county than came in.

These counties, the net-loss counties and the net-out-migration counties, are the areas in America where the current hoopla about the population sounds a bit hollow. These are the areas, mostly rural and small town, that are trying to attract industry, areas where a smokestack or a traffic jam signifies not pollution but progress, areas that have more open space around them for hunting and fishing than before, and areas where the older people are a little sad because, as they tell you, "the young people don't stay around here anymore."

This human plaint tells us what has been happening demographically in the United States in recent years. It has not been a population explosion, but a population redistribution. And the place people have been redistributing themselves *to* is a place we call "suburb":

### American Population by Residence

|  | Population | | Increase |
|---|---|---|---|
|  | 1950 | 1968 | 1950-1968 |
| Residing in Central city | 35% | 29% | 6 million |
| Residing in Suburb | 24% | 35% | 32 million (!) |
| Residing in small cities, towns and rural | 41% | 36% | 9 million |
|  | 100% | 100% | 47 million |

In less than two decades the proportion of Americans living in suburbs has gone from less than a quarter to more than a third.

But even the total increase in population – rural, city, and suburb – is misleading. The big gains in population occurred ten and fifteen years ago; today growth is much slower. Thus, in calendar year 1956, the US population grew by 3.1 million, while in calendar year 1968 population went up by 2.0 million – and in a nation with a larger population base.

What has happened, simply, is that the baby-boom has ended. When the GIs came home after World War II, they began begetting large quantities of children, and Americans went on begetting at high rates for about 15 years. The best index of population growth in the US is the fertility rate, that is, the number of babies born per thousand women aged 15-44. In 1940, the fertility rate was 80, just a few points above the 1936 Depression all-time low of 76. Ten years later, in 1950, the baby-boom had begun and the fertility rate had soared to 106, an increase of 32 percent in just ten years. It kept climbing. In 1957, it reached 123, up more than 50 percent in two decades.

But since 1957, the rate has gone steadily down: to 119 in 1960, to 98 in 1965, to 85.7 in 1968, not very much higher now than in Depression times. The estimated fertility rate for 1969 was down slightly to 85.5 and there is no reason now to think it will go up, although, as we shall see, it may sink further.

When measured by another yardstick, the "percent national population growth" (birth plus immigration less deaths), the American population is now growing by about 1.0 percent per year; just a decade ago it was growing by 1.8 percent per year. That may not sound like much of a difference, .8 percent, but in a nation of 200 million people it means 16 million fewer people over a single decade!

With all this, however, comes another important set of facts: our population *is* still growing. At the reduced growth rate there are now about two million people being added to our population each year. This may even go up somewhat in the next few years as the baby-boom babies become young adults and – roughly simultaneously – parents. Moreover, a growing population, even a slowly growing population, grows by larger numbers as it grows. As the two hundred million Americans become two hundred and fifty million Americans there is a proportionately greater number of potential mothers, more babies, and the incremental two million new Americans per year can rise to $2^1/_2$ or 3 million new Americans even with a relatively low growth *rate*.

The current, most likely projection of the Census Bureau of the US population in the year 2000 – three decades hence – hovers somewhere in the 280-290 million range. That means there will be about 75-85 million more Americans than today, which is many millions more indeed, although not quite the round "hundred million" figure everyone is talking about.

It must be stressed, however, that this is only a projection: it could be high, it could be low. The figure is derived from a series of four alternate projections based on different levels of fertility rates issued by the Census Bureau in 1967. Already the highest two projections – calling for 361 million and 336 million – are out of the question. The third projection called for 308 million and that too now seems high, as it called for a fertility rate of 95 in 1970 – about 10 points higher than the 1969 rate. The lowest of the four projections calls for a fertility rate of 84.6 in 1970 (roughly where we are) and yields a population of 283 million in the year 2000.

But even that is not an immutable figure by any means. Just as the first three of the alternate projections quickly proved themselves false, so it may be that Series D may prove high. After all, the Hoover Depression, in an era with far less effective birth control technology, brought fertility rates down to 76. What might a Nixon Recession do in an era of pills, loops, diaphragms, liberalized abortion?

Already the Census Bureau – quite properly – is preparing to revise its projections for the future. The new set of alternate projections – which will bracket the newer, lower, fertility rates – will unquestionably be lower, with a low-end possibility in the general area of 265 million for the year 2000. That too will only be a projection, based on assumptions which may or may not prove valid. But if such a low fertility rate does indeed occur, population in the US would then begin to level off after the year 2000 as the last of the baby-boom babies have completed their own families. The US might then be in an era of near-stable population along the lines of many Western European nations.

But even that is sixty million more Americans in just three decades – more than the population of Great Britain today.

Those, then, would seem to be the elementary facts. More Americans, although probably not as many as we may have been led to believe. More Americans, but not necessarily inhabiting a statistically crowded country.

With these facts, we can now turn to the premise set forth by the Explosionists i.e., more Americans are bad.

Are they? My own judgment is – not necessarily.

There are a number of points made by the Explosionists and they can only be briefly examined here.

Because population growth is currently being linked to environmental problems, we can look there first. The Explosionists say people, and the industry needed to support people, causes pollution. Ergo: fewer people – less pollution.

On the surface, a reasonable enough statement; certainly, population is one of the variables in the pollution problem. Yet, there is something else to be said. People not only cause pollution, but once you have a substantial number of people, it is only people that can solve pollution. Further, the case can be made that *more people* can more easily and more quickly solve pollution problems than can fewer people. For example: let us assume that $60 billion per year are necessary for national defense. The cost of defense will not necessarily be higher for a nation of three hundred million than for a nation of two hundred million. Yet the tax revenues to the government would be immensely higher, freeing vast sums of tax money to be used for the very expensive programs that are necessary for air, water, and pollution control. Spreading constant defense costs over a large population base provides proportionately greater amounts for nondefense spending. The same sort of equation can be used for the huge, one-time capital costs of research that must go into any effective, long-range anti-pollution program. The costs are roughly the same for 200 or 300 million people – but easier to pay by 300 million.

Lake Erie, the Hudson River, the Potomac, are ecological slums today. If the US population did not grow by one person over the current 205 million Americans, these bodies of waters would *still* be ecological slums. These waters, and any others now threatened, will be decent places only if men are willing to devote resources to the job. That is not a function of population growth, but of national will. It can be done if we, as a nation, decide that we want it done and are willing to pay for it. It is as simple as that and it has relatively little to do with whether the national decision involves 200 or 250 or 300 or 350 million Americans. It should also be remembered that pollution occurs in underpopulated places as well: in Sydney, Australia today, in medieval Europe in ancient Rome.

Next, the Explosionists view more people as a crisis because of all the demands they will make upon the society. So many new schools, so many more hospitals, more libraries – services and facilities which we are having difficulty providing right now. Similarly with "new towns." If we are to avoid vast and sprawling megalopolitan swaths, we are told, we must build 100 brand-new towns in 30 years. Unfortunately, we've only been able to construct a few in the last couple of decades – so, alas, what possible chance do we have to make the grade in the years to come?

What this argument ignores, of course, is that it is not governments who really create schools, hospitals, libraries and even new towns. It is *people* who create and build. People pay taxes; the taxes build and staff the schools; the more people, the more need for schools, *and* the more taxes. In an uncanny way it usually works out that every child in America has his own set of parents, and a school to attend. In a nation of a hundred million there were roughly enough schools for the children then present, at two hundred million the same was true and, no doubt, it will hold true at three hundred million. Nor will quality suffer because of numbers; quality suffers if taxpayers aren't willing to pay for quality and it is not harder for 300 million Americans to pay for quality schools for their children than it is for 230 million to buy quality schooling for their offspring.

And those "new towns"? *People* make them too. That's just what's been happening in America in the last few decades. We call them "suburbs," not "new towns," and as the earlier data showed, 32 million Americans opted for this "decentralization" over the past eighteen years, long before it became a fashionable, political fad-word. People did this because people are not damn fools and when they had a chance to trade a rural shack or an urban tenement for a green quarter acre in suburbia, they did so, even though the faddists then were saying that suburbia was not "decentralized" (which is allegedly good), but "conformist" (which is allegedly bad). What smug town-planners like to call urban sprawl, represents uncrowded, gracious living for the former residents of city slums and the quality of such suburban life doesn't necessarily deteriorate if another new suburb rises down the road a mile.

Now, suburbs are not identical to the new town concept. The new towns, in theory, are further away from big cities, they are largely self-contained and they are designed from scratch. But, curiously, as many jobs move from the central cities, suburbs are becoming more and more self-contained; as metropolitan areas get larger, the newer suburbs *are* quite far from central cities; and there are some fascinating new start-from-scratch concepts in planning that are now materializing in suburban areas, particularly in some of the massive all-weather, multi-tiered, multi-malled shopping centers.

All this is not to denigrate new towns or the idea of population decentralization. Far from it. The effort here is only to point out that people often act even faster than their governments in seeking their own best interests. If it is new towns near a babbling brook that Americans feel they want, if the country remains prosperous, some patriot will no doubt step forward and provide same, and even have salesmen in boiler rooms phoning you to sell same. The process is mostly organic, not planned/governmental. It works with 200 or 250 or 300 or 350 million Americans.

There is next the "resources" argument. It comes in two parts. Part one: many of our resources are finite (oil, coal, etc.); more people obviously use more resources; the fewer the people, the less the drain on the resources. Part two: we Americans are rich people; rich people use more resources; therefore, we must cut back population particularly fast, and particularly our rich population.

The resources problem is difficult to assess. A demographer now in his sixties seemed to put it in perspective. "Resources are a serious problem," he said, "We've been running out of oil ever since I was a boy."

The fact is, of course, sooner or later we *will* run out of oil; perhaps in thirty years or fifty years, or a hundred years or two hundred years. So too will we run out of *all* nonrenewable resources – by definition. We will run out of oil even if population growth stops today and we will run out of oil, somewhat sooner, if population growth continues. Whether oil reserves are depleted in 2020 or 2040 or 2140 does not seem to be of critical importance; in any event a substitute fuel must be found – probably nuclear. If no adequate substitute is developed, then we (all us earthmen) will suffer somewhat regardless of numbers.

Part two, that *rich* people are the real menace both resource-wise and pollution-wise, has recently been particularly stressed by Dr. Jean Mayer who advises the President hunger-wise but would not seem to be fully up to date demography-wise.

For the simple fact is that wealthier people generally have far fewer children than poorer people. With current mortality rates, population stability is maintained if the typical woman has on the average 2.13 children. In a 1964 Census Bureau survey among women who had completed their child-bearing years, it was shown that families with incomes of $10,000 and over had 2.21 children, just a trifle over replacement. This compared with 3.53 children for the poorest women. Since 1964, fertility rates have gone down among young women, and it is possible that when these lower rates are ultimately reflected as "completed fertility" we may see that affluent American women of the future just barely replace their own number, if that.

In short, current population patterns show that affluent people do not cause rapid population growth. And if the entire population were entirely affluent, we certainly would not be talking about a population explosion. Further, if the entire population were affluent *and* committed to combatting pollution, we wouldn't be talking about a pollution explosion either.

What then is Dr. Mayer's prescription? Is he against affluent people having babies but not poor people, even though the affluent have relatively few anyway? Or perhaps is it that he is just against the idea of letting any more poor people become affluent people, because they too will then consume too many resources and cause more pollution?

There are two important points that run through most of the above. First is that the simple numbers of people are not in themselves of great importance in the United States. There is no "optimum" population as such for the U.S., not within population ranges now forecast in any event. Whether we have 250 million people or 350 million people is less important than what the people – however many of them there are – decide to do about their problems. Second the population problem, at least in the United States, is an extremely long-term proposition, and in a country of this size and wealth, there is more flexibility in solving the potential demographic problems than might be assumed from the current rhetoric-of-crisis.

To be sure, much of the concern about population growth is sane, valid, and important. Certainly the concept of family planning – which for years had been a political stepchild – is now coming into the mainstream, and properly so. That every family in America should at least have the knowledge and the technology to control the size of its family as it sees fit seems beyond question. This knowledge and this technology, previously available largely to middle-class and affluent Americans, is now being made available to poorer Americans through growing federal programs. Some of the more militant black leaders have called it "genocide," but that is a rather hollow charge when one realizes a) that the poorest American women now have about 50 percent more children per capita than do middle-class Americans and b) that more-children-than-can-be-properly-provided-for is one of the most classic causes of poverty in America and around the world.

Certainly too, population growth must sooner or later level off. While America could support twice its current population and probably four times its current population – growth can obviously not go on forever and it is wise to understand this fact now rather than a hundred years from now. It is also wise to begin to act upon this knowledge, as indeed we have begun to act upon it. It is, accordingly, difficult to complain about the suggestions for legislation to make conditions easier for women to get and hold decent jobs – the thought being that easier access to employment will slow the birth rate. Our problems in the future probably will be easier to handle with somewhat fewer people than with somewhat greater numbers.

But what is wrong, and dangerous, and foolhardy is to make population a crisis. Doing so will simply allow too many politicians to take their eyes off the ball. When Explosionists say, as they do, that crime, riots, and urban problems are caused by "the population explosion," it is just too easy for politicians to agree and say sure, let's stop having so many babies, instead of saying let's get to work on the real urban problems of this nation. (As a matter of general interest it should be noted that the riot areas, the high-crime areas, the areas of the most acute urban problems *are areas that are typically losing population.* For example, special censuses in Hough and Watts showed population *loss.* Given that kind of data it is hard to accept the Explosionist notion that crowding causes crime.)

When the Explosionists say, as they do, that Yosemite and Yellowstone are crowded and that there is a vanishing wilderness because of too many people – they are wrong again. When visits to national parks have gone up by more than 400 percent in less than two decades, while population growth has gone up by about 30 percent, over the same time, then Yosemite isn't crowded because of population but because of other factors. When you have a nation where a workingman can afford a car, and/or a camper-trailer, when you give him three weeks paid vacation, provide decent roads – there would be something to say for the fact that you have indeed set up the society that Old Liberals, Trade Union Variety, lusted for, and who is to say that is bad? Again, if the population-crisis rhetoric is accepted it becomes too easy to say that the way to an uncrowded Yosemite is to have fewer people, and forget about the hard and far more costly problems of creating more recreation areas, which are needed even if our population does not rise.

When the Explosionists say, as they do, that it's because we have so many people that Lake Erie is polluted then once again we are invited to take our eye off the tens-of-*billions*-of-dollars ball of environmental safety and we are simultaneously invited to piddle around with 25-*million* dollar programs for birth control, which are nice, but don't solve anything to do with Lake Erie.

Finally, we must take note of the new thrust by

the Explosionists: population control. Note the phrase carefully. This is specifically not "family planning," where the family concerned does the planning. This is *control* of population by the government and this is what the apocalyptics are demanding, because, they say, family planning by itself will not reduce us to a zero growth rate. The more popular "soft" position of government control involves what is called "disincentives," that is, a few minor measures like changing the taxation system, the school system and the moral code to see if that won't work before going onto outright baby licensing.

Accordingly, the demographer Judith Blake Davis of the University of California (Berkeley) complained to a House Committee: "We penalize homosexuals of both sexes, we insist that women must bear unwanted children by depriving them of ready access to abortion, *we bind individuals to pay for the education of other people's children, we make people with small families support the schooling of others. . . ."* (Italics mine.)

Now, Dr. Davis is not exactly saying that we should go to a private school system or eliminate the tax exemption for children thereby penalizing the poor but not the rich – but that is the implication. In essence, Senator Packwood recently proposed just that: no tax exemptions for any children beyond the second per family, born after 1972.

The strong position on population control ultimately comes around to some form of governmental permission, or licensing, for babies.

Dr. Garrett Hardin, a professor-biologist at the University of California, Santa Barbara, says, "In the long run, voluntarism is insanity. The result will be continued uncontrolled population growth."

Astro-physicist Donald Aiken says, "The government has to step in and tamper with religious and personal convictions – maybe even impose penalties for every child a family has beyond two."

Dr. Melvin Ketchel, professor of physiology at Tufts Medical School writes in *Medical World News:* "Scientists will discover ways of controlling the fertility of an entire population . . . the compound . . . could be controlled by adjustments in dosage, [and] a government could regulate the growth of its population without depending upon the voluntary action of individual couples . . . such an agent might be added to the water supply."

And Dr. Paul Ehrlich of Stanford: "If we don't do something dramatic about population and environment, and do it immediately, there's just no hope that civilization will persist. . . . The world's most serious population-growth problem is right here in the United States among affluent white Americans. . . ."

What it all adds up to is this: why have a long-range manageable population problem that can be coped with gradually over generations when, with a little extra souped-up scare rhetoric, we can drum up a full-fledged crisis? We certainly need one; it's been months since we've had a crisis. After all, Vietnam, we were told, was "the greatest crisis in a hundred years." Piker. Here's a crisis that's a beauty: the greatest crisis in two billion years: we're about to breed ourselves right into oblivion.

**F**inally, look at it all from Mr. Nixon's point of view. It's beautiful. You (Mr. Nixon) take office and the major domestic problems, generally acknowledged, are the race situation and the (so-called) crisis of the cities. They are tough problems. They are controversial problems. They are problems that have given way only gradually, painstakingly, expensively, over the years. Your opponents are in a militant mood. They have been co-opted in Vietnam and you fully expect them to hold your feet to the fire on these tough domestic problems.

Apprehensively, you await the onslaught. And what is the slogan? No, it . . . can't be – but yes, it is. It's coming into focus. Read it: "Lower Emission Standards"! And in the next rank is another militant sign; and what does it say? It says, "Our Rivers Stink."

Full circle. The opposition sloganeers have gone from the "New Deal" to the "Fair Deal," to the "New Frontier" to the "Great Society," and now they march to a new banner: "No Shit"!

Beautiful. Of course the environment *is* a real problem, an important problem; we knew that from Senator Muskie. Of course your President will respond to it, particularly since almost everyone is for it, particularly if it takes the heat off elsewhere. But even the environment issue is massively expensive – too expensive to do everything now that ought to be done now.

So wait a minute, you say, your opponents have been good to you so far, let's see how really helpful they'll be. And behold, here comes the cavalry.

And what do they say? The problem of pollution is really the problem of too many people. Let the opponents divide among themselves and let the opponents fight among themselves. Let there be a children's allowance, say some of your opponents. Nay, let there not be a children's allowance, it will encourage population growth. Let there be better public schools, say some of your enemies. Nay, let each family pay for their own schooling to discourage population growth. Let us help the poor, say the opponents; nay, let us penalize the poor for having too many children. Let then the Secretary of HEW go forth to the people and say, "Ask not what your country can do for you, ask what you can do for your country – you shall have two children no more, no less, that is your brave social mission in America."

I imagine there have been luckier Presidents, but I can't think of any.

# WORLD POPULATION*

## By COLIN CLARK

### Director, Agricultural Economics Research Institute, Oxford

IF not impeded, the probability of conception in fertile human couples appears to average 0·1 per menstrual cycle, higher for first conceptions, but otherwise irrespective of age. From a minimum of 3 per cent, the proportion of infertility rises rapidly with age from 25 onwards. Infertility, at any given age, appears greater among coloured than among white races. The assertion that natural human fertility rises with under-nourishment rests upon no evidence whatsoever.

This probability of conception, allowing for some miscarriages,. and some temporary sterility during lactation, implies the birth of a child for every $2\frac{1}{2}$ years of married life, as observed in England a century ago, or in some peasant communities now.

'Total fertility', defined as the number of children born to an average woman by the end of her reproductive period, in the circumstances most favourable for reproduction, when every woman marries young, and with surplus males waiting to re-marry any widows, assuming the onset of infertility on the average twenty years after marriage, should be 8 (that is to say, $20/2\frac{1}{2}$). This rate is indeed found among those (very few) Irish women who are married young, to young husbands, and who are not widowed ; rates of 6 or 7 are found among primitive nomadic peoples, and among peasant populations in Asia and Latin America ; considerably lower figures are found in Africa, where the percentage of infertility is unaccountably high. The highest total fertility ever recorded was 10, for the early French-Canadian settlers ; but they were a group specially selected for vigour and hardihood. Evidence from India indicates that the consummation of marriage below the age of seventeen tends, in the long run, to reduce rather than to increase total fertility.

Writing in 1798, Malthus taught that populations always tend to increase up to the limits of their food-producing capacity, whereupon population growth must necessarily be checked, if not by late marriage (which he recommended) then either by 'misery' or by 'vice'. In the same year Jenner was publishing his proposals for vaccination against smallpox, which probably did more than any other single factor to

* Based on the Newmarch Lectures given in University College London, during February 1958.

bring about the great rise in population in the nineteenth century. Malthus, however, stated that Jenner's work was a waste of time, because the "principles of population" indicated that, even if he were successful, it was inevitable that some other disease would spring up to take the place of smallpox. Instances of populations growing rapidly until they reach the limits of food supply have occurred, but exceptionally, and certainly not generally in the history of mankind.

For the greatest proportion of mankind's time upon Earth our ancestors lived the life of nomadic hunting peoples, which involves high mortality, with few people surviving to the age of forty. In these circumstances, a total fertility of 6 or 8 will only just suffice to maintain the population. This is observed among some primitive tribes to-day. The present world average rate of population increase is $1\frac{1}{2}$ per cent per annum, as against 1 per cent in the nineteenth century. From approximate figures of world population (errors in them will not affect the order of magnitude of our results) we deduce, between the first and the seventeenth centuries A.D., an average growth-rate of only 0·05 per cent per annum; and from the beginning of the human race to the beginning of the Christian era 0·005 per cent per annum. These low growth-rates, while populations were far smaller than those now supported by the same agricultural methods in the same areas, were clearly not due to the world's inability to produce food.

In a settled peasant community, population increases at the rate of about $\frac{1}{2}$ per cent per annum, but only so long as there are no widespread epidemics, and peace and order can be preserved. "Better fifty years of Europe than a cycle of Cathay"; India and China for thousands of years have been slowly building up population, and then losing most of it again in recurring periods of war and disorder. In Europe, where total fertility may have been reduced to 5 by the custom of later marriage, population growth proved to be slow, too. The Black Death was only the first of a cycle of epidemics which checked the growth of population all over Europe. In France, which also suffered greatly from the Hundred Years' War, the population-level of the fourteenth century was not regained until the eighteenth. Egypt, and many other regions in the Middle East, had less population in the nineteenth century than they had had 2,000 years earlier. The spread of malaria, sometimes adduced as a cause, is better regarded as a consequence of social disorder; *Anopheles* only secures a hold when irrigation channels are neglected. Sustained growth of population, at the rate of 1 per cent per annum or more, which began in the British Isles and Scandinavia with the improvement of medical knowledge in the late eighteenth century, began in China only with the establishment of peace under the Manchu Empire in the seventeenth century, in India with the establishment of the British Empire, in Latin America not until the nineteenth century, and in Africa not until the present century.

Prospects did not look good at the time when Malthus wrote. Real wages were low and did not rise until the middle of the nineteenth century. Nevertheless, the British courageously refused to listen to Malthus. Had they done so, Britain would have remained a small eighteenth-century-type agrarian community; and the United States and the British Commonwealth would never have developed. No great degree of industrialization would have been possible. The economics of large-scale industry demand large markets and a first-class transportation system, only obtainable with a large and growing population.

The country which did listen to Malthus was France, where size of family began to decline early in the nineteenth century. "If population limitation were the key to economic progress," as Prof. Sauvy said at the World Population Conference, "then France should be the wealthiest country in the world by now." France, which seemed to be on the point of dominating the world in 1798, has since seen her influence steadily decline; and the recurring inflations which France has suffered are an economic consequence of the excessive burden of pensions and other overhead costs which an ageing country has to carry.

When we look at the British in the seventeenth and eighteenth centuries, at the Greeks in the sixth century B.C., the Dutch in the seventeenth century, and the Japanese in the nineteenth century, we must conclude that the pressure of population upon limited agricultural resources provides a painful but ultimately beneficial stimulus, provoking unenterprising agrarian communities into greater efforts in the fields of industry, commerce, political leadership, colonization, science, and (sometimes but not always, judging from Victorian England) the arts.

But if a country fails to meet the challenge of population increase, it sinks into the condition known to economists as 'disguised unemployment' or rural overpopulation. The simpler forms of agriculture, using hand tools (as in China or Africa), can economically occupy 50 able-bodied men per sq. km. (246 acres), or 20 men per sq. km. using draught animals. A man working for a full year, using hand tools, produces at least two tons of grain-equivalent (expressing other products as grain at their local

**3**

exchange values) ; twice that with draught animals. Minimum subsistence requirements can be estimated at 275 kilos of grain-equivalent per person per year (225 kilos of grain plus a few other foods and textile fibres). So one agricultural worker, even with hand tools, can produce subsistence for seven or eight people, that is to say, he can feed himself and his dependants at better than subsistence-level, and have some food to exchange for clothing, household goods, etc., so that an urban population can begin to grow up. (One Canadian grain grower, however, could feed 750 at subsistence-level.) Where, however, the densities of agricultural population exceed these limits, as in southern Italy, India, Egypt, etc., the marginal product of this additional labour is very low, and the consequence is that many men consume only a subsistence diet, are idle for a considerable part of their time, and have little surplus to exchange for industrial products.

Lord Boyd-Orr's statement that "a life-time of malnutrition and actual hunger is the lot of at least two-thirds of mankind" is simply an arithmetical error, based on confusing two columns in a statistical table. Malnutrition exists in the world, but it is impossible to state its extent until physiologists can be more precise about food requirements, and statisticians about agricultural output and body-weights.

Countries the population of which has outrun their agricultural resources can industrialize, and exchange manufactures for imported food, as did Britain and Japan, and as India can—if they have a large population and a good transport system. Experience in both India and the U.S.S.R. has shown that, with modern engineering knowledge, capital requirements for establishing an industrial community are less than was previously supposed. This solution, however, is not open to the smaller and more isolated islands, away from the main channels of world trade. If they become overcrowded they must seek relief in emigration, which from an island such as Porto Rico is as high as 2 per cent of the population per annum.

Some fear, however, that the agricultural resources of the world as a whole may soon be exhausted. The world's total land area (excluding ice and tundra) is 123 million sq. km., from which we exclude most of the $42\frac{1}{2}$ million sq. km. of steppe or arid lands, discount anything up to half the area of certain cold or sub-humid lands, but could double 10 million sq. km. of tropical land capable of bearing two crops per year. We conclude that the world possesses the equivalent of 77 million sq. km. of good temperate agricultural land. We may take as our standard that of the most productive farmers in Europe, the Dutch, who feed 385 people (at Dutch standards of diet, which give them one of the best health records in the world) per sq. km. of farm land, or 365 if we allow for the land required to produce their timber (in the most economic manner, in warm climates—pulp requirements can be obtained from sugar cane waste). Applying these standards throughout the world, as they could be with adequate skill and use of fertilizers, we find the world capable of supporting 28 billion people, or ten times its present population. This leaves us a very ample margin for land which we wish to set aside for recreation or other purposes. Even these high Dutch standards of productivity are improving at a rate of 2 per cent per annum. In the very distant future, if our descendants outrun the food-producing capacity of the Earth, and of the sea, they will by that time be sufficiently skilled and wealthy to build themselves artificial satellites to live on.

'Total fertility' is an accurate measure of reproductivity, but we cannot measure it directly until the generation in question has reached the end of its reproductive period. In interpreting current data, a difficult mathematical problem is involved, because the probability of any given family producing a child depends upon : (1) the mother's age, (2) the duration of the marriage, (3) the number of children already born ; and these three variables are highly intercorrelated. Crude measurements, such as birth-rates and reproduction-rates (so-called), can give gravely misleading results when there have been temporary fluctuations in the marriage-rate, or in the age-structure of the population. Henry has devised an elegant mathematical technique whereby, from the birth data of a single year, it is possible to integrate the probabilities for all future years that a family containing $n$ children will expand to $(n + 1)$. By multiplying together these probabilities the ultimate total fertility of the generation can then be estimated.

During the past century reproductivity has fallen heavily in all the economically advanced countries. During the past two decades, however, there has been a dramatic reversal of this trend in several countries, particularly in France, and in the United States and the British Commonwealth countries, the populations of which are now growing faster than India's ; but not in England. Mortality-rates throughout the world, after declining fairly steadily for a century, greatly accelerated their fall in the 1930's and 1940's, through the discoveries of sulpha-drugs and penicillin. We must therefore certainly expect a further acceleration in the rate of growth of world population.

We have as yet little understanding of the economic, social, historical and religious factors lying behind either the past decline in fertility, or its recent recovery. Most familiar generalizations have proved to be erroneous. It used to be held that it was the wealthier, more educated and more urbanized communities which most reduced their fertility. This was true in the past ; but in the English-speaking and Scandinavian countries the educated are now beginning to have larger families than the uneducated. The urban-rural difference in reproductivity disappeared in France fifty years ago, and is now disappearing in Britain and the United States. We have little understanding of those profound motives which make people willing to face the hardships and inconveniences of bringing up a family, motives often of a religious or similar character. An irreligious community is rarely a reproductive one.

# 1. Zero Population Growth: What Is It?

*By Frank W. Notestein, Ph.D.*

Zero population growth, as platitude, sales slogan or urgent goal, has caught the public by storm—and included in that public are many biologists and economists, as well as a considerable number of sociologists and demographers.

From one point of view, favoring zero population growth is somewhat like favoring the laws of motion. Anyone who knows how to use a table of logarithms must be aware that in the long run the average rate of population growth will approach zero as a limit. If, for example, the world's population had grown at its present rate since the beginning of the Christian era, the water content of the human race would fill a sphere having a radius more than ten times that of the earth. Zero growth is, then, not simply a desirable goal, it is the only possibility in a finite world. One cannot object to people who favor the inevitable.

There is another group that values zero population growth because it is a powerful sales slogan. They are willing to accept—even to promote—the slogan despite its ambiguity, because of the energy and resources it brings to the subject of population. Some of these supporters foster the popular impression that population growth could be stopped quickly by acceptable means if only the public were alerted to the dangers of the situation; and a few of them advance this line despite their private opinions to the con-

Frank Notestein is President Emeritus of the Population Council, and a member of the Planned Parenthood-World Population Board of Directors and the National Advisory Council of the Center for Family Planning Program Development. This article is adapted from a paper presented at the 1970 meetings of the Population Association of America. The paper will be published along with the comments of the discussants in the July-September 1970 issue of *Population Index*.

trary. They justify this lack of candor on the grounds that egregious overstatement is necessary to arouse public interest. They seem to feel that it takes massive advertising to sell both soap and the ecological necessity for a prompt end to population growth. With that I am inclined to agree. But it is a sad day when we see professionally expert distortions of the truth peddled to the public under the highest scientific auspices, as if truth can be fostered best by untruth. When scientists become concerned with reform, as I think duty indeed requires, they will at their peril abandon the ardent respect for truth that lies at the basis of their professions. It is hard enough to stick to the truth when one tries. Fortunately, this huckstering group is only a small part of those who see zero population growth as a slogan that arouses interest in objectives perceived to be both timely and important. To this there can be no objection. It is our obligation to stick to the truth, but we are not compelled to be dull about it.

Many of its most earnest advocates obviously see zero population growth as more than a slogan, and more than a platitude about long-run objectives. They want, or at least some of them want, zero growth, if not yesterday, at least now. They want it moreover, if not on any terms, at least with the sense of urgency that makes them willing to accept many second and third order effects without careful examination. It is to these questions that we must turn our most careful attention. This means that we must ask with what urgency it is necessary to seek zero growth under varying circumstances. What are the advantages and disadvantages of attaining the goal with varying speeds, and what are the advantages and disadvantages of using

various methods for its attainment? The assessment of the means is quite as important as the assessment of the goal.

There may be different answers for the technologically more developed and less developed countries, because of differences in the severity of the problem as well as differences in the availability of means for their solution. Let us consider first the problem in developed countries, and particularly the United States.

## ZPG in the Developed Regions

Here the ecologists take the hardest line. Some of them seem to be saying that we now stand in mortal danger if our population continues to grow; indeed, that we already have too much population and should start reducing the size. On matters of resources, energy and ecology I am outside of my professional field, but I have read some and listened more and find these ecologists' case wholly unpersuasive. There are no substantial limits in sight either in raw materials or in energy that alterations in the price structures, product substitution, anticipated gains in technology and pollution control cannot be expected to solve.* Subject to one condition, my statement seems to be in agreement with the overwhelming

*The very extensive literature is summarized in a nutshell by R. Philip Hammond in a letter to *Science*, 167:1439, 1970, reading in part as follows: "Even 20 x 10⁹ people, each producing 20 kilowatts of heat (twice the U.S. average), would add only 1/300 of the present atmospheric heat load. This would raise the average temperature of the earth by about 0.25° . . . At an energy budget of 20 kilowatts per person, we could maintain a worldwide living standard near the present U.S. level even when we have exhausted our high-grade mineral resources. We could do this without placing an impossible heat load on the earth for a very large population, but not for an 'unlimited' one."

Reprinted by permission of the author and the publisher from *Family Planning Perspectives* 2(3):20–24, June 1970.

weight of professional opinion. The limitation arises from the fact that on the side of resources and technology we can only look ahead about a generation in terms of specific technology and known raw materials. Obviously our human interests run much farther into the future; but we cannot spell out the nature of a technology not yet developed. One can, however, on the assumption of an ordered world, reasonably predict immensely powerful developments based on cheap and virtually unlimited energy, and, thanks partly to that, on an enormously expanded availability of conventional and new raw materials.

Much of the pessimistic argument is based on the idea that there are nonrenewable resources in our finite world. This seems to me to miss the point. Basically resources are not material; they are socially defined. Coal did not become a resource until a few centuries ago. It is barely one hundred years since petroleum had any but medical and magical uses. Nuclear energy is only beginning to become a resource although it has almost unlimited prospects. We talk of diminishing returns with non-renewable resources, but so far as I know almost all materials usually put in that category have declined in relative worth. Even with modern machinery it no longer pays to clear land in the United States. Indeed, land has never been so abundant. The fact is that basically we have only one non-renewable resource, and that is space. Otherwise mankind's basic resources are knowledge and skill, mainly of the organizational kind.

Nor do I share in that ocean of guilt now flooding the literature because our small fraction of the world's population consumes the lion's share of the world's resources. I hope our share becomes smaller as others gain, but I do not want a reduction of our per capita consumption. Thanks, indeed, to the high consumption of the developed world we have generated the knowledge and techniques that have greatly expanded both the supplies and the reserves of such raw materials in the world. There has often been outrageous waste but, on balance, our heavy use is expanding the world's resources, not diminishing them. We can get into intricate discussions about whether the more developed regions have paid enough for the raw materials they have purchased from the less developed regions,* but we cannot fail to see that sub-

*Land has never been so abundant . . . Our basic resources are knowledge and skill.*

stantial reductions of our purchases from those regions would bring them to economic chaos and greatly retard their development. Our sin is not use. Instead, it is the failure to pay the costs of use by avoiding pollution and by recycling minerals instead of further degrading them. I think it is time that social scientists look at resources in the same dynamic terms with which they have become accustomed recently to study population.

If we consider the evidence, not just the inchoate fears, there is not the slightest indication that per capita income in the United States would be consequentially different if we had 50 or 100 million more people than we have, or 50 or 100 million fewer people. At present, the costs of both energy and raw materials represent such a small proportion of our total costs that they could be drastically increased with a negligible effect on per capita income.

Moreover, the current excitement about the size of population as a cause of pollution is almost completely without merit, save in the sense that there can be no pollution without polluters. That there is severe pollution is all too evident; but it is equally evident that pollution is related almost exclusively to mismanagement and to our high standard of living. It is related negligibly to our numbers. If we had half the population and the same per capita income, we would have much the same kind of urban concentration, and much the same local pollution. Australia is sparsely populated but has 80 percent of its people concentrated in huge cities, and has much the same

kind of smog and other pollution as do we.

Moreover, it is silly to suggest that reductions in population would drastically help in attacking pollution while we continue to raise our per capita incomes. There has been a vast increase in use of electricity in this country since World War II—a fact which has worried those concerned with heat and air pollution. But if we wished to achieve the per capita use of electricity of 1960 without increasing the total produced above the 1940 level we would need to reduce our U.S. population below 25 million. Pollution control of all kinds will involve social and economic changes of considerable magnitude, but manipulation of the numbers of people in the society to solve this problem is probably not a realistically open option.

Nor, incidentally, does the exhortation that people should stop aspiring to lift their standards of living come gracefully from college professors, already sitting comfortably in the top ten percent of the income distribution of the richest nation on earth. I doubt that we members of the international jet set will be very effective in telling others that they should not aspire to live half as well as we do lest pollution destroy our narrowly balanced ecology.

In political terms, relating pollution to population may have done harm to a

*By more developed regions, I mean Europe, the Soviet Union, Japan, Northern America, temperate South America, Australia and New Zealand. The remainder of the world comprises the less developed regions.

*Zero Population Growth*

serious attack on both pollution and on population growth. It weakens interest in the present by concentrating on a distant goal. The effective approach to pollution is to make the polluters pay, and to start doing so as soon as possible. This will cost all of us money, for we are all polluters. We also need research on a vastly increased scale. That, too, is expensive. Particularly, we need research in ecology. It is time for some solid information to replace the bad dreams of the enthusiasts, their yearnings for traditional biological equilibria and their reasoning by analogy. It is a distraction from an immediate attack on pollution to concentrate attention on the importance of stopping population growth in, say, 20, 30 or 50 years. Similarly, it is a distraction from legitimate concern for the nation's population policy to base the attack on ecological ghost stories instead of the actual inhumanities of our reproductive process. The present population-pollution axis, by raising false issues, deters rather than helps realistic and urgently needed efforts in both fields.

## We Don't Need More People

My own interest in speeding the end of population growth in the United States is based on much less urgent problems than the constraints of dwindling resources and energy or the risk of insoluble ecological problems. It is clear that growth must stop sometime, both here and in the world as a whole. It does not seem that we are likely to grow in national effectiveness by virtue of increasing numbers. At least I have difficulties thinking of any national need for which we do not have enough population to provide the economies of large scale production. On esthetic grounds it seems to me that we should avoid becoming a highly crowded nation. Europe is much more densely settled, but we are a more mobile people and more space will almost certainly add to our enjoyment. I would like to come to zero population growth, but with no great haste and without making important sacrifices in the process of accomplishing it.

It is also clear that some costs will be entailed if we come to an end of growth. I shall not detail them, because they are well set out in the pre-war literature on stagnation. I doubt that the costs of stopping growth will be nearly as high as then envisioned. Much has since been

learned about managing the level of economic activity. But some adjustments will have to be made. Our entire economy has developed in a period of population growth with the relatively young populations that high birth rates produce. Nevertheless, this is an adjustment that must be made sometime unless we start lifting the death rates of the oldsters drastically—a proposal with which I have an understandable lack of sympathy. In short, I would like to see population growth come to a gradual end in the United States. But my lack of a sense of great urgency makes me unwilling to accept drastic means such as those often proposed by the people to whom the problems of energy, resources and ecological protection have high saliency.

I would be happy if, for example, we could reach replacement level of reproduction in 10 or 15 years and stay there until the end of the century. After that I would have no objection to an intrinsic rate of natural decrease of a quarter of one percent for a time. If we did this we would still come to a maximum population of something like 300 millions in some 70 to 90 years. These to me are acceptable goals as to numbers. They are not very important, however, compared to the means for their attainment.

The rates of population change and the factors determining them are very much more important than the *size* of the population. Family planning represents a new and important freedom in the world. It will surely be a happy day when parents can have and can avoid having children, as they see fit. We are coming close to realization of that goal —a goal that has given new dignity and new importance to the individual. We have not yet arrived at it. Bumpass and Westoff[1] have shown that the proportion of unwanted births was substantial in the first half of the 1960s. It was very much higher in the lower educational groups, in the lower income groups and, partly as a consequence of this, among Negroes. It is a matter of major importance that this kind of new freedom to choose, now existing for the bulk of the population, should be extended to its most disadvantaged parts. If it were extended, reproduction would be brought fairly close to the replacement level. However, I would advocate the right to choose even if I thought the demographic consequences would be highly adverse, because it will always remain possible to manipulate the environment in which the choice is made.

I happen also to favor the repeal of laws against abortion in the belief that parents should control the destiny of the nonviable products of their bodies. I do not favor it on demographic grounds, and hope that when abortion becomes legal no one will advocate it as anything but the personal tragedy which it inevitably is. One may expect, however, that easy abortion will further reduce the birth rate.

It is not at all beyond belief that, with contraceptives of ever increasing efficiency and legal abortion, fertility may fall below the replacement level. And, of course, it also may not. But, lacking a sense of urgency in matters of population size and believing in the importance of voluntary parenthood as a human freedom, I hope we do not accept drastic proposals to reward or penalize reproduction. We should wait at least until all of the population has ready access to effective contraception, and we can see under these conditions how the trend is going.

It seems to me dangerous to endeavor to penalize reproduction by various economic constraints because almost certainly the political process would result in maximum pressures on the most defenseless sectors of the population. There is too often willingness on the part of the bulk of the population to blame its troubles on the poor and ignorant minorities. But economic sanctions taken against the poor to compel a reduction of fertility seldom work. Generally, fertility does not fall in response to the lash of poverty. The most fertile sectors of the population will reduce their fertility with maximum speed if they can have easy access to competent contraception and the kind of support that brings them into the mainstream of the economy and society. At least in the present temper of the times, I would rather accept growth than step up the constraints which we have reason to expect would fall most heavily on the poor and their children.

It must also be recognized that the actual adoption of drastic programs designed to restrict fertility would, if they were successful, contain the seeds of their early reversal. If we could imagine a program that would drop the crude birth rate to the crude death rate in five years, we would have, as Frejka[2] has shown, to imagine a net reproduction rate of less than 0.6—not a two-child, but a one-child family—which if maintained for a few years would evoke the specter of rapid population decline, cries of race suicide and a turn-about. It is to be noted that no nation, however heavily populated and poor, has adopted a policy for population decline. At best they want to bring the rates of growth down to two or even one percent, and just possibly to become stationary in the long run. It is interesting to note that Japan is already talking of the dangers of slow growth, that Rumania 1 pealed its liberal abortion law because of plummeting birth rates, and that in Hong Kong one hears a great deal of talk about a labor shortage. Quickly successful policies of a drastic nature would certainly contain the seeds of their own reversal. I think there is every reason to believe that the quick way to a stationary population is the gentle one, both in action and in propaganda. And herein lies the weakness of the hucksters. Their line is successful until people realize that they have been misled. Then even sensible discussion suffers, for people once burned are twice cautious.

## ZPG and the Less Developed Regions

The situation of that two-thirds of the world's population living in the less developed regions contrasts sharply with that of the United States. In general, in the less developed regions the economy rests heavily on subsistence agriculture and other extractive industries; per capita income and literacy are very low, birth rates are very high and death rates range from the world's highest to the world's lowest, as does the density of population. Rates of growth vary from a little under two percent to well over three percent. Moreover, where the increase is relatively low, as in parts of Africa, it is clear that it will rise as soon as rudimentary health protection can be introduced.

It is evident that most of these populations are already too large to rise from poverty on the basis of a traditional subsistence agriculture. Their only hope of achieving reasonable per capita incomes, literacy and health lies in the modernization of their economies. Such modernization entails heavy investment in productive equipment, transport, education and health. Rapid progress in this direction is considerably deterred by the necessity of meeting the costs of rapid population

growth at the same time. Indeed, I think that there is grave danger that population growth will so retard economic transformation and the improvement of living conditions that there will be a breakdown of civil order in a number of large countries. This risk gravely threatens the lives of tens, perhaps scores, of millions of people.

It seems difficult to exaggerate the importance of reducing the rate of population growth as soon as possible throughout most of the less developed regions. Indeed, even the areas now viewed as too sparsely populated might well benefit from the reduction of the rate of increase. In these circumstances, wisdom may enjoin favoring development at the expense of population growth where possible. This is not the place to discuss the issue, but it is my impression that there are extremely few places in the less developed regions that would not be aided in their struggle for modernization by a slower rate of population growth.

From my point of view, then, the need for slowing population growth is vastly greater in the less developed than in the more developed regions. A rapid decline of fertility for some decades until there is even a small negative rate of increase would be desirable. But zero growth, as a meaningful proposal in the near term, is idle talk. It could only be achieved by a rise in the death rate, which no one will accept as a goal of policy for his own people. During the next century, for theoretical purposes, zero growth is not low enough and, for practical purposes, it is too low. Although the problems of the less developed regions are much greater, unfortunately the opportunities for relevant action are far fewer than in the rest of the world.

A rather large and growing number of countries in the less developed regions have national policies designed to foster the reduction of the birth rate and thereby a slowing of population growth. But even in these countries there would be minimal support for zero population growth. Policies in support of family planning have been widely adopted because the provision of services to the citizens who want them entails few political risks, and much of the top leadership realizes that the unprecedented speed of growth is blocking efforts at development. It is one thing to favor a reduction of the pace of population increase, and another thing to ask for a complete stop. When one begins to talk

about growth rates less than one percent, attention quickly shifts to the rate of growth of the traditional enemy or rival. Israel's victories in the Six-Day War did much to devalue large populations as a source of power; but the rivalry of numbers remains. It is possible that, among small countries, Hong Kong and Singapore would be content to stop growing fairly soon; and, among large countries, India and Pakistan might accept the idea at the level of top leadership. I can think of no other countries where this position would be accepted. Even where leadership agreed on the long-run objective, it would almost certainly wish not to advertise that fact, because more limited objectives would be expected to attract more widespread political support and serve program needs as well.

A number of scholars have been critical of people of my persuasion who advocate voluntarism through family planning as a means of slowing population growth and who have concentrated efforts on contraceptive methods, information and service. They hold that since the difficulty lies in the lack of motivation for restriction, it makes little sense to concentrate on the means while failing to strengthen the motives.

Naturally, I think that my approach represents the first and most effective step in strengthening the motivation for fertility restriction. Obviously, there are large numbers of people who are behaving in the traditional manner, governed by the values of the traditional society. But the number is larger in the minds of the leadership than it is in reality. Surveys, trials and national experiences show that major proportions—often, indeed, a heavy majority—of the population expresses an interest in limiting their fertility. To be sure, they generally want more children than are needed to maintain a stationary population. To be sure also, many aspects of their society still foster the ideal of the large family. I am aware that values influence behavior, but I am also aware that behavior influences values. It seems to me that the example of successful fertility limitation set by those now motivated is probably the most effective means of fostering both new values and innovative behavior. Moreover, I am greatly impressed by the speed with which the restrictive behavior has spread where family planning programs have been skillfully introduced.

*Zero Population Growth*

I am happier than the critics with the progress that has been made, possibly for two reasons. On the one hand, I view the ultimate constraints to population growth as less narrowly drawn than they do. On the other hand, in the light of the situation a decade ago, I think there has been great and accelerating progress. By contrast, I am much less hopeful than are the critics of voluntarism about the feasibility of using more drastic measures to lift incentives for the restriction of fertility. The leadership would accept them in very few countries. Indeed, even in many of the countries having policies to foster family planning, the opposition in influential parts of the leadership group remains substantial — more substantial, I think, than among the people. In the near term more drastic means will be entirely unacceptable almost everywhere.

In the less developed regions, moreover, it would, simply for administrative reasons, be impossible to introduce even such measures as fiscal sanctions and rewards. Even now, weak administration is proving more of an obstacle to the spread of family planning than lack of public interest. Almost all of the governments are far too poor and weak to carry out a drastic program. Few of them can even count the number of their births and deaths, or have more than rudimentary medical services and facilities, or social security systems. It is hard to remember how poor they are. Canada, for example, with some 21 million people, has a larger national income and federal budget than the Government of India with more than 500 million people. It is at best idle to talk of governments in this position drastically coercing their people's reproductive behavior. They are governments that can do something to educate and lead, but, save in the most primitive matters of public order, they cannot coerce.

The inability to coerce is perhaps fortunate in this field. I think we have reason to believe that voluntarism through education and service is the most direct route, as it is certainly the most civilized.

My own reaction to zero population growth, therefore, comes out about the same way for the less developed regions as for the more developed regions. The countries that could apply drastic constraints to human fertility do not need to; the countries that need drastic constraints cannot apply them; and in any case, the path of voluntarism through family planning is likely to be both more efficient and civilized.

If zero population growth means the down-grading of voluntarism and the strident demand for a quick end to population growth, then it will do more harm than good. If on the other hand it is taken as an organizing focus for research and educational efforts concerning the importance of a worldwide trend to a stationary population and the means by which it is ultimately to be achieved, then it should be enthusiastically welcomed.

**References**

1. L. Bumpass and C. F. Westoff, "The 'Perfect Contraceptive' Population: Extent and Implications of Unwanted Fertility in the U.S.," *Science* [in press].

2. T. Frejka, "Reflections on the Demographic Conditions Needed to Establish a U.S. Stationary Population Growth," *Population Studies,* 22:379, 1968.

# Redefining the Population Problem

Lester R. Brown

When Thomas Malthus published his gloomy treatise in 1798, he defined the population problem primarily in terms of food supplies and the threat of famine. Ever since, the threat of overpopulation has been perceived largely in his terms. In the 1960's, when national and international leaders were preoccupied with food scarcities in the poor countries, the population problem was regarded as virtually synonymous with the food-population problem. The two terms were often used interchangeably.

But as we enter the 1970's we are faced with a need to re-define the population problem. After nearly two centuries, it is time to move beyond our legacy from Malthus.

Two independent phenomena, both bearing directly on the population issue, are forcing us to change our conception of it. The first is the agricultural breakthrough in the poor countries. Although this is by no means a solution to the population problem, it is diminishing the prospects of famine in the near future and buying time—perhaps an additional fifteen years—in which to develop the technologies, the will, and the strategies to stabilize global population growth.

While the threat of famine is diminishing, the number of young people entering labor markets is rising very rapidly. This is the second phenomenon. The population explosion began in most poor countries fifteen or twenty years ago and

Reprinted by permission of the author and the publisher from *Seeds of Change*, Chapter 14, pp. 121–133. Praeger Publishers, New York, 1970.

resulted in an almost immediate demand for additional food. But, since babies do not require employment, there is a grace period of fifteen or twenty years on the job front that does not exist for food. As we enter the 'seventies we approach the end of this grace period. The food-population problem of the 'sixties is becoming the employment-population problem of the 'seventies. Feeding the increased numbers of people will not be easy, but it is likely to prove much more manageable than providing jobs.

### THE EMPLOYMENT-POPULATION EQUATION

With more and more young people entering the job market, the day of reckoning with the explosion in population growth has arrived. In some countries the number of young people coming of employment age will nearly double in a matter of years. If these millions of young people are not able to find jobs, the "labor force explosion" could pose an even greater threat to peace and stability than did the threat of famine in the 'sixties.

As we saw in Chapter 12, the Green Revolution can be a tremendous source of additional jobs. Selective mechanization coupled with intensive cultivation can provide millions of new farm jobs. Even more jobs will be created if the poor countries are admitted into competition for the agricultural markets of the rich countries. Still more will be created as industries grow up to provide the farmer with the new inputs he needs to process and market his products. Finally, as the farmer becomes an ever-better customer for the products of industry, industry will need to expand to meet his demands.

But just as mechanical power can be substituted for manpower on the farm, at great social cost, so machines can be substituted for men throughout the industrial sector, with unfortunate effects. The labor force explosion demands that virtually all governments in the poor countries give priority to job creation in the 'seventies equal to that finally accorded to food production in the 'sixties.

Nor is this a problem for governments only. The International Labor Organization, in a document on *The World Employment Program* that helped it earn the Nobel Peace Prize in 1969, argues eloquently that employment creation should be the objective of the international development-assistance effort of the 'seventies. Certainly the hopes of those who are concerned with the population problem will rest on the ability of society to create vast numbers of new jobs.

We are late in coming to this realization. Even the concepts of employment and unemployment in poor, transitional societies remain vague. In all poor countries, the bulk of the population still follows traditional pursuits that keep people in society but out of the labor force as we know it. Modern economic activity exists side by side with traditional or subsistence activities, with all manner of gradations in between. That human energy is not put to productive use, as economists apply the term, is not necessarily a source of discontent in traditional societies. To the contrary, a distinctive feature of this type of society is that it gives its members a sense of place and belonging regardless of their "productivity." But in today's technical society, there is an urgency to the labor-force explosion that derives from the fact that millions of young people are breaking away from the shelter of traditional society to seek a place in modern life.

The ILO hopes to develop some useful ways to quantify the employment problem in poor countries—in the words of Director General David Morse, to "define concrete and realistic employment objectives for economic development policies." This is a complex research task; it is very difficult, given our current knowledge, to think of devising useful indices of unemployment for a country like India that are modeled on the indices used in rich countries.

Despite the difficulty of defining precisely what constitutes the labor force, the fact remains that there are a great many people in the poor countries whose labor potential is under-utilized by any standard. Large numbers, especially in the rural areas, are only bystanders in the process of economic growth. The magnitude of the future problem is suggested by Figure 3, which shows the age structure of populations in selected geographic regions. The pyramid-shaped forms for South Asia and Latin America, contrasting sharply with the industrial regions, indicate dramatic, continuing increases in the numbers of young people entering the job market.

What this means for rural areas can be illustrated by the case of West Pakistan. Between 1951 and 1961, non-farm employment grew at the rate of 4.5 per cent per year, a rate which, in the postwar period, appears to have been exceeded only in Taiwan.[1] Even if this rate of growth were to continue until 1985, workers in the rural sector would still increase only from 7.4 million (in 1961) to 12.2 million. The situation will be worse in many other poor countries. Hundreds of millions of jobs must be created in the coming decade if the world's poor are to have a chance to improve their lives.

The need to develop new technology to create modern *labor-intensive* economic opportunities presents a challenge to economists and planners. We in the rich countries are accustomed to equating modern economic activity with labor-saving economies; in the poor countries we must think in terms of labor-creating economies. The pragmatic need is to encourage as much modern, labor-intensive economic activity as can be produced using the combined resources of the poor and the rich countries.

Capital and other resources from the rich countries can be transferred through government or private channels to create jobs for the burgeoning numbers of young people in the poor

[1] B. F. Johnston, *Agriculture and Economic Development: The Relevance of the Japanese Experience,* Stanford, Calif.: Food Research Institute Studies, Vol. 6, 1966, p. 274.

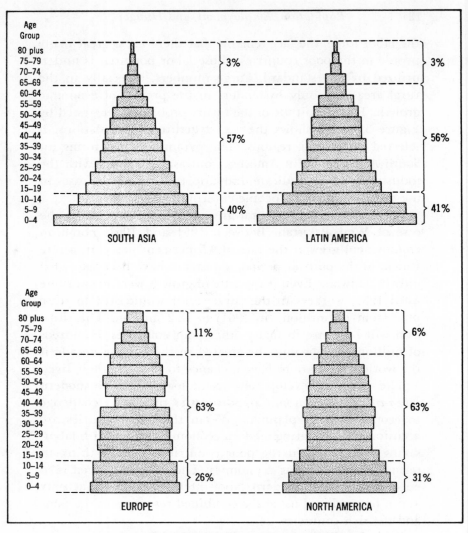

Figure 3.  AGE STRUCTURE OF POPULATION IN SELECTED REGIONS
(Width of bars indicates proportion of total population in age group.)

countries. But the prospective transfers of public resources cannot begin to create the necessary numbers of jobs. If the poor countries are to provide jobs for their young people, they must turn to the private sector for new sources of capital and expanded participation by the multinational corporations.

In the second half of the twentieth century, the multinational corporation has demonstrated its capacity to create economic opportunities in poor countries. There is no larger pool of risk capital, managerial talent, and technical knowledge. Most important, the goal of agricultural modernization, to which more and more countries that use the new seeds are subscribing, cannot be achieved unless the poor countries become much more active participants in the international markets, first for cereals and other farm products, and later for labor-intensive industrial exports. Insofar as the multinational corporation brings with it an international marketing network for the products of the poor countries, it becomes indispensable to them. No other institution is even remotely comparable in its capacity to create the jobs they need so desperately.

In dealing with the population problem in the years ahead, we must avoid repeating the errors of the past by not focusing exclusively on one dimension of the problem, whether employment or food. Although employment looms large for the immediate future, it is far from the only one that must be considered.

## The Ecology of Population Growth

Man, in his search for food, is altering his environment at an accelerating pace. In the poor countries particularly, efforts to produce food are destroying the environment. Rich countries have had this experience, too, but the ecological implications of man's quest for food are still only beginning to be understood.

As population grows, an ever-expanding area is cleared of natural cover as the land is used for cultivation. As a result of rising needs for fuel for heat and cooking, the forests are cut far in excess of natural replenishment. The areas thus stripped of forest include the Indian subcontinent, where much of the population must now use cow dung for fuel. Livestock populations tend to increase along with human population, and forage needs for cattle now far exceed replenishment in many poor countries, denuding the countryside of grass cover.

As population pressure builds, not only is more land brought under the plow, but the land remaining is less suited to cultivation. Once valleys are filled, farmers begin to move up hillsides, creating serious soil-erosion problems. As the natural cover that retards runoff is reduced and soil structure deteriorates, floods and droughts become more severe.

Denudation of the countryside and the resulting soil erosion is widespread in much of the developing world. The relationship between man and the land from which he derives his subsistence has become very unstable in large portions of India, particularly in the north and west, and in parts of Pakistan, the Middle East, North Africa, and Central America. Millions of acres of crop land are so severely eroded that they are being abandoned. Many of the displaced farmers and their families are moving to urban areas, swelling the slums.

In addition to destroying soils, severe erosion can impair and eventually destroy irrigation systems as well. The overcutting of forests in Java, an island of 70 million people, causes silting of the irrigation canals and steadily reduces the capacity of existing irrigation systems. Each year the damage from floods, droughts, and erosion becomes more severe.

West Pakistan provides an unfortunate example of the cost of denudation of the countryside. The recently completed

Mangla Reservoir, in the foothills of the Himalayas, cost $600 million dollars to construct. Its life expectancy is currently estimated at less than 50 years, only half the span anticipated in the feasibility study which justified its construction. The Mangla watershed is eroding rapidly as Pakistan's fast-growing human and livestock population bares the country-side. Gullies cutting through the fertile countryside within a half hour's drive of Rawalpindi are so deep that they have become minor tourist attractions.

If man presses nature too hard, the results can be disastrous. The "dustbowl" years of the 1930's offer an example very close to home. Only after some 20 million acres of crop land were set aside for fallow each year and after thousands of miles of windbreaks were planted was a reasonably stable situation re-established in the southern Great Plains. The United States was lucky to have the resources necessary to correct the mistakes man had made, particularly the ability to withdraw large areas of land from cultivation each year. These options are not readily available to the poor countries.

The pressure of population not only causes man to move onto marginal land but also forces him to intensify agricultural production. This in turn involves the use of fertilizer and pesticides, both of which can seriously pollute the environment. Among pesticides, the chlorinated hydrocarbons, such as DDT and dieldrin, pose a serious threat in that they are both toxic and break down slowly or not at all. Thus the amount in the environment keeps building, reaching damaging concentrations in some situations.

DDT tends to concentrate in the predatory forms of life, including man. Such concentration adversely affects the reproductive capacities of certain birds, such as eagles and hawks, and some types of fish. Its precise effect on human life at current levels of concentration in the environment is not known.

Suffice it to say that biologists and medical experts are

worried about the potentially harmful effects of DDT on man and other forms of life. Some countries (e.g., Sweden, Denmark, and the United States) and some states (Michigan and Wisconsin) have already partially or totally banned its use, at least temporarily, and others are expecting to do so.

Meanwhile USDA researchers are hard at work attempting to develop biological controls. The release of sterilized male insects has succeeded in reducing pest populations in some experimental situations. Breeding disease-resistant plants has eliminated the need for chemical pest controls in others.

The heavy use of fertilizer causes the accumulation of nitrates in bodies of water, which stimulates excessive growth of certain kinds of plant life, upsetting the ecological balance and, in so doing, destroying many if not all species of fish. Perhaps the most tragic example of this is Lake Erie, once one of the world's fine inland lakes.

## PROSPECTS OF REDUCING BIRTH RATES

The population problem needs to be redefined, but its essential nature remains: until birth rates are decreased, it will be with us.

The spread of modern medical technology during the 1940's raised the global rate of natural population increase well above 1 per cent. By 1960, it had reached 2 per cent, where it has since stabilized. But perhaps even more serious than the sheer numerical increase—70,000,000 people annually—is the fact that fully four fifths of this number are being added in the poor countries. Birth rates in the aid-recipient countries are now virtually twice those in the rich countries. In Latin America as a whole, the rate of annual increase has reached an incredible 2.9 per cent, which means that the population will double in only 24 years.

Three alternative projections used by United Nations demographers yield anticipated populations of 5.4, 6.1 and 7.0 billions by the end of the century. World population is currently growing slightly faster than the second of these projections. This means we must prepare for nearly three billion more people between 1970 and 2000, a billion per decade.

The old adage, "the rich get richer and the poor get children," clearly applies in the rich and poor countries. Economic growth in the poor countries is required merely to provide for population increase, leaving little scope for improvement in individual welfare. The reverse is true in the rich countries, where populations grow slowly and most economic progress improves individual welfare. Population growth thus turns out to be the principal contributor to the widening gap between rich and poor.

Birth rates in the rich countries are declining steadily from the post-World War II highs. In the two largest industrial countries, the United States and the Soviet Union, birth rates have declined steadily since 1957. Remarkably parallel trends have dropped crude birth rates to 18 per thousand per year in each, resulting in a yearly rate of natural increase of just under 1 per cent. These trends and similar declines in high-income countries in Europe and in Japan, Australia, and Canada are encouraging.

Successful national family-planning efforts in the poor countries are thus far limited to a few smaller ones, all in East Asia: Taiwan, South Korea, and Hong Kong. If recent trends continue, the peak rates of population growth experienced in these countries should be cut in half by 1975.

In Singapore, a city-state of about two million, population grew at an average of more than 3 per cent a year between 1957 and 1965. Then, the dynamic and energetic Prime Minister, Le Kwan Yew, threw his weight behind an intensive program to promote family planning. The Singapore telephone book today lists 28 family-planning clinics that are advertised as being open 24 hours a day, seven days a week. Virtually all mothers in Singapore have at least one baby at a single large urban hospital, making it easy to reach them with family-planning information and contraceptives. Population growth in Singapore was expected to drop below 2 per cent in 1969, one of the most rapid declines any city of this size ever experienced in peacetime.

But these success stories have occurred in only a few places in the less-developed world. Major deceleration in world population growth awaits a significant reduction in births in India and Pakistan, which together contain nearly 700 million people. (Mainland China should also be included, of course, but reliable statistics from that vast country are hard to come by.) The target of India's family planners is that the population, now approaching 550 million, might be stabilized at 750 million. That would involve reducing today's 2.5 per cent annual growth to about 2 per cent in 1975, and to zero by 1985! Put another way, it requires reducing a birth rate of 41 per thousand to 11 per thousand.

The Indian program attempts to popularize all types of contraceptives. Raising the legal age of marriage, legalized abortions, and even compulsory sterilization for those with three or more children are all being advocated seriously.

An India of 750 millions, of course, will not be free of population pressure. The consequences of crowding three quarters of a billion poverty-stricken people into an area the size of the United States east of the Mississippi are certainly not going to be easy to contend with.

Considering the fantastically high economic returns that can be expected from successful investments in family planning, much greater efforts are justified. The Ford Foundation estimates that worldwide research expenditures on fertility control, currently $25 to $30 million a year, should be increased five- or sixfold. The argument is convincing; until medical researchers find a new contraceptive technology, it will be difficult to achieve a widespread reduction in population growth rates in low-income countries. The major spon-

sors of contraceptive research today are the Rockefeller and
Ford Foundations, the National Institute of Health, the U.S.
Agency for International Development, and the Swedish government. Considering the economic and social dividends at
stake, a strong case can be made for a much larger contribution by international agencies which thus far have failed to
come to grips with the problem. It would be a major tragedy
if the time bought by the Green Revolution were wasted only
because the relatively modest sums needed were not forthcoming.

### THE GREEN REVOLUTION AND FAMILY PLANNING

Breakthroughs in food production and the prospects for
effective family-planning efforts in poor countries are not
unrelated. In addition to providing time in which to develop
new contraceptive techniques, expanded food supplies can
have a widespread effect on attitudes toward family planning.
The lack of interest in family planning by most couples in
these countries is largely due to their feeling that they must
bear many children if a few are to survive to adulthood. With
less malnutrition, much larger numbers should survive. If
assured food supplies are a precondition for the widespread
adoption of family planning, as many sociologists believe,
then this hurdle is now being crossed in some of the poor
countries. Paradoxically, more food could eventually mean
fewer people.

Reinforcing this contribution of the Green Revolution to
family planning is the likelihood that those who adopt the
new seeds will become much more susceptible to change in
other areas, including the planning of their families. Once
an individual breaks with tradition in agriculture, it becomes
easier for him to accept other kinds of change.

The most significant contribution of the Green Revolution
to the population debate is likely to be the new context in
which that debate will be carried on in the 1970's. The Green

Revolution has, at least temporarily, laid the spectre of famine to rest, permitting an employment crisis of vast proportions to surface in its place. Discussion of the urgency of limiting populating growth must shift its focus from food to jobs.

Thoughts on Feeding the Hungry

# More or Less People

## by Wayne H. Davis

Population alarmists tell us that it is urgent that we increase food production, doubling or tripling today's harvests by the year 2000 in order to feed adequately the burgeoning billions. People like the Paddock brothers, Georg Borgstrom, and René Dumont imply that the production of food for the expected seven billion people is man's greatest challenge. Dumont and Rosier in their recent book, *The Hungry Future*, even go so far as to say that the world population explosion would not be a serious problem if food production were keeping pace. This is nonsense.

They and others who write about our numbers doubling in the next 35 years are extrapolating the human population growth curve, assuming that growth will continue uninterrupted at 2 percent per year. But when I look at the population growth curve (printed on pg. 20), I view it as a population ecologist and recognize it as an unstable and temporary phenomenon which cannot continue. That population will crash before the year 2000.

George Wald, Nobel prize-winning biologist at Harvard, was recently quoted as saying that life on earth is threatened with extinction within the next 15 to 30 years. When a scientist makes a statement like that, you can figure that either he is a nut or he has carefully studied the situation and knows what he is talking about. Before you write George Wald off as a nut you should stop to think that nearly every other scientist who has been studying these problems is also predicting massive tragedy for mankind. Remember that medicine has not conquered the virus diseases, that as people become more crowded diseases spread more readily, and that our modern transportation system could distribute an infectious disease around the world within a few days.

If thermonuclear war or disease do not control our population, toxic products of our civilization will. With our overpopulated world, rising industralization and modern agriculture, we are releasing into the environment ever increasing quantities of hundreds of toxic substances, such as lead, arsenic, mercury, carbon monoxide, oxides of sulphur and nitrogen, pesticides, herbicides and radioactive wastes. All of these have already caused serious problems at various places on our spaceship earth, resulting in the death of plants or animals, or death or diseases in man.

Anyone in the health profession knows that for a toxin the critical factor is concentration; as concentrations rise, more trouble will appear. Those who wonder why the sudden concern about pollution should realize that concentrations of toxins are just now getting high enough to be critical.

Modern biology teaches us that basic life processes are essentially the same in all species. A toxin interferes with basic life processes. A substance that's toxic to one organism is toxic to others; only the degree of sensitivity varies. Therefore when we realize the concentrations of DDT in our environment are now high enough to have set the stage for extinction of the brown pelican, bald eagle, peregrine falcon, and other birds, it should be plain that the ecosystem upon which man's survival depends is doomed. These birds are equivalent to the canaries taken down into the coal mines to test for poisonous gas.

Although we in the United States recognize that DDT is dangerous, and our use of it has declined steadily, your friendly poison peddlers in this country produce it in even greater quantities. In 1968 they produced 69,000 tons, up one third from the previous year. Nearly 80 percent was exported and half of it went for the malaria control programs which have been so successful in lowering human deaths from this disease, and which, combined with our food giveaway program, have allowed these people in the malaria infested regions to increase their numbers by about 50 percent over the past 15 years.

The food production boys tell us that in order to feed themselves, the so-called underdeveloped nations of the world will have to increase their use of pesticides sixfold. Since DDT is the cheapest and these nations the poorest, that pesticide will be used. Yet it is common knowledge that DDT adversely affects species in the various links of the marine food chain from algae to fish and birds. New and more drastic effects are seen each year. DDT is the probable cause of the collapse of the herring fishery of the North Sea where Iceland's major industry has fallen by more than 90 percent since 1966. It is likely involved in the decline of our haddock landings from 50,000 tons in 1964 to 10,000 in 1969 due to spawning failures. As little as 10 parts per billion of DDT in ocean

WAYNE H. DAVIS *teaches in the school of biological sciences at the University of Kentucky.*

Reprinted by permission of the author and the publisher from *The New Republic*
162(25):19–21, June 20, 1970. © 1970, Harrison-Blaine of New Jersey, Inc.

water inhibits photosynthesis in marine algae. Not only are algae the base of the food chain upon which all other marine life depend, but they also produce 70 to 90 percent of the world's oxygen. It has been argued that oxygen production is inconsequential because upon decomposition the plant demands oxygen equal to the amount released. However, the standing crop of green plants represents oxygen released to the air; their death and decay would remove it. Thus the death of the oceans, foreseen by Paul Ehrlich within a decade or so, may mean the end of the ball game. Certainly, it will bring major tragedy, for the food production boys tell us we must double the harvests from the ocean by 1989 to provide food for people.

DDT is just one example of a toxin whose concentration has been rising until it threatens the existence of man. So many other factors are reaching critical levels, and are decending upon us all at once, that piecemeal solutions cannot save us. Unless population growth is stopped or we have a population crash soon, our efforts to control pollution are a waste of time.

Air pollution levels are now critical. Not only do radio stations announce when it is unsafe for children to play outdoors in Chicago and in Los Angeles—and air pollution is killing trees 60 miles from the cities—but within the past year there have appeared three papers in the scientific literature describing the effects of recent developments in air pollution on weather patterns in the United States. Two of these have most ominous forebodings. One describes the effects of filth plumes over the great cities in seeding clouds and causing premature precipitation. When one recognizes that the rainfall for our prairie farm belt originates over the Gulf of Mexico, he should be disturbed as pollution levels rise in Houston or New Orleans.

Another paper described the effect of tiny particles such as are produced by your idling auto at a rate of one billion per second (whose numbers apparently are enhanced by antipollution devices on cars and smokestacks), in creating a mist which decreases the amount of sunlight reaching the earth. For years air pollution has decreased the amount of sunlight coming into the cities, but this new development is reported from the wilderness areas. In other words, air pollution problems are no longer restricted to the industrial areas, and since plant growth is dependent upon sunlight, crop production can be directly inhibited.

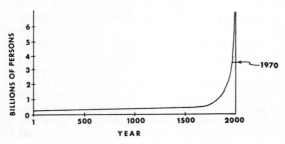

Thus the technologists who, in their book, *The Next Hundred Years*, foresee a 25-fold increase in the use of fossil fuels by a totally industrialized world for the decades ahead, are as ignorant of basic ecology as are the agronomists. So are the power tycoons with Consolidated Edison and the AEC who tell us that power demand in the United States will double within this decade. I think power usage will be less than it is today. We could increase the prospects of our survival by outlawing advertising designed to increase power consumption and reversing the discriminatory rate structures that reward those who consume the most power. And don't let them fool you with ideas about unlimited supply of clean nuclear power. Garrett Hardin's basic ecological law ("You can never do just one thing") applies here. That the rush to more and ever larger nuclear reactors may be the most ecologically insane thing we've come up with yet has been noted by Sheldon Novick in *The Careless Atom*.

**I**t is sometimes said that the problem of feeding people is one of distribution, not production. Although this is true, it is an oversimplification. Let's examine in some detail the Great Wheat Glut and its lesson to those who advocate the redistribution of food so as to feed the hungry people of the world.

The major wheat producers of the world are Russia, the United States, Canada, Argentina and Australia. Russia, by far the largest producer, does not supply the starving free world. In fact, she usually imports wheat from Canada. The latter four nations are the world's only significant exporters.

The harvest of 1969 was the greatest mass of wheat the world has ever known. This was due primarily to the chance occurrence of favorable weather in all the wheat countries, but in part to the influence of better practices and new strains in Mexico, India and Pakistan. The result is a massive surplus and a crash of world market prices. In Canada, where storage bins were full with a record 850 million bushels, a new crop of 650 million bushels was harvested. Her communist customers canceled their annual standing order because their own wheat crops fulfilled their needs. So one might think that this year the hungry people of the world will be well fed and able to produce a larger crop of children. But the world's wheat surplus will not go to feed hungry people. With a wheat glut and falling prices the exporter nations cannot afford to give their grain to starving people even if they wanted to. Only the US has been able to give away grain.

The Canadian farmer is in serious trouble because of wheat prices. With $65 million in last year's loans still unpaid the Canadian government has increased its cash advances against unsold wheat to $6000 per farm. Obviously the Canadians must sell their wheat to the highest bidder and take their losses; the wheat will go to produce meat for Americans and Europeans. Here we can see one of the simple lessons of agricultural economics which should help the reader to understand why the farmers never get a fair deal and why we are always hopelessly bogged down in federal controls, price supports and crop surpluses. The farmer's customers are every person on earth. But with most of the world's people in grinding poverty which deepens every year, the average customer cannot be expected to provide daily margin of profit which could be considered a generous contribution to the standard of living of a Canadian farmer. On the other hand, he who markets automobiles, jewelry or furs has only selected customers who are known to be well off and his margin of profit is substantial. As long as our system demands that every person alive be fed but not that he be supplied with automobiles, jewelry, furs, etc., the farmer will be poor while the merchants become wealthy.

So we will feed the wheat to farm animals. Wheat is not a feed grain; feeding it exclusively leads to digestive problems in livestock. Nevertheless, farm experts have developed programs to use up the wheat which the starving people cannot afford. Thus the *Farm Journal* for October says to feed wheat to cattle and in November to feed wheat to pigs. It also says that Canada plans to export grain surplus as beef. She brings in feeder cattle from the United States, fattens them on wheat, and sells them back to us.

We also have hungry people in the United States, generally estimated at about 15 million. They are hungry for the same reason as are people in the rest of the world; they can less afford grain to eat than the affluent can afford it to feed to pigs.

The White House Conference on Food Nutrition and Health on November 29, 1969, said that hunger in America is so widespread and serious that President Nixon should declare a state of emergency under the disaster relief act. They asked that such action be taken to provide funds to eliminate hunger in this nation in 1970 and poverty within the next few years. Implementing these requests would show the nation once again a strange paradox: you cannot eliminate hunger simply by feeding hungry people. They reproduce, and reproduction is as rapid as the level of nutrition intake will allow.

Let me illustrate this. In the United States and Canada is a small religious sect called the Hutterites on which good demographic data are available. Since they are fanatically opposed to birth control, are never killed in auto accidents or wars, and take advantage of the best in modern medicine, they should be the most rapidly growing human population on earth.

The average completed family size of the Hutterite family is 10.4 children. Thus the average couple has 108 grandchildren, 1125 great grandchildren, and lives to see the first few of their 11,703 great, great, grandchildren arrive. Crude birth rates and death rates for

the Hutterites are 45.9 and 4.4 per thousand, respectively. However, there are 34 hungry nations which have birth rates as high as or higher than the Hutterites. These include some larger nations such as Nigeria with a population of 54 million and a birth rate of 50, and Pakistan with 131 million people and a birth rate of 52.

These nations have rather high infant mortality rates indicating that modern medicine still has much progress to make there. The death rate in Nigeria is 25. Now if our missionaries will go over there and work on this high death rate problem we might bring it down to 5 (the current rate in Hong Kong and Singapore). Then we could give these people the benefit of a growth rate which would double their numbers in 16 years and give them 3.6 billion people, the current population of the world, within a century. Apply the same sound practice of medical care plus food for the hungry to Pakistan and she would have a rate of increase that would give her a potential of over 13 billion people within 100 years.

Thus hungry people can outbreed the ability of this nation or any other to supply their food. We learned this once before with public law 480 with which we provided $15 billion worth of food to the hungry nations. The result was a dramatic increase in the number of hungry people, lowering of per capita food consumption and general living conditions, and a decline in the efforts of these nations to feed themselves. Recognizing this fact, an editorial in the February 1969, *Bioscience* said, "Because it creates a vicious cycle that compounds human suffering at a high rate, the provision of food to the malnourished populations of the world that cannot or will not take very substantial measures to control their own reproductive rates is inhuman, immoral, and irresponsible."

The above statement is just as sound when applied to Americans as to Egyptians. To guarantee to feed all the descendents that the poor can produce is to make certain that we cannot uphold the guarantee. Not only will such a program assure an ever increasing proportion of people on welfare (according to *Time* the number in New York City alone doubled during Mayor Lindsay's first term; in Kentucky the doubling time is less than 7 years for the number of children on welfare despite efforts to screen new applicants most closely) and the collapse of society; it also blots out the chances of the hungry ever to attain a decent standard of living. The more children in a family the more the money required to raise them, and the less the chance of the family ever becoming self-sufficient.

It is time we faced our responsibilities. Those who call for increased food production in the world are asking that we make a grave problem still more grave. Responsible people must oppose any food distribution plan that is not tied to a program of birth control and a genuine effort to help the recipients break the poverty cycle.

# SOCIAL PROBLEMS
# AND POPULATION GROWTH

# THE SOCIAL CONSEQUENCES
# OF POPULATION GROWTH

### By Dr. Benjamin Viel

*It has been demonstrated that families lacking access to contraceptive means of birth control, particularly in Latin America, often turn in desperation to the harsh alternative of abortion. Some evidence for this fact is presented in the following provocative essay by a distinguished Chilean physician. According to Dr. Viel, the rate of induced abortion in Latin America is highest among the middle classes, which do not practice contraception on a wide scale. Extremely poor families, he asserts, seldom resort to abortion or contraception because "ignorance and demoralization probably destroy the capacity of poor women to combat family growth." Under such circumstances, birth rates are very high.*

*The most disturbing part of Dr. Viel's essay is his hypothesis that women in large, poor families may unconsciously wish for the death of their newest-born children. While the evidence for this hypothesis is still inconclusive, it merits further attention. The degree to which unconscious infanticide exists in Latin America— and the degree to which it may occur among large families in the United States and elsewhere—can only be ascertained through research. Such research is urgently needed.*

*The following essay is abridged from a paper Dr. Viel delivered at the Third Dialogue on Population, sponsored on Long Island last June by the Population Reference Bureau and the Tinker Foundation. Dr. Viel is a professor with the School of Preventive Medicine at the University of Chile in Santiago.*

WHEN WE REFER to population growth and its effects, we should differentiate clearly between normal growth, which parallels the increase in the means of subsistence, and accelerated growth, which takes place more rapidly than the increase in resources available to support life. Far from stimulating progress and giving rise to evolutionary processes, accelerated growth has been the cradle of wars and revolutions. It has slowed down production and vastly increased human misery and hunger.

Starting somewhat arbitrarily with the year 1930, we have had normal growth in the developed regions of the world and accelerated growth in all the regions we call underdeveloped or developing. In the latter areas, mortality rates have dropped swiftly as a result of techniques imported from the industrialized world. Populations have consequently grown fast,

but there has been no parallel growth in productivity or in the sources of employment.

Latin America today is a typical victim of this speedup in population growth. Its predicament has been caused largely by the reduction of infectious diseases through new drugs and more effective methods of administering and distributing medical resources. Both the new drugs and the improved methods are imports from abroad. Instead of creating a biological balance between the South American and his environment, they have helped to destroy the equilibrium already in existence. Death rates have dropped much faster than they would have fallen through improvements in nutrition brought about by an increase in the means of subsistence.

Between 1930 and 1968, the population of Latin America more than doubled, and at the present rate of growth, it will have tripled between 1960 and the end of this century.

What are the social implications of this enormously rapid growth? In offering an analysis, I will, as a doctor, start with those effects which lie closest to the field of medicine.

**Unconscious Infanticide**

It comes as a shock to realize that infanticide has grown more widespread during the twentieth century. This phenomenon exists at a frequency and in a form that is unknown to the great majority of people in Latin America.

I do not speak of deliberate infanticide such as the outright killing of the newborn, which is very rare, or the abandonment of infants, which is tragically on the increase, at least in Chile. Rather, I refer to infanticide of the unconscious type, in which the mother allows her child to die without even admitting to herself that she desires the child's death.

In a careful study in Santiago, Dr. Aníbal Faúndes found that for first-born infants, 60 of every 1,000 died during their first year. Among the third- or fourth-born, however, infant deaths rose to about 100. After 10 or more children were born to the same couples, the number of deaths during the first year of life reached 300 for every 1,000 infants. Since there is no biological phenomenon that entirely explains this increase in mortality, we must consider the possibility that a major cause is the growing lack of concern on the part of the mother towards additional children who burden her with more work than she can endure.

This hypothesis is supported by the experience of almost any pediatrician. Mothers come to him when they detect the least symptoms of illness in their first-born children. After they have had five or six children, however, these same mothers bring in their infants only when they are seriously ill.

In developing countries such as those of Latin America, the multiplicity of births per family may provoke unconscious infanticide and thereby serve as an important cause of high infant mortality rates. High mortality, moreover, continues through the pre-school years. We must face the shameful fact that out of every 100 deaths in Latin America, 44 are of persons less than five years old. In Argentina and Uruguay, where birth rates are lower than elsewhere in the continent, mortality rates in the younger ages are also lower. Only 18 out of every 100 deaths in these two countries occur among children under five.

**Induced Abortion**

When the mother's life is not imperiled by pregnancy or childbirth, induced abortion is considered illegal throughout Latin America. Both the mother who submits to such an abortion and the person who performs it are liable to punishment. Yet we have had an extremely high rate of induced abortion. The result has been widespread non-enforcement of the law. If the law *were* enforced, we would soon face a grave shortage of police, judges and jails.

How common are induced abortions in Latin America? Their illegal status has led to vast under-reporting, and we must therefore resort to indirect means of evaluating their frequency.

Assuming that in 1960 the use of reliable contraceptives was very rare among Latin American women and that the age distribution was "young" in all Latin American countries except Argentina and Uruguay, we may then state that the theoretical birth rate (without abortion) in these countries could not have been lower than 50*. From the differences between this theoretical rate and the actual birth rates in 1960, as shown in Table 1, we can obtain a rough idea of the frequency of induced abortion.

**TABLE I: DIFFERENCE BETWEEN THEORETICAL AND ACTUAL BIRTH RATES, 1960.**

| Country | Actual Birth Rate | Difference from Theoretical Birth Rate of 50 | Percentage of Population Urban |
|---|---|---|---|
| Brazil | 33.0 | − 17.0 | 40.4 |
| Chile | 33.0 | − 17.0 | 66.2 |
| Perú | 38.2 | − 11.8 | 47.1 |
| Venezuela | 42.8 | − 7.2 | 63.7 |
| Colombia | 44.6 | − 5.4 | 50.6 |
| México | 44.7 | − 5.3 | 50.7 |
| Honduras | 47.2 | − 2.8 | 22.5 |
| Salvador | 48.5 | − 1.5 | 38.5 |
| Costa Rica | 49.2 | − 0.8 | 34:5 |

This table indicates that induced abortion is more frequent in Brazil, Chile and Perú than in other countries. Although the relationship is not very close, the table also suggests that the actual birth rate tends to be higher where the percentage of urban population is smaller. In other words, the incidence of provoked abortion rises with urbanization.

In 1964, the U.N. Regional Center for Demographic Training and Research (CELADE) conducted a random-sample survey of abortion and contraception among women of reproductive age in several Latin American cities. Table 2 gives the results. San José, the capital of Costa Rica, had an abortion rate of 33 per 1,000 woman-years; Caracas and Mexico City also had very high rates. Comparing these results with those of Table 1, we may state that where the frequency of abortion is low at the national level, it is very often high in urban areas. The varying rates of abortion in different countries therefore tend to reflect the varying degrees of urbanization.

* Birth and death rates are given per 1,000 people per year.

Table 2 also reveals an inverse relationship between the abortion rate and the percentage of women in each sample using contraceptives.

## TABLE 2: ABORTION, CONTRACEPTION AND FAMILY SIZE IN SEVEN LATIN AMERICAN COUNTRIES, 1964.

| City | Abortions per 1,000 Woman-Years | Percentage of Women Using Contraceptives | Average Number of Children |
|---|---|---|---|
| Mexico City | 37 | 13.7 | 3.3 |
| Caracas | 34 | 24.4 | 3.0 |
| San José of Costa Rica | 33 | 27.2 | 3.0 |
| Bogotá | 26 | 21.8 | 3.2 |
| Panama City | 24 | na | 2.7 |
| Rio de Janeiro | 21 | na | 2.3 |
| Buenos Aires | 21 | 41.8 | 1.5 |

Other investigations bear out the urban-rural differential in provoked abortion. Surveys by the population department of the Colombian Association of Medical Schools reveal that the rate of induced abortions reached 16 per 100 pregnant women in Bogotá and 20 or more in other cities, while in rural communities it averaged only about 8. Likewise, in Santiago, Chile, the induced abortion rate as determined by surveys reached 35, while in the rural community of Calera it was less than 7.

What are some of the reasons for this urban-rural differential? In the rural areas, particularly where the climate is favorable as it is in most of Latin America, children do not constitute a great housing problem; they use the home mainly for sleeping. Even before they reach the age of 15, moreover, they help with the farm work. But in the cities, conditions are much different. Children remain in the home for a much longer time, creating a serious housing problem. Far from contributing substantially to the family's income, they constitute a financial burden even after the age of 15. Moreover, they are increasingly born into families where the mother works outside the home. It is under such circumstances that women turn to abortion when they lack effective contraceptive devices. In the cities, too, it is much easier to find the facilities for abortion.

Considering the fact that in Latin America there is a growing trend towards urbanization, it is easy to conclude that, unless an attempt is made to prevent them, induced abortions will become tragically more prevalent in the next decade.

The trend towards a gradual increase in illegal abortions in Chile can be traced as far back as 1937. In that year, records first became available of the number of women hospitalized for complications which arose from illegal abortions performed outside the hospital. Certainly such cases represent only a fraction of all illegal abortions, since illegal abortions without complications are not recorded. It should

also be noted that these hospital cases do not represent all the socioeconomic classes. They are heavily weighted towards the low-income groups. When complications of abortion arise in women who are economically well off, the patients are usually hospitalized in private clinics where it is easy to falsify the diagnosis.

The Chilean record reveals a gradual increase in hospital abortion rates, nationwide, and in Santiago, between 1937 and 1967. It also reveals that abortion is more frequent in Santiago than in the rest of the country. Outside Santiago, the problem appears to have been minimized by the low rate of abortion in the rural areas, even though the rate in other Chilean cities is as high as in Santiago—sometimes even higher. Since 1966, the level of hospital abortions has stabilized, particularly in Santiago. This stabilization appears to have been caused by a birth control program which has been in effect since 1965 and which has been applied more extensively in Santiago than elsewhere.

In conjunction with studies of hospital abortions in Chile between 1937 and 1967, a decrease has also been observed in infant mortality rates. It is thus clear that there is an inverse relationship between abortion and infant mortality. While infant mortality rates have dropped, the frequency of illegal abortion has risen. There is a logical explanation to this relationship. Years ago, high infant mortality severely limited the size of families. In recent decades, however, medical advances and the availability of powdered milk have decreased infant mortality without stimulating any significant change in the economic conditions of the home. Women, the most responsible members of Latin American society, are attacking the problem of excessive family size by resorting more and more to illegal abortions.

It is interesting to note that the greatest frequency of induced abortion exists among married women. From studies recently conducted in Santiago and San José, we can see that the yearly rate of induced abortions for married women was 49 per 1,000 women in Santiago and 26.5 in Costa Rica, while for single girls it was only 19 in Santiago and 11.5 in Costa Rica. The old belief that illegal abortion is resorted to mainly by single women who wish to hide premarital relationships is erroneous. This practice undoubtedly exists, but its extent is very small compared with the number of married women with children who seek abortion to prevent a further increase in family size.

### Abortion and Socioeconomic Class

It has been shown that a definite relationship exists between socioeconomic class and the frequency of abortions. If we assume that fertility is roughly equal in all classes, then abortion must be considered a rare phenomenon in the extreme classes and a very common one in the middle-income classes. Wealthy women resort less often to abortion for the simple reason that they use contraceptive methods to a much greater extent than other women. Middle-income women submit to illegal abortion much more frequently because they seldom use contraceptives to prevent unwanted births. In the very low-income classes, however, abortion is rare and the birth rate is extremely high. The ignorance and demoralization caused by destitution probably destroy the capacity of the poor woman to combat family growth.

In studying the frequency of abortion, researchers use the degree of education as a measure of socioeconomic status. Table 3 shows the percentage of women in three educational groups who have resorted to abortion in three Latin American cities.

## TABLE 3: ABORTION AND EDUCATIONAL STATUS

| Level of Education | Percentage of women having resorted to one or more abortions. | | |
|---|---|---|---|
| | Santiago | Bogotá | México City |
| None | 27.3 | 26.0 | 29.6 |
| Primary School | 39.3 | 28.8 | 34.2 |
| Secondary School and above | 24.3 | 19.1 | 24.8 |

If we assume that educational levels roughly coincide with economic classes, then Table 3 bears out the statement that abortions are sought primarily by women in the middle socioeconomic classes.

Throughout Latin America, women in these classes generally hire domestics who, in addition to receiving a salary, live in the homes of their employers. Practically every middle-class family has one or more domestic workers. For this type of hired help, abortion can be called a professional disease. Faced with pregnancy, domestics must chose between losing their jobs and resorting to induced abortion. Most well-off families will not hire domestics who are mothers.

In the methods as well as the frequency of abortion, we can discern distinct differences according to socioeconomic class. When a woman from the high-income group decides to have an abortion, she seeks out a professionally trained doctor and she generally pays an expensive fee. At a somewhat lower economic level, however, the woman resorts to a non-professional whose competence is as low as the fee he charges. This woman may suffer complications from the methods used by the unskilled practicioner.

In the poorest classes, a woman is likely to perform a crude abortion on herself by inserting a stiff implement or sewing needle through the neck of the uterus. She seeks help only when hemorrhaging begins.

While complications requiring hospitalization may result from abortions performed by unskilled "specialists," they almost always follow from abortions performed by the pregnant woman herself.

The foregoing conclusions, based on research in Chile, reflect practices throughout Latin America.

Illegally induced abortions result in the deaths of many young women. They are the cause of an incalculable number of gynecological infections that lead to a serious interruption of medical practice, because proper attention for women during childbirth and for newborn children is made difficult by the need to care for so many complications of abortion. Medical care for these complications drains a large fraction of the funds allocated to health programs by the Latin American countries.

We may conclude that unless something is done to reduce the problem, abortion will continue to increase in direct proportion both to the rate of urbanization in our countries and to the expected drop in infant mortality.

## Control of Illegal Abortion

The punishment of abortion by law in Chile has failed miserably, even though authorities have long had access to the names and addresses of women who are hospitalized each year because of complications of illegal abortion. Since no attempt has even been made to initiate court proceedings, many people ask: "Why not adopt the policy of Japan and make all abortions legal?" This proposal reflects a very superficial analysis of the problem. First of all, there are strong moral objections to making abortions legal. Secondly, such a policy would be completely impractical. It is true that the Soviet Union and Japan, among many other countries, have legalized abortions, but in the Soviet Union there is a doctor for every 460 people, and in Japan the ratio of doctors to the total population is only slightly smaller. In Chile, one of the medically more advanced countries in Latin America, there is only one doctor for every 1,600 persons. If doctors were authorized to practice abortion, and even more importantly, if they had the legal *obligation* to practice abortion on request, Chile would not have enough doctors to handle the demand. Nor would there be enough hospital beds—even for one day of hospitalization—unless Chile accepted a significant reduction in the present insufficient number of beds used for normal obstetric care.

There is, finally, a strong medical objection to legalizing abortion. Giving a woman the means to exercise very high fertility is incompatible with her good health and with the normalcy of her last-born children. Therefore, an indiscriminate policy of legalizing abortion is not an acceptable solution.

What about other proposed remedies? There is no doubt that reducing abortion by abstinence would require a return to the harsh times of Malthus. No one could seriously consider such an approach. It is equally wrong to maintain that abortion can be prevented by improving the living standards of the family and guaranteeing the education of children. Housing space is becoming continuously smaller because every day there are more people to be housed. Education is expensive, and government programs are seldom on a par with the educational requirements of countries having high birth rates.

The truth is that a humane, effective solution to the very serious problem of illegal abortion cannot be other than the use of contraceptives. This brings together the two demographic goals which must be sought in today's world—first, the reduction of the rate of population increase to the point where it parallels the rise in production, and second, the reduction of the population explosion within the family which forces women to expose themselves to a cruel operation.

Those persons who are against birth control join forces with those seeking legalized abortion to maintain that the contraceptive methods known today are incapable of replacing abortion and reducing the birth rate to any significant extent. It is even argued that illegal abortion tends to increase when a birth control plan based on contraception is started. The evidence, however, is to the contrary.

In our own experience with a birth control program in the western district of Santiago between 1964 and 1968, we observed a considerable drop in the number of induced abortions that resulted in complications requiring hospital care. Table 4 shows the estimated population of fertile women (aged 15-44) in the area studied, the cumulative number and percentage of women using intrauterine devices, the number of hospitalized abortions, and the percentage of women in the 15-44 age group who resorted to abortion.

### TABLE 4. ABORTION AND CONTRACEPTION IN WEST SANTIAGO, 1964-1968

| Year | Females Aged 15-44 | Women Using IUD's (Cumulative Number) | Percent | Hospitalized Abortions | Percent of 15-44 Age Group |
|------|------|------|------|------|------|
| 1964 | 81,642 | 4,073 | 5.0 | 5,282 | 6.5 |
| 1965 | 84,747 | 8,222 | 9.9 | 6,237 | 7.4 |
| 1966 | 87,994 | 14,579 | 17.1 | 4,731 | 5.4 |
| 1967 | 101,909 | 26,147 | 28.5 | 4,265 | 4.2 |
| 1968 | 104,283 | 36,377 | 38.3 | 3,727 | 3.6 |

The number of hospitalized abortions in 1968 amounted to only about 70 percent of those in 1964. This drop can only be attributed to the free distribution and use of the intrauterine device and other effective contraceptives.

In maintaining that a contraceptive program can reduce the number of illegally induced abortions to the extent shown in Table 4, we do not claim that abortion can be eliminated. The contraceptives available today, even the most effective ones, involve a certain percentage of failure and are not suitable for all women.

Abortion will therefore continue to be a serious problem. Nevertheless, a reduction in abortions to the point where they do not require the use of over 10 percent of the beds in gyneco-obstetric wards would be a real triumph.

## Population Growth and Employment

Despite high infant mortality and the increasing use of illegal abortions, Latin American countries are experiencing very rapid population growth at rates which, with the exception of Argentina and Uruguay, range between 2 and 3.5 percent annually.

Sustained high fertility has raised the percentage of young people in Latin America, and the majority of the Latin American nations find that over half their people are under 20. Every year the number of new job candidates is so great that the labor market cannot absorb all of them. The consequence of this phenomenon is increasing unemployment.

When Europe experienced a decline in its mortality rates as a result of better hygiene and improved nutrition, she also enjoyed the benefits of an extraordinary economic expansion arising from a successful industrial revolution. Furthermore, Europe had a safety-valve—emigration—which enabled her to colonize other continents when her own labor market failed to absorb all the new candidates for employment. Conditions in Latin America today are much different.

Latin America's labor market is growing too slowly to absorb all the workers which modern medicine and public health measures have saved from premature death. Furthermore, the continent lacks almost completely the migratory outlet which Europe long enjoyed.

There is another point of comparison which is unfavorable to Latin America. When the population growth rates of the European nations increased—and they were never as high as those occurring today in Latin America—the industrial machinery of that time required a large number of human laborers. But the slow economic expansion of Latin America today is being achieved through more automated industrial machines which are continuously replacing muscle power. Every day we see how factories which once employed 1,000 workers are modernizing their machinery and producing more and better products with only half as many workers.

The mechanization of agriculture has increased productivity and reduced the number of farm laborers. Those who do not find new jobs in the rural environment must migrate to the cities, where they face very serious problems created by a type of industrial production which requires fewer and fewer workers and which selects only the most qualified persons. Skills are demanded which cannot be acquired in the rural environment.

The continent's cities are growing, partly as a result of their own natural increase, but largely because of rural migration caused by the mechanization of agriculture. The growing mass of urban unemployed is seriously inflating the service expenditures of the Latin American countries, and it is disturbing the social peace.

This trend affects not only the city laborer and the farm worker. Intellectuals are also victims of technological progress. Without a doubt, if Latin America had the capital to purchase many more electronic computers, the middle classes would be as seriously riddled with unemployment as the classes of blue-collar workers and farm workers are now.

What are the political consequences of population growth which is too rapid for the economy to absorb? If a young man cannot find work, his natural reaction is to blame the socioeconomic system. It is not strange that his energy is spent in resisting the economic and social structures prevalent today.

The intense and growing political activity of the youth of Latin America, which has assumed more and more violent forms in recent times, is the natural reaction to the uncertain future which is faced by young people who cannot find employment in the labor market.

For young intellectuals, the circumstances of the unemployed man give further incentive to protest and rebellion. Universities join in the violence. Strike after strike interrupts the periods of study. Students who should leave our universities technically trained are handicapped by an inadequate preparation, and thus they help widen the gap between the high-technology developed world and the low-technology underdeveloped world.

### The Loss of Values

Youth has always been rebellious, but perhaps in no period of history has its rebellion been more vehement than now. In former times, fathers spoke to their sons with absolute faith in the moral and intellectual values which had guided their own lives. Today, men who are approaching 50—the generation holding power—sense that their faith is wavering.

They can no longer hand down a given set of values to their sons with complete sincerity.

The multicellular family which constituted the basis of Latin American life in the past has been swept away by the population increase. The ancestral home of the grandparents, parents and grandchildren has been replaced by the apartment in the cooperative which the new generation views less as a home than as a bedroom.

We were taught in the cradle that work was a virtue, and that every person should cultivate his talents to the maximum. But we are living in a world in which overzealous work, far from being virtuous, is anti-social. One man's excessive work leaves another man unemployed.

We were taught that savings would guarantee the education of our children, that they would be an insurance against our old age. But we are living at a time when inflation has so thoroughly destroyed savings that anyone who saves what he earns is destined to be poor.

Having lost faith in the moral values which were absolute pillars of our upbringing, we do not understand the upcoming generation. We have lost the confidence to promote an evolutionary movement which will deliver us from a revolutionary force of dire consequences. If the Latin American population continues to grow ever more rapidly, a revolution led by illiterate and impoverished masses will be the logical result.

Given this dangerous prospect, it is very difficult to understand those traditional elements of Latin American society which so vehemently resist the effort to reduce the rate of population growth. Yet this rate must come down if we are to relieve the family tensions that lead mothers to unconscious infanticide and abortion. And it must come down if we are to relieve the social tensions which lead men to rebellion and violence, seeking changes which are possible only in a climate of peaceful dialogue.  □

# POPULATION, RESOURCES AND THE GREAT COMPLEXITY

**"It is too late to solve today's problems," states a noted ecologist. "Tomorrow's problems can be solved only if we agree to be responsible for them." As human crowding gives rise to an exponential increase in social and economic crises, Americans would do well to reconsider their national obsession with growth.**

### By Durward L. Allen

OVER THE PAST QUARTER-CENTURY, an increasing body of scientific leadership has been concerned with the accelerating increase of world population. Since the early 1940's major advances in the control of infant mortality and epidemic disease, as well as aid to areas of food shortage, have reduced death rates in many tropical countries by about half. Humanity as a whole is in a logarithmic phase of the population curve. The 3.5 billion people now inhabiting this globe are on the way to doubling by the end of the century. Unless strenuous counter-measures are taken, in the United States our 200 million citizens will grow to more than 300 million in the same period.

It is a looming threat that already more than half the world's people are underfed. Although food-production technology has made important recent gains and food scientists are making every effort to rescue mankind from major disaster, there appear to be few authorities who expect such efforts to overtake the irruption of human numbers. There is, instead, a growing consensus that the chance of avoiding a demographic reckoning in the so-called "developing" countries is small, and that within 20 years hundreds of millions of people will be faced with a debacle of starvation and its associated ills.

This is the context in which we must consider our policies and programs in North America. We are deeply involved at present in food shipments to the needy, and our technology is being exported at an increasing rate. Unfortunately, while there is a growing belief that population limitation is essential and inevitable in this nation and elsewhere, our leadership in these matters is not in depth. It is a leadership of a few informed and concerned individuals, diluted by the attitudes of the many who, with an ear to the political ground, do not yet hear the tramp of approaching millions.

Although some sociologists and economists will not agree, I postulate that the problems of human welfare are biological, behavioral and economic—in that order. There are no interfaces where one leaves off and another begins. Understanding these problems requires both the detailed knowledge of the specialist and the broad appraisal of the generalist. Such a generalist is usually a biologist who has extended his interests far enough into the problems of human society to communicate with the specialists. The time is not far ahead when generalists will be appointed to high government commissions and committees.

My present purpose is to suggest relationships

Reprinted by permission of the author and the publisher. *Population Reference Bureau Selection No. 29*, 6 pp., August 1969.

that can help us understand many of the problems that plague mankind increasingly with each passing year. It may be that we do not fully grasp what is happening to us and that a re-examination of primordial adjustments will be profitable. Long before the human line became human there were millions of years of evolution in which the ancestral stock occupied its functional niche in the ecosystems in which it was found. We probably pay penalties when the primitive inner man is outraged too far, and there could well be clues to rights and wrongs in the social and habitat adaptations of some of our common animals and birds. A few of these characteristics are worth reviewing, for they are nearly universal.

## Biological Analogies

In our latitude, the young of most species are born in spring and summer, and they develop to a "subadult" stage in late summer and fall. These adolescents commonly wander widely in a "fall shuffle," evidently seeking a place to live. The farther such individuals move in strange country, the higher their mortality rate. They are at every kind of disadvantage, including the need to invade desirable space already occupied by their own kind.

When the wanderer finds a location where food, cover and other requisites are in useful combination, it settles down into a "home range." This is a unit of habitat where the animal becomes familiar with the terrain, develops its routes of travel, knows the location of every necessity, and is best able to escape from its enemies. Seasonally, at least, it does not leave the security of its home range. Here it has relationships of tolerance with other individuals of the same species whose ranges overlap. A high quality home range is a small one, where daily needs can be fulfilled with a minimum of movement. Both economic security and behavioral ease are found by the animal in its own familiar surroundings. Residents tend to display antagonistic behavior toward strangers.

Let us now consider a human analogy—the resident of a small town in rural America, perhaps in the more simple times of 40 years ago. This person

*Dr. Durward L. Allen is a distinguished Professor of Wildlife Ecology with the Department of Forestry and Conservation at Purdue University. The author of several books, including* Our Wildlife Legacy *(1954) and* The Life of Prairies and Plains *(1967), he has recently been noted for his studies of wolves, moose and other species in the unique habitat of Lake Superior's Isle Royale. This* Selection *is adapted from a paper which Dr. Allen delivered at the Thirty-Fourth North American Wildlife and Natural Resources Conference in Washington, D.C. in March 1969. Early this fall, the full paper will be published by the Wildlife Management Institute in the conference transactions.*

has a high degree of self-sufficiency. He has a garden and a cellar stocked with food. He has a well, his own outdoor plumbing, and his supply of fuel for heat and lighting. He disposes of his own trash and garbage.

His home range is small; he commonly gets to his work or wherever else he needs to go by walking. He recognizes most of the people of his community. Here he has feelings of security and comfort. There is, he says, no place like home. His high degree of independence becomes particularly evident under "emergency" conditions. He can ride out a winter blizzard with composure, and he can meet most of the dislocations that affect him with his own efforts. He needs a minimum of public service.

Compare his situation with that of a dweller in one of our large cities today. Passing over the social and economic enclaves that produce something akin to small-town conditions, I select an individual who is representative of urbanized man. Wherever he lives, he is dependent on a wide range of public services. His food, water, fuel and power are brought to him, and his wastes are taken away. His work is likely to be many miles removed from his home. To fulfill a specialized function in his community, he must meet a rigid transportation schedule in getting to his place of employment and returning home daily. Likely enough, he passes through territory that is largely unexplored and unfamiliar, and he has continual contacts with individuals with whom he is unacquainted. He has lurking anxieties in dealing with a wide range of unpredictable situations. He may develop the social callouses and aggressive behavior frequently observed in the residents of large cities. In a measure, the city dweller has lost his identity in a social melange that is diffuse and uncertain.

This individual is dependent for many things. He is vulnerable to every kind of public emergency. A drought or power failure, a strike or riot, a heavy snow that ties up traffic, can immobilize him and jeopardize his security. In this aggregation of largely strange humanity, he finds many of his activities organized and regulated. In turn, he needs protection from his fellow men. Aberrant and antisocial behavior must be dealt with. Health hazards must also be guarded against. It is testimony to the unusual adaptability of man that he can so often tolerate these essentially unnatural conditions reasonably well.

## The Density Determinant

Since all "higher" animals are socialized in some degree, a measure of association between individuals is beneficial. It follows that with the increase of numbers an optimum density is reached in terms of behavioral needs and available habitat resources. At still higher concentrations, we see the development of competition for space and other necessities and the breakdown of normal social relationships.

*Technology has an insatiable appetite. "The inhabitants of North America—only seven percent of humanity—are using about half the world's yield of basic resources."*

The behavioral and logistic attrition that builds up can be described conveniently by the term "stress." Eco-social stress is an elusive phenomenon—difficult to define, analyze and quantify. For good reasons, scientists have largely avoided this baffling universe of inquiry in their investigations of population mechanics and animal relationships, although the physiology of stress is somewhat better understood. The physical and psychic well-being of the individual is tied closely to environmental conditions.

To appraise the nature of high-density stress in human society, we may review, for want of more appropriate terms, some of the findings of Alfred Korzybski, known for his innovations several decades ago in the field of general semantics. In a paper of 1943, largely drawn from three earlier sources, Korzybski explored the increase in complexity of functional relationships or problems as individuals are added to a managerial system. He cited the work of V. A. Graicunas, who calculated the growth of problems faced by a supervisor as assistants with related work were added to his responsibilities. Deriving an appropriate formula, Graicunas solved for the increasing relationships as follows:

| Number of assistants or functions | Number of possible relationships |
|:---:|:---:|
| 1 | 1 |
| 2 | 6 |
| 3 | 18 |
| 4 | 44 |
| 5 | 100 |
| 6 | 222 |
| 7 | 490 |
| 8 | 1,080 |
| 9 | 2,376 |
| 10 | 5,210 |

We need go no further than ten in the series, since it illustrates beyond question that the addition of individuals or functions in this relatively simple organization gives rise to some kind of exponential increase in relationships. "At the root of the problem," said Korzybski, "lies the significant fundamental difference in the *rate of growth* between arithmetical progression, which grows by addition, for example, 2, 4, 6, 8, 10, etc., and geometrical progression, which grows by multiplication, for example, 2, 4, 8, 16, 32, etc." He stated further: "My whole life's work, and particularly since 1921, has been based on the *life implications* of this neglect to differentiate between the laws of growth of arithmetical and of geometrical progres-

sions." In effect, he despaired that those who govern could find the wisdom and means to meet their proliferating managerial tasks satisfactorily.

It seems evident that concentrations of people and, more generally, the growth of nations, produce a great complexity that expands in geometric proportion to the buildup of population density. If, for example, our present world population of 3.5 billion doubles by the year 2000, it might be supposed that the problems of government and social affairs would be twice as great. Using the scale of the Korzybski example, however, we can see that such a concept would fall far short of reality. The buildup of eco-social stress would undoubtedly take place much more rapidly.

### The Costs of Overpopulation

Americans customarily think of mass production as a means of attaining efficiency and lowering the cost per unit—an approach that clearly does not apply to human beings. As people multiply and concentrate, they require more protection and services of every kind, and they are correspondingly more costly.

Thus, a significant question: Is this great and burgeoning complexity related to our increasing costs of government, our deficits, our inadequacies in dealing with social problems—especially the rising rates of mental and psychosomatic disease and crime? Does it help to explain why municipalities and state governments find it progressively more difficult to collect enough taxes to carry out their commitments to education and other multiplying functions?

If population growth beyond an optimum begets problems that increase more rapidly than human numbers, it might be assumed that this only bespeaks the immaturity of our social and economic science—that in due time, man and his computers will handle the dilemma and produce a higher living standard despite the difficulties. To an extent, such optimism may be justified. But whether management skills can overtake a problem that is growing geometrically—and whether they can do so soon enough to be a relief to this generation and those immediately ahead, is highly questionable.

It is particularly evident that many of the high-density problems of humanity exist in the world's cities. Ironically, many educated Americans hold the view that the rural populations of the "underdeveloped" countries must be gathered into cities and their land given over to large-scale mechanized agriculture. It is assumed that industrialization in our image will bring this two-thirds of the world the blessings of modernity.

Yet, to an impressive degree, we have ourselves fallen far short in dealing with the challenge of urban complexity. Some 70 percent of the American people now live in cities of more than 50,000—a proportion that is increasing. The President's Council on Recreation and Natural Beauty has remarked: "No major urban center in the world has yet demonstrated satisfactory ways to accommodate growth. In many areas, expanding population is outrunnning the readily available supply of food, water, and other basic resources and threatens to aggravate beyond solution the staggering problems of the new urban society."

Perhaps the most widely evident sign of our overabundance is degradation of the environment. The technological "explosion"—a term that suggests a consciousness of some of the exponentials involved —has been accompanied by a corresponding reworking of the face of the land. The widespread pollution of water and air, and the despoliation of natural beauty need no particular documentation here. The solid wastes to be disposed of now aggregate 4.5 pounds per American per day. Thermal modification of natural waters as a result of power production is doubling in ten years. There is ample evidence that in North America we have exceeded the capacity of the biosphere to degrade and assimilate our wastes. Not only should we be making strenuous efforts to avoid further population increases, but real and rapid progress toward better standards of life in America probably must await the attaining of a negative growth rate.

Finally, the concept that American-style industrialization can be the salvation of overpopulated and impoverished peoples seems to neglect the fact that the U.S. system is based on an abundance of native and imported wealth. *The inhabitants of North America—only seven percent of humanity— are using about half the world's yield of basic resources.* Sociologist Philip M. Hauser has stated that, at our standard of living, the total products of the world would support about half a billion people. This seems a dim outlook for the 3.5 billions now alive and those yet to come.

## Our Growth Obsession

Nowhere in the state of nature do we find animals prospering so well, surviving in such large numbers, living so long, and reproducing so abundantly as when a population is expanding to fill a vacant environment. Of course, this is what has happened to our own species in North America during the past 300 years. The white man displaced the Indian and took over his resources for use at a "higher" cultural level that could support many more people. It is perhaps understandable that modern Americans have developed an expansionist euphoria that attributes collective weal to the growth process itself, rather than relating it to the availability of re-

sources on which growth can take place. The "expanding economy" idea has passed from the stage of useful realism to one of economic dogma.

Two of the "easy" approaches to success in business and industry have become routine. First, we have assumed the right to pollute air, water, and land or to mutilate the scenery as a valid part of the profit-taking process. Secondly, and because we have always had it this way, it is assumed that every enterprise has the "right" to expand through continuous increases in customers—which takes place through additions to the population. The view that this process should go on indefinitely and that it holds the key to the "American dream" is behind the huge promotion now under way to "attract new industry" and build population in practically every community that can support more people through private or public development.

We need to understand clearly that human numbers do not grow in thin air. Their increase is a response to the broadening of the resource base and the opening of vacant or sparsely occupied areas through developments that support new communities. This is one way in which population can be manipulated—by creating more centers of buildup or, in the other direction, by deliberately preserving our open spaces for less intensive uses. We have no legitimate incentive to increase population, yet our planning is consistently in this direction.

## Mania for Development

One who reads the transactions of the Western Resources Conferences will learn that, as of 1960, there were $22 billion worth of water development projects for 17 states in the files of the Bureau of Reclamation—plans that engineers considered "feasible." These projects are scheduled for construction by the year 2000. It is assumed that every river system must come under complete control, with the total water supply utilized to establish new agriculture, new industry, and more people in all of the "undeveloped" open space that can be found. There are many enthusiastic promoters of this program in Congress, and, needless to say, in the local electorates.

I do not imply that all such enterprises are against the public interest. But to make these far-reaching resource decisions, our representatives in Congress must have access to every kind of information. Today they draw much of their information from—and are frequently reminded that they represent—the construction beneficiaries who move the earth and pour the concrete. But our harried Congressmen also represent every taxpayer who supports the great works, with their wonderful and baffling cost-benefit ratios. They represent the millions of people at large who make use of the scenic and recreational features of this land—people who have little concept of what is happening to their environment. Most

*"In the sum total of their ecological malpractice, the elders are heading humanity toward the damnation of the lemmings."*

Americans know only that we are dedicated to "progress." Where that progress leads, or what kind of world it is contriving, they are never told. Has someone decided for them that we are to have no hinterland? Are there to be smokestacks in every wilderness, a smog over every countryside, the threat of extinction over every flowing stream?

There is another concept of resource management that sees our continent as a composite of environmental types, each with its own character and its particular contribution to the national scene. The latter view presupposes that there are many and diverse ways to achieve a pleasant life and that various regions have much to offer in their existing features and natural assets.

The wild creatures of this earth have survived because each performs a useful function in a reasonably stable ecosystem. Any living thing that is too successful destroys the sources of its livelihood and disappears with the community on which it depends. Man's vast power play in using, if not inhabiting, nearly every environment on this planet could be self-defeating if he does not have the insight to impose his own controls and work for that necessary stability in his ecosystem.

The 1968 report of Congressman Emilio Q. Daddario, Chairman of the Subcommittee on Science, Research and Development, observed that ". . . the population explosion is fundamental to the requirement for environmental management. Population must come under control and be stabilized at some number which civilization can agree upon. Otherwise, the best use of natural resources will be inadequate and the apocalyptic forces of disease and famine will dominate the earth."

Stability and an "agreed-upon" population level are indeed worthy objectives in realistic planning for the future. For now, a curb on the birth rate by every acceptable means and a major reduction of the government-sponsored environmental onslaught are two requisites of the greatest urgency. It is heartening to see signs that these are getting attention in Congress.

## Demands of Crisis

We have come to a threshold in world and national affairs where there is immediate need to apply sophisticated, up-to-date thinking if we are to mitigate, rather than augment, the growing miseries of mankind. Around the earth, much that needs to be done is blocked by a massif of ignorance. However, it certainly is true that the wars of history have made greater personal demands on men of many countries than what must be asked of the world's

people in the years ahead. The population issue does not brutalize the masses and inflict hardship on the innocent. It calls for an appeal to reason backed by all the skills social science can muster. In our own nation, public acceptance of new ideas is of such great urgency that every effort must be applied in bringing it about. Many of our old traditions, assumptions and slogans need a searching review with open-minded willingness to innovate.

Most of us are all too aware of the unrest of the new generation of our citizenry. I make no case for those who march and protest with no real effort at problem solving. But we probably can ascribe some of their social malaise to the frustrating complexity of the world in which they find themselves.

### The Failure of Education

There is, to be sure, an "establishment" devoted to high-sounding maxims that are supposed to be worthy and venerable by definition, but which seem to confuse rather than simplify our problems. In the sum total of their ecological malpractice, the elders are heading humanity toward the damnation of the lemmings. If young people do not see this at once, there are good reasons; for no one has given them any rational concept of man's relationship to the earth or any basic ethos of human respectability. In our overgrown institutions of higher education, the husbandry of intellects is monitored by humanists who are not biologists and biologists who are not humanists. They learn marvelous techniques but are the why of nothing.

This is to identify one of our overshadowing difficulties. In this time of television, moon exploration, and the imminent availability of nearly unlimited sources of energy, it is obvious that accomplishments in engineering and its supporting sciences are awe-inspiring testimony to the human mind's capacity.

Attending all our technical triumphs, however, is a growing realization that we have a critical area of weakness. While we know how to do fantastic things, we frequently do not know when and where —nor indeed why—to do them. The problem transfers itself from physical science in the development and use of hardware to another sphere in which we are less competent—that of the biology and ecology of man.

The nature and proportions of this problem actually bespeak the relative complexity of the systems of nature. Even though the physical characteristics of matter and energy are inconceivably involved, they are far less so than the limitless intricacies of the world of living things. Biological systems include all the variables of physical science plus the endless elaborations of more than two billion years of organic evolution. To the structure and physiology of the living organism are added the organization of ecosystems and the behavioral adaptations that are essential to survival.

In these dimensions were the origins of man, and now his culture has taken over to reorient his own speciation and vastly modify the habitat in which he developed. If, with the tools now at his disposal, he blunders unaware into the throes of overpopulation and environmental ruin, he could in a tick of the geological time clock be carried away to oblivion by the mechanical monster he has created.

Pessimism often has a hollow ring. But where so much is at stake there is more safety in planning to cope with the worst than in idly hoping for the best. The truth is that it is already too late to solve today's greatest problems. We have failed for lack of foresight. Only tomorrow's problems can be solved, and only if we of today agree to be responsible for tomorrow. ☐

---

# READINGS IN POPULATION

*With this* Selection *the PRB begins a new service for its readers—occasional listings of recent books and noteworthy articles and speeches in the field of population. This service has been prompted by the veritable explosion of population writings in the 1960's—a phenomenon which represents a first step toward dealing with the grave and continuing explosion in human numbers. Appearing from time to time in our* Bulletins, Profiles *and* Selections, *briefly annotated lists, such as the one below, will hopefully give our readers a useful sampling of works in this vital, fast-growing category.*

Behrman, S.J., Leslie Corsa, Jr., and Ronald Freedman, Editors. *Fertility and Family Planning: A World View.* Ann Arbor: University of Michigan Press, 1969. 503 pages, $12.50. Twenty scholars discuss social, economic bases of past and present fertility trends, implications for developing countries, medical aspects of fertility control, family planning programs, etc.

Bogue, Donald J. *Principles of Demography.* New York: John Wiley and Sons, Inc., 1969. 917 pages, $16.50. Nearly a thousand pages of exploration in depth of all aspects of world demography, with extensive charts and tables; exercises and detailed bibliography accompany each chapter.

Borgstrom, Georg. *Too Many: A Study of Earth's Biological Limitations.* New York: The Macmillan Company, 1969. 369 pages, $7.95. A distinguished scholar explores the alternatives which man faces in accommodating population growth to global resources.

Fisher, Tadd. *Our Overcrowded World.* New York: Parents' Magazine Press, 1969. 256 pages, $4.50. A notable essay introducing the lay reader to the world population crisis; includes suggested readings.

Kammeyer, Kenneth C. W. *Population Studies: Selected Essays and Research.* Chicago: Rand McNally & Co., 1969. 481 pages, $5.95 (paper). Twenty-seven essays on population issues reprinted from various sources, including two *Population Bulletins;* discussions of the study of population, demographic data, migration, mortality and morbidity, fertility, and world population trends.

*Spanish-language publication:*

Asociación Colombiana de Facultades de Medicina, División de Estudios de Población, Estudios Socio-Demográficos. *Urbanización y Marginalidad.* Bogotá, Columbia: Population Reference Bureau, Inc., Calle 45A, No. 9-77, 1969. 154 pages, $2.00. Papers presented at the First National Conference on Urbanization and Marginality (Colombia, 1968) cover many aspects of the problem of integrating rural migrants into urban society; Colombia is given special attention.

# Science, Birth Control, and the Roman Catholic Church

### Jeffrey J. W. Baker

Since it has long been a hobby, I have done quite a bit of research and writing on the history of the American Civil War. Before coming to the University of Puerto Rico, I was on the faculty of The George Washington University in Washington, D.C. While there, I took my wife to Ford's theater. We stood and looked at the balcony where, on the night of 14 April 1865, a man sat watching a popular play of the time, "Our American Cousin." At approximately 10:20 p.m., a tiny ball of lead, no more than one-half inch across, penetrated the man's skull, traversed his brain, and lodged behind his right eye. Nine hours later, President Abraham Lincoln was dead.

An autopsy was performed in the White House. The attending physicians were shocked to find that this one small bullet had shattered the president's skull. Two lines led from the point of impact and passed through the eye sockets until they met at the front. With very little else done, the top half of Lincoln's skull could have been separated from the bottom. Indeed, later it was, so that the brain could be removed and the bullet recovered.

The men performing the autopsy on Lincoln were surprised at the bone-shattering ability of the tiny bullet because they were practicing physicians, not scientists. Any good physicist, familiar with the traversing of solid matter by shock waves, might have predicted the nature and extent of the damage with nearly complete accuracy. Indeed, many men killed in the Civil War with similar wounds had shown just such damage. Thus, what was a completely natural and predictable consequence to a 19th century scientist was a surprising phenomenon to his nonscientist counterpart.

Adapted from a speech delivered March 1969, as part of a lecture series entitled "The Social Responsibility of the Scientist" commemorating the 66th anniversary of the founding of the University of Puerto Rico, where the author was a Visiting Professor of Biology. He is presently at Wesleyan University, in Middletown, Connecticut.

In December 1968, I attended the meetings of the American Association for the Advancement of Science in Dallas, Texas. While there, I walked with a friend to Dealey Plaza. We stood on the curb a scant 4 feet from the spot where another president was murdered. I looked up at the Texas School Book Repository Building from which the fatal shot came and recall being surprised at how very easy it must have been. My mind flashed back to Wesleyan University in Middletown, Connecticut, where I was that terrible November 1963. I recalled discussing with a physicist the hopelessness of the case, once it was known what kind of rifle was used. For this was no 19th century pistol, but one of the most powerful rifles ever developed by man. When the mass and velocity of the bullet are fed into the proper equations, the result is inevitable—even a surface head wound might be sufficient to turn the entire brain to jelly. With penetration of the skull, the shock waves could explode a man's head and, in President Kennedy's case, they did. Thus, because of a particular bit of routine scientific knowledge, a scientist could know before a nonscientist that Kennedy could not possibly survive.

The gap in terms of technological know-how between John Wilkes Booth's Derringer pistol and Lee Harvey Oswald's Mannlicher-Carcano rifle is a fantastically wide one. But, in terms of what has happened to our world in the past 100 years, the technological gap cannot begin to compare with the scientific one. And, again, the gap between scientist and nonscientist looms frighteningly large.

#### A Problem of Perception

In a speech delivered at Bard College in January 1967, Novel* Laureate Albert Szent-Gyorgyi pointed out that the central nervous system of a living organism can be compared to a computer. In "lower" forms

\* Nobel

of animal life, the behavior seems largely instinctive. In other words, these animals are born with their computers already programmed. However, as we move to consider progressively "higher" forms of animal life, organisms seem less programmed and more amenable to environmental modifications of behavior, i.e., "learning." Man, who ranks himself the highest form of life, seems the least programmed, instinctively, among organisms. But through certain kinds of education, he may become very much so. In Szent-Gyorgyi's analogy, the aim of a liberal education is simply to program man's computer to play a fair game of life in what is now a rapidly changing environment. Thus we must be very careful not to program the computer too completely. We must program only to the point that the individual is free to choose his or her own circuits in the future, and thereby have the potential of leading a truly intellectual life. Too often, we have overprogrammed to the extent that the individual is no longer free to adapt or adjust to a changing society. In today's world, such an individual is doomed to intellectual extinction. *The same can apply to overprogrammed institutions made up of overprogrammed individuals.*

Szent-Gyorgyi went on to point out that while science has, almost overnight, drastically changed man's world, in the past 50,000 years his brain has not changed much at all. Instead, it evolved to fit the exceedingly primitive conditions under which early man lived. Biologically speaking, man's brain was not made to search for "truth," but to distinguish between enemy and friend—to tell a cave bear from a rock. Thus our brains were made for only short-range "truths"; those which permitted survival. Even at the heart of the so-called Christian era, most of those who deviated from short- to long-range "truths" were imprisoned or burned at the stake.

Reprinted by permission of the author and the publisher from *BioScience* 20:143–151, February 1, 1970.

Again, Szent-Gyorgyi pointed out that the doorways from our brains to the environment—the senses—are not made so as to reveal the nature of things as science has revealed them to us. Our eyes do not see a chair or a table for what, to science, they really are—empty space, with here and there a particle with electrons buzzing around it. What modern science has done is to show man what, to that science, is the "real stuff" out of which the universe is made—the electrons, protons, neutrons, elementary nuclear particles, etc. In so doing, science has forced man into a world of dimensions which his brain was not made to detect or directly comprehend.

Consider temperature. Almost everyone knows what it is like to be burned with a match or boiling water at 100 C. But 15 million degrees, the temperature of the interior of the sun or a hydrogen bomb, means nothing to us—we simply have no machinery in our heads to even imagine it.

Consider force. As men, we can only conceive of force in terms of that which we can apply—the quantity of mass we can lift, the amount of physical work we can do, and so on. But when we are told that the explosive force of a 40-megaton atomic bomb landing in the center of 100 × 35-mile Puerto Rico will totally destroy all its villages, towns, and cities, we can only shake our heads. We are amazed—but we still cannot really conceive of such a force. And so we remain unmoved.

Consider speed and velocity. We know how fast we can run and how fast our cars can go. But the speed of light and the supersonic speeds with which technology now deals routinely simply lie beyond the pale of our comprehension.

Most frightening of all is the fact that, even when dealing with life and death, our minds can only comprehend those situations dealing with low quantities. Thus the death of a child will sadden all of us, and the perishing of almost an entire family in a boating accident off Isla Verde beach fills us with horror and pity for the bereaved. But when we are told the same 40-megaton bomb that could destroy every Puerto Rican village, town, and city will also kill all of the island's almost 3 million inhabitants, the same emotional chords or feelings remain untouched. Our brains have simply not had time to evolve the capacity to feel grief and sadness in such huge dimensions. Indeed, we have actually become rather hardened to large-scale death, and scarcely notice that our news reports blithely and habitually report the military progress

of the United States in Vietnam in terms of the number of counted enemy dead.

When one mentions temperature, force, velocity, etc., one is essentially talking about physical phenomena. But matters of life and death, although ultimately the expression of physical forces, must be dealt with in terms of biology. The Intercontinental Ballistic Missile systems being developed by the United States, the Soviet Union, and Red China, in terms of the physical forces involved, are frightening enough. But to the biologist, the situation is more than tense—it is perilous. Our ever-increasing ability to transmit death and destruction great distances has greatly lessened the factors which could prevent their ever being used.

An example is probably pertinent here. In certain species of animals, fighting among males is common during the breeding season. The observation of this fact was one of many that led Darwin to his "survival of the fittest" hypothesis. The idea of fighting for the female fits in well with the chivalrous views of manhood and womanhood fashionable in the Victorian Era, and was also harmonious with the later Freudian concept of sex as a primary drive. And thus the hypothesis survived for a very long time. .

It is now fairly well established, however, that males will fight when no female is involved, and that more often than not it is food or territory, not fair womanhood, for which they fight. Further, and most important for the thesis being developed here, the loser of the fight is rarely, if ever, killed. For those few species who actually do engage in direct combat, each has its own built-in surrender signal. The rat and wolf present submissive postures to their rivals, who immediately cease being aggressive. Many other animals adopt the age-old technique of simply running away. Whatever the surrender behavior that has evolved, unnecessary slaughter is prevented by their presence.

Man, too, has surrender signals, and it is certainly no accident that they have been incorporated into our military systems. Thus the raised hands or the traditional white flag are familiar internationally and their violation is looked upon with vehement disapproval by most nations of the earth. But, here again, our evolution has been too slow. Within a scant 150 years—far too short a period for organic evolution by natural selection—we have gone from the ability to kill only a few men a few hundred feet away.(where their surrender signals are plainly detectable) to our present-day potential of killing

millions on the other side of the earth, where a surrender signal cannot be seen or, if transmitted, may come too late. A very real, essentially biological safety valve is gone.

It is, perhaps, their knowledge of these facts that accounts for the relatively recent extensive political activity on the part of scientists, not as politicians themselves (for which scientists seem remarkably unsuited) but as citizens whose special type of education necessarily makes them more aware of the very real perils mankind faces.

Having given several examples of essentially scientific but now political situations which our minds and senses are not really capable of fully grasping, it is necessary to proceed to another situation which many feel is by far the most serious facing mankind. This is the situation which Paul Ehrlich (1968), Professor of Biology at Stanford University, aptly termed *The Population Bomb*.

### The Statistics

In the year 1 A.D., the population of the earth was approximately 250 million persons. But even that number is hard to imagine in terms of individuals. It is easier, perhaps, if it is considered in terms of 500 San Juans, or if it is said that the population of the earth in the year 1 A.D. was just a little greater than that of the United States as it will be in 1972.

In the year 500 A.D., the population of the world was 300 million people. Note that the increase is only 50 million persons, or 100 San Juans, in five centuries.

By the year 1000, there were still only 450 million persons in the world—an increase of only 150 million. Of course, 150 million is three times as great an increase in five centuries as the 50 million in the previous five centuries. But then there were still whole vast areas of the rich earth's surface unexplored and uninhabited, and so there did not seem much to worry about. Nor was there much to be concerned about in the 16th century during the time of the Council of Trent, for the world was still inhabited by less than 600 million persons.

(The reader will perceive here an intentional point: the Council of Trent, a reactionary council establishing much of the basis of current Roman Catholic theology, was held in a world populated with far fewer persons than can be found today within the boundaries of mainland China alone.)

But this is still several hundred years

ago. Moving closer, by 1900, the earth's population had become one and three-fourths billion persons.

Now we are truly in the realm of numbers that our minds cannot comprehend in terms of concrete realities. And so, as with the force of the atomic bomb, we talk about it as if it were something quite ordinary.

Or, we simply ignore it.

Note that with the first two 500-year time jumps, the population increase was only 50 and 150 million persons, respectively. The time jump from 1500 to 1900 is only 400 years. Yet, the population increase is 1 billion, 205 million persons.

Now we need jump only 60 years, not 400. And, in 1960, the earth was populated with 2 billion, 800 million people—an increase in less than a man's lifetime of over one billion persons.

There are more than enough figures available now to extrapolate a mere 31 years. In 1960 it was predicted that unless drastic population control measures were taken immediately, the population of the world would rise to 6 billion, 35 million people in the year 2000, an increase of 3 billion, 650 million. Now, in 1969, with very few really meaningful steps having been taken in the direction of population control programs, we can tell that this estimate has likely been too conservative and that the population increase may actually be far greater.

It is frustrating, but giving such statistics is usually quite futile, for one is forced to deal with figures that none of us can really comprehend—again, our brains were simply not designed to do so. It is possible that the present population growth rate becomes a bit more meaningful when it is realized that had it been going on at the same rate since the time of Christ there would be over 2000 persons per square foot on the surface of the earth.

Since this discourse deals at least partly with the Roman Catholic Church, perhaps it would help still more if the population growth rate is put in Professor Garrett Hardin's (1968) units of Vatican time.

**June 1963.** Giovanni Battista Montini became Pope Paul VI. In June 1964, just one year later, the Pope increased the size of the Vatican's own carefully selected Birth Control Commission to a total of 60 members. In the meantime, the world's population increased by 63 million people —a number roughly equal to the population of the entire nation of Nigeria.

**October 1965.** Pope Paul spoke before the United Nations and referred to birth control as "irrational." By this time, the

world's population had increased by an amount equaling the population of East and West Germany combined.

**March 1966.** The Pope created a Commission of 16 bishops to review the 60-man Birth Control Commission Report. By this time, the world's population had increased by an amount equaling the population of the Phillipines.

**June 1966.** The 16-bishop Commission submitted its report to the Pope. In the meantime, a number of persons equal to the population of the Congo was added to the world. Now it seemed as if there would finally be some action. The reign of Pope John XXIII had given the world reason to hope that at last the Roman Catholic Church was ready to face reality.

But, no, in November 1966, Pope Paul said he needed more time to "study the matter." He selected a 20-man Commission for further investigation of the problem. In the meantime, the world's population had increased by an amount equal to the population of South Vietnam.

**April 1967.** An historic month. Members of the Birth Control Commission, realizing (it would be nice to believe) that every day's delay spelled tragedy for millions, leaked their recommendations to the press. Now Rome's hand was forced, for it became publicly known that the vast majority of the Birth Control Commission—all Roman Catholics, and including theologians and nontheologian advisors—favored any means of birth control other than abortion for Catholics. By this time, a number of persons equal to the entire population of Italy had been added to the earth.

**December 1967.** The 20-man Commission reported to the Pope. In the meantime, the world's population had grown by an amount equaling the population of Turkey.

**25 July 1968.** Pope Paul issued his birth control encyclical, *Humanae Vitae*.

To total this segment of Vatican time, from the time of Pope Paul's ascension to the throne to the issuance of this incredible encyclical, the population of the world had increased by an amount equal to *the entire population of six United Kingdoms.*

And, 20 million persons died of malnutrition.

But now we are back to those same inconceivable numbers again. And, while the San Juan newspaper *El Mundo* can print a truly excellent series of articles at Christmas time on the poverty and misery suffered by a few Puerto Rican families with more children than they can possibly

feed properly, there seems to be no way man's emotions can be similarly stirred when he learns that there are literally millions of such families living in the same or worse conditions.

### Rational Escapism

Faced with the reality of the inconceivable, we resort to simplistic explanations or solutions which our minds *can* comprehend. We look to international politics and say that the problem is due to wealthy nations not sharing their wealth with the less fortunate. Most certainly, this is part of the problem. But this overlooks the fact that wealth of nations is measured in terms of gross national product or the standard of a nonedible substance—gold. Needed are vital macromolecules—proteins, lipids, and carbohydrates—produced most efficiently by living organisms within a *properly balanced* natural system.

We say that if nations behaved in a more "Christian" manner, and shared their riches, things would be better. Most certainly they would, but inasmuch as only in the movie *The Shoes of the Fisherman* has even the Vatican (itself wealthier than some nations of the earth) seen fit to do so in any meaningful way, is it realistic to sit by and watch people starve to death while we wait for this Christian action on the part of nations making less pretentious claims to righteousness?

We say that the agriculturists are going to save us, that new farming techniques, mining of the sea, and other get-rich food schemes are going to provide the solution. An effective rebuttal to this argument is provided by an analyst in the Puerto Rican Office of Economic Opportunity who writes: "Articles appear regularly in the press that the utilization of fertilizers, oceans, and solar energy can provide food for many more millions of people. These science-fiction possibilities do not, however, make today's poor feel less hungry." Equally effective is the obvious fact that at our present population growth rate the space needed for this miraculous farming will have to be used by man to live on and pollute. There also remains the opinion of more than a few that, despite improvement in food production efficiency, if all the food available today were evenly distributed among the world's peoples, everyone would go hungry. Further, even if we *were* able to give every man on earth enough to eat for an indefinite period into the future, there is substantial research evidence showing that an organism's behavior patterns become decidedly abnormal when subjected to extended periods of high population density. Finally, in an overpopulated, unbalanced system, the overall quality of life is greatly decreased.

The overpopulation problem is bringing man face-to-face with the harsh realities of the laws of thermodynamics, bioenergetics, and ecology which no scientist, Catholic or non-Catholic, can deny; and it is no accident that the scientific advisors to Pope Paul's Birth Control Commission were the ones most vocal in their support of birth control. In essence, we are faced with having to live on a planet which has only a certain input of useful potential energy. Additional energy is pumped into the earth every day by the sun, of course, but only at a rate which cannot keep up with the pace at which our expanding population must continue to use it in order to survive.

For the scientist, it is far easier to sit smugly in the laboratory and say that such matters lie in the political rather than the scientific realm. Often, far too often, this is what has been done. But three events in recent history have forced scientists to speak out and participate in problems of vast political and sociological significance. The first is the development of nuclear weapons. The second is the misuse and pollution of our natural environment. The third is a natural extension of the first two, and one that must first be solved before the others can be adequately handled. This is the checking of the human population growth rate.

This third event has also brought about an historical first; one foreshadowed, perhaps, by an editorial appearing in the highly respected journal, *New Scientist* (1 August 1968), just one week after the birth control Encyclical was released by Pope Paul VI:

> Bigotry, pedantry, and fanaticism can kill, maim, and agonize those upon whom they are visited just as surely as bombs, pogroms and the gas chamber. Pope Paul VI has now gently joined the company of tyrants, but the damage he has done may well outclass and outlast that of all earlier oppressors.

In the following months and continuing up to the present, it has become clear from articles appearing in other journals that a large portion of the scientific academic community, particularly the biologists, find themselves in direct conflict with a certain segment of the Roman Catholic Church hierarchy—unfortunately, by far the most powerful segment. It is a conflict that *Humanae Vitae* forces upon us. It is a conflict that science

cannot lose. The only question is, *can it be won in time?*

### Science vs. the Church

In the time that the reader has spent on this article thus far, a few things have happened. For one thing, many people have starved to death. For another, the perennial optimist in most of us tends to bring to the surface several points on which, hopefully, this article is incorrect or perhaps overly pessimistic.

Some of these points can be anticipated. For one, it was stated that this is the first time that science finds itself in conflict with the Roman Catholic Church, a statement that certainly seems incorrect on the basis of several other events, most notably the infamous case of Galileo. But the Galileo case has not been overlooked. Indeed, it is on the basis of that case that we can feel confident that science will win over *Humanae Vitae*.

A brief review of the Galileo case is highly pertinent here. In 1633, Galileo was summoned to Rome to face charges of teaching the Copernican-Kepler view of the universe rather than the Church-approved Ptolemaic version. Basically at issue was whether the earth was the center of the universe and everything revolved around it, or whether the earth was in orbit itself around some other central body, notably, the sun. As everyone knows, under threat of torture and imprisonment, Galileo was forced to recant and refute his own scientific evidence supporting the latter hypothesis.[1]

But two points are important here. First of all, while in the Galileo case the Church made a very sharp attack upon science, in general, the attack was not returned. Nor has it ever been. Until *Humanae Vitae*, science has done little more than observe with detached interest the opinions of the Papacy on certain scientific hypotheses. Occasionally there would be some minor stir, as in the case of statements on Adam and Eve and human evolution made by Pope Pius XII which made a few biologists, especially Catholic biologists, cringe. But after all, if some Roman Catholics, or all of them, chose to take seriously what Pius XII had to say about evolution, that was certainly their own business, not science's.

In general, then, science ignores Roman Catholicism, and there are several good reasons for this. First, Roman Cath-

olicism is easily the most dogmatic of the Christian religions and, of course, dogmatism has no legitimate place in science. In March 1954, Pope Pius XII decreed that the belief that Mary's body did not decay but was assumed into heaven, body and soul, was a necessary part of the Christian religion. In his encyclical announcing this, he finished by stating that, " . . . if anyone, which God forbid, should dare wilfully to deny or call into doubt that which we have defined, let him know that he has fallen away completely from the divine and Catholic faith." One can imagine what would happen to a scientist if he tacked anything like that onto one of his research papers (e.g., if anyone, God forbid, should dare deny or call into doubt that the degree of actinomycin D binding to chromatin is related to the degree of repression of the chromatin and that removal of histone increases the capacity of repressed, condensed chromatin to bind actinomycin D, let him know that he is no longer a biologist). But further, in the Galileo case, it really did not matter very much if the average man-in-the-street believed that the earth orbits the sun or vice versa—at the time, neither belief greatly affected the welfare of mankind.

The most important point is the second one. The Roman Catholic Church based a great deal of its theology on an earth-centered universe; at stake was an entire concept concerning the relationship of God and man. The argument went something like this: God made man in his own image and therefore man and the earth he inhabits must be at the center of things. Further, in the scriptures it says that Joshua made the sun stand still—he could hardly have done so if it was the earth that moved, and not the sun. Thus the Church crawled further and further out on a limb and lashed out more and more paranoically at Galileo, just as Pope Paul VI is now doing against those Roman Catholic priests and bishops who have had the courage to point out that *Humanae Vitae* puts the Church out on a limb even shakier than the one Galileo selected.

As everyone knows, the Church was wrong—dead wrong—and Galileo was right. And, slowly, the Church began to crawl back along the limb until the safety of the main trunk was reached and the theology could be readjusted to a non-homocentric universe, and a bit of history could be rewritten.

But it took the Church 189 years to admit it was wrong (on 11 September 1822). Even then, it did not admit Galileo was right. It merely said that it was no longer a

---

[1]Often a new pope selects the name of a previous pope whose life and deeds he particularly admires. One wonders if there is any significance in the fact that Galileo was first checked by Rome during the reign of Pope Paul V.

serious sin against God to think that he *might* be right. Not until 203 years had passed were the works of Kepler, Copernicus, and Galileo removed from the Index of forbidden books. As far as I know, the Roman Catholic Church to this day has never publicly admitted that the earth really does go around the sun (possibly that is why the United States sent astronaut Borman to the Vatican). Professor Hardin has wagered that if the Church ever does retry Galileo (which has been seriously suggested), it will find him guilty again.[2]

As stated previously, it does not make much difference if the Roman Catholic Church chooses to believe that the sun orbits the earth, instead of *vice versa*. But it does greatly affect mankind if very many persons take seriously the idea that to use an artificial contraceptive is a grave sin against God. This, then, is certainly one reason why the scientific community, as well as the rest of the academic world, has been so shocked by *Humanae Vitae*. Mankind simply cannot afford to wait for two centuries for Rome to admit its error—the present population growth rate and the accompanying death rate by disease and starvation simply will not permit it.

On 29 December 1968, a strong protest statement against *Humanae Vitae*, instigated by the author, Professor Ehrlich, and Professor Ernst Mayr (Harvard University), was released to the press. At that time, over 2600 scientists, Roman Catholic and non-Roman Catholic, had signed this statement (the resulting publicity has greatly increased this number). In discussing this action, one priest told me he thought it to be a waste of time because those Roman Catholics who have had the benefit of a good education pay no attention to the Pope and use contraceptives anyway.

This is true enough. Indeed, recent surveys indicate that almost 80% of Roman Catholics in the United States practice means of birth control forbidden by the Church. But the United States is not the world. It is the world's uneducated that will suffer the most from the fear of eternal punishment in the flames of Hell in the hereafter—and they are the ones who stand at the bottom of the economic ladder and who can least afford to have large numbers of children.

Another stock argument used in defense of the Pope is that the birth rate in many Catholic countries is often the same or even lower than birth rates in such non-Catholic countries as India, where the Pope has no authority. This is possibly true. But is it right to use the existence of poverty and misery in non-Catholic countries as an excuse to block attempts to correct slightly less miserable situations in Catholic countries? Further, do these birth rate statistics take into account the over 900,000 abortions a year in Catholic Italy, where contraceptives are outlawed? Does it account for the frequent use of infanticide by women in Catholic Columbia, where access to knowledge of any other means to limit family size has been denied by the Church and government? The same press release that gave out the comparative birth rates in Catholic and non-Catholic countries also pointed out that in Catholic Austria, Belgium, and France, it is estimated that there is at least one abortion for every live birth. According to Alvaro Garcia-Pena, Director of the Population Reference Bureau's Latin American Department, in Uruguay the ratio is three abortions to every live birth. In Latin America, 78% of the abortions performed (many of them fatal) are carried out on married women.

### The Cause for Concern

Since it is evident that most Roman Catholics, even those who publicly defend *Humanae Vitae*, privately ignore it, and that even if the Pope reversed his stand tomorrow, it would have little immediate effect on the world's alarming birth rate, it is still reasonable to probe further to understand why there is such concern in the academic community about the birth control encyclical.

One does not have to look far. The great danger of *Humanae Vitae* lies in the support it gives to organized conservative Catholic resistance to the initiation of publicly financed population control programs. In the past, opposition by such groups has effectively prevented or slowed population control programs through the United Nations, *even to non-Catholic nations*, such as India. This, it will be seen, *does* give the Pope some authority in non-Catholic nations. In the United States, conservative Catholic opposition helped defeat Senator Gruening's efforts to pass a law promoting the dissemination of birth control information—just the *information*, mind you, not the contraceptives themselves—to those who wanted it. Some of the testimony delivered against this legislation makes pitiful reading indeed.

The President's Scientific Advisory Committee, in its massively documented three-volume report, *The World Food Crisis*, stated that, "The solution to the problem that will exist after about 1985 *demands* that programs of population control be initiated now." The "now" was 2 years ago, and no such programs have been initiated. *Section XXIII of Humanae Vitae specifically encourages renewed interference in governmental efforts to disseminate birth control information*. This fact renders ridiculous the charge that those non-Catholics who have protested against the Encylical are interfering in the private affairs of the Roman Catholic Church. I suspect that as far as most non-Roman Catholics are concerned, the Church could return to believing that the sun goes around the earth for all they care. But they are quite within their rights to protest when, through political activity, it attempts to limit their freedom to think and act otherwise.

### Political Interference: A Case History

Except for a few regions, it is difficult for a person living in the United States to fully comprehend what Roman Catholic political interference means. But those who live in Puerto Rico are well aware of the extreme coercive tactics to which the Church has resorted in its fight against birth control by means that it does not find acceptable. Failing to convince the laymen of the "immorality" of contraception, the Church in Puerto Rico turned to "spiritual retreats" for government and civic leaders, doctors, nurses, social workers, etc. In reality, these retreats were mostly indoctrination courses in Catholic thinking on the subject of birth control. Associations were formed of Roman Catholic physicians, Roman Catholic nurses, Roman Catholic lab technicians, etc., all opposed, of course, to birth control aid.

Despite repeated official statements by the then-in-power Popular Democratic Party (PDP) that the government was not promoting any birth control programs and that for strict health reasons only were contraceptive services being given, the Church continued its attack against the government, mainly because it wished the "Neo-Malthusian" laws of 1937 repealed.[3]

[3]These laws simply made it no longer a felony to advertise contraceptive methods or provide contraceptive services and enabled the Commissioner of Health to regulate the teaching of birth control in health centers, maternal hospitals, and clinics to married couples or those living together publicly. Under government regulation, sterilization was also permitted on the advice of physicians. The fact that the Medical Association and the Association of Graduate Nurses, as well as many members of the University academic communities, backed this legislation led to the formation of the aforementioned Catholic organizations.

[2] In Scranton, Pennsylvania, a priest was reprimanded for five points in his writings, one of which was that he was too lenient in his interpretation of Galileo. The year? 1969.

Partly because of the 1937 legislation and partly because of the tabling of a bill which would have authorized the release of public school children during school hours to receive religious instruction, the Society of the Holy Name initiated a movement for the formation of the "Christian Action Party." The movement was given the green light by Archbishop Davis, who saw this party as a means to "define*the rights of the faithful." The reigning Popular Democratic Party was labeled by the bishops of Puerto Rico and others of the hierarchy as "Godless, immoral, antichristian, and against the Ten Commandments" . . . certainly a notable record for any political party. In a pastoral letter to the laity· dated 18 October 1960 and read from the pulpit in all Roman Catholic Churches in Puerto Rico, Archbishop Davis and Bishops McManus and Aponti forbade Catholics from voting for the PDP because its philosophy was "antichristian, anticatholic, and based upon the modern heresy that the popular will and not Divine Law decides what is moral or immoral." (The "immoral" practices the good bishops had in mind were the birth control services provided at public hospitals, clinics, and health centers.)

The response of the PDP was simply and reasonably to point out that the birth control laws were not compulsory but simply allowed those individuals who wished birth control *information* to obtain it without breaking the law. As one PDP leader put it, "The government should not be subordinated to an exclusive creed or moral interpretation of a specific religious group which condemns or prohibits the moral beliefs of other groups, and should not interfere with purely moral questions, like the use of birth control devices, which pertain to the free will of the individual."

Governor Muñoz Marín, founder of the PDP and a Roman Catholic, made his reply to the 18 October pastoral letter sharper and still more to the point:

> The statement of the Catholic bishops is an incredible and unjust intervention in the rights and the political freedom of citizens in Puerto Rico. It has the characteristics of medieval obscurantism.
>
> We could not believe that in the modern world, nor in a country intimately associated with the United States, such a document could be issued. When the Popular Party states that it is not possible to sanction punitively those acts over which there is no general consensus, it is referring to the differences between Catholics and those of other Christian denominations.
>
> The bishops' document assumes or pretends to assume that in Puerto Rico there is an established Church, and that

that Church is theirs. Neither in Puerto Rico nor in any part of the U.S. democracy is there one church established, and we have the duty to respect the differences of opinion that exist between Christians.

The reaction of the hierarchy to these statements was typical. On 22 October, a few days before the election, a pastoral letter was read from the pulpit stating:

> For a Catholic to vote in favor of the Popular Democratic Party is to vote in favor of the anti-Catholic morality proclaimed by the Popular Party, is to vote in favor of the destruction of the Ten Commandments of the Law of God, is to act against his own Catholic convictions and, whether the Bishops say it or not, it is a sin to act contrary to one's own convictions. If the faithful should not heed the warning of the Bishops, that is a matter for their consciences, but they . . . are committing a sin. With penalties or without penalties from the Bishops, they violate the Law of God which prohibits favoring a morality without God, which is clearly a disobedience against God and is evidently a sin.

The results of the elections were an anticlimax. The Popular Democratic Party was victorious, with the Christian Action Party receiving little more than 5% of the total vote cast. Proof of wholesale fraud connected with voter registration for the Christian Action Party—defended because of the overriding moral issues involved (! ! !)—led to an investigation in which more than 3000 fraudulent registrations were uncovered. In 1964, two of the three bishops (with some urging) went elsewhere, and were replaced. The one remaining, Aponti, continues his fulminations against birth control, but one gets the impression that not even *he* takes anything he says on the matter very seriously anymore. But meaningful birth control programs in Puerto Rico are still being crippled by the political extortions of the Church.

The·happy outcome of the Puerto Rican elections should in no way be used to justify lessened concern about the fact that *Humanae Vitae* specifically encourages such nonsense. The 1960 Puerto Rican elections were a very special case. Governor Marín was a very popular and powerful political leader. Further, while its quality varies widely, public education in Puerto Rico is widespread. Thus most Puerto Ricans have generally been educated beyond the stage of being frightened by threats of eternal hellfire and damnation. Such is not the case in much of Latin America or countries such as Spain or

Italy. Even in liberal Puerto Rico, the Executive Director of the Family Planning Association, an intelligent and courageous woman, has been slandered, threatened, and attacked from the pulpit in the presence of her children. One priest told his congregation that "a woman with a Satanic purpose in mind has been visiting the community." Threats were made to bar any Catholic from the Church who attended birth control meetings. Even after the 1960 election debacle, the San Juan Chancery attempted to bar from the sacraments and church services those who had disobeyed the hierarchy's voting instructions.[4]

### The Theology of *Humanae Vitae*

For a person trained in science to delve into theology, especially Roman Catholic theology, is a dangerous venture. Until very recently, orthodox theological research has been primarily apologetic; certain assumptions are never challenged, only supported. For example, the scriptural evidence which supports belief that God really meant for Peter and his "successors" to be Popes is marshaled in full strength, while scriptural and historical evidence casting doubt upon this belief is downplayed or "explained" away. Days spent by this writer in the Library of Congress trying to wade through a vast entanglement of Roman Catholic theological literature in an attempt to understand how a *Humanae Vitae* could ever have happened were dismaying ones, and the complexities of the scientific research literature seemed like paradise in comparison. Only two thoughts prompted me to continue. The first was a belief that the most effective way to tackle a serious problem is to go to its roots—and the roots of *Humanae Vitae* are, or claim to be, primarily theological. The second thought was a comforting one: whenever the Roman Catholic Church has passed judgment upon scientific matters, it has almost invariably managed to be wrong. Thus, I could feel confident that my own batting average could hardly be much worse.

Just how firm a theological basis does the Church's opposition to birth control have? An incredibly weak one. The first really powerful Papal decree indicating disapproval comes not from the time of Christ, but from Pope Sixtus V on 29 October 1588. Here, the using or giving of contraceptives was equated literally with

---

[4]Archbishop Davis, undoubtedly chastened by thoughts of drastically reduced collections in the plate, later denied statements issued from the Chancery to this effect.

\* defend

murder and was punishable as such.[5] Sixtus V Bull *(Effraenatum)* proved more embarrassing than successful, and was quietly laid to rest a few months after its author by his successor, Gregory XIV. The sort of reasoning behind it, however, did not die. It was to appear again in the mid-19th century under St. Pius IX (the same who proclaimed as dogma the Immaculate Conception of Mary and Papal infallibility). But it was not until 1930 that Rome really resurrected Sixtus V, with the issuance of Pius XI's *Casti connubii,* a masterful distillation of past doctrinal statements. St. Augustine's famous passage on the "cruel lust" of couples avoiding procreation is cited, as is the Thomistic view of the nature of coitus. But probably the tone and intent of *Casti connubii* are best conveyed by its statement that " . . . those who do such a thing (i.e., practice contraception) are masked with a grave and total flaw" (yes, "flaw"!).

There were, however, still some grounds for hope. Even in 1930, many of the clergy were openly critical of *Casti connubii* and the French, in particular, tried to prevent it. Thus, prior to *Humanae Vitae,* the Church had really been inching its way back out on a limb on this matter for only about 35 years. Pope Paul could have easily enabled the Church to retreat rather gracefully, as well as perform a tremendous service to humanity. Indeed, as soon as Paul began to examine the birth control issue, the Patriarch of Antioch said to his Cardinal colleagues, "I beg of you, my brothers; let us avoid a new Galileo case: one is enough for the Church." But Pope Paul elected to ignore the lessons of history.

If contraception is really such a serious sin for Christians, one would have expected Christ to have devoted at least a little attention to it. He did not; nor did the apostles. In truth, as one Roman Catholic priest put it concerning *Humanae Vitae,* "Since there is no scripture and no history, there can be no theological ground either."

Early birth control bans gave as scriptural justification an obscure passage in the Old Testament book of Genesis, Chapter 38. Here is related the "Sin of Onan." In the story, Onan is ordered by his father to have sexual intercourse with his brother's widow. Onan does so but, not wishing to have his own sperm follow that of his brother, withdraws before having an

orgasm and, as the Bible puts it, "spills his seed upon the ground." God then "slew" him.[6]

I invite any reader to read the story of Onan for himself. According to the Church, the incident showed that God disliked birth control. But this is a classic case of out-of-context interpretation. Once one reads the *entire* story of Onan, not just the part cited by the Church, it becomes perfectly evident that Onan was slain for his refusal to meet his responsibility to his brother and the clan, rather than for the means he used in not doing so. Even the Church now seems to realize it was a mistake to use Onan in support of antibirth control activity, and it is perhaps a credit to Pope Paul that *Humanae Vitae* wisely omits any reference to it.

In terms of being consistent, the Church lost much of the strength of its argument against birth control when it allowed rhythm as a means of limiting family size. This meant the Church had changed its tune—it was no longer implying that for man to limit his numbers was necessarily wrong, but only the use of "unnatural" means of doing so was a "grave sin." Indeed, *Humanae Vitae* is quite explicit on this point. But what *are* these "unnatural" means? Even the Church admits that in some cases it does not know. There are certain means, such as the use of diaphragms, condoms, intrauterine devices, etc., that the Church says are definitely "unnatural." But even the pill is banned as "unnatural," which implies that the Church knows more about the precise biochemical means by which the pill works to effect birth control than do the scientists who developed it.

Thus, to date, the only method of birth control now considered as "natural" is rhythm. Ironically, the Roman Catholic physician John Rock, who had written a definitive paper on rhythm years before, recently expressed regrets that he had done so and clearly labeled rhythm as unnatural! Biologically speaking, it certainly is. The only thing that separates man sexually from the vast majority of lower animals is that he does not have certain periods of nonmating. In other words, man has no breeding schedule. Rhythm puts man right back onto a breeding schedule. Rome gets around this difficulty by suggesting that periods of abstinence be looked upon as personal sacrifices to the glory of God. But this merely reflects

the scarcely hidden opinions of sex as dirty and immoral held by St. Paul and St. Augustine. ("Better to marry than to burn," is the way St. Paul is quoted.) Even as late as March 1954, Pius XII was stating in his encyclical, *Sacra Virginitae,* that marriage was not as high a state of life as holy virginity! Until very recently, obsession with the "evils" of sex permeate Catholic theology—indeed, Pope Paul IV insisted that for his coronation, loincloths be put upon Michelangelo's cherubs on the ceiling of the Sistine Chapel. It is not until 1874 that one finds a Roman Catholic theologian making any connection between sexual intercourse and love, and it is only since the reign of Pope John XXIII (1958-63) that this anti-Augustinian, anti-Thomist heresy has crept in any significant way into the Church's viewpoint on these matters. Thus, while it is difficult to prove, one gets the impression that Rome has long considered sex as a necessary evil in order to have children, and that "if the chance of the procreation of life no longer remains open," then the act of sexual intercourse may be simply done because it's fun . . . and that's a "no no." And so the attacks of the Church against birth control have paralleled in intensity the rate at which birth control practices have become available to mankind.

### The Catholic Scientist

Where does all of this leave the Roman Catholic scientist? In my opinion—and events since the encyclical has come out tend to support it—the Catholic scientist has three choices.

The first is to simply ignore both the Pope and the problem. This is no more nor less than many educated Roman Catholic laymen are doing, and many of them frankly admit it. But the person who *privately* feels the birth control encyclical is wrong, yet refuses to speak out against it, is adopting an unchristian form of behavior, for it is an intrinsically selfish one. The Catholic scientist who ignores the encyclical (which according to the encyclical is the same as disobeying it) may himself be intellectually free to do so. But he is guilty of turning his back on the vast majority of his fellow Catholics who have been deprived of a good education and who live out their lives in an environment which is both physically and intellectually a replica of the 13th century. To such persons, fears of the "fires of Hell" are both real and frightening.

As Bernard Hollowood put it in *Punch* (14 August 1968):

---

[5] Sixtus V seems to have had an obsession to continue a pet project of Pope Paul V to stamp out prostitution in Rome, and actually had a woman who had procured for her daughter executed.

[6] "Slewing" people seemed to be almost an obsession with the God of the Old Testament, often on rather vaguely worded charges. Indeed, we read that Onan's brother was struck down merely for "displeasing" God. The American Civil Liberties Union would have been driven absolutely wild.

Unfortunately, those who will suffer most from this philosophical nonsense will be the poor and underprivileged, those who lack the strength of mind and body to resist religious enslavement. Many of them will obey out of fear and ignorance, and as they do so they will bring increasing hardship upon themselves, increasing misery, and hopelessness. Religion is a terrible and terrifying force when it can be so abused.

The second type of Roman Catholic scientist is the one who goes right down the line with the Church and publicly says so. While I do not myself see how any scientist can square what is now known with what is written in *Humanae Vitae*, I can say that I admire this sort of Roman Catholic scientist a great deal more than one who simply ignores the encyclical. At least the former has the courage of his convictions and speaks out for them.

The third kind of Roman Catholic scientist is the one our protest petition was written to support. The following words of a Roman Catholic biologist perhaps best describes this type of person.

My first duty as a Catholic is to do what I believe is morally correct. There is no doubt in my mind that the position of the Church with respect to birth control is morally wrong. The price of doctrinaire insistence on unworkable methods of birth control is high. It contributes to misery and starvation for millions and perhaps the end of civilization as we know it. As a scientist I know that Catholic doctrine in this area is without biological foundation. It is therefore my duty, both to myself and to my Church, not just to ignore this doctrine, but to do everything within my power to change it. After all, without drastic world-wide measures for population control in the near future, there will be no Church anyway. If the Church, or for that matter, any organized religion is to survive, it must become much more humanitarian in focus. If it does, the theology will take care of itself.

As if to echo these words, and in reference to *Humanae Vitae*, another scientist writes:

Whilst respecting individual beliefs, the world can no longer afford to tolerate such undemocratic, authoritarian pronouncements which claim universal obedience. The great hope, as has been aptly shown in the past few weeks, is that people—Roman Catholics and others—are beginning to see the Roman Catholic Church for what it is—an institution concerned primarily with the maintenance of its own authority in a world it does not comprehend, and where the need to preserve the dogma of bygone centuries has priority over a concern for man.

## What Can Be Done

It is too late, of course, to prevent *Humanae Vitae*. But it is not too late to prevent at least some of the tragedy and misery which will result from it.

In matters such as foreign policy, arms control, etc., the voice of the scientific academic community has had considerable effect. The same voice can be used to good effect in this matter also. Recently, three Roman Catholic biologists, one a priest, sent a copy of the scientists' protest statement to the 150 U.S. Roman Catholic bishops and stated in their accompanying letter their own conviction that "no leader, religious or otherwise, who speaks irresponsibly, can be allowed to go unchallenged." Twenty members of the Catholic University of Washington, D.C., signed a protest statement against the encyclical as soon as it was issued. The University is currently considering whether or not to take disciplinary action; if it does so, surely some sort of censure should be attempted by the academic community, both Catholic and non-Catholic. Indeed, it is the former who should be the most concerned, because any action of a punitive nature taken against faculty members acting out of intellectual and moral conviction would make the Catholic University's claim to academic respect a laughable one and, indeed, would be a serious blow to the intellectual respectability which some Catholic universities have only recently attained. In any community pretending to be an academic one, the channels of debate must be kept open on both sides of the question; if this is done, *Humanae Vitae* will collapse on its own merits (or lack of them).

There is a strong liberalizing force now at work in the Roman Catholic Church, a force attempting to make the Church adjust to the 20th century. While the problem is an internal one, more the concern of Catholics than non-Catholics, incidents such as *Humanae Vitae*, the dictatorial methods of Washington, D.C.'s Cardinal O'Boyle in suspending those priests who protested it (methods recently supported by Pope Paul VI in a letter to O'Boyle), and other such transgressions on the rights of free men certainly offer focal points at which the non-Catholic academic community could and should lend its support.

Meetings of the American Roman Catholic bishops are usually followed by statements such as "American Roman Catholics believe . . . ," "American Roman Catholics will not support . . . ," etc. But

the situation has obviously changed for the better; on birth control and other issues, Roman Catholics are now thinking for themselves. The medieval dogmatism which characterized the Church in the past is slowly dying out; ironically, *Humanae Vitae* seems to be hastening its demise. Just this year, the Dutch Roman Catholic clergy stated that "love is the only absolute and eternal law."

*Humanae Vitae* is not based upon love; as were statements made in the past by the Church, it is based upon biological ignorance. It thus is a perversion of the very religion it claims to represent. As is stated in the last sentence of the scientists' protest statement, "The fact that this incredible document was put forth in the name of a religious figure whose teachings embodied the highest respect for the value of human dignity and life should make the situation even more repugnant to mankind."

### References

Pope Paul VI. *Humanae Vitae,* dated July 25, 1968, released to press July 29, 1968.

Fremantle, Ann (ed.). 1963. *The Papal Encyclicals in their Historical Context.* Mentor-Omega Books, New York & Toronto. This book extends only to the "Pacem in Terris" of Pope John XXIII, and thus does not contain *Humanae Vitae.* Mrs. Fremantle is a Roman Catholic and the book carries the "Nihil Obstat" of John A. Goodwine, J. C. D., Censor Librorum, and the "Imprimatur" of the late Francis Cardinal Spellman, Archbishop of New York. A full reading of encyclicals is absolutely essential before one can begin to understand the sort of reasoning behind them. As the book's title suggests, the point is made that in order to be fully appreciated, the Papal encyclicals must be read in the context of the period in which they were written. This is certainly correct, but when one realizes that both *Humanae Vitae* and Pius X's encyclical, *Lamentable Sane* (which "condemns the errors of the Modernists"), were both written in the 20th century, one's "appreciation" is apt to be of another sort. On 31 May 1954, incidentally, Pope Pius XII canonized Pius X a saint, a happening that would appear to make the future bright for Paul VI.

Getlein, Frank. 1964. *The Trouble with Catholics.* Helicon Publishers of Baltimore, Maryland & Dublin, Ireland. This book is written by a Roman Catholic layman in a delightfully humorous tone. Mr. Getlein retains his faith in the Roman Catholic Church's ability to get over what he calls "its love affair with the 13th century." (This book was written before *Humanae Vitae.*)

Ehrlich, Paul R. 1968. *The Population Bomb.* Ballantine Books, New York. This book has received wide circulation, due primarily to the interest shown in it by many natural history societies, conservation groups and ecological societies. Professor Ehrlich has been a leading figure in putting in layman terms the danger of the current population growth rate.

*Genesis*, Chapter 38. Related in this chapter is the "Sin of Onan," which the Roman Catholic Church once used to justify scripturally its opposition to birth control.

Noonan, John T., Jr. 1965. *Contraception*. Mentor-Omega Books, New York & Toronto. A well-researched book, the author traces the history of the Church's oppositon to contraception from its origins in gnosticism, stoicism, and paganism to its modern day status in the Church.

Hardin, G. 1968. Remarkable reversal of time at 41.52 N. 12.37 E. *New Sci.*, September 5, 1968. A delightful tongue-in-cheek article by biologist Garrett Hardin of the University of California, Santa Barbara, in which the author sees *Humanae Vitae* as a case of time reversal leading to scientific predictability.

152

# Growth versus the Quality of Life

Our widespread acceptance of unlimited growth
is not suited to survival on a finite planet.

J. Alan Wagar

In economics, as in most other matters, past experience provides a major basis for current decisions, even though changing circumstances may have diminished the appropriateness of such experience. Such use of "conventional wisdom" may explain our continuing emphasis on economic and other types of growth despite the many problems created by such growth.

When the United States was sparsely populated, emphasis on growth made good sense. Growth of many kinds permitted exploitation of the rich environment at an accelerating rate and provided a phenomenal increase in wealth.

Growth still increases material wealth but has a growing number of unfortunate side effects, as each of us tries to increase his own benefits within an in-creasingly crowded environment. These spillover effects, which were of minor importance when settlement was sparse and neighbors farther apart, are now of major consequence. For example, a firm may make the most money from a downtown tract of land by erecting a tall office building there. Construction of the building will add to the gross national product, and the builders will be hailed for their contribution to "progress." However, the building will add to traffic congestion, exhaust fumes, competition for parking, the need for new freeways, and social disorder. These problems, which must be handled by someone else, become part of the "environmental mess" or "urban crisis."

When this article was written, the author was leader of the Cooperative Recreation Research Unit maintained by the Intermountain Forest and Range Experiment Station, Forest Service, U.S. Department of Agriculture, in cooperation with Utah State University, Logan. Since then, he has become leader of a similar unit maintained by the Pacific Northwest Forest and Range Experiment Station in cooperation with the University of Washington, Seattle.

Too few people have recognized the connection between uncontrolled growth and our environmental ills. Growth has become so widely accepted that, in *The Costs of Economic Growth*, Mishan (*1*) found it necessary to emphasize at some length that his criticism of economic growth was to be taken seriously. Yet, because rising levels of congestion, pollution, and social and biological disorder accompany our growing material wealth, an increasing portion of what passes for progress is illusory. We face the choice either of using more of each gain to offset the problems of growth or of accepting such threats to the quality of life as smog, rising crime rates, dead fish, and vanishing species. Rather than getting full measure for our resources and toil, we seem to be on a treadmill that makes us run faster and faster just to inch forward.

Growth is not an unmixed blessing, and the purpose of this article is to argue that growth is no longer the factor we should be trying to increase.

Unfortunately, growth is as deeply entrenched in our economic thinking as rain dancing has been for some other societies. In each case there is faith that results will come indirectly if a capricious and little-understood power is propitiated. Thus, instead of concentrating directly on the goods and values we want, we emphasize growth, exploit the environment faster, and assume that good things will follow by some indirect mechanism.

From time to time, the correlation between rainfall and rain dancing must have been good enough to perpetuate the tradition. Similarly, the correlations between exploitation of the environment, growth, and progress were usually excellent in our recent past. So great have been the successes of our economic habits that they have become almost sacrosanct and are not to be challenged.

However, here in the United States as in most of the world, the relationships between people and environment have changed drastically, and past experience is no longer a reliable guide. While we rush headlong through the present with frontier-day attitudes, our runaway growth generates noxious physical and sociological by-products that threaten the very quality of our lives. Although we still seem confident that technology will solve all problems as they arise, the problems are already far ahead of us, and many are growing faster than their solutions (*2*).

We cannot return to some golden and fictionally perfect era of the past, and we certainly should extend the knowledge on which not only our comfort but our very existence depends. However, to cope with the future, we may need a fundamental reanalysis of the economic strategy that directs our application of knowledge. Instead of producing more and more to be cast sooner and sooner on our growing piles of junk, we need to concentrate on improving our total quality of life.

If environmental resources were infinite, as our behavior seems to assume, then the rate at which we created wealth would depend mainly on our rate of exploitation, which is certainly accelerated by growth. However, the idea of an unlimited environment is increasingly untenable, in spite of our growing technological capacity to develop new resources.

Boulding has beautifully contrasted the open or "cowboy" economy, where resources are considered infinite, with the closed "spaceman" economy of the future (*3*). He has pointed out that, as the earth becomes recognized as a closed space capsule with finite quantities of resources, the problem becomes one of maintaining adequate capital stocks with the least possible production and consumption (or "throughput"). However, this idea of keeping the economic plumbing full, with the least possible pressure and flow, is still almost unthinkable. Experience to the contrary is still too fresh.

## Cult of Growth

The economic boom of World War II, in contrast with the stagnation of the Great Depression, seemed to verify the Keynesian theory that abundance will follow if we keep the economy moving. As a result, continuing growth has been embraced as a cornerstone of our economy and the answer to many of our economic problems. At least for the short run, growth seems to be the answer to distribution of wealth, debt, the population explosion, unemployment, and international competition. Let us start with the distribution of wealth.

Probably no other factor has contributed as much to human strife as has discontentment or competition concerning wealth. Among individuals and nations, differences in wealth separate the "haves" from the "have-nots." The "have-nots" plot to redress the imbalance, and the "haves" fight to protect their interests and usually have the power to win. However, the precariousness of their position, if recognized, demands a more just balance. But, rather than decrease their own wealth, they find it much more comfortable to enrich the poor, both within a nation and among the nations. Only growth offers the possibility of bringing the poor up without bringing the rich down.

In our market society, the distribution of wealth has come to depend on jobholding, consumption, and, to an increasing extent, on creating dissatisfaction with last year's models. Unless this year's line of larger models can be sold, receipts will not be sufficient to pay the jobholders and assure further consumption. Inadequate demand would mean recession. We have therefore been urged: Throw something away. Stir up the economy. Buy now. And if there are two of us buying where there had been only one, wonderful! Rapid consumption and a growing economy help to distribute income and goods and have been accepted as part of "progress."

Problems of debt also seem to be answered by growth. To keep up with production, consumption may need to be on credit, or personal debt. But debt is uncomfortable. However, if we are assured that our income will grow, then we can pay off today's debt from tomorrow's expanded income. Growth (perhaps with just a little inflation) is accepted as an answer.

The same reasoning applies to corporate debt, the national debt, and the expansion of government services. As long as debt is not increasing in proportion to income, why worry? Debt is something we expect to outgrow, especially if we can keep the interest paid.

The population explosion is growth that is finally causing widespread concern. Yet many businessmen can think of nothing worse than the day our population stops growing. New citizens are the customers on which our economic growth depends. Conversely, economic growth can meet the needs of added people—if we are careful not to look beyond our borders.

Growth might also handle unemployment problems, and Myrdal (*4*) has indicated that only an expanding economy and massive retraining can incorporate our increasingly structural "underclass" into the mainstream of American life.

Finally, there is the problem of international competition. In an era when our sphere of influence and overseas sources of economic health are threatened, strength is imperative. Yet our main adversary has grown from a backward nation to a substantial industrial and military power. To counter the threat, we expect to outgrow the competition.

The evidence suggests that growth is good and that we have always grown. Isn't it reasonable to believe that we always will? This question takes us from the short run to the middle and long run.

## Dynamics of Growth

Viewed in the most general terms, growth will continue as long as there is something capable of growing and the conditions are suitable for its growth. The typical growth pattern starts slowly because growth cannot be rapid without an adequate base, be it capital, number of cells or organisms, or surfaces for crystallization. However, if other conditions are suitable, growth can proceed at a compound rate, accelerating as the base increases. But growth is eventually slowed or stopped by "limiting factors." These factors can include exhaustion of the materials needed for growth. They can also include lack of further space; the predation, disease, or parasitism encouraged by crowding; social or psychological disorganization; and concentrations of wastes or other products of growth. For example, the concentration of alcohol eventually limits the growth of yeast in wine.

Perhaps it is worth examining the U.S. economy within this frame of reference. Although its vigor has been attributed solely to free enterprise, or to democracy, or to divine grace, it fits the general growth model of a few well-adapted entities with growth potential (settlers) landing on an extremely rich and little exploited growth medium (North America).

Our settlers had, or soon acquired, the technological skills of Europe. They also had the good fortune to inherit and elaborate a political philosophy of equality, diffused power, and the right to benefit from one's own efforts. So armed, they faced a rich and nearly untouched continent. The growth we are still witnessing today is probably nothing more than the inevitable.

But the end of growth is also inevitable. In a finite environment no pattern of growth can continue forever. Sooner or later both our population growth and our economic growth must stop. The crucial questions are When? and How will it come about?

Malthus once saw food shortages as the factor that would limit population growth. At least half of the world lives with Malthusian realities, but the technological nations have so far escaped his predictions. To what extent can technology continue to remove the limiting factors? Will we use foresight and intelligence? Or will we wait until congestion, disease, social and psychological disorganization, and perhaps even hunger finally limit our growth? Perhaps there is little time to spare (5). Many factors already in operation could stop or greatly curtail the economic growth of the United States within the next 10 to 30 years. Furthermore, the multiplier effect of many economic factors could transform an apparently low-risk decline into an accelerating downward spiral. If devastating results are to be avoided, the adjustment from a rapidly growing to a much slowed economy will take time, and we should examine the problems and possibilities far enough in advance to be prepared.

## The Case for Pessimism

Some of the very problems we hope to outgrow result in part from growth. Certainly the rapid changes brought by a growing economy contribute strongly to unemployment, migration to the cities, and the uneven distribution of wealth. A great deal of our debt can also be attributed to growth, as people try to keep up with what is new. Even the population explosion may result in part from confidence that the future offers increasing abundance. By trying to inundate the problems with more growth, we may actually be intensifying the causes.

If there were no other powers in the world, technology might be sufficient to sustain our growth, replace our shortages, and keep us ahead of the problems. Boulding (6) has suggested that we may have a chance, and probably only one, to convert our environmental capital into enough knowledge so that we can henceforth live without a rich natural environment.

But we are not alone. The Communists have vowed to bury us, one way or another, and can be expected to do whatever they can to upset our applecart. We can expect competition in many places in a struggle for spheres of influence and the roots of power. The nation or bloc that can extend its influence can gain raw materials and markets and can deny them to its competitors.

It is doubtful that we can retain the hegemony enjoyed in the late 1940's, and technology cannot fully fill the breach. Our competitors have access to the same technology that we do, and, if they gain control of rich resources and markets while ours are declining, they can increase their power relative to ours.

Closely related to competition for spheres of influence are the rising nationalism and aspirations of the underdeveloped countries. Extractive economies have seldom made them wealthy, and they aspire increasingly toward industrialization. As elements in the global struggle for power, they can demand technological assistance by threatening to go elsewhere for it if refused. From their point of view, it would be rational to put their resources on the world market, to try to get enough for them to support aspirations toward technology, and to let us bid without privileged status.

The problem is compounded by rapid communication and increasing awareness by the aspiring nations that wealth and consumption are disproportionate. The United States, for example, has about 6 percent of the world's population and consumes about 40 percent of the world's annual production. Until such differences in wealth are substantially reduced, they will create constant tension and antagonism. While enduring the many frustrations and setbacks of incipient economic growth, the aspiring nations may be happy to do whatever they can to reduce our wealth. The possible effect is suggested by England's economic woes since she lost her empire and her control over vast resources and markets.

If the aspiring nations and the Communists are not enough to slow us down, perhaps our friends will add the finishing touch. Western Europe is becoming increasingly powerful as an economic bloc and will compete for many of the resources and markets we would like to have. From another quarter, we can expect increasing competition from the Japanese.

In addition to these external forces, there are processes within our own nation that could slow our rate of growth. One of them is the increasing recognition that the products of runaway growth can damage the quality of living, especially for adults who remember a different past. When our rivers are choked with sewage, our cities are choked with automobiles and smog, and our countryside is choked with suburbs, some people begin to wonder if "the good life" will be achieved through more growth and goods. When goods are so abundant and the environment so threatened, will people continue to want even more goods at the expense of environmental quality?

Even the growth promised by automation may be self-limiting. The machines used by "management" to replace "labor" are not going to engage in collective bargaining. However, labor outnumbers management at the ballot box and may well counter such threats by demanding government control of automation and the protection of jobs, even at the cost of slowing our economic growth.

We already have a rising number of permanently unemployed and unemployable people who probably threaten our domestic tranquillity far more than "have-not" nations threaten international stability. Our traditions of self-reliance seem increasingly inadequate now that jobholding depends largely on technological skills that are so much easier to acquire in some settings than in others.

In addition to such technological unemployment, Heilbroner (7) has listed three other factors that may slow our growth. The first is the extent to which we now depend on defense expenditures to maintain growth and the likelihood that these outlays will eventually stabilize. His second point is that capitalism is inherently unstable, even though the factors that caused the Great Depression are now better understood and largely under control. His third point concerns the size of government expenditures that might be needed for anti-recession policy in the future. If investments in plant, equipment, and construction are all low in 1980, he has estimated that government expenditures of $50 to $75 billion per year may be required to maintain growth and that Congress may well balk at such appropriations.

Another factor that could slow growth was suggested by Brown (8). Growth can be slowed by the increasing amount of energy and organization required for subsequent units of output from resources of decreasing richness. So far, as we have used up the richest mineral resources, improved technology, imports, newly located deposits, and the redefinition of resources have

kept us ahead of the problem. But, if the difficulty of extracting essential materials from the environment should ever happen to increase more rapidly than our technological efficiency, our economy could become static and then decline.

Perhaps of greater importance, Brown predicted that the level of organization needed for a very populous society would become so interdependent that failure at one point could trigger failures elsewhere until a chain reaction led to total collapse. In relation to his prediction, the chain reaction aspects of power failures in the Northeast, the Southwest, and elsewhere are sobering. Also sobering is the growing power of strikes to disrupt our economy.

As stated earlier, growth must inevitably stop, and the major uncertainties are When? and How? Despite these uncertainties, the factors examined above could limit our growth within the next few decades, and they merit careful thought. Because growth has become such an integral part of our economy, any sudden setback is greatly feared and could be disastrous. Nevertheless, transition from accelerating growth to some other economic pattern must eventually be made, and it is desirable that we make a smooth transition to something other than total collapse. Perhaps there is an acceptable alternative to growth or collapse.

## A Simplified Calculus for "The Good Life"

If we look only at the production side of economics, it is easy to visualize the average standard of living (SL) as the sum of material goods that have been produced divided by the total population (9):

$$SL = \frac{\Sigma \text{ production}}{\text{population}}$$

It follows that the average standard of living can be raised only by increasing production faster than we increase population. Quite conceivably, we could have a static or even declining population and a rising standard of living. For example, the Black Death, which decimated the population of Europe in the 14th century, has been credited with providing the surplus that kicked off the Renaissance. However, other factors are involved.

Goods often have a limited useful life and are depleted by a variety of losses. Thus, for a better computation

of the average standard of living, we can subtract the total of everything that has been lost from the total of everything that has been produced and divide this difference by the population:

$$SL = \frac{\Sigma \text{ production} - \Sigma \text{ losses}}{\text{population}}$$

The per capita share of wealth now includes antiques, the serviceable old, and the new. From this relationship it appears that we can increase the average standard of living by reducing losses as well as by increasing production. However, in our economy, production is closely related to consumption, and we face the seemingly illogical fact that we can increase the standard of living by increasing waste! Such losses as normal wear and tear, designed obsolescence, and accidents can increase consumption enough to stimulate production.

Even if we grant that technology can create and exploit new resources as needed, we must deal with the quality of living (QL) as well as the purely material standard of living. In addition to material goods, the quantity and quality of both services and experiences available to each person will be included. The model must therefore be expanded to

$$QL = \frac{\Sigma \text{ production} - \Sigma \text{ losses}}{\text{population}}$$
$$+ \frac{\text{services/time}}{\text{population}} + \frac{\text{experiences/time}}{\text{population}}$$

As material comforts increase, it is likely that "the good life" will be defined to a greater degree by services. And, as services become more abundant, the emphasis may shift toward experiences. Services may well increase in abundance and excellence with continued growth. The quantity of experiences may also increase. However, the quality of many experiences is likely to decline, especially if the environment deteriorates seriously.

Our values will undoubtedly shift toward what is available, but this shift will lag enough to leave many desires for things that are remembered and cherished but no longer available. This "memory gap" between what is remembered and wanted and what is available will mean a decrease in the quality of living unless it is at least offset by new advantages. Right now, for example, how many families no longer have a "view" from their picture window because of growth? What will be the impact of added growth on activities that let the imagination run free without an overdose of organization, regulation, and spectatorship? As growth continues, how many of us will long for such things as a picnic by an unpolluted lake, fishing in a clear stream, room for a family dog, or even places to walk, ride, boat, or fly with a minimum of regulation and traffic?

In mastering the details of production and distribution we seem to forget the environmental base on which our productive forces and many enjoyable experiences depend. Even in our outdoor recreation, we still tend to emphasize access to new areas rather than management of existing areas for continued enjoyment. One wonders if the rise in our standard of living can be sustained or whether it is the result of a rising rate of exploitation of a limited and exhaustible environment. To what extent are we drawing on the capital as well as the interest of our global savings account? Can technology replace environmental capital? Can it do so in time?

We may grow into a "Brave New World" where pleasures come from happiness pills and electrodes in the brain. Conversely, we may grow into a "1984," where repressive measures are necessary to keep society from falling apart. As a third alternative, we may exhaust the resources or disrupt the organization needed for a dynamic technology and then collapse to a thin population of subsistence farmers. To find a better alternative, we may have to rethink our entire economic strategy. How can we do it?

## Some Criteria for a Future Economy

As the product of a long and often stormy evolution, our economic system is not something that can be overhauled by a few armchair critics. Yet one need not be an expert to identify some difficulties with our present system and to suggest what it ought to be doing for us. Too often we seem to view the economy as a mysterious creature operating by its own inscrutable laws and to which we humans must be subservient. Instead, we should see it as a human institution which must serve human needs as directly as possible.

Now that we are so capable of fouling our own nest, dare we assume that an "invisible hand" will somehow guide us automatically along the correct course to survival? Although modern technology can work many wonders, it can also permit enormous mistakes to be made before we have learned the consequences of our actions. Now that we are on the threshold of such things as weather modification and massive transfers of water between regions, one wonders how sure we can be of avoiding unexpected and undesirable side effects. Yet shortages induced by rapid growth may force us to act before we understand the full implications of our actions. As examples, DDT killed many fish and threatened many species of birds before we knew that it would, and some Eskimos ingested dangerous amounts of cesium-137 from what were considered harmless tests of nuclear devices. Smog alerts, epidemics of hepatitis, unemployment, riots, and other problems already demonstrate that personal greed does not necessarily aggregate to public good in a populous and highly interrelated society.

A few criteria for an ideal economy are obvious. It must provide a decent quality of living for every citizen. For the foreseeable future, it must also maintain enough national strength to prevent another nation from overwhelming us. Beyond these criteria, perhaps our major concern with any future economic system is that it not repress individual freedom any more than is inevitable because of population density and technological complexity.

Two factors seem of particular importance in maintaining individual freedom. The first is representative government. Although many voters are apathetic and poorly informed, it would be an awful and probably irreversible step to lose the power to turn an unsatisfactory government out of office by peaceful processes. Yet, as we speculate on the future, it is not difficult to imagine political instability and chaos as the electorate votes "no confidence" in the economic policies of successive governments that deal unsuccessfully with resource and environment problems. Problems resulting from population growth, worldwide as well as domestic, seem especially likely to create a serious challenge to representative government everywhere in the years ahead.

A second factor of importance to individual freedom is diffused decision-making. There is safety in a redundant system in which many suppliers estimate needs and many purchasers select among competing goods and services. Such redundancy guards against a crisis in one sector mushrooming into total collapse throughout a highly interdependent technological society. As society becomes more complex, it is unlikely that centralized decision-makers, even with the best computers, can foresee all our needs and all the effects of each decision. In addition, the centralization of decision-making is likely to decrease individual freedom.

Self-interest is also important as a strong motive force that needs to be retained in any future economy. However, in a complex society where one person's actions affect many other people, self-interest must operate within the constraints needed to guard the interests of the total society.

The market system is probably still the most effective means of maintaining the abundance, individual freedom, redundant decision-making, and self-interest we desire. However, it is less effective than it could be in achieving high levels of human benefit. For example, as we chase the rainbow of economic growth, our marketplace decisions are usually based only on the costs incurred by the individual or firm and ignore the costs borne by society in general. Thus industries have been allowed to save money by dumping their wastes, often untreated, into the atmosphere, lakes and streams, or onto the land. But the costs are borne by the public in terms of respiratory disease, dead fish, and lost amenity and recreation opportunities.

Perhaps rather subtle controls on the economy would enhance the quality of our living by forcing a consideration of *all* costs of economic activity. Included would be such social costs as air and water pollution, building surburbs on prime agricultural land, and spoiling scenic or recreation areas.

One means of bringing hidden costs into the market system would be to tax or charge the responsible party for the full costs of repairing, replacing, or cleaning up whatever was damaged by his economic activity (*10*). Water users might be required either to return water of equal quality or to pay a pollution charge. Road builders might be required to provide lands of quality and acreage equal to park lands taken for highways. Such costs would simply enter into the total allocation process. If protection of the environment were accepted as a legitimate cost of production, many abuses would simply become too expensive to perpetuate and some activities that are now profitable would become uneconomic.

A second difficulty results because marketplace decisions are usually short-run decisions that de-emphasize the future. Currently we usually discount every future benefit by assuming that it can be equated to whatever present investment would give the same value at a selected rate of interest. For example, at an interest rate of 6 percent, each dollar in benefits 50 years from now would discount to a present worth of approximately 5 cents.

Such discounting may be perfectly appropriate for decisions that can be readily reversed. However, irreversible decisions should not be based on discounting. For example, the depletion of soils, water tables, minerals, interesting species, and space and amenity values must be curbed if future generations are to have a rich life.

I am not saying that we must go "back to nature," which is clearly impossible. A technological society can live only by greatly modifying nature on much of its land. But at some point we must admit that future people are just as important as present people and that we cannot justly discount the value of their environment. Unless we use the environment responsibly, we will greatly reduce the range of opportunities and alternatives available to our descendants.

Again, some fairly subtle controls on the economy might be effective. Tax laws are already being used to encourage or discourage specific practices, and some changes in direction might become essential. For example, to accelerate the discovery and exploitation of mineral resources, we now give generous depletion allowances. However, to encourage more efficient use of such resources, we may need to institute resource depletion taxes. We might also need a space depletion tax to encourage effective use of land and to discourage our urban sprawl.

There may be some merit in a replacement tax for durable goods. By taxing people on the frequency with which they replace things, we might encourage them to make things last as long as possible and might reestablish a belief that durability means quality. This belief might in turn improve the quality of living by greatly weakening the link we have developed between waste, production, and distribution in our economic system. For example, if each automobile lasted twice as long, we could have just as many automobiles per family by producing only half as many cars. The effect could be less industrial smoke, fewer junkyards, and fewer new scars on the landscape due to mining. It could also mean that more resources, energy, and leisure would be

available for purposes other than building automobiles.

Yet, true to the assumption that man is subservient to the economic system, we hear waste defended as necessary for our prosperity. Surely we can organize our economy efficiently enough to avoid having to throw things away to have more! Are we inescapably on such a treadmill?

As we approach the "spaceman" economy suggested by Boulding, we must come into better equilibrium with the environment instead of trying to sustain the continual disequilibrium implied by our treadmill pattern of growth. We have tried to keep our economic plumbing full by increasing the pressure and flow rather than by fixing the leaks. Improved knowledge, efficiency, and durability can repair the leaks in the economic vessel that contains society's wealth, and their achievement will probably always be a desirable kind of progress. But we face enormous problems if we continue to insist that everything must grow.

First we must stop the population growth that is the major stimulus to many other kinds of growth. Thus far we have been unwilling and unable to take this step, and it seems tragic that we may reproduce ourselves back into scarcity just as we are within reach of affluence for all. Unless population growth is slowed on a worldwide basis, the "have" nations may soon face the ethical dilemma of reducing their own per capita wealth by sharing with the "have-not" nations or reverting to increasing "defense" operations to control desperate people who are trying to better their own lot.

In addition to stabilizing population levels, we need to recycle our environmental resources. For some structural purposes, we might develop reusable polymers that can be assembled, used, separated into constituents, and reassembled with minimum losses. Such materials seem well within reach of foreseeable technology and might be preferable to the problems of unscrambling and reusing alloyed metals. Human wastes should go back to agricultural lands rather than into our water supplies. Because fossil fuels will not last long if the rest of the world begins to consume them at anywhere near our own rates of consumption, much of our energy may have to come from the sun. At current levels of technology, nuclear fission and fusion may both be too dirty for widespread use. Petroleum may need to be conserved primarily for lu-

brication, with reprocessing after use, or perhaps for aircraft use where other energy sources might be too heavy.

My comments may amount to a redefinition of "progress." Too often, progress has been equated with mere growth, change, or exploitation rather than with a real improvement in the per capita quality of life. Thus a new smokestack has usually passed as progress, and the odors generated by new factories have been said to "smell like money." But getting rid of the stacks already in town may now be a more rational view of progress. Developing a smokeless process, a product that lasts longer, or a process that requires less expenditure of human energy, or something that makes life more meaningful—all these may better qualify as progress.

In its time the treadmill pattern of growth was progress enough and served us well. But as the relationships change between human numbers and the total environment, we must abandon unregulated growth before it strangles us.

The essential tasks ahead are to stabilize human population levels and to learn to recycle as much of our material abundance as possible. Ideally, the change to new ways would be by incremental, evolutionary, and perhaps experimental steps, although some writers believe an incremental approach may not work (11). But if steps of some kind are not started soon, they may well be outrun by the pace of events. Unless we can slow the treadmill on which we have been running faster and faster, we may stumble—and find ourselves flung irretrievably into disaster.

### References and Notes

1. E. J. Mishan, *The Costs of Economic Growth* (Praeger, New York, 1967).
2. Although we have generally assumed our well-being to be a linear function of total size ($X$), it has turned out to be the curvilinear function $Y = a + bX - cX^n$, where $n$ is greater than 1. Thus at some point we can expect added growth to decrease our wellbeing rather than add to it.
3. K. E. Boulding, in *Environmental Quality in a Growing Economy*, H. Jarrett, Ed. (Resources for the Future, Washington, D.C., 1966), pp. 9–10.
4. G. Myrdal, *Challenge to Affluence* (Pantheon, New York, 1963).
5. For a summary of threats to our survival, see J. Platt, *Science* 166, 1115 (1969).
6. K. E. Boulding, in *Future Environments of North America*, F. F. Darling and J. P. Milton, Eds. (Natural History, Garden City, N.Y., 1966), p. 234.
7. R. L. Heilbroner, *The Future as History* (Grove Press, New York, 1959), pp. 136–140.
8. H. Brown, *The Challenge of Man's Future* (Viking, New York, 1954), pp. 222–225.
9. To be precise, we should exclude production used to replace capital goods. However, the general logic of this analysis does not depend on such refinement.
10. M. M. Gaffney, *Bull. At. Sci.* 21 (6), 20 (1965); A. V. Kneese, *Pap. Proc. Reg. Sci. Ass.* 11, 231 (1963).
11. B. L. Crowe, *Science* 166, 1103 (1969).

# Can We Prepare for Famine?

## A Social Scientist's View

### E. James Archer

Since the writings of Malthus, we have heard that the growth of the world's population will outstrip our ability to feed that population. Almost as frequently we have heard from the optimists that in view of our great technological advances "something will turn up" to prove Malthus wrong. Perhaps the optimists will be correct, but on the chance that they will be wrong, it might be prudent to consider some alternatives.

With increasing frequency we are reminded of our exploding population and our much slower progress in increasing our food production. If one were an optimist, he would dismiss the prediction of widespread famine, but if one were more cautious, he would look at the evidence which has prompted Paddock and Paddock to write the book, *Famine 1975! America's Decision: Who Will Survive* and the President's Science Advisory Committee (PSAC) to issue a three-volume report entitled, "The World Food Problem."

The Paddock and Paddock book concentrates on the exploding population. It points out four principal population dynamics and several false hopes for controlling the population growth. I would like to identify these four population dynamics and some of the false hopes:[1]

### 1. The Death Rate

Most people think that the population explosion is due to an *increased*

A paper presented at the Midwest Conference on Graduate Study and Research, March 26, 1968, Chicago, Ill. The author is a Professor of Psychology at the University of Colorado, Boulder.

[1] Except where noted all quotes are from Paddock and Paddock.

birth rate, i.e., number of births per 1000 people. This is a gross oversimplification. As Robert Cook, the president of the Population Reference Bureau said, "We've been trying for years to get people interested in death rates, to get people to understand that the 'explosion' is due primarily to falling death rates and not to changing birth rates."

The relationship is quite simple: *Only* live people have babies and live people *do* have babies. The more people you save from death due to typhoid, cholera, diphtheria, smallpox, malaria, and bubonic plague, the more people will be around to have babies.

In many underdeveloped countries the death rate has been cut in half since World War II. The relationship between death rate and population explosion is nicely illustrated by the following observation, "If by 1975 the death rate in Guatemala fell somewhere near the 1950 United States level (9.6) — a not unlikely development — this alone would increase the number of women reaching the beginning of the child-bearing period by 36 percent and the number at the end of the child-bearing period by 85 percent."

### 2. The Younger Generation

Nearly one-half of all the people in the underdeveloped countries are under the age of 15. Young people marry and married people have babies. One statistical prediction presents the case: by 1975 there will be 60% more marriages formed in Latin America than in 1960. Sixty per cent more marriages formed in 1975 will mean 60% more babies in 1976. Again, it is not the

birth rate, i.e., births per 1000 population, which accounts for the explosion, rather there are just more people in the child-bearing ages.

### 3. The Birth Rate

For many years it was thought that a birth rate of 45 per thousand was the physiological maximum. This figure was based on the observation that of 1000 people 500 will be women. Of that number, 410 were either too old or too young or sterile. Of the remaining 90, we could find another 45 who were pregnant or who just had a child and had not had time to conceive and deliver another child. However, with a shift to a lower average age (Population Dynamic Number Two) we find a few instances of birth rates exceeding the "classical limit" of 45/1000. For example, in 1963, Costa Rica had a birth rate of 50.2/1000.

We also see an interaction of some of these Population Dynamics in that those techniques which lower the death rate generally also improve the health of the individual and people who are both young *and* healthy, are more fertile, have more frequent intercourse, and if a child is conceived, it is more likely to come to full term, i.e., there will be fewer miscarriages and still births.

### 4. Man's Reproductive System

"Man has been evolving and reproducing for a million years. Those who expect science to be able to find quickly a birth control method which can successfully circumvent this million years of such single-mindedness both overestimate modern science and under-

Reprinted by permission of the author and the publisher from *BioScience* 18:685–690, July 1968.

estimate the efficiency of the reproductive system which evolution has provided man."

Now the optimists will react with a list of things that will assure themselves that all is well. For example, they might cite the control of population in Japan, but that is a very special case and not applicable to other areas. Specifically, Japan has a literacy rate which is so high that they don't even bother with this measure in their census taking today. In 1948 Japan showed an illiteracy level of 1.1%. In contrast, Africa's is 84% and Latin America's is about 40%. Japan also had legalized abortions in 1948. The impact of this decision is best seen in the following statistics: In 1955 there were 1.2 million abortions performed. Even assuming the higher proportion of males at birth, because these 1.2 million conceptions did not come to full term, Japan will have approximately 0.5 million *fewer* women entering the child-bearing age next year than would have occurred in the absence of the abortions which took place in 1955.

Japan has a large medical profession as compared to the underdeveloped nations. If we look at the number of inhabitants per physician ratio, we see Japan's is 900:1, but Mexico's is twice that ratio. Pakistan has a ratio of 11,000:1 and Ethiopia has 96,000:1. If you think the intrauterine device (the IUD) is the answer, you have another problem. Who will insert it?

The IUD is another false hope of avoiding widespread famine due to the exploding population. Consider these data. The designer of the most widely used IUD claims it can be inserted in 6 minutes. One well trained team even managed to insert 75 IUD's in a 3-hour session — that is one IUD insertion every 2 minutes and 24 seconds. While this sounds good, it must be recognized that 850,000 women entered the child-bearing age in India alone last year and the number will increase in succeeding years. You cannot insert IUD's fast enough.

The hope of the Pill is equally discouraging. Its use requires daily attention plus motivation. Remember also when a woman goes off the Pill, or forgets to take it regularly, her fertility is actually increased. Furthermore, because of the undesirable side-effects, the

Pill is not recommended for all women. Until a "morning after" or monthly pill is developed, the Pill as it is now known is only promising and not an answer.

Let me mention a few other hopes which the optimists cite but which also appear to be *false* hopes. We have frequently heard, and the PSAC report emphasizes this point, that what we need to do is to improve the agricultural production of the developing countries. One way to do this is to send them seeds, stock, and fertilizers; then they can raise more food to feed their exploding population and all will be well.

First, many strains of wheat and corn which do very well in the United States either perform poorly or even fail to come to seed in other climates and on other soils. You cannot export seed; you have to develop the appropriate strains and agricultural technology in the field where the grain is to grow. For example, it is estimated that corn production in Mexico has been increased about 200% by the work of the Rockefeller Foundation program. This sounds great and may seem to be the obvious solution, i.e., we export the know-how and all will be saved. There are a few hitches, however. First, half of the increased yield was due to double cropping (but getting in two growing seasons is not always possible). Second, the research program did *not* find just *the* right strain of corn to grow in Mexico. The soils, micro-climates, macro-climates, and irrigation conditions are so different in different areas that about a dozen different strains are needed — each appropriate to its growing conditions. Third, the program took 25 years. We just do not have 25 years.

Look at it this way — in the best of our agricultural research and training institutions, how long does it take you to train one plant pathologist? One geneticist? And remember, he comes from and lives in an environment that financially supports him, offers rewards for successful work, and has a supporting intellectual climate of chemists, biochemists, cell biologists, plant physiologists, biophysicists, and agricultural engineers. Finally, he has the elaborate infra-structure of an agricultural extension system to communicate his work to the point of meaningful effect — the farmer. Even if we had all of the per-

sonnel, equipment, and financial resources available, we do not have the time — no matter how many chickens sit on an egg, it still takes 21 days to hatch it. The same principle applies to successive plant breeding tests.

Some of the optimists will feel safe because man will solve his food problems by "harvesting" the sea. Paddock and Paddock point out the special relish with which the word "harvest" is used. Hoping to harvest the sea in time to avoid major famines is truly a false hope. How little we know of the sea is shown in another PSAC publication entitled "The Effective Use of the Sea," which appeared in 1966. We are a long way from ever understanding the processes of turbulence which contribute to the essential stirring of the sea. The sometimes cyclic churning action brings necessary organic material to intermediate depths to provide food for plankton, which becomes food for shrimp, which become food for larger fish, which become food for man. We do not even have a satisfactory buoy network technology to enable us to study the microclimate of the seas. If you do not understand the climate on land, you will be a poor farmer and if you don't understand the "climate" in the ocean, you will be at least as poor a harvester of the sea. How long will it take to train an oceanographer? The climate for such personnel development is nowhere comparable to that which exists for training a plant pathologist.

Even if I have not persuaded the optimists that there is cause for concern about the population explosion, I hope I have brought the matter to their attention.

Let us now look at another aspect — the world's food supply. A few years ago this country was troubled with crop surpluses. You do not hear of these anymore because they no longer exist. Whereas we used to be concerned with the cost of storing our surplus crops, we now find that we could ship one-fourth of each year's production to India alone — and that would not be enough.

The PSAC report focuses its attention on the need to improve the economic development of the developing countries so as to produce the capital to invest in improving agricultural development. The PSAC report offers

46 recommendations. It is significant, disturbingly significant, that of the 46 recommendations, only one refers specifically to the population problem.

Here is a quotation and comment on this particular recommendation: *Population and Family Planning.*

"This policy has been stated forcefully and adequately in recent messages by the President and the Panel strongly endorses these statements. Family planning should be encouraged because of the long-range needs to decrease the rate of population growth and because of its value in improving economic benefits per capita. The Panel *cautions, however, that family planning will not in itself be a solution to the world food problem,* and that family planning alone will probably not significantly reduce the problem of the food needs within the next 20 years in the developing countries. Population numbers in the developing countries will continue to increase rapidly during the next 20 years because nearly half of the present population is less than 15 years old. In spite of the fact that population control is one of the greatest problems facing mankind, there is an immediate need for increased supplies of food and better nutrition."

I disagree! First, the recommendation directs its attention at the **effect** rather than the cause. Developing countries need more food *because* of their exploding population — they would need less food if there were fewer people. Second, what is family planning? It is a decision made by a man and a woman about the size of their family. It is a decision based upon their personal wishes independent of their food supply. It is a decision based upon cultural norms as perceived by the procreating couple. For example, if Chilean couples are asked what they consider an ideal family size, they reply four children. They have no need for "planning" until they have had their fourth child. It takes very little arithmetic to see what this means in terms of population growth. *We do not need "family planning"; we need population management.* India has come to realize this problem too late and unless it adopts a proposal of compulsory sterilization of every man who has fathered two children, it will not manage its already excessive population.

Third, the PSAC report states, "In spite of the fact that population control is one of the greatest problems facing mankind, there is an immediate need for increased supplies of food and better nutrition." This, I believe, is remarkably short sighted. If we were to supply more food and improve nutrition, we would improve the health and fertility of an already mismanaged population. We would only exacerbate an already critical problem. How critical the problem is can be seen from a close-up view of Calcutta. It is so overpopulated now that 600,000 of its people sleep on the sidewalks. It is estimated that two-thirds of Calcutta goes to sleep hungry. Calcutta has a birth rate of 41 per 1000 now. Imagine the birth rate if the nutrition were improved.

The general tone of the PSAC report is best described by quoting two sections: One is just inside the cover and reads, ". . . Feed Them Also and Lift Them Up . . ."—Psalms 28:9, the other is Section 3.10.1 entitled "Why?"

In the Panel's view, the concern of this country for the hungry nations is threefold:

"1. *Humanitarian.* We should help the less fortunate simply because they need help and we are able to help them. The benefits of altruism are by no means unilateral. The challenge of a difficult task and the moral uplift that comes only from doing for others are needed to temper and balance the leisure and affluence of American life. The real successes of the Peace Corps center in the fundamentally inspired, collective aim that is exemplified in the late Albert Schweitzer's dictum, 'It is only giving that stimulates.'

"2. *Security.* Populations in the developing countries double in 18 to 27 years; 55 to 88 years are required for populations to double in developed countries. By the year 2000, if present rates of growth continue, there will be more than four times as many people in the developing countries as are in the developed nations. To avoid a threat to the peace of the world as well as to our own national security, we cannot afford to be too little and too late with our development assistance. The expectations of the poor are demanding fulfillment. It is to be hoped that some measure of their ambitions can be realized by peaceful means."

(I must interrupt here and challenge the logic of this statement. It assumes that the population increase *will* take place and we should prepare to feed that increased population. It even seems to imply that an ever-increasing population for us in the United States is both inevitable and may be even desirable. It implies that our security is tied to the *number* of people we have rather than the quality of the life future generations live. It is remarkably condescending since it implies that those countries which are now "developing" will still be only developing in the year 2000, they will still be poor and we hope "some measure of their ambition can be realized.")

Continuing with the Panel's reasons for our improving the world's food supply, we have the third and most disturbing reason.

"3. *A Better Tomorrow for Us, Too.* This is a long-range goal, an economic reason for investment. An important way to expand our own economy in the future will be through further specialization and trade. As nations develop, they become trading nations and through trade, both parties to a transaction benefit. Trading partners are likely to be peaceful protagonists."

This *reason* sounds disturbingly like economic exploitation or it can easily be so interpreted by others. I suggest that we are less in need of a study of "The World Food Problem" with the PSAC orientation than we are in need of a study of "The World Population Problem" with an orientation which recognizes that this world has a finite size. We must recognize that the world's population may have already exceeded the allowable limits and, finally, that if man is going to live in an environment of high quality, he must learn to be a part of his environment — interacting with it and not just consuming and in some cases destroying it.

When we speak of the population explosion, we usually imply some other nation's explosion, but we had better start looking at our own population. Unless we can demonstrate that we can manage our own population, we can hardly hope to have others manage theirs. Why should they? The population of the United States has increased from 130 million in 1930 to over 200 million in 1967. The day the census clock ticked off the 200 millionth U.S. citizen, the President celebrated the event with a speech. He might well have used the occasion to ask, "Where are we going?" This is an increase of over 70 million in less than 37 years. With this enormous growth we have polluted our air, streams, lakes, and sea shores to a degree that in some cases they have been irreparably spoiled. We are consuming natural resources faster than they can be replaced and we are putting impossible pressures on our recreational and cultural facilities. Ecologically, we seem hell-bent on creating as degraded an environment as possible for those future generations who might survive us and we seem equally motivated to make sure that that future population is enormous.

What can we do about this problem? First, we need to decide if we want to do something about the problem. If you are a confirmed optimist then there is no problem. If, however, you have been persuaded that we have a problem, I suggest we decide to do something about it. *That* is the first step.

Secondly, I suggest that the universities are in the best position to deal with the problem. Just as some universities in the United States formed the University Corporation for Atmospheric Research (UCAR) to operate the National Center for Atmospheric Research (NCAR), so also could we establish a National Center for Population Studies. Such a Center could develop at least three major programs. One of these programs would be in the field of public information; the second would be in research on the biological, social, and humanistic problems; the third would serve as a legislative reference service.

The first would deal with public information. Here I see a very critical problem. The solution to the long-range problem of population management will depend on an informed and concerned public. Unless the majority of people in this country are convinced that there is a problem and that we can and should do something about it, there will be little hope of success. I would suggest that the Public Information Program of the Center could produce a series of television documentaries which would present the scope of the problem as it now exists and what would seem to be

realistic predictions. As a starter, the producer of the documentaries could even consider televising the Paddock and Paddock book. I suggest television as the medium of communication to the public since this is the medium which will bring the information to the public. Few of my colleagues even know of Paddock and Paddock and, I suspect, fewer still have read the exchanges of letters on this general problem which recently have appeared in *Science*. Unfortunately, the average citizen is even less likely to be aware of the problem and the prediction of the future. I believe a series of televised documentaries could correct this lack of information and understandable lack of public concern.

Unfortunately, the task of educating the public will be difficult and the difficulties are compounded by such TV programs as the recent NBC television special entitled "Feeding the Billions" (Frank McGee, Friday, February 23, 1968). This hour-long program spent the first 53 minutes on the many pilot programs underway for developing synthetic foods, improving marine aquaculture, and fresh-water fish farming. Only in the last 7 minutes did we get to hear from Drs. James Bonner and Harrison Brown of Cal Tech that we faced unavoidable famines and that our synthetic food production technology, our fertilizer plant projects in underdeveloped countries, and our "harvesting" from the sea would take more time than we had available.

Curiously, many people who were interviewed on that NBC Special freely admitted that we were coming up with too little and it would be too late, but the commentator smoothed over these rough spots with heavy doses of optimism.

The research programs of the Center would need to be quite diversified. In the *biological* research programs some effort might be directed to the general problems of contraception, but since other agencies are already providing considerable support in this area, it might be better to look at population genetic problems, especially behavioral genetics. As you know, whenever you impose any bias or limitation on procreation of a population, you will produce a pattern of changes as that population reproduces. Some of these changes in

blood chemistry are reasonably easy to recognize. Some of the behavioral changes are less easily identified, however. For example, how a man or woman reacts to stress will be determined by many variables and one of these is genetic makeup. Unfortunately, the nature of the inheritance is not as simple as brown eyes are dominant over blue eyes. The genetic characteristic which is transmitted provides a disposition of the individual to react in a particular way *if* the social situation is appropriate and if the individual has not already learned some counter-reaction to stress. In short, the variables in behavioral genetics are at once more complex, show a greater degree of interaction, and are more important for the high quality survival of future generations than brown eyes are dominant over blue eyes.

For the social research programs, we have many problems to consider. Many of them deal with attitude assessment and attitude change. The following questions indicate the scope of appropriate research programs that need to be considered by social scientists. What are the factors which account for family size preference? How do these factors operate to determine family size? What can be done to modify the effect of these factors? What will be the secondary repercussions of modifying family size? For example, if the size of the school age population would become much more predictable, providing for educational facilities could be done with greater reliability. If the school boards and state legislators knew the size of the school age population in 1980, 1990, and 2000, they could better plan expenditures for education and would have less reluctance in doing so.

There are very serious problems to consider in the field of race relations. A population management program could easily be misinterpreted as a poorly disguised program of race extermination. In fact, if population management controls were applied differentially to the races, it *would* be a form of prenatal genocide. There would be many problems in "selling" a population management program, but if the people were informed, I am hopeful that they would demand such a program.

It is unfortunate that my discipline

of psychology has not made greater efforts to study the factors which make for a human environment of high quality. Some of our research is far removed from this very critical problem. The factors which promote or inhibit the acquisition of a conditioned eyeblink are interesting, but knowledge of factors which will better enable man to resolve conflicts is more important. Discovering the factors which interfere with the learning of a list of nonsense syllables can be challenging, but determining the changes in human relations which result from commuting to work in a dirty, smelly, crowded, and noisy subway will be more important for both our survival as a species and our development as humane human beings.

Psychology, sociology, and anthropology should rise to the occasion and study human development under different environments. It is interesting to know of the warlike ways of the Mayutecs in Amazon country, but what are the factors in ghettos in our big cities which make for warlike subcultures?

The field of urban planning has assumed new prominence in the past few years because of our growing concern with the city and its core which is frequently found to be deteriorating. There is little evidence of an interest in building cities which strive to attain environments of high quality. While it is true that expediting the flow of traffic through or around a city adds a measure of pleasure, consider the ugliness that surrounds you as you come down the Kennedy Expressway from O'Hare Airport. It is an ugliness which overwhelms the visitor; but worst of all, the citizen of Chicago adapts to it (he has to), and he becomes insensitive to it. That insensitivity enables him to tolerate the ugliness of visual and auditory and olfactory noise which he finds in the Loop and many, many other parts of this and other cities. (I feel I can criticize Chicago's ugliness since I was born and raised here.)

Humanists frequently refer to the sanctity and dignity of each human individual — but what are they doing about it? What efforts are they making to assure that dignity? What efforts are they making to prevent man from sinking to a caged animal existence in the cities where the effects of our ever increasing population are so sharply seen? Could not the humanists and the behavioral scientists study the problem of determining maximum population density? Or more precisely, do we not need to formulate the relationship between population density and availability of recreational and cultural facilities which will contribute to a human environment of high quality?

My point is that the humanists have limited themselves to academia or to showplace cultural centers; the humanities have had pitifully little impact on man and his development of his environment. As we start to consider the kind of environment we want to live in, the humanities must play a more significant role than they have in the past. The humanities need to become a force in shaping our future, making the most of what has been and can be man's best efforts.

A National Center for Population Studies would employ the best available biological and social scientists and humanists. The latter two fields would be especially critical because the problems is *not* just a biological problem but rather one of social and cultural change.

We urgently need our most able humanists to turn their attention to the questions of the human environment. The humanists need to consider how and to what degree we can change our morality, as change we must, and still remain humane; they need to consider how we can make each man and woman aware of his role in a society without also destroying the qualities of individuality we hold so dear (and which in fact are essential to the continued development and improvement of our human environment); they need to participate in the planning of a human environment of the highest quality. Traditionally, humanists have been concerned with evaluating man's past and their occasional anticipations of the future have been deemed utopian. We live in a time when their function has become essential and utterly practical — man will not adjust biologically until his spirit demands it. We are in a time when the wisdom of the past should be used to divine man's future.

The third very important functional program of my proposed National Center for Population Studies would be a legislative reference program. There is going to be a need for appropriate state and federal legislation in many areas of population management. For example, last year the Legislature of the State of Colorado passed a "liberalized" abortion law. The law was not meant to manage our population, but it is a start in changing attitudes toward an even greater acceptance of abortion as a form of population control. It is only relatively liberal but is far ahead of anything like it in other states. If and when other states want to consider such legislation, they need not only a copy of the Colorado bill but they will need to know of its successes and its failures. In addition, they will want to know what has been tried or is being considered in other states and countries.

Your first reaction may be that *we* could never legislate how many children someone has, but this is not true. We actually pay a bonus to people for having children. Every April 15th you may discount $600 from your taxable income for each child you have. While the concept of a bonus may not have been intended, this is the effect.

Finally, I have deliberately chosen to restrict my proposal to a *National* Center rather than try for an *International* one. I am not being a provincial or an isolationist. I think our best contribution is not exporting foodstuffs to underdeveloped countries or even fighting wars in which they themselves do not believe. Rather, I think we should take a page from the Department of Housing and Urban Development approach which is trying to develop "model cities." We should try to develop a "model country" where overcrowding, pollution of all sorts, and inhumanity toward one another is eliminated. The forced regulation of the lives of other people is imperialism. We will best serve a better world by showing leadership in developing a society worthy of emulation. We certainly cannot lead in any effective way if our own strength is sapped away while we "help" others.

I think that Paddock and Paddock are right when they conclude that there are some underdeveloped countries which are making so little progress in population control and so little progress in increased agricultural production that we cannot help them to avoid widespread famine without destroying our own society. Paddock and Paddock go so far as to suggest that the under-developed countries need to be divided into three groups: They draw the analogy of triage.

" 'Triage' is a term used in military medicine. It is defined as the assigning of priority of treatment to the wounded brought to a battlefield hospital in a time of mass casualties and limited medical facilities. The wounded are divided on the basis of three classifications:

(1) Those so seriously wounded they cannot survive regardless of the treatment given them; call these the 'can't-be-saved.'

(2) Those who can survive without treatment regardless of the pain they may be suffering; call these the 'walking wounded.'

(3) Those who can be saved by immediate medical care."

This concept can and must be applied to nations when the time of famines comes. Paddock and Paddock see the analogy as follows:

"(1) Nations in which the population growth trend has already passed the agricultural potential. This combined with inadequate leadership and other divisive factors makes catastrophic disasters inevitable. These nations form the 'can't-be-saved' group. To send food to them is to throw sand into the ocean. . . . Nor can the national interests of the United States be excluded, whether political, military, or economic. American officials when applying triage decisions and shipping out *American* food are surely justified in thinking beyond only the food requirements of the individual hungry nations. They are justified, . . . , to consider whether the survival of a specific nation will:

(a) help maintain the economic viability and relative prosperity of the United States during the time of famines.

(b) help maintain the economic stability of the world as a whole.

(c) help create a 'better world' after the troubles of the time of famines have ended."

Let me put the problem another way. At the present time we have many people demonstrating and engaging in civil disobedience because of a war they feel is immoral. It is immoral, they say, to kill one or two thousand people on both sides a week. How will they react to triage? How will they react when it has become a national policy to let a particular group of nations suffer widespread famine while we withhold food from them? Panics? Riots? What unfriendly nations will fish in troubled waters and offer military weapons including ICBMs to large starving nations to blackmail us into sharing? How will the "moralists" react then?

The question is not *"Can* we prepare for famine?" The real question is "Are we *willing* to prepare for famine?"

# ECONOMICS
## AND POPULATION GROWTH

# Birth Control for Economic Development

Reducing human fertility can raise
per capita income in less-developed countries.

Stephen Enke

There is a growing interest in the possibilities of lowering birth rates in order to raise per capita incomes in many of the less-developed countries. Described below is one economic-demographic method of assessing what reduced human fertility might contribute to increased economic development. Justifications of government programs to increase voluntary contraception are also considered (1).

In less-developed countries, one-half or more of annual increases in national output is being "swallowed" by annual increases in population, with income per head rising very slowly. Most of these countries have natural increases of from 2 percent to 3 percent a year. Hence they are doubling their populations every 35 to 23 years. This results not from rising birthrates but from falling death rates during the past 25 to 40 years—mostly attributable to improved health measures.

Some of their governments have decided that they cannot afford to wait for a spontaneous decline in fertility, resulting perhaps from more education, greater urbanization, and improved living. Instead, a few governments are

The author is manager of economic development programs at TEMPO, General Electric's Center for Advanced Studies, Santa Barbara, California.

encouraging voluntary use of contraceptives. The objective is economic development.

Many questions remain. How effective in raising incomes per head is reducing fertility as compared with other investments of resources? Could and should governments of less-developed countries encourage voluntary contraception?

## Income per Head

One measure of successful economic development is a rising income (output) per head of population (2). It is ordinarily associated with other indicators of increasing welfare such as greater annual investment. Another measure is fewer people living in poverty.

Income (output) per head is a ratio. Governments have sought to raise this ratio by increasing its numerator—investing in factories, dams, and highways, and the like—in order to increase the annual national output of goods and services. However, where politically feasible, governments can also raise the ratio of output per head by decreasing the denominator. A comparison of economic effectiveness can

be made of changing the denominator as well as the numerator.

In a very simple arithmetic calculation, an imaginary less-developed country may be expected, in 1980, to have a national output ($V$) of $2500 million and a population ($P$) of 12.5 million for a yearly output per head ($V/P$) of $200. The government may decide to spend an extra $2.5 million a year for 10 years starting in 1970 to raise $V/P$. It can use these funds to increase output ($\Delta V$) or to decrease population ($\Delta P$) from what they would otherwise be (3). If the significant rate of return on traditional investments is 10 percent annually, an investment of $25 million from 1970 to 1980 will yield a $\Delta V$ in 1980 of $2.5 million, so that $\Delta V/V$ is 0.1 percent, or 1 in 1000.

Alternatively, the $2.5 million per year might have been spent on birth control. If the annual cost of an adult practicing contraception is $5 (4) and the annual fertility of contraceptive users is otherwise typically 0.25 live births, then in 1980 the population (12.5 million) would be 1.25 million smaller than expected. Thus $\Delta P/P$ is 10 percent or 1 in 10.

Apparently the amount of money spent each year on birth control can be 100 times more effective in raising output per head than the amount of money spent each year on traditional productive investments—for $V\Delta P/P\Delta V$ here equals 100. Had the rate of return on investments been 20 percent annually instead of 10 percent, had the annual cost of birth control been $10 instead of $5, or had the otherwise fertility of "contraceptors" (5) been 0.125 instead of 0.25, this superior effectiveness ratio would have been 50 to 1 instead of 100 to 1. Had all three parameters been altered by a factor of two to weaken the argument, the expenditures on birth control would still appear 12.5 times more effective.

The explanation is that it costs fewer

resources to prevent a birth than to produce a person's share as a consumer in national output. Calculations of this kind do not convince everyone, however, for they exclude so many of the economic and demographic interactions that could be expected from reduced fertility (6).

## Developa: A Less-Developed Country

In order to assess the impacts of declining human fertility, a more complete economic-demographic model is needed as is applied here to a typical less-developed country named Developa. Any computer model should include at least the demographic and economic interactions shown in Fig. 1.

Specifically, the demographics involve projections of rates of mortality and fertility by age and sex, and data on the initial age and sex distribution of the less-developed country. Age and sex distributions can be calculated at 5-year intervals. Given the labor force participation coefficients by age and sex, the available labor force (L) can be computed.

The economics involve a national production function that relates number of employed workers (N), capital stock (K), and improving technology (t) to national output (V). Annual savings that increase K are related positively to V and negatively to P. An increasing K not only raises output per worker but reduces the surplus labor ratio (L/N).

A frequently used national production function is of the type

$$\log V = \log z + n \log N + k \log K + y \log (1 + t)$$

where V, N, and K are defined as above, z converts for units, y is years, and n and k are so-called output elasticities of labor and capital respectively. Thus, if n is 0.5, a 10-percent increase in N will occasion a 5-percent increase in V. In this formulation t is an annually compounded shift factor that increases the productivity of labor and capital by the same multiplier.

In such a model the demographics affect the economics through a changing age distribution. Declining fertilities reduce the ratio of children (who consume but do not produce) to workage adults (who do produce when employed with enough capital). Also more is saved and invested from a given V when P is smaller (7).

Let us consider a nonexistent nation

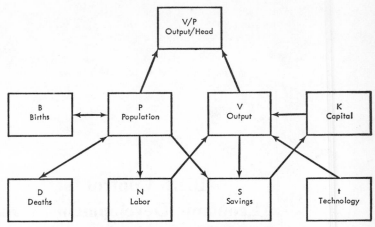

Fig. 1. Population and output per head.

called Developa with the attributes typical of a less-developed country which has, in 1970, a population of 10 million and an income per head of $150. The crude birthrate is 44 per 1000 a year. When this model is used, what are the economic consequences of alternative fertility projections, given various parameters? Only two conditions are considered for fertility. When fertility is high the gross reproduction rate is 3.025 throughout (8). When fertility is low the gross reproduction rate falls from 3.025 in 1970 to 1.95 in 1985 and 1.48 in A.D. 2000. (The crude birthrate falls from 44 to 31 and 26, respectively.) Life expectancy at birth increases slowly from 53.4 years in 1970 to 56.6 in 1985 and 59.0 in A.D. 2000.

The consequences of these contrasting projections for fertility over 30 years are shown in Table 1, starting with 1970 as a common base, for 1985 and A.D. 2000 (9). In both cases there is an improvement in output per head because of increasing capital per worker and contributions from improving technology—the latter compounding to 1.56 over the 30 years. However, when fertility is high, annual V/P increases only 1.63 times to $245, whereas when fertility is low it increases 2.36 times to $354 by A.D. 2000.

The number of persons living in "poverty"—defined arbitrarily as the state of being able to afford not more than $75 worth of goods and services a year—hardly changes when fertility is high. Saving-from-income increases nationally from 6.6 percent in 1970 to 18.1 percent by A.D. 2000 when fertility is low. The capital per worker

Table 1. Declining fertility for economic development.

| Item | 1970 | 1985 | | 2000 | |
|---|---|---|---|---|---|
| | | High fertility | Low fertility | High fertility | Low fertility |
| P, population (10⁶) | 10.0 | 15.9 | 14.1 | 25.9 | 18.1 |
| V, output ($10⁹) | 1.50 | 2.92 | 2.99 | 6.33 | 6.43 |
| V/P, income per head ($) | 150 | 183 | 212 | 245 | 354 |
| L, available labor (10⁶) | 3.86 | 6.09 | 6.09 | 9.77 | 8.66 |
| N, employed labor (10⁶) | 3.28 | 5.41 | 5.49 | 9.01 | 8.26 |
| Unemployment rate (%) | 15.0 | 11.2 | 9.8 | 7.8 | 4.6 |
| K, capital stock ($10⁹) | 3.50 | 6.08 | 6.39 | 14.2 | 16.7 |
| K/N, capital per worker ($) | 1066 | 1126 | 1165 | 1572 | 2023 |
| SV, savings from income (%) | 6.60 | 10.3 | 12.3 | 14.5 | 18.1 |
| Earnings per worker ($) | 228 | 270 | 273 | 352 | 389 |
| Return on capital (%) | 15.0 | 16.8 | 16.4 | 15.7 | 13.5 |
| Children/population (%) | 40.4 | 44.5 | 37.4 | 51.9 | 30.6 |
| Dependency rate* (%) | 88.8 | 90.8 | 68.9 | 92.8 | 54.4 |
| Living in "poverty"† (10⁶) | 2.50 | 2.53 | 1.45 | 2.20 | 1.18 |

* Young and aged divided by work-age population.    † Personal income of less than $75 per year.

increases from \$1066 to \$2023. Hence in A.D. 2000 a worker earns \$389 a year with low fertility as against \$228 in 1970.

These various estimates are only suggestive. Their exact magnitudes are unimportant. What is significant is that combinations of alternative parameters indicate that declining fertility rates do contribute to economic welfare (10). The absolute population size does not matter as much as the population growth rate. If a population doubles in 25 years, it does not mean that output will also double in that period. The labor force may double, but not all may be employed as productively if there is not a doubling of capital. Twice as much labor and capital will not double output if there is a scarcity of equally useful land. Were it not for a slow improvement in technology, most rapidly growing populations would be hard put to raise their per capita incomes (11).

Conversely, a slowing rate of population growth accords more economic benefits than a slow growth rate, and hence part of the former's gains cannot last beyond a few decades. As fertility rates decline, the ratio of unproductive children to work-age population declines substantially. With low fertility in Developa, this ratio decreases from 0.83 in 1970 to 0.49 in A.D. 2000. With high fertility the ratio rises from 0.83 to 0.87. Fewer children per family give each family member more potential consumption from the same family income. But actual consumption should rise less than potential consumption. The difference is "released" for investment.

With low fertility Developa can have a population of 18.1 million by A.D. 2000. Table 2 indicates what would happen if its leaders for some reason wanted this same population sooner, by 1989 instead, and so encouraged a continuation of the high-fertility rates of 1970. In 1989 $V/P$ is \$197 instead of \$354 in A.D. 2000 and $S/V$ is 11.5 percent instead of 18.1 percent. A worker's average annual earnings are \$287 instead of \$389. The ratio of the sum of the young and old dependents to the number in the work-age population is 0.914 instead of 0.554. Technology has had only 19 years instead of 30 years to make its contribution. This comparison at the same population size indicates that a slower population growth favors economic welfare.

## Costs and Benefits

The stipulated decline in fertility might be due entirely to increased use of contraceptives. It should then be possible to estimate very approximately, from the reduction in births, the number of women using contraceptives and the cost in resources of their doing so. How do these costs compare with the economic benefits?

It is hazardous to estimate the number of adults who must be using contraceptives in order to achieve a given birth decrement. And the cost per "contraceptor" a year is sensitive to the mix of methods used—a coil being cheaper than pills after several years, for example. Nevertheless very crude estimates of the cost for contraceptors in Developa, assuming conditions of low fertility, are that in A.D. 2000, for instance, there will be 2.8 million "contraceptors" whose use of contraceptives will cost \$14 million (12).

Estimating benefits is simpler if there is agreement on how to define them. Contraception results in a smaller population commanding more income per head because national output is little affected. It seems reasonable to ignore persons who would otherwise have been born, had it not been for contraception, and to consider only the living population. Thus Developa in A.D. 2000, with low fertility, has a population of 18.1 million and an income per head \$109 higher than it would have been without contraception. The economic "benefit," defined

as population times positive difference in income per head, in that year is \$1.97 billion.

How can benefits and costs be compared? The ratio of benefit to cost in a particular year has little meaning. In A.D. 2000 it happens to be 146, but the benefits enjoyed in that year were due to previous expenditures, whereas the costs of that same year will only bring benefits afterward. If benefits and costs are accumulated over the 30-year period, which makes a comparison more meaningful, the ratio is 82 to 1. This understates the case, for with no subsequent costs there will be benefits after A.D. 2000. Possibly significant to policy-makers with short time horizons is that the benefit-cost ratio is already 22 to 1 in the 5th year (1975).

## Extent of Program

Still in Developa, the low-fertility policy requires widespread use of contraceptives, so much so that the practicality of such a birth control program must be questioned (13).

The resource costs of the program are comparatively insignificant. From 1970 to A.D. 2000, the costs that yield \$16.6 billion of benefits are \$202 million, a figure about 0.2 percent of the accumulated national income of the 30 years. These costs per head of population range from under 20 cents in the 5th year to slightly over 75 cents in the 30th year and average about 50 cents annually.

Hence, birth-control programs are not a serious rival for funds. Most less-developed countries annually use for economic development resources worth approximately \$10 per capita. Even an extensive contraceptive program would leave about 95 percent of development budgets available for traditional spending (14).

The real question is not adequacy of funds, or even of specific resources such as paramedics and clinics eventually, but whether enough women and men will voluntarily practice effective contraception. Under a policy of low fertility the gross reproduction rate should decline steadily from 3.025 and is halved by A.D. 2000. In 1985 22 percent of the population between 15 and 49 years of age would have to be practicing birth control. In A.D. 2000 this group would be about 30 percent of the men and women of these ages.

Table 2. Unfavorable economic results of fast population growth (at same population).

| Item | 1989 (High fertility) | 2000 (Low fertility) |
|---|---|---|
| $P$, population ($10^6$) | 18.1 | 18.1 |
| $V$, output (\$$10^9$) | 3.57 | 6.43 |
| $V/P$, income per head (\$) | 197 | 354 |
| $L$, available labor ($10^6$) | 6.89 | 8.66 |
| $N$, employed labor ($10^6$) | 6.22 | 8.26 |
| $L-N/L$, unemployment rate (%) | 9.8 | 4.6 |
| $K$, capital stock (\$$10^9$) | 7.44 | 16.7 |
| $K/N$, capital per worker (\$) | 1196 | 2023 |
| $S/V$, savings from income (%) | 11.5 | 18.1 |
| Earnings per worker (\$) | 287 | 389 |
| Return on capital (%) | 16.8 | 13.5 |
| Children/population (%) | 44.7 | 30.6 |
| Dependency rate* (%) | 91.4 | 54.4 |
| Living in "poverty"† ($10^6$) | 2.37 | 1.18 |

* Young and aged divided by work-age population. † Personal income of less than \$75 per year.

These percentages are considerably below comparable estimates for developed countries. But they are far above anything yet achieved in any less-developed country.

A less extreme and more attainable program would reduce the gross reproduction rate from 3.025 in 1970 to 2.60 in 1985 and 2.25 in A.D. 2000. With medium fertility $V/P$ by A.D. 2000 is $285, compared to $245 with high fertility and $354 with low fertility. Assuming medium fertility, among women and men 15 through 49 years old, necessary contraceptive users would be approximately 8 percent in 1985 and 16 percent in A.D. 2000.

How large a percentage of the relevant population will ever practice contraception voluntarily is unpredictable. Fortunately, no minimum participation is necessary to attain some benefits, with even 5 percent practicing being better than none. And clearly this percentage can be influenced by government.

## Other Ways To Hasten Development

The economic-demographic model described above demonstrates that there are other ways of raising individuals' incomes than that of reducing human fertility. If families saved and invested slightly over twice the percentage of their incomes than was assumed, the same increases in income per head would be approximated with unchanged fertility. Or, if families would innovate technological improvements a little less than twice as rapidly as supposed, about the same economic gains could be realized without birth control (15).

However, calculations of the proportionate increases in saving and technology that would give the same income increases per head as fertility reduction have no practical significance. Arithmetical equivalents are not real alternatives in this case. Families will not save and innovate more because they do not have fewer children.

If there is any association at all among progeny, savings, and innovation, it is more probably one that favors birth control. One could argue that the sort of family that chooses among alternatives, can discipline itself, and manages its affairs is likely to have fewer children, invest more savings, and innovate more improvements. The doing of one may indirectly even induce the others.

## Governmental Encouragement of Contraception

Could and should the government of a less-developed country encourage contraceptive use? Any such government could do many things to increase contraceptive practice. A government can at least have information and devices available at clinics. But it can also subsidize the retail sale of contraceptives and pay doctors to insert coils and perform vasectomies. It can pay bonuses to married women who remain nonpregnant, to "finders" who bring women to clinics for a coil insertion, and to fertile men or women who volunteer for sterilization. It can also educate and exhort through various advertising media.

A given expenditure that reduces fertility contributes so many times more to raising personal incomes than conventional development investments that a government can afford many activities if it increases the number of "contraceptors." If the percentage of adults using contraceptives remains small, despite government encouragement, at least something will have been gained. Government must then resort more exclusively to traditional investments for dams, and the like.

Many people raise the objection that promoting birth control is not a proper activity of government, arguing that whether adults do or do not have more children is their affair alone. Yet many governments encourage larger families. Some almost seem to have a policy of compulsory pregnancy and birth, with laws not only against abortion but also against furnishing contraceptive information or devices. Governments also have many programs that incidentally favor larger families —programs such as free schooling, public housing, and military conscription (which takes away the labor of sons).

A government that really wished to be neutral with regard to family size would often have not only to legalize contraceptive distribution but also to offset the incidental encouragement of fertility by social welfare programs through subsidizing birth control to some extent. Finally, if governments wish to give people more control over their lives, public health programs should not only reduce the risks of premature death but also the risks of unwanted progeny (16).

## Summary

Most less-developed countries have population increases approaching 3 percent a year. Death rates have fallen dramatically in the past several decades, but annual birthrates remain at around 4 percent of population. Income per head is rising slowly.

Enough is known about the main parameters that a demographic-economic computer model can be used to assess the effects of declining fertility rates on various indices of economic welfare in a typical less-developed country. Thus halving in 30 years a 3.025 gross rate of reproduction results in income per head increasing 3.0 percent a year instead of 1.7 percent a year with no fertility change. Halving fertility also results in a third more capital per worker after 30 years.

A large birth-control program might directly cost about $5 a year per "acceptor." About 25 percent of the population aged 15 through 49 would have to practice contraception on an average to halve the gross reproduction rate in 30 years. During this period the total cost might be roughly $200 million for a less-developed country that started with a population of 10 million. Accumulated benefits could be $16 billion. The benefit to cost ratio is roughly 80 to 1.

### References and Notes

1. Many of the ideas and calculations presented here stem from research under contract and on overhead at TEMPO, General Electric's Center for Advanced Studies, in Santa Barbara, California, where my colleagues A. De Vany, W. E. McFarland, and R. A. Zind furnished valuable assistance.
2. National income is national output except for international debt service.
3. This 10-percent rate of return is not compounded for two reasons. First, such compounding would imply that income from capital is entirely saved and invested, although it is otherwise assumed that only a small and varying fraction of income in general is saved and invested. Second, investments have a so-called "gestation period" in reality, the increment in output not commencing sometimes for several years after the investment of funds begins (for example, construction of factories). For simplicity, and because these two considerations are countervailing, they have been ignored. Their net effect if included would have favored the argument.
4. Contraceptive pills, wrapped and packaged, are now available to governments for about 25 cents a monthly cycle; distribution probably doubles this cost. Latex condoms wrapped in aluminum foil are available to governments at about $2.50 in the United States and $1.25 in Japan per gross. The new plastic condoms may be cheaper. Distribution costs through regular commercial channels could be around $0.60 per dozen. The intrauterine device costs about a penny to make and from $5 to $10 to insert (by public health doctors). In India, vasectomies are being performed at a direct cost less than $10. Direct costs per acceptor-year are sensitive to the mix of methods used and the number of years that a person uses each method. If half of all acceptors use

condoms or pills and the other half take intrauterine devices or vasectomies, over a 5-year period the direct acceptor-year cost is less than $4.
5. A "contraceptor" is a person who voluntarily accepts (uses) contraceptives.
6. The above numerical example was the basis for President Johnson's statement to the United Nations General Assembly in San Francisco that $5 spent on birth control was worth $100 used for economic development.
7. The original precursor of the model used here was described by S. Enke [*Raising Per Capita Income Through Fewer Births*, General Electric-TEMPO, Santa Barbara, Calif., 1968)].
8. The gross rate of reproduction is the number of female live births a representative woman would be expected to have if she survived to age 50.
9. In these calculations $t$ is 0.015, $n$ is 0.5, and $k$ is 0.35. That $n$ and $k$ sum to less than unity implies diminishing returns to workers and capital because of land-resource scarcity. Annual savings for investment equal 0.25 $V$ minus $35 $P$ approximately.

10. Income per head of population slightly exaggerates improvements in economic welfare when it rises because of shifts in age distribution from children to work-age adults. In equivalent consumer units a child is here 0.75 of a work-age adult. In the low-fertility case the increase in income per equivalent consumer is from $171 in 1970 to $394 in A.D. 2000.
11. S. Enke, *Quart. J. Econ.* **77**, 55 (1963).
12. Suppose the birth decrement is $X$ and the fertility rate is $y$. Then a first crude approximation of the number of "contraceptors" is $X/y$. However, there may have to be three fewer conceptions for each two births, because of abortions and miscarriages. And of every three women of fertile age, only two may be at risk of pregnancy, with the other one being either not exposed to intercourse, sterile, or already pregnant at the time. Given these ratios, these two effects cancel, leaving the $X/y$ relation. Few contraceptive methods are perfectly reliable in practice, and this may raise $X/y$ by 1.1 times. Thus, if $y$ is 0.2, for every one birth less there must be 5.5

women attempting contraception. At $5 per contraceptor a year, the cost of preventing a birth is then $27.50.
13. K. Davis, *Science* **158**, 730 (1967).
14. See S. Enke, *Econ. J.* **76**, 44 (1966).
15. S. Kuznets stressed savings and innovation as substitutes for contraception [*Proc. Amer. Philosoph. Soc.* **3** (No. 3), 170 (1967).
16. Useful readings include B. Berelson *et al.*, *Family Planning and Population Programs* (Univ. of Chicago Press, Chicago, 1966); P. Demeny, *Demography* **2**, 203 (1965); P. M. Hauser, *The Population Dilemma* (Prentice-Hall, Englewood Cliffs, N.J., 1963); E. M. Hoover and M. Perlman, *Pakistan Develop. Rev.* **6**, 545–566 (Winter 1966); G. Ohlin, *Population Control and Economic Development* (Organisation for Economic Cooperation and Development, Paris, 1967); C. Tietze, "Effectiveness, Acceptability and Safety of Modern Contraceptive Methods," *Paper No. 205* (World Population Conference, Belgrade, 1965) and *Studies in Family Planning* (occasional papers published by the Population Council, New York).

# Optimum World Population

## H. R. Hulett

The population explosion is now widely recognized as a worldwide problem. Many have attempted to calculate the ultimate supportable population of the world, with resulting numbers ranging from a few to many times the current population of about 3.5 billion (Schmidt, 1965). There is no reason to believe that such a population is optimum, unless it is assumed that it is innately desirable to have as many people as possible. On the other hand, there are many reasons why such a population would not be optimum—reasons concerned with such aspects of the quality of life as pollution, loss of open space and wildlife, overcrowding, and lowered individual allotments of food and other raw materials. It is probably impossible to come to any quantitative conclusions as to the most desirable value for any of these parameters. However, the average U.S. citizen would certainly assume that the amount and variety of food and other raw materials available to him are not greater than optimum. The ratio of current world production of these materials to current average American consumption then can be used as a rough indication of the upper limit of optimum world population at present production rates. This optimum population can increase no more rapidly than the production of these essential raw materials can increase.

## Food

Food is probably the most useful indicator of supportable population. Even at

The author is in the department of genetics, Stanford University School of Medicine, Stanford, Calif. 94305.

current levels, which over most of the world entail much lower quantity and quality than American diets, there is not enough food in many areas to provide an adequate diet for the present population (F.A.O., 1968). The picture is much darker when the American diet is used as a reference standard. We each purchased about 3200 kcal/day in 1966, probably corresponding to about 2600 kcal/day consumed (USDA, 1968). Of this 3200 kcal/day about one-third came from meat, milk, eggs, and other animal products, with the remainder, about 2100 kcal/day or $7.5 \times 10^5$ kcal/yr, directly from plants. The animal products required $750 \times 10^9$ feed units (corn equivalent pounds) or about $6.3 \times 10^6$ kcal/person/yr, so total requirement was slightly over $7 \times 10^6$ kcal/person/yr—about six times what it would have been on a strictly vegetarian diet.

The increased primary calorie requirements because of use of animal products are not strictly comparable to calories available from cropland, since much of the land used by animals for grazing is not suitable for cropland, and its produce would be wasted if it were not grazed. Some 1 billion acres are used for grazing in the United States, but its caloric yield is only equivalent to about 200 million cropland acres (Landsberg et al., 1963). There is an additional 16 million cropland acres equivalent from grazing on previously harvested fields, but about 66 million acres of cropland are included in the grazed area, giving a caloric output equivalent to that from about 150 million cropland acres from grazing areas not suitable to crops. There are a total of 465 million acres presently suitable for crops. Thus the increased yield from grazing is about one-third.

There is more grazing and cropland in the United States relative to total area than in most countries, but the ratio of the two is not far from average (Schmidt, 1965). However, let us assume optimistically that caloric output throughout the world from grazing land is equal to that from present cropland. The production of

plant crops in the world is about $1.2 \times 10^6$ kcal/person yr or about $4.2 \times 10^{15}$ kcal/yr (Schmidt, 1965). If this is doubled to include grazing by domestic animals, the total production would be less than $10^{16}$ kcal/yr, enough to provide for only about 1.2 billion people at American food standards. Other methods of calculation, based on present protein consumption in various areas, together with the efficiency of conversion of plant food by individual animal species, gives very similar results. These figures show the impossibility of lifting the rest of the world to our dietary standards without a several fold increase in world food production or a massive reduction in population.

In addition to food from the land, man utilizes some of the food in the ocean. However, the amount is relatively small—less than 1% of the total food calories and less than 4% of the total protein in the global diet (Schmidt, 1965). It may be possible to increase the harvest from the oceans in the future, but at present it has only a minimal effect on available food.

## Other Renewable Resources

The other major renewable resources are lumber and other forest products such as paper. Here again the picture is dim. On a world basis, forest reserves are probably shrinking. Total worldwide wood production in 1965 was $2.0 \times 10^9$ m³. Of this about $0.33 \times 10^9$ m³ were used in the United States (USDA, 1968; UN Statistical Yearbook, 1969). If the present cut could be maintained, it would supply a world population of a little over one billion people at the U.S. level of consumption. The energy content in the wood used, estimated at 0.65 g/cm³ of carbohydrate equivalent is about $4 \times 10^6$ cal/yr for each U.S. inhabitant, a large fraction of that utilized for food. If the energy in the wasted roots, branches, and leaves is included, the total is undoubtedly more than that used for food.

Of course the basic limitation on renewable resources is the photosynthetic process. Man tries to convert solar energy

Reprinted by permission of the author and the publisher from *BioScience* 20:160–161, February 1, 1970.

into various plant and animal products. Unfortunately, he is not yet able to attain high efficiency in the conversion. When irrigation water "makes the desert bloom," or when large-scale fertilizer applications remove natural limitations on plant food, man increases photosynthetic production. However, in many cases where agricultural crops are substituted for natural ecosystems, total photosynthesis is decreased because man keeps certain plants out of available ecological niches where they would utilize sunlight which is otherwise wasted. In addition, we take land out of production for cities and highways, vast areas of the earth have been made deserts by man's activities, and environmental pollution has drastically reduced plant growth in some areas. On balance, photosynthesis has been reduced by man.

Recent estimates of net photosynthetic production on land include about $10^{10}$ tons of carbon fixed/year (Lieth, 1963), $2.25 \times 10^{10}$ tons (Wassick, 1968), and 2.2 to $3.2 \times 10^{10}$ tons (Vallentyne, 1966). These figures correspond to between 2.5 and $10 \times 10^{10}$ tons of dry plant material as carbohydrate. With a caloric value for such material of about 4 kcal/g, this is a total conversion of about 1 to $4 \times 10^{17}$ kcal of solar energy into available plant energy. If all 3.5 billion inhabitants of the world utilized this energy for food and forest products at the same rate as U.S. citizens, from 10 to 40% of all material photosynthesized on land would be used for humans. When it is realized that most of the solar energy goes into roots, stalks, leaves, and other materials which are currently unusable by man, it is obvious that either the efficiency of photosynthesis will have to be greatly increased or some other energy source will have to be developed if the growing world population is to adopt U.S. patterns of using renewable resources.

### Nonrenewable Resources

The picture is even bleaker in terms of present production and use of many nonrenewable resources (UN Statistical Yearbook, 1969). World production of energy in 1967 was equivalent to about 5.8 billion tons of coal, that of the United States was equivalent to almost 2 billion tons. Thus, fewer than 600 million people could have used energy at the rate we did. In theory, coal, oil, and gas can be considered renewable resources since they are derived ultimately from photosynthesis. If all the material currently photosynthesized on land were burned, it would provide energy at the U.S. rates of consumption for about one to four billion people (and, of course, there would be nothing left for food). Steel consumption of the world in 1967 was 443 million tons, in the United States, about 128 million. About 700 million could have used steel at this rate. Fertilizer use in the world was 44 million tons, in the United States, about 10 million. About 900 million people could have used fertilizer at our rate. Aluminum production was 7.5 million tons, U.S. production, almost 3 million. Thus, only 500 million people could have used aluminum at the rate we did. All other mineral resources show similar ratios. The world's present industrial complex is sufficient to provide fewer than a billion people with the U.S. standard of affluence. Production of all these substances can be increased, but the increases will be slow because of the heavy capital investment required. In addition, of course, the increased production is accompanied by more rapid depletion of mineral reserves, and in many cases, by increased environmental pollution, certainly not a component of optimum conditions.

In all the areas treated, it appears that of the order of a billion people is the maximum population supportable by the present agricultural and industrial system (and the present work force) of the world at U.S. levels of affluence.

It would obviously be very difficult to produce food and raw materials at the present rate with the smaller work force consistent with a world population of about a billion people; therefore, this number is, if anything, too large to be self-supporting at U.S. affluence levels. As our technology, knowledge, and industrial and agricultural systems expand so can the optimum population, although it might be more desirable either to channel the increased production into an increased standard of living or to reduce the depletion rate of our nonrenewable resources rather than simply to produce more bodies. The differences between one billion people and the present world population is an indication of the magnitude of the problem caused by the population explosion.

### References

F.A.O.: Third World Food Survey, Freedom from Hunger Campaign, Basic Study #1, 1963; *Mon. Bull. Agr. Econ. Statist.*, **17**: 1 (#5), 1968.

Landsberg, H. H., L. L. Fischman, and I. L. Fisher. 1963. *Resources in America's Future.* The Johns Hopkins Press, Baltimore, Md.

Leith, H. 1963. The role of vegetation in the carbon dioxide content of the atmosphere, *J. Geophys. Res.*, **68**: 3887-3898. ($1.5 \times 10^{10}$ tons C exchanged, with 30% lost on short time basis through respiration and direct exchange.)

Schmidt, W. R. 1965. The planetary food potential, *Ann. N.Y. Acad. Sci.*, **118**: 647-718.

United Nations Statistical Yearbook 1968. Statistical Office of the U.N., Department of Social & Economic Affairs, New York, 1969.

U.S. Dept. of Agriculture. 1968. *Agricultural Statistics.* Govt. Printing Office, Washington, D.C.

Vallentyne, J. R. 1966. New primary production and photosynthetic efficiency in the biosphere, p. 309. In: *Primary Productivity in Aquatic Environment*, C. R. Goldman (ed.), University of California Press.

Wassink, E. C. 1968. Light energy conversion in photosynthesis and growth of plants, p. 53-66. In: *Functioning of Terrestrial Ecosystems at the Primary Production Level*, F. E. Eckhardt (ed.), UNESCO.

# A Simulation Study of Population, Education, and Income Growth in Uganda*

PHILLIPS FOSTER AND LARRY YOST

Increases in educational level tend to increase income. Higher community income in turn can enable more resources to be put into education. However, increases in population tend to spread scarce educational resources over more children, thereby inhibiting the rise in level of living that can come through increasing the educational investment in each individual. This paper analyzes for a developing economy how changes in birth and death rates affect population growth and educational and economic development. A simulation model of these demographic, educational, and economic processes, based on empirical data from the Buganda tribe in Uganda, is used to study the extent and timing of the responses. Both the method and the empirical results should have relevance for readers concerned with growth and development.

THIS STUDY attempts to clarify the relationship between population growth, expenditure on education, and economic development in an underdeveloped rural economy.

The problem was to estimate, through simulating the growth of a micro-socio-economic system a number of times, the probable impact of differential rates of population growth on the rate of growth of per capita income in a rural community in Uganda. We began with the hypothesis that over an extended period of time, such as 30 years, an inverse relationship exists between the rate of growth of rural population and the rate of growth of its per capita income. Implicit in this hypothesis was the assumption that formal education would play a crucial role in the relationship, should it exist.

A model was developed containing the economic relationships thought to be relevant to the problem. The economic model then became the basis for an econometric model which was used in simulating the behavior of the economy through time. The basic logic of the economic model used in this study borrows heavily from work by Coale and Hoover [1]. The method of simulating the growth of a population through time was suggested by Orcutt [4]. What is methodologically new in this study is the grafting of an economic model of a peasant economy to the population

* Scientific Article Number A1473 and Contribution Number 4108 of the Maryland Agricultural Experiment Station. The authors wish to express their appreciation to the Agricultural Development Council for making possible the field work for this project and to the University of Maryland Computer Science Center for underwriting most of the cost of the computer time involved.

PHILLIPS FOSTER *is professor of agricultural economics at the University of Maryland, and* LARRY YOST *is the Parkersburg area program chairman, West Virginia University Extension.*

Reprinted by permission of the authors and the publisher from *American Journal of Agricultural Economics* 51:576–591, August 1969.

simulation technique developed by Orcutt et al. The econometric model that resulted from this fusion uses a combination of the Markov Chain[1] and Monte Carlo techniques.

### General View of the Model Used

The model used in this study, diagrammed in Figure 1, has three decision-making components: demographic, educational, and income, each consisting of a set of three decision-making units—individuals, families, the community. Each unit can vary from year to year as status variables, and each participates in the operation of the model in combination with one or more sets of probabilities or functional relationships. As the decision-making components operate and interact through time, they produce outputs that in turn influence the operation and interaction of the decision-making components.

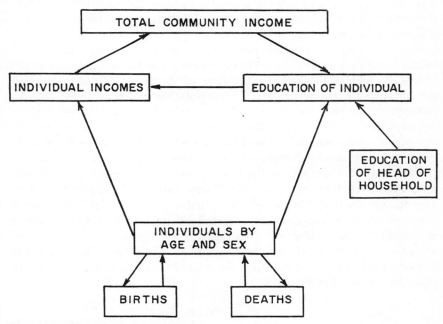

Figure 1.  Basic economic model

The demographic decision-making component contains individuals whose status varies by age, sex, marital status, and, for females, the time interval since the last child was born. Changes in age and sex take place each year as births and deaths occur. Birth rates are a function of both

---

[1] Individuals in the study community have certain probabilities of moving from one set to another from year to year, within certain constraints.

the age and sex structure of the population and of the age specific fertility rates[2] of the community. Given a set of birth probabilities, the number of births changes as the age and sex composition of the population changes. Likewise, the number of deaths is dependent upon the age and sex makeup of the population, given a fixed set of death probabilities.

The educational decision-making component uses all three decision-making units. An individual's educational level is a function of his age and sex, the education of the head of household,[3] and the total community income. The amount of money available for education, which is dependent upon the total community income, is a key constraint on the level of education. Generally, the greater the amount of money available for education, the higher is the level of education attainable in the community, and vice versa.

The income decision-making component of the model is built up from individual income and total community income. An individual's income depends on his education, age, and sex, while total community income is the sum of the individual incomes.

It is the complexity of the interactions among the components of this model through time that makes the simulation technique used appropriate to testing the hypothesis that is the focus of this paper. These interactions generated three major outputs: (1) population structure of the selected community for each year over a 30-year period; (2) annual educational achievement in the community within the estimated demographic, income, and other constraints; and (3) annual incomes in the community, given the estimated demographic, educational, and other constraints.

Each output is affected by the three decision-making units, whose characteristics vary from year to year. Those varying characteristics necessary to our econometric model are called status variables. The year-to-year operation of the model is affected by its annual outputs, such as births, deaths, marriages, etc. The decision-making units and status variables, as well as types of probabilities, functional relationships, and annual outputs used in our model as they are related to the decision-making components, are listed in Figure 2.

## The Study Community

Kako community of the Buganda tribe in Uganda was selected for this study. The area, known informally as Kako Hill [2], is located about

---

[2] The age specific fertility rate is the total number of live births per 1,000 female population of a given age cohort. This rate can be converted to the age specific birth probability by dividing it by 1,000.

[3] The educational level of the head of any household is not an independent variable, as Figure 1 suggests, but actually depends on other variables that in the past have influenced the education of the individual. These relationships are not indicated in Figure 1, however, in order to keep the diagram relatively simple.

| Decision-making component | Decision-making unit | Status variables | Examples of probabilities and/or functional relationships | Examples of annual outputs |
|---|---|---|---|---|
| Income | Individual | Age<br>Sex<br>Marital status<br>Educational level<br>Income | Income step production function | Individual income |
| | Community | Population | | |
| Demographic | Individual | Age<br>Sex<br>Marital status<br>Interval since last child | Marriage rules and constraints<br>Sexing probabilities | Births<br>Deaths<br>Family formation |
| | Community | Age specific birth rates<br>Age specific death rates | Age specific birth probabilities<br>Age specific death probabilities | |
| Education | Individual | Age<br>Sex<br>Educational level | Starting-school index<br>Staying-in-school index | School entrants<br>School leavers |
| | Family | Education of head of household | | |
| | Community | Total income<br>Proportion of community income spent on education | | Amount spent on education |

**Figure 2. Decision-making units, status variables, probabilities, functional relationships, and annual outputs as related to decision-making components**

seven miles northeast of Masaka and 70 miles southwest of Kampala, the capital of Uganda. In 1965, at the time of the field work, 1,677 persons in 423 households lived there, a base population small enough to allow a complete census of the current relevant decision-making units, status variables, and outputs, as shown in Figure 2.

Agriculture provides the economic base for Kako Hill. When the census for this study was taken, over 95 percent of its households were growing at least a few crops, and fewer than one-tenth of the working population worked off the farm. In addition, many of the off-farm occupations were closely related to agriculture. To some extent, the community was an economic enclave, with an estimated per capita income in 1965 of 596 shillings, or $84 [3].

Kako Hill has four schools (one has only grade 1; two have grades 1–8; and one, grades 9–12), with five additional schools (all offering grades 1–6) near its boundary. Residents can send their children through high school without sending them away to boarding school. At the time of our field work, over half the school-age population was in school and 18 percent of the income of the community was being spent on educating its children. The possible age range for the school population was 4 through 29 years; however, the oldest person who actually was in school at the time of the census, or who was simulated to be in school by the model, was a 25 year old person who was in graduate school in India in 1965.

580 / PHILLIPS FOSTER AND LARRY YOST

In 1965, Kako's birth rate was 38.5 per thousand people; its death rate, 21.5 per thousand; its population growth rate, 1.7 percent per year.

## Decision-Making Components of the Model

As previously indicated, there are three major groups of decision-making components in the model: demographic, income, and educational.

### Demographic component

The demographic decision-making component includes death probabilities, birth probabilities, sex probabilities for new babies, selection of women of child-bearing age, and the marriage function.

Sex and age specific death probability tables were prepared for the community from survey data, supplemented by data from the two most recent government censuses. The data in these tables showed the probability of death or of having a baby for persons in 24 age-sex categories.

During the simulation, when an individual was brought into the system for processing, his death probability was selected from the table of death probabilities depending on his age and sex. A random number generator then provided a number between zero and one. If the number was equal to or less than his death probability, he did not die, but was passed on through the other operations of the system.

The birth probabilities furnished the decision-making components that determined when a woman of child-bearing age gave birth. The associated status variables were the woman's age and years since she had her last child. The birth probabilities were calculated as follows:

$$\frac{B_{ij}}{W_{ij}} = P_{ij}$$

where

$B_{ij}$ is the number of women in age category $i$ ($i = $ 10–14, 15–19, 20–24, 25–29, 30–34, 35–39, and 40–50) and years since last child category $j$ ($j = $ 0–2, 3–5, and over 5) who gave birth to a child in 1965;

$W_{ij}$ is the total number of women in age category $i$ and years since last child category $j$ in the population in 1965; and

$P_{ij}$ is the probability that a woman in age category $i$ and years since last child category $j$ will give birth to a child.

The probabilities thus generated were used in the simulation to determine whether a woman gave birth to a child during the year under consideration. The procedure was similar to that used for the "death determination" described earlier.

The sex of each new baby was determined by the use of a sexing probability in combination with the random number generator.

The marriage function required that both the man and the woman be single before either could be considered for marriage and that the man be between 3 years younger and 12 years older than the marriageable woman. This was consistent with the marriage age customs observed during the field work.

## Income component

The step production function for income for males not in school is shown in Table 1. Other income production functions were calculated for females not in school, and for males and females in school. The method for estimating farm and off-farm income and for allocating income among individuals is discussed elsewhere [3, p. 11–28]. In the simulation, any individual ten years old or older was processed through the labor force operation. An income was selected for him from one of the income production function tables based on his age, sex, education level, and whether or not he was in school. This income figure was then added to the sum of the incomes of all individuals who had already gone through the labor force operation during that year's run. When every member of the population had been passed through the system that year, the total community income was calculated.

**Table 1. Annual incomes for males not in school[a]**

| Years of schooling of individual | Age of individual | | | | | |
|---|---|---|---|---|---|---|
| | 10–14 | 15–19 | 20–29 | 30–44 | 45–65 | 66 and over |
| 0 | 114 | 373 | 464 | 558 | 554 | 397 |
| 1–4 | 229 | 628 | 870 | 696 | 527 | 723 |
| 5–8 | 220 | 879 | 1,049 | 1,728 | 2,312 | 1,361 |
| 9–12 | 294[b] | 1,417[b] | 3,687 | 2,920 | 10,107 | 6,893[b] |
| 13 and over | — | 14,486[b] | 27,000 | 15,600 | 25,600 | 15,000 |

[a] Incomes are stated in East African shillings.
[b] Calculated by interpolation or extrapolation.

## Educational component

If an individual was between the ages of four and ten and had not yet dropped out of school, a starting-school index number was calculated for him. This index was developed from our survey data and was based on the child's age and the years of schooling of the head of his household. Field data indicated that sex does not seem to influence starting-school probabilities.

The index was calculated as follows:

$$\frac{R_{ij}}{R_{ij} + N_{ij}} = P_{ij}$$

582 / Phillips Foster and Larry Yost

where

$R_{ij}$ is the number of individuals age $i$ ($i = 4, 5, \ldots 10$) who entered school in 1965 and whose heads of households had $j$ ($j = 0$, 1–4, 5–12, and over 12) years of education,

$N_{ij}$ is the number of individuals in the population age $i$ who were not in school in 1965 and whose heads of households had $j$ years of education,

$P_{ij}$ is the index for a possible school entrant age $i$ and whose head of household had $j$ years of schooling.

A staying-in-school index was also calculated, based on field observations relating the student's age and sex and the years of education of his household head. Sex was included as a relevant factor in this index because in Uganda, a girl who reaches senior secondary school is much less likely to remain in school than a boy of the same age with similar family characteristics.

The staying-in-school index was calculated as follows:

$$\frac{R_{ij}{}^k}{R_{ij}{}^k + N_{ij}{}^k} = P_{ij}{}^k$$

where

$R_{ij}{}^k$ is the number of individuals sex $k$ ($k$=male, female,) and age $i$ ($i$ =5–7, 8–10, 11–12, 13–14, 15–16, and over 16), whose heads of household had $j$ ($j$=0, 1–4, 5–12, and over 12) years of schooling and who were in school in 1965,

$N_{ij}{}^k$ is the number of individuals sex $k$, age $i$, and whose heads of household had $j$ years of schooling who were not in school in 1965,

$P_{ij}{}^k$ is the index for an individual having the possibility of remaining in school of sex $k$, age $i$, and whose head of household had $j$ years of schooling.

During the simulation, when an individual who met the criteria for starting or staying in school came into the system, a starting-school or staying-in-school index was calculated for him. When all individuals in the population had entered the system for that year and those who met the starting-school or staying-in-school criteria had been assigned an index, they were arrayed from the individual with the highest index to the one with the lowest. Individuals were then picked from this array, one at a time, from the highest downward, until the cumulative cost of education for the individuals equalled the amount of money available for education that year. The rest of the individuals in this array either did not enter school that year (if they were potential entrants) or were dropped out of school (if they had been in school last year).

The school costs function was made up of the cost estimates for educating a student for one year in each of grades 1–21.[4] It was assumed that a few students would go on to college, some even to graduate school or professional school, and that much of their support at those levels would come from the local community in which they were brought up.

The money available for education in any year of the simulation was calculated by multiplying the total community income of the previous year by 18 percent, the proportion of community income spent annually for education.

### Population Expansion Patterns

Five alternative population expansion patterns were produced by making arbitrary changes in the birth and death probabilities. The first pattern was the result of using birth and death probabilities obtained from the field survey. The simulation production run using these probabilities had an average annual population growth rate of 2.3 percent. (This run was therefore labelled run 2.3; other runs were labelled similarly.) This average population growth rate during the 30-year simulation was higher than the growth rate at the time of the field work because of the relatively large number of females then about to move into the childbearing years (Figure 3). The age structure of the population when our simulation was begun suggests that rate of population growth spurted upwards about 15 years earlier. This could have been due as much to a drop in the infant mortality rate as to an increase in the fertility rates; whatever its cause, the demographic impact of the resulting broadly based population pyramid is evident in each of the simulation runs.[5]

In the second simulation, the death probabilities were arbitrarily lowered enough to reduce the 1965 crude death rate ten points (from 21.5 to

---

[4] There were actually 12 grades in the primary through senior secondary school levels. Higher school, college, technical school, and graduate school were considered in the study on the basis of the number of years of school beyond the twelfth grade. Since it was assumed that anyone going on to college and graduate school could finish a Ph.D. or M.D. degree in 9 years or less, 21 years or grades of schooling were assumed possible in the simulation.

[5] The age specific fertility rates for the 20–29 year old females were understandably much higher than for the other age ranges. This, plus the relatively large number of females between 0 and 14 years of age when the simulation began, caused the crude birth rate in the census year to be lower than it would have been for a more "normal" female age distribution with the same set of fertility rates. Therefore, after each simulation had progressed about six years, the relatively large number of females who were in the 0–14 age range during the survey year began moving into the 20–29 age range. The movement of a large number of women into this high birth probability range caused the birth rate to increase. With the death rate fluctuating relatively less than the birth rate, the population growth rate of each simulation began a noticeable increase after the first six years or so of simulation. After some 20 years, the original 0–14 year old cohort of females had moved through or into the 20 to 29 year range and population growth rates started to level off or recede.

182

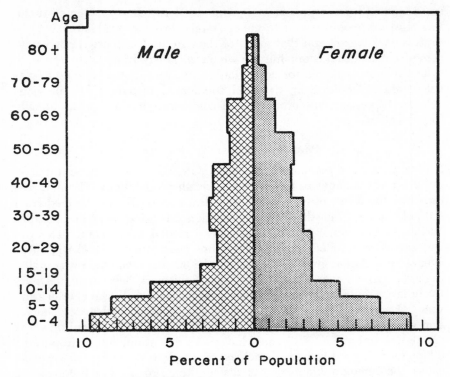

Figure 3.   Age-sex pyramid at the start of each simulation

11.5 per thousand).[6] This production run yielded an average annual population growth rate of 2.7 percent.

For the third simulation, the age specific fertility probabilities were arbitrarily lowered enough to reduce the 1965 crude birth rate 10 points (from 38.5 to 28.5 per thousand) and the death probabilities were held at the same level as in the first run. The average annual population growth rate during this 30-year run was 2.1 percent.

The fourth simulation was made using birth and death probabilities associated with base year birth and death rates of 18.5 and 11.5 per thousand, respectively; that is, the 1965 crude birth rate was lowered 20 points and the crude death rate 10 points. This run was to show the simulation output results when population was growing at a low rate. The average population growth rate resulting from this run was 1.2 percent. It should be noted that, although this was the slowest population growth rate of all

[6] With improvement in nutrition, medical facilities, and sanitation, it is probable that the Kako crude death rate will be reduced to somewhere between 10 and 15 per thousand during the next few years.

the simulations, it is still faster than the present population growth rates of Europe and the United States.

For the final simulation, fertility probabilities were increased to yield a 1965 birth rate of 51.5, and death probabilities were adjusted to yield a 1965 death rate of 11.5. These changes were made in order to give a set of birth and death probabilities that would yield a high population growth rate. This run produced a 3.7 percent annual growth rate.

These five runs provided results within a farly wide range of realistic annual population growth rates, from 1.2 to 3.7 percent.

## Results of the Simulations

The simulation technique used investigates the relationship between income growth and population growth derived from the following feedback loop: Educational level, age, and sex determine an individual's income and hence the total income of the whole group of individuals; the total community's income is allocated in a fixed proportion to producing educational services for the school age population; the amount of education provided the school age population heavily influences its income after it leaves school. The loop is thus closed. With a different set of birth and death probabilities assigned to each production run, the differential results obtained are attributable to the different ways the population grew.

Total population at the beginning of each simulation was 1,677. At the end of the five simulations, it ranged from a low of 2,379 to a high of 4,632 (Figure 4).

The dependency ratio (proportion of population under 15 years of age) of the five runs varied from 31 percent at the end of 30 years for run 1.2 to 53 percent for run 3.7 (Figure 5). At the end of the sixteenth year the spread was even greater—24 percent versus 52 percent.

All the dependency ratios, except the one associated with the fastest rate of growth of population, experienced a general depression centering roughly on year 15 of the simulation. As explained above, this occurred because the population pyramid with which the simulation began had an especially broad base. Our simulation suddenly stabilized the age specific fertility rates and the result, among the slower growing population simulation runs, was a tendency for the dependency ratio to fall as the "oversized" younger cohorts moved into older cohort status. Then as these same "over-sized" cohort groups moved into the most fertile child bearing age, they sent the birth rate back up and the dependency ratio thus began moving up again. This phenomenon is depicted clearly in Figure 6, especially in run 1.2 and run 2.1.

The average years of schooling of the community population over the 30 years continually increased for all five runs (Figure 7), but the rate of increase differed. At the end of the 30-year period, the average level

586 / Phillips Foster and Larry Yost

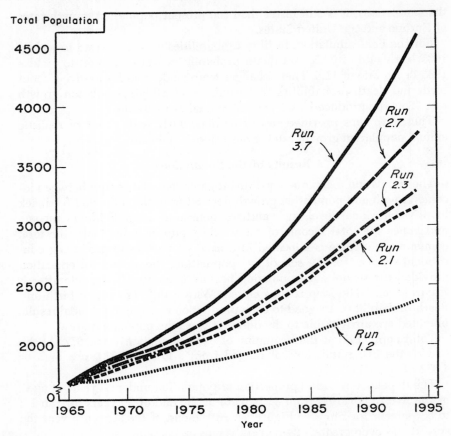

Figure 4. Total population annually for each simulation

of education ranged from a low 5 years for run 3.7 to a high of over 7 years for run 1.2. Using this data, an equation was fitted by least squares. The resulting equation was $y = 4.75 - .50x$; $(R^2 = .93)$, where

$y$ is the annual percentage increase in average educational level,[7]

---

[7] Annual percentage increase in average education level was calculated by the formula

$$PL = FL/(1 + r)n$$

where
$PL$ = present average educational level,
$FL$ = average education level in year $n$ $(n = 30)$,
$r$ = annual percentage increase in average education level, and
$n$ = number of years over which the calculation is made, i.e., years between $PL$ and $FL$.

185

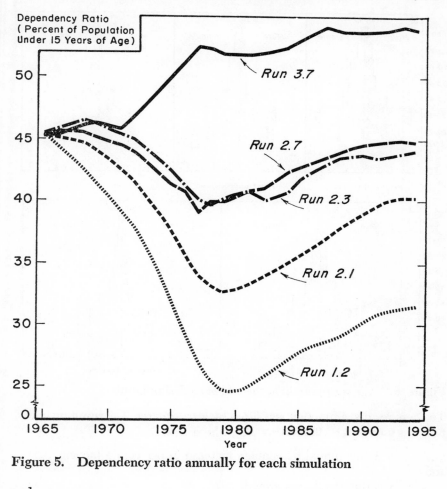

Figure 5. Dependency ratio annually for each simulation

and

$x$ is the population growth rate.

The per capita income increased during each of the five simulations (Figure 8). At the end of the 30 years, it ranged from a low in run 3.7 of 1,429 shillings to a high in run 1.2 of 2,972 shillings.

The percentage increases in annual per capita income (rate of economic development) varied from a low of 3.04 percent (run 3.7) to a high of 5.56 percent (run 1.2). Runs 2.1, 2.3, and 2.7 had increases in annual per capita incomes of 4.93 percent, 4.84 percent, and 4.85 percent respectively.[8]

---

[8] These figures were calculated by use of the formula

$$PI = FP/(1 + r)n$$

588 / PHILLIPS FOSTER AND LARRY YOST

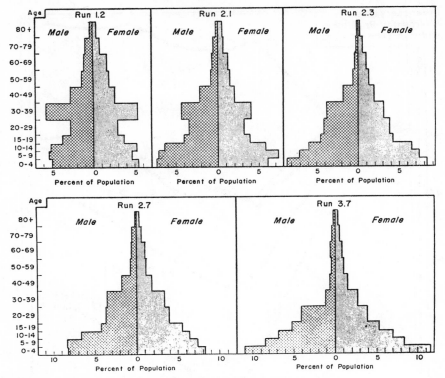

**Figure 6.** Age-sex pyramid at the end of each simulation

To these results, a function was fitted by least squares. The resulting equation was $y = 6.42 - .98x$; $(R^2 = .88)$, where

> $y$ is the annual percentage increase in per capita income,

and

> $x$ is the population growth rate.

This equation summarizes the most important finding of our study. It suggests that in Kako community in Uganda, over a 30-year period, a reduction in the rate of growth of population from, say, 3 percent annually to 2 percent will, in and of itself, increase the annual rate of growth of per capita income from 4.0 percent to 4.98 percent. Conversely, an increase in rate of growth of population from 2 percent annually to 3 per-

where

PI = per capita income in year one,
FP = per capita income in year n (n = 30),
r = percentage increase in annual per capita income, and
n = the number of years over which the calculation was made.

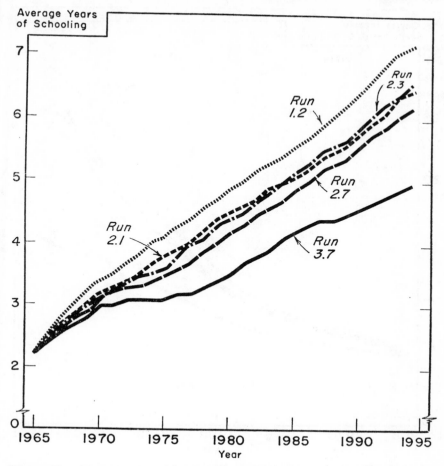

Figure 7. Average years of schooling annually for each simulation

cent annually will result in a decrease in rate of growth of per capita income from 4.98 to 4.0 percent.

Put less precisely, but perhaps more understandably, this equation suggests that, for each percentage point or fraction of a percentage point development planners can reduce the rate of growth of population in this community, they can expect an approximately equal increase in rate of growth of per capita income. Conversely, for each percentage point or fraction of a percentage point development planners allow the rate of growth of population to increase in this community, they can expect an approximately equal decrease in rate of growth of per capita income.

188

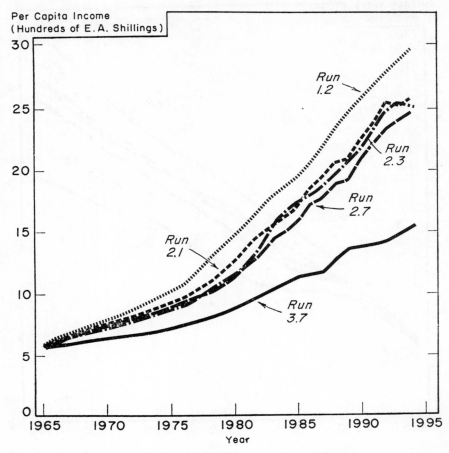

**Figure 8.   Per capita income annually for each simulation**

### Summary and Implications

Through time in Kako community in Uganda, a marked inverse relationship apparently exists between population growth rate and rate of increase in per capita income. This relationship seems to be closely associated with the inverse relationship, suggested by our simulation results, between population growth rate and the capacity of Kako community to educate its children. A high population growth rate in this community will probably be seriously deterimental to economic development, its dampening effect increasing in degree as the population growth rate increases.

The econometric model we developed to simulate our economic model through time could be used for a country or regional population on a

POPULATION, EDUCATION, AND INCOME GROWTH IN UGANDA / 591

sample basis. The results from such simulations could have even greater value to economic development planners than our present study. Furthermore, our econometric model can be altered for a number of different research interests and may thus have many possibilities for further use.

## References

[1] COALE, ANSLEY, AND EDGAR HOOVER, *Population Growth and Economic Developments in Low Income Countries—A Case Study of India's Prospects,* Princeton, Princeton University Press, 1958.

[2] FOSTER, PHILLIPS, AND LARRY YOST, *Buganda Rudimentary Sedentary Agriculture,* Maryland Agr. Exp. Sta., Misc. Pub. 590, May 1967.

[3] FOSTER, PHILLIPS, AND LARRY YOST, *Population Growth and Rural Development in Buganda,* Maryland Agr. Exp. Sta., Misc. Pub. 621, April 1968.

[4] ORCUTT, GUY H., et al., *Microanalysis of Socioeconomic Systems: A Simulation Study,* New York, Harper, 1961.

# Toward a New Economics: Questioning Growth

by Herman E. Daly

"He looked upon us as a sort of animal to whose share, by what accident he could not conjecture, some small pittance of reason had fallen, whereof we made no other use than by its assistance to aggravate our natural corruptions and to acquire new ones which nature had not given us; that we disarmed ourselves of the few abilities she had bestowed, had been very successful in multiplying our original wants, and seemed to spend our whole lives in vain endeavors to supply them by our own inventions."
Jonathan Swift.

Excerpted from an article entitled "Toward a Stationary-State Economy," in *The Patient Earth*, John Harte and Robert H. Socolow, eds., to be published by Holt, Rinehart and Winston in 1971 and printed with their permission.

Any discussion of the relative merits of a stationary, no-growth economy, and its opposite, the economy in which wealth and population are growing, must recognize some important quantitative and qualitative differences between rich and poor countries and social classes. Consider the familiar ratio of gross national product (GNP) to total population (P). This ratio, per capita annual product (GNP/P), is the measure usually employed to distinguish rich from poor countries. In spite of its many shortcomings, it does have the virtue of reflecting in one ratio the two fundamental life processes of production and reproduction. Two questions must be asked of both numerator and denominator for both rich and poor nations: namely, what is the quantitative rate of growth, and qualitatively, exactly what is it that is growing?

The rate of growth in the denominator P is much higher in poor countries. While mortality is tending to equality at low levels throughout the world, fertility in poor nations is roughly *twice* that of rich nations. No other social or economic index divides the world so clearly and consistently into "developed" and "undeveloped" as does fertility.

Qualitatively, the incremental population in poor countries consists largely of hungry illiterates, while in rich countries it consists largely of well-fed members of the middle class. The incremental person in poor countries contributes negligibly to production, but makes few demands on world resources. The incremental person in a rich country adds to his country's GNP, but his high standard of living contributes greatly to depletion of the world's resources and pollution of its spaces.

The numerator, GNP, is growing at roughly the same rate in rich and poor countries—around 4 or 5 per cent annually, with the poor countries probably growing slightly faster. Nevertheless, because of their more rapid population growth, the per capita income of poor countries is growing more slowly than that of rich countries. Consequently the gap between rich and poor widens over time.

Incremental GNP in rich and poor nations has very different qualitative significance. At some point, probably already passed in the United States, an extra unit of GNP costs more than it is worth. Extra GNP in a poor country, assuming it does not go mainly to the richest class of that country, represents satisfaction of relatively basic wants (food, clothing, shelter, basic education, etc.), while extra GNP in a rich country, assuming it does not go mainly to the poorest class, represents satisfaction of relatively trivial wants (more electric

Reprinted by permission of the author and the publisher from *Yale Alumni Magazine* 33(8):47–52, May 1970.

toothbrushes, yet another brand of cigarettes, more force-feeding through advertising, etc.).

The upshot of these differences is that for the poor, growth in GNP is probably still a good thing, while for the rich it is probably a bad thing. Growth in population, however, is a bad thing for both: for the rich because it makes growth in GNP less avoidable, and for the poor because it makes growth in GNP, and especially per capita GNP, more difficult. The following discussion is concerned exclusively with a rich, affluent-effluent economy such as that of the United States, and will seek to define more clearly the concept of a stationary-state economy, see why it is necessary, consider its economic and social implications, and finally, comment on an emerging political economy of finite wants and nongrowth.

## The Art of Getting On.

The term "stationary state" has had two quite different meanings in the history of economic thought. The original sense in which the classical economists used the term was that of an actual state of affairs toward which the real world was tending, a state in which growth in wealth and population will have ceased. The stationary state was the eschatology of political economy, the doctrine of the ultimate working out of the evolutionary forces of capitalism. The later meaning assigned to the term by the neo-classical school was that of an epistomologically useful fiction, an idealized abstraction like the frictionless machine of mechanics or the ideal gas of chemistry, which would serve as a stable analytical reference point in the study of the progressive or growing economy, but without any eschatological vision as to where the progressive economy would end. The latter sense is the one most current in economics today. However, it is the former, classical sense that is relevant to this discussion. Of course, adoption of the classical sense does not imply rejection of the neo-classical concept since the two are entirely different ideas.

This change in meaning was part of the general intellectual shift from teleology to mechanism. One cannot escape the impression that the neo-classical abstraction rose from servant to master as economists became more and more fascinated with working out all of the logical properties of this and other mechanistic abstractions and less concerned with the problems of the real world and just where "progress" was taking us. This drive towards logical purity and rigor in economic theory has cost a heavy price in terms of what Whitehead calls the "fallacy of misplaced concreteness," which "consists in neglecting the degree of abstraction involved when an actual entity is considered merely so far as it exemplifies certain [pre-selected] categories of thought."

The classical economists, on the other hand, were less rigorous, but not so prone to the fallacy of misplaced concreteness. Over a century ago John Stuart Mill, the great synthesizer of classical economics, spoke of the stationary state in words that could hardly be more pertinent today:

"It must always have been seen, more or less distinctly, by political economists, that the increase in wealth is not boundless: that at the end of what they term the progressive state lies the stationary state, that all progress in wealth is but a postponement of this, and that each step in advance is an approach to it.

"I cannot . . . regard the stationary state of capital and wealth with the unaffected aversion so generally manifested towards it by political economists of the old school. I am inclined to believe that it would be, on the whole, a very considerable improvement on our present condition. I confess I am not charmed with the ideal of life held out by those who think that the normal state of human beings is that of struggling to get on; that the trampling, crushing, elbowing, and treading on each other's heels which forms the existing type of social life, are the most desirable lot of human kind. . . . The northern and middle states of America are a specimen of this stage of civilization in very favorable circumstances . . . and all that these advantages seem to have yet done for them . . . is that the life of the whole of one sex is devoted to dollar-hunting, and of the other to breeding dollar-hunters. . . .

"I know not why it should be a matter of congratulation that persons who are already richer than anyone needs to be, should have doubled their means of consuming things which give little or no pleasure except as representative of wealth. . . . It is only in the backward countries of the world that increased production is still an important object: in those most advanced, what is economically needed is a better distribution, of which one indispensable means is a stricter restraint on population. . . . The density of population necessary to enable mankind to obtain, in the greatest degree, all the advantages both of cooperation and of social intercourse, has, in all the most populous countries, been attained. . . . It is not good for a man to be kept perforce at all times in the presence of his species. . . . Nor is there much satisfaction in contemplating the world with nothing left to the spontaneous activity of nature. . . . If the earth must lose that great portion of its pleasantness which it owes to things that the unlimited increase of wealth and population would extirpate from it, for the mere purpose of enabling it to support a larger, but not a happier or better population, I sincerely hope, for the sake of posterity, that they will be content to be stationary, long before necessity compels them to it.

"It is scarcely necessary to remark that a stationary condition of capital and population implies no stationary state of human improvement. There would be as much scope as ever for all kinds of mental culture, and moral and social progress; as much room for improving the Art of Living and much more likelihood of it being improved, when minds cease to be engrossed by the art of getting on. Even the industrial arts might be as earnestly and as successfully cultivated, with this sole difference, that instead of serving no purpose but the increase of wealth, industrial improvements would produce their legitimate effect, that of abridging labor."

The direction in which political economy has evolved in the last hundred years is not along the path suggested in the quotation. In fact, most economists are hostile to the notion of stationary state and dismiss Mill's discussion as "strongly colored by his "social views" (as if the neo-classical theories were not so colored!); "nothing so much as a prolegomenon to Galbraith's *Affluent Society*"; or "hopelessly dated." The truth of the matter, however, is that Mill is even more relevant today than in his own time.

## Discovering an Invisible Foot

Stationary state signifies a constant stock of physical wealth (capital), and a constant stock of people (population). Naturally these stocks do not remain constant by themselves. People die and wealth is physically consumed (worn out, depreciated). Therefore the stocks must be maintained by a rate of inflow (birth, production) equal to the rate of outflow (death, consumption). But this equality may obtain, and stocks remain constant, with a high rate of throughput (inflow equal to outflow) or with a low rate.

This definition of stationary state is not complete until the rates of throughput by which the constant stocks are maintained are specified. For a number of reasons the rate of throughput should be as low as possible. For an equilibrium stock the average age at "death" of its members is the reciprocal of the rate of throughput. The faster the water flows through the tank, the less time an average drop spends in the tank. For the population, a low rate of throughput (low birth and death rates) means a high life expectancy and is desirable for that reason alone—at least within limits. For the stock of wealth, a low rate of throughput (low production and low consumption) means greater life expectancy or durability of goods and less time sacrificed to production. This means more "leisure" or non-job time to be divided into consumption time, personal and household maintenance time, culture time, and idleness. This too seems socially desirable.

But to these reasons for the desirability of a low rate of maintenance throughput, must be added some reasons for the impracticability of high rates. Since matter and energy cannot be created, production inputs must be taken from the environment, leading to depletion. Since matter and energy cannot be destroyed, an equal amount of matter and energy in the form of waste must be returned to the environment, leading to pollution. Hence lower rates of throughput lead to less depletion and pollution, higher rates to more. The limits regarding what rates of depletion and pollution are tolerable must be supplied by ecology. A definite limit to the size of maintenance flows of specific materials is set by ecological thresholds that, if exceeded, cause system breaks. To keep flows below these limits we can operate on two variables: the size of the stocks and the durability of the stocks. As long as we are well below these thresholds, economic cost-benefit calculations regarding depletion and pollution can be relied upon as a guide. But as these thresholds are approached, "marginal cost" and "marginal benefits" become meaningless, and Alfred Marshall's motto, "nature does not make jumps," and most of neo-classical marginalist economics becomes inapplicable. The "marginal" cost of one more step may be to fall into the precipice.

Of the two variables, size of stocks and durability of stocks, only the second requires further clarification. Durability here means more than just how long a commodity lasts. It also includes the number of times that the waste output can be reused as input in the production of something else. Nature has furnished the ideal model of a closed-loop system of material cycles powered by the sun. To the extent that our technology can imitate nature's solar-powered closed-loop, then our stock of wealth will tend to become as durable as our water, soil, and air which are the real sources of wealth since it is only through their agency that plants are able to capture vital solar en-

49

ergy. The ideal is that *all* physical outputs should be usable either as inputs in some other man-made process, or as non-disruptive inputs into natural material cycles.

The stationary state of wealth and population is maintained by an inflow of low entropy matter-energy and an outflow of an equal quantity of high entropy matter-energy. ( Low entropy matter-energy is highly structured, organized matter and easily usable free energy. High entropy matter-energy is randomized, useless bits of matter, and latent, unusable energy.) Stocks of wealth and people feed on low entropy. Low entropy inputs are received from the environment in exchange for high entropy outputs to the environment. In this overall sense there can be no closed loop or recycling of both matter and energy because of the second law of thermodynamics. However, within the overall system there can be subsystems of individual processes arranged so that their material input-output links form a closed loop. Conceivably all processes in the stationary state could be arranged to form a material closed loop. But the recycling of matter through this closed-loop "world engine" requires energy, part of which becomes irrevocably useless as it is dissipated into heat. Actually, industrial material cycles cannot be 100 per cent closed as this would require an uneconomical, if not impossible expenditure of energy. Thus some of the high entropy output takes the form of randomized bits of matter, and some takes the form of heat. The limit to using energy to reduce material pollution is the resulting localized thermal pollution, not the very long run, universal thermodynamic heat death. Thus it is important to bear in mind that the expenditure of energy needed for recycling necessarily pollutes.

The mere expenditure of energy is not sufficient to close the material cycle, since energy must work through the agency of material implements. To recycle aluminum beer cans requires more trucks to collect the cans as well as more energy to run the trucks. More trucks require more steel, glass, etc., which require more iron ore and coal, which require still more trucks. This is the familiar web of inter-industry interdependence reflected in an input-output table.

All of these extra intermediate activities required to recycle beer cans involve some inevitable pollution as well. If we think of each industry as adding recycling to its production process, then this will generate a whole chain of direct and indirect demands on matter and energy resources that must be taken away from final demand uses and devoted to the interme-

diate activity of recycling. It will take more intermediate products and activities to support the same level of final output. The advantage of recycling is that it allows us to choose the least harmful combination of material and thermal pollution.

The classical economists thought that the stationary state would be made necessary by limits on the depletion side, but the main limits now seem to be in fact occurring on the pollution side. In effect, pollution provides another foundation for the economic law of increasing costs, but has received little attention in this regard since pollution costs are social while depletion costs are usually private. On the input side the environment is partitioned into spheres of private ownership. Depletion of the environment coincides, to some degree, with depletion of the owner's wealth, and inspires at least a minimum of stewardship. On the output side, however, the waste absorption capacity of the environment is not subject to partitioning and private ownership. Air and water are used freely by all and the result is a competitive, profligate exploitation—what biologist Garrett Hardin calls the "commons effect," what welfare economists call "external diseconomies," and what I like to call the "invisible foot."

Adam Smith's "invisible hand" leads private self-interest unwittingly to serve the common good. The "invisible foot" leads private self-interest to kick the common good to pieces. Private ownership and private use under a competitive market give rise to the invisible hand. Public ownership with unrestrained private use gives rise to the invisible foot. Public ownership with public restraint on use gives rise to the visible hand ( and foot) of the planner. Depletion has been partially restrained by the invisible hand while pollution has been encouraged by the invisible foot. It is therefore not surprising to find limits occurring mainly on the pollution side.

## Mini vs. Maxi

The economic and social implications of the stationary state are enormous and revolutionary. The physical flows of production and consumption must be *minimized, not maximized,* subject to some agreed upon minimum standard of living and population size. The central concept must be the stock of wealth, not as presently, the flow of income and consumption. (Kenneth Boulding has been making this point since 1949, but with no effect on his fellow economists.) Furthermore, the stock must not grow. The important issue of the stationary state will be distribution, not pro-

duction. The argument that everyone should be happy as long as his absolute share of the wealth increases, regardless of his relative share, will no longer be available. The arguments justifying inequality in wealth as necessary for savings, investment, and growth will lose their force. With income flows kept low, the focus will be on the distribution of the stock of wealth, not on the distribution of income. Marginal productivity theories and "justifications" pertain only to flows and therefore are not available to explain or justify the distribution of stock ownership.

It is hard to see how ethical appeals to equal shares can be countered. Also, even though physical stocks remain constant, increased income in the form of leisure will result from continued technological improvements. How will it be distributed if not according to some ethical norm of equality? The stationary state would make fewer demands on our environmental resources, but much greater demands on our moral resources. In the past a good case could be made that leaning too heavily on scarce moral resources, rather than relying on abundant self-interest, was the road to serfdom. But in an age of rockets, hydrogen bombs, cybernetics, and genetic control, there is simply no substitute for moral resources and no alternative to relying on them, whether they prove sufficient or not.

With constant physical stocks, economic growth must be in non-physical goods, particularly leisure. Taking the benefits of technological progress in the form of increased leisure is a reversal of the historical practice of taking the benefits mainly in the form of goods and has extensive social implications. In the past, economic development has increased the physical output of a day's work while the number of hours in a day has, of course, remained constant, with the result that the opportunity cost of a unit of time in terms of goods has risen. Time is worth more goods, and a good is worth less time. As time becomes more expensive in terms of goods, fewer activities are "worth the time." We become goods-rich and time-poor. Consequently we crowd more activities and more consumption into the same period of time in order to raise the return on non-work time to equalize it with the higher returns on work time, thereby maximizing the total returns to total time. This gives rise to what Staffan Linder has called the "harried leisure class."

Not only do we use work time more efficiently, but also personal consumption time, and we even try to be efficient in our sleep by attempting subconscious learning. Time-intensive activities ( friendships, care of the aged and children, meditation and reflection) are sacrificed in favor of commodity-intensive activities (consumption). At some point people will feel rich enough to afford more time-intensive activities even at the higher price. But advertising, by constantly extolling the value of commodities, postpones this point.

From an ecological view, of course, this is exactly the reverse of what is called for. What is needed is a low relative price of time in terms of commodities. Then time-intensive activities will be substituted for material-intensive activities. To become less materialistic in our habits, we must raise the relative price of matter. Keeping physical stocks constant and using technology to increase leisure time will do just that. Thus a policy of non-material growth, or leisure-only growth, in addition to being necessary for keeping physical stocks constant, has the further beneficial effect of encouraging a more generous expenditure of time and a more careful use of physical goods. A higher relative price of material-intensive goods may, at first glance, be thought to encourage their production. But material goods require material inputs, so costs as well as revenues would increase, eliminating profit incentives to expand.

In the 1930's the late Bertrand Russell proposed a policy of leisure growth rather than commodity growth and viewed the unemployment question in terms of the distribution of leisure. The following words are from his essay, "In Praise of Idleness":

"Suppose that, at a given moment, a certain number of people are engaged in the manufacture of pins. They make as many pins as the world needs, working (say) eight hours a day. Someone makes an invention by which the same number of men can make twice as many pins as before. But the world does not need twice as many pins. Pins are already so cheap that hardly any more will be bought at a lower price. In a sensible world, everybody concerned in the manufacture of pins would take to working four hours instead of eight, and everything else would go on as before. But in the actual world this would be thought demoralizing. The men still work eight hours, there are too many pins, some employers go bankrupt, and half the men previously concerned in making pins are thrown out of work. There is, in the end, just as much leisure as on the other plan, but half the men are totally idle while half are still overworked. In this way it is insured that the unavoidable leisure shall cause misery all round instead of being a universal source of happiness. Can any-

thing more insane be imagined."

In addition to this strategy of leisure-only growth, we can internalize some pollution costs by charging effluent taxes. Economic efficiency requires only that a price be placed on environmental amenities, it does not tell us who should pay the price. The producer may claim that the use of the environment to absorb waste products is a right that all organisms and firms must of necessity enjoy, and whoever wants air and water to be cleaner than it is at any given time should pay for it. Consumers may argue that the use of the environment as a source of clean inputs of air and water takes precedence over its use as a sink, and that whoever makes the environment dirtier than it otherwise would be should be the one to pay. Again the issue becomes basically one of distribution—not what the price should be, but who should pay it. The fact that the price takes the form of a tax automatically decides who should receive the price—the government. But this raises more distribution issues, and the solutions to these problems are ethical, not technical.

Another possibility of non-material growth is to redistribute wealth from the low marginal utility uses of the rich to the high marginal utility uses of the poor, thereby increasing total social utility. Joan Robinson has noted that this egalitarian implication of the law of diminishing marginal utility was "sterilized mainly by slipping from utility to physical output as the object to be maximized." As we move back from physical output to non-physical utility, the egalitarian implications become unsterilized.

Traditional Keynesian full employment policies will no longer be available to palliate the distribution question since they require growth. By allowing full employment, growth permits the old principles of distribution (income-through-jobs) to continue in effect. But with no growth in physical stocks and a policy of using technological progress to increase leisure, full-employment is no longer a workable principle of distribution. Furthermore, we add a new dimension to the distribution problem—how to distribute leisure.

A stationary population, with low birth and death rates, would imply a greater percentage of old people than in the present growing population, although hardly a geriatric society as some youth worshippers claim. Since old people do not work, the distribution problem is further accentuated. However, the percentage of children will diminish, so in effect there will be mainly a change in direction of transfer payments. More of the earnings of work-

ing adults will be transferred to the old and less to children.

What institutions will provide the control necessary to keep the stocks of wealth and people constant, with the minimum sacrifice of individual freedom? It would be far too simpleminded to blurt out "socialism" as the answer, since socialist states are as badly afflicted with growthmania as capitalist states. The Marxist eschatology of the classless society is based on the premise of complete abundance; consequently economic growth is exceedingly important in socialist theory and practice. And population growth, for the orthodox Marxist, cannot present problems under socialist institutions. This latter tenet has weakened a bit in recent years, but the first continues in full force. However, it is equally simpleminded to believe that our present big capital, big labor, big government, big military type of private profit capitalism is capable of the required foresight and restraint, and that the addition of a few effluent and severance taxes here and there will solve the problem. The issues are much deeper and inevitably impinge on the distribution of income and wealth.

Why do people produce junk and cajole other people into buying it? Not out of any innate love for junk or hatred of the environment, but simply in order to earn an income. If—with the prevailing distribution of wealth, income, and power—production governed by the profit motive results in the output of great amounts of noxious junk, then something is wrong with the distribution of wealth and power, the profit motive, or both. We need some principle of income distribution independent of and supplementary to the income-through-jobs link. A start in this direction was made by Oskar Lange, who attempted to combine some socialist principles of distribution with the allocative efficiency advantages of the market system. However, at least as much remains to be done here as remains to be done in designing institutions for stabilizing population. But before progress can be made on these issues we must recognize their necessity and blow the whistle on growthmania.

### Stunting Growthmania

Although the ideas expressed by Mill have been totally dominated by growthmania, there are an increasing number of economists who have frankly expressed their disenchantment with the growth ideology. Arguments stressing ecological limits to wealth and population have been made by Kenneth Boulding and Joseph Spengler, both past presidents of the American Economic Association. Recently E.J. Mishan, Tibor Scitovsky, and Staffan Linder have made penetrating anti-growth arguments. There is also much in Galbraith that is anti-growth—at least against growth of commodities whose desirability must be manufactured along with the product.

In spite of these beginnings, most economists are still governed by the assumption of infinite wants, or the postulate of non-satiety as the mathematical economists call it. Any single want can be satisfied, but all wants in the aggregate cannot be. Wants are infinite in number if not in intensity, and the satisfaction of some wants stimulates others. If wants are infinite, growth is always justified—or so it would seem.

Even while accepting the above hypothesis, one could still object to growthmania on the grounds that given the completely inadequate definition of GNP, "growth" simply means the satisfaction of ever more trivial wants, while simultaneously creating ever more powerful externalities that destroy ever more basic environmental amenities. To defend ourselves against these externalities, we produce even more, and instead of subtracting the purely defensive expenditures, we add them. For example, the medical bills paid for treatment of cigarette-induced cancer and pollution-induced emphysema are added to GNP, when in a welfare sense they clearly should be subtracted. This should be labeled swelling, not growth. The satisfaction of wants created by brainwashing and 'hogwashing" the public over the mass media also represents mostly swelling.

A policy of maximizing GNP is practically equivalent to a policy of maximizing depletion and pollution. This results from the fact that GNP measures the flow of a physical aggregate. Since matter and energy cannot be created, production is simply the transformation of raw material inputs extracted from the environment; consequently, maximizing the physical flow of production implies maximizing depletion. Since matter and energy cannot be destroyed, consumption is merely the transformation into waste of GNP, resulting in environmental pollution. One may hesitate to say "maximal" pollution on the grounds that the production inflow into the stock can be greater than the consumption outflow as long as the stock increases as it does in a growing economy.

To the extent that wealth becomes more durable, the production of waste can be kept low by expanding the stock. But is this in fact what happens? If one wants to maximize production, one must have a market. Increasing the durability of goods reduces the replacement demand. The fas-

ter things wear out, the greater can be the flow of production. To the extent that consumer reaction and weakening competition permit, there is every incentive to minimize durability. Planned obsolescence, programmed self-destruction, and other waste-making practices so well discussed by Vance Packard are the logical result of maximizing a marketed physical flow. If we must maximize something it should be the stock of wealth, not the flow—but with full awareness of the ecological limits that constrain this maximization.

But why this perverse emphasis on flows, this flow fetishism of standard economic theory? Again the underlying issue is distribution. There is no theoretical explanation, much less justification, for the distribution of the stock of wealth. It is a historical datum. But the distribution of the flow of income is at least partly explained by marginal productivity theory, which at times is even misinterpreted as a justification. Everyone gets a part of the flow—call it wages, interest, rent, or profit—and it all looks rather fair. But not everyone owns a piece of the stock, and that does not seem quite so fair. Looking only at the flow helps to avoid disturbing thoughts.

But even if wants were infinite, and even if we redefine GNP to eliminate swelling, infinite wants cannot be satisfied by maximizing physical production. As people grow richer they will want more leisure. Physical growth cannot produce leisure. As physical productivity increases, leisure can be produced by working fewer hours to produce the same physical output.

Even the common-sense argument for infinite wants—that the rich seem to enjoy their high consumption—cannot be generalized without committing the fallacy of composition. If all earned the same high income, a consumption limit occurs sooner than if only a minority had high incomes. The reason is that a large part of the consumption by plutocrats is consumption of personal and maintenance services rendered by the poor, which would not be available if everyone were rich. By hiring the poor to maintain and even purchase commodities for them, the rich devote their limited consumption time only to the most pleasurable aspects of consumption. The rich only ride their horses—they do not clean, comb, saddle, and feed them, nor do they clean the stables. If all did their own maintenance work, consumption would perforce be less. Time sets a limit.

The big difficulty with the infinite wants assumption, however, is pointed out by Keynes, who in spite of the use made of his theories in support of growth, was certainly no advocate of unlimited growth,

as seen in the following quotation:

"Now it is true that the needs of human beings seem to be insatiable. But they fall into two classes—those needs which are absolute in the sense that we feel them whatever the situation of our fellow human beings may be, and those which are relative in the sense that we feel them only if their satisfaction lifts us above, makes us feel superior to, our fellows. Needs of the second class, those which satisfy the desire for superiority, may indeed be insatiable; for the higher the general level, the higher still they are. But this is not so true of the absolute needs—a point may soon be reached, much sooner perhaps than we are all of us aware of, when those needs are satisfied in the sense that we prefer to devote our further energies to non-economic purposes."

Lumping these two categories together and speaking of infinite wants in general can only muddy the waters. The same distinction is implicit in Mill, who spoke disparagingly of "consuming things which give little or no pleasure except as representative of wealth. . . ."

The source of growth lies in the use made of surplus. The controllers of surplus may be a priesthood that controls physical idols made from the surplus and used to extract more surplus in the form of offerings and tribute. Or they may be feudal lords, who through the power given by possession of the land extract a surplus in the form of rent and the corvée. Or they may be capitalists (state or private) who use the surplus in the form of capital to gain more surplus in the form of interest and quasi-rents.

If growth must cease, the surplus becomes less important and so do those who control it. If the surplus is not to lead to growth, then it must be consumed, and ethical demands for equal participation in the consumption of the surplus could not be countered by productivity arguments for inequality as necessary for accumulation. The surplus would eventually enter into the customary standard of living and cease to be recognized as a surplus. Accumulation in excess of depreciation, and the privileges attached thereto, would not exist.

We no longer speak of worshipping idols. Instead of idols we have an abomination called GNP, large parts of which, however, bear such revealing names as Apollo, Poseidon, and Zeus. Instead of worshipping the idol, we maximize it. The idol has become rather more abstract and conceptual and rather less concrete and material, while the mode of adoration has become technical rather than personal. But fundamentally, idolatry remains idolatry.

# Growing Populations
# and Diminishing Resources

*Preston E. Cloud, Jr.*

Since Americans in general think well of other people and envisage their country in terms of the thriving populace from which much of its prosperity arises, they are also inclined to think of people as a good thing and the more of them the better. Prizing democratic principles and individual freedoms, we skirt discussion of population control and talk hopefully of family planning, although without some sort of population control we run the risk eventually of losing all other freedoms. Many of us, moreover, do not appreciate hearing about places where America might be falling short, not even when such information comes from a well-informed popular hero like Charles Lindbergh.

We find it very hard to concede that there might be problems that lie beyond the capabilities of American technology or ingenuity.

People who call attention to unpleasant realities risk being dismissed as naive or mischievous. Thus, questions of population control and of limitations in our ability as a nation or a world to support unlimited population growth have strong emotional overtones. That is all the more reason for trying to think about and discuss such problems as concretely as possible.

My response to your questions, therefore, will stress the limitations that are placed on supportable population densities and level of living by the availability of natural resources. In so responding, however, I wish to emphasize that I speak mainly of limitations that, if we are alert and skillful in dealing with imminent shortages, will probably not apply during the current century. Unless corrected by our own deliberate and active choice, the consequences of our deteriorating physical, biological, and psychological environment, and of inadequacies in the management and distribution of resources, may well limit the growth of populations before absolute limitations of resources become critical.

The author is with the Department of Geology of the University of California at Santa Barbara.

Reprinted by permission of the author from *Effects of Population Growth on Natural Resources and Environment*, pp. 3–7. U.S. Government Printing Office, Washington, D.C., September 1969.

Let me state my conclusions at the outset and then give you some of the reasons for them. I define an optimum population as one that is large enough to provide the diversity, leisure, and substance whereby the creative genius of man can focus on the satisfactory management of his ecosystem, but not so large as to strain the capabilities of the earth to provide adequate diet, industrial raw materials, pure air and water, and attractive living and recreational space for all men, everywhere, into the indefinite future. I take it as self-evident under this definition that there is an optimum population, or at least optimal limits.

I believe, moreover, that the present world population of more than 3.5 billion substantially exceeds this optimum and that the present U.S. population of more than 200 million is beyond the optimum for our own country. Inasmuch, therefore, as the number of births needed to maintain the population at its present level is about 2.3 per fertile female, the number of children that couples ought to want—for the good of these children and the society in which they will live—is, at least until populations show signs of stabilizing, no more than two.

Unfortunately, the populations of the Nation and the world are going to get larger before they level off or become smaller, no matter what we do short of nuclear, chemical, or biological warfare, and no matter how fast we do it. This follows from the age structure of existing populations and the inadequate understanding that most people still have of the dimensions of the problem or what to do about it. That is all the more reason for thinking hard and carefully about what might be done and for getting on with it as rapidly as possible.

Now let me outline the reasons for these views.

The resources of the earth as an abode for man are large, but they are not infinite. No matter how discrepant or how large informed estimates of these resources may be, they must all agree that there is some annual harvest of food that cannot be exceeded on a sustained basis, some maximal quantity of each mineral and chemical resource that can be extracted and kept in circulation.

Technology and economies of scale result in the situation that these maximal quantities differ for different models of industrial civilization although the models that give the largest ultimate quantities also consume them at higher rates.

Thus it is possible to think of man in relation to his renewable resources of food, water, and breathable air as limited in numbers by the sustainable annual crop. His nonrenewable resources—metals, petrochemicals, mineral fuels, et cetera—can be thought of as some quantity which may be used up at different rates, but for which the quantity beneath the curve of cumulative total consumption from first use to exhaustion does not, in the final analysis, vary significantly.

In other words, the depletion curve of a given nonrenewable raw material, or of that class of resources, may rise and decline steeply over a relatively short time—as seems to be the case with petroleum, mercury, and helium —or it may be a flatter curve that lasts for a longer time. This is a choice that civilized industrialized man expresses, consciously or unconsciously, whenever his collective judgment takes form in a given density of population and per capita rate of consumption.

The ultimate extraction and consumption of all useful metals, and of mineral raw materials as a class, must eventually be limited by the quantity we can get under the curve. This, of course, depends to an important extent on the development and intensity of mineral exploration and extractive technology, and on economics, but it has intrinsic limitations that cannot be set aside. For any given quantity and rate of use, we can also flatten and thus extend the depletion curve by recycling, cladding, substitution, and other conservative and innovative measures. It is axiomatic, however, that nothing can expand indefinitely on our finite spaceship earth—or beyond it to other and hostile planets within our finite solar system.

Data available on the ultimately accessible and extractable reserves of most mineral resources are not yet good enough to say what the ultimate limits may be. But they are good enough, together with data on use rates and prospective demands on both food and mineral resources, to cast some ominous shadows.

Consider the limitations on ultimate human populations, and on the quality of human life that result from limitations of food, of industrial raw materials, and of the resiliency of the physical and biological environment to degradation.

The Committee on Resources and Man studied the ultimate capability of an efficiently managed world to produce food, given the cultivation of all potentially arable and marginal lands and an optimal expression of scientific and technological innovations, both on land and in the sea. Its results imply that world food supplies might eventually be increased to as much as nine times the present, provided that sources of protein were essentially restricted to plants, and to seafood mostly from a position lower in the marine food chain than is now customarily harvested—and provided metal resources and mineral fertilizers are equal to the task.

Given equitable distribution, such an ultimate level of productivity might sustain a world population of 30 billion, at a level of chronic malnutrition for the great majority. That places a maximal limit on world populations, at a figure that would be reached by about the year 2075 at present rates of increase—by which time, given concerted effort and luck, the maximal sustainable level of food production might have been reached.

Many students of the problem do not believe that it is possible to sustain 30 billion people, and I have no dispute with them. Here I seek simply to establish some theoretical outside limit based on relatively optimistic assumptions, both about what could be possible and what we may do about it. More important attributes than a starvation diet would be sacrified by a world that full.

Similarly optimistic assumptions about demographic balances that might ensue from the present wave of concern, however, led the Committee on Resources and Man to judge it likely that world population might level off at around 10 billion by about the year 2050. Yet, in my view, even such a leveling off would still result in a world population of about 3 billion more than might eventually—and temporarily—be supported at a general level of living comparable to that enjoyed by developed nations at a modest state of affluence. That is the number of people—7 billion—that continuation of current rates of population increase would place on earth by the end of this century.

Granting the far from established assumption that such a population can be nourished adequately, and accepting the often-expressed American goal of development for all now underdeveloped countries, what would it take to bring a world population of 7 billion to an average level of living comparable to that of the United States in 1969?

It can be calculated that this would require keeping in circulation more than 60 billion tons of iron, about a billion tons of lead, around 700 million tons of zinc, and more than 50 million tons of tin—about 200 to 400 times the present annual world production of these commodities. Assuming these metals were placed in circulation, efficiently recycled, and demand stabilized, it would still take large quantities of new metals annually merely to replace those lost by unavoidable oxidation and friction—about 400,000 tons of new iron a year, for example. The needed quantities of lead, zinc, and tin, moreover, not to mention other metals, greatly exceed informed estimates of eventually recoverable quantities—that of tin, for instance, by at least two and one-half times.

As it is not possible to increase metal production by anywhere near the suggested amounts by the end of the century, if ever, the revolution of rising expectations among the people of the earth is doomed to bitter disappointment without population control and eventually reduction in population to present or lower levels.

We in the United States will be hard pressed to support the raw materials needs of our own growing population without some reduction in per capita demands for minerals, expected, according to Interior Assistant Secretary Hollis M. Dole, in a news release issued the 31st of July, to triple by year 2000.

With determined effort, with a well-trained and well-staffed earth science profession and mineral industry, and with luck, Assistant Secretary Dole expects that domestic mineral production can also triple by the end of the century. But the projected demands will then be four and a half or more times the present. Even assuming a tripled production, we cannot meet these demands without ever-increasing imports—not even with the help of unlimited quantities of cheap energy from fully breeding nuclear reactors yet to be perfected.

Thus, growing populations of Americans will be confronted with the hard choice of forgoing some of their affluence or continuing to import, at increasing rates, the raw materials on which the underdeveloped countries might base their own industrial growth. At the same time Americans, and the people of other developed nations, will have other agonizing problems: What to do about the ever-growing pressures against their gates by the less privileged. How to cope with the increasing burden of pesticides, nuclear wastes, urban and atmospheric pollution, and noise. How to endure the necessary increase of regulatory measures flowing from competition for resources, space, recreation, transportation, housing, educational facilities, and privacy.

These things and others make it essential, in my view, to recognize two new fundamental human rights:

1. The right of the fetus not to be conceived or, if conceived, not born into a world where its presence assures additional misery and privation. It seems to me in some deep sense uncivilized to consider babies as things that people are entitled to propogate at will, regardless of the kind of life the growing child and adult is likely to live.

2. The right of society as a whole to determine the density of population that best assures a continuing flexibility of options and access to necessary resources of food, clean air and water, recreation, and essential raw materials.

Failure to insist on these rights is to jeopardize all others—either as a result of the steady growth of regulatory measures that will be necessary to assure the essentials of existence and opportunity for livelihood, or because of social and political anarchy.

In closing, I invite your attention to the 26 recommendations made in the report on "Resources and Man." I particularly stress the following: Recommendation No. 5, which urges that population control be added to family planning as a weapon in the war on hunger and deprivation; recommendation 6, which stresses the need for national and global natural resources policies; recommendation 19, calling for searching study of the nonmaterial factors that affect man's use of and demand for resources; and recommendation 26, calling for the establishment of a national resources council or board to maintain continuing surveillance of both renewable and nonrenewable resources and to recommend actions that will avert or ameliorate crises of supply, environmental stress, and international harmony.

To these I would add at this time only the suggestion that the population, the urban, and the educational crises in this country might all be helped concurrently by attempting to nucleate the new cities that are so much in the air these days around a new type of urban-grant university oriented toward environmental studies. When we keep both the long-range and the short-range crises in view, they take on mind-boggling dimensions.

To accommodate the 120 million or so new and mainly urban Americans expected by the year 2000, as well as to renovate some existing facilities, calls for the completion by then of new housing, urban transportation, communication, and educational facilities equivalent to all of those already in existence. To try to do all of this within existing urban centers would only aggravate their already grave problems. To try to crowd even the 3 million new college and university students expected by 1977 (Carnegie Commission on Higher Education) onto existing overcrowded campuses is unthinkable. But 120 new cities with eventual populations of a million each, nucleated around 120 new urban grant universities with eventual enrollments of 25,000 each, would just accommodate the new students expected by 1977, and new citizens expected by the end of the century.

Such universities, having no traditions to hamper them, dispersed throughout the country, and charged to create new and better cities, might find it easier than established ones to relate to the surrounding communities, to pioneer new modes in urban revolution and resource management, and to educate the people toward a more constructive outlook on their role as custodians of the spaceship earth, including the need for population control and equalization of opportunity throughout the world. To meet at last the challenge of learning to live in harmony with our total environment is both worthy of our finest effort and essential for our survival. If we could do, beginning now, what our predecessors did with the land-grant colleges, beginning in 1862, we would have made an important move in that direction.

# The Myth of Our Vanishing Resources

*Traditional fears about scarcities are unwarranted;
technology makes fuller use of resources*

HAROLD J. BARNETT

". . . We have timber for less than 30 years, . . . anthracite coal for but 50 years. . . . Supplies of iron ore, mineral oil, and natural gas are being rapidly depleted. . . ." Or so thought Gifford Pinchot in 1910 when he argued in *The Fight for Conservation* that America was gorging itself to death on a diet of natural resources.

Obviously, the nation did not choke nor later starve from its ravenous appetite. More than 10 billion cubic feet of timber were cut in 1965, for example, while about 15 million tons of anthracite and 500 million tons of soft coal were mined that same year. Nor has a scarcity of iron ore, oil, or gas developed. Taconite iron resources are now economical, proved oil reserves in 1965 were 24 percent higher than 15 years earlier, while natural gas reserves were 55 percent greater than those known in 1950.

Yet only recently, Lord Robens, chairman of England's National Coal Board, raised the same specter again. Present proved worldwide resources of oil, gas, and uranium, he warned, will not meet "more than 20 years consumption at the established rates of growth." Population experts like Robert C. Cook see an exploding world population imploding on agricultural resources. Some conservationists and ecologists believe that a scarcity of natural resources not only hinders economic growth, but that we should change the "basic philosophy, indeed, religion of modern man" with respect to growth. Pinchot was wrong, and these modern-day prophets of resources doom may also be.

According to classic economic reasoning, a scarcity of natural resources leads to diminishing incremental returns for economic effort. Thus, for example, it tends to cost more and more over the years, in terms of labor and capital, to mine another ton of coal or to grow another bushel

Reprinted by permission of the author and the publisher from Trans-*action* 4(7):6–10, June 1967.

of wheat. This view of diminishing returns, however, is not justified by the facts. Since 1870 in the United States the record shows *increasing* returns, averaging 1 to 2 percent a year. Moreover, the favorable trend in natural resource industries is stronger in the past 40 years than in the earlier period when the nation's natural resources were less fully utilized.

The voices of the past—and perhaps some of the present ones too—overlooked the cornucopia of scientific advance and technological change. These have created a virtually unlimited "knowledge bank" for an endless stream of new cost-saving innovations. There has operated what Gunnar Myrdal calls the principle of "circular and cumulative causation," or change fostering further change in the same direction. This new reality sharply contrasts with the classical school's contention that natural resources are "fixed" or unchangeable.

Mechanical transformation of resources, moreover, is no longer the principal means of using them. Atoms and molecules and their energies, not fields and trees and fossils, are the building blocks of our time. Nature's availability should be measured in these units, not in acres or tons. The new technology is able to tap resources—including low-grade mineral deposits or sea water—with a skill and level of productivity never conceived 100 years ago. And the world's oceans are a vast farmland, waiting to be developed and harvested if needed.

This is why the long-term upward trend of economic growth will not be halted by availability of extractive goods, as Pinchot and many others before him predicted. And why new, cheap contraceptive devices could bring a timely end to the specter of unabated population growth.

### The Persistence of Pessimism

It is not surprising, however, that the natural resource scarcity "conventional wisdom" has persisted so long. "The ideas of economists and political philosophers, both when they are right and when they are wrong, are more powerful than is commonly understood," wrote John Maynard Keynes.

The persistence of such ideas about resources is understandable on two accounts. First, because there is extensive interest in the social problems stemming from the relation of natural resources to man's welfare. There are more than 500 private and public bodies, including the massive agriculture and interior departments, concerned with the conservation of natural resources. In addition, the list of publications and research studies is seemingly endless. (The Pinchot collection alone in the Library of Congress includes about one million papers.) Established public policy, buttressed in platform statements every presidential election year, is based on the view that natural resources play a significant role in the nation's welfare.

Second, the authors of the classical school of economic reasoning are impressive in their logic. And their premises have not been proved wrong for all time, nor can they be. Thomas Malthus' now legendary dilemma, first advanced in 1798, held out the gloomy prospect of a rapidly expanding population pressing on limited agricultural land. Future generations, he warned, would be afflicted with diminishing returns when all farm land was in use.

About two decades later, David Ricardo observed that natural resources varied in physical properties. It followed, Ricardo reasoned, that society would employ those resources in the order of declining economic quality—richer farm land would be cultivated before marginal acres. Thus, growth would be hampered long before the Malthusian limits were reached, by the need to resort to inferior acres as population grew.

John Stuart Mill subsequently restated the now two-pronged doctrine. The Malthusian limit was the ultimate problem, Mill agreed, but Ricardian limitations of declining quality resources were operating even as Mill wrote in the mid-nineteenth century. These predictions of the classical economists gave to the growth theory of economics its essential character and reputation as "the dismal science."

In the 1860's W. Stanley Jevons extended the Ricardian-Mill conceptions of agricultural land in a study of coal—the chief reason, in his opinion, for Britain's economic growth. Jevons foresaw coal depletion as creating a Ricardian-type problem of declining quality of resources. Thus minerals exhaustion became another powerful force in the doctrine of natural resources scarcity.

At the same time, George Perkins Marsh observed that man's influence had greatly damaged the limited and ecologically balanced natural resource environment. This, in turn, was the door opener for the American conservation movement of 1890-1920 led by Pinchot and later by President Theodore Roosevelt.

### The U.S. as an Emerging Nation

Let us examine the record from 1870 to 1957. At the beginning of the period, the U.S. was an "underdeveloped" country with a population of under 40 million. Since then, population has multiplied fourfold, the annual output of goods and services is roughly 20 times as great, and consumption of the products of agriculture, mining, and forests is six times larger.

During this period, the U.S. also passed from an underdeveloped to an advanced economic status by the close of World War I. While the process was continuous, the decade of World War I stands out as a landmark. The war effects were significant. The first conservation movement ended about then, final homestead entries hit a peak and declined thereafter, immigration dropped off sharply, and the nation ceased to be a net exporter of extractive products.

Look at the record in agriculture, where the net output expanded better than threefold in the period 1870-1957. According to the scarcity doctrine, increasing resource scarcity would force the "unit cost" of farm output—the cost

"Mechanical transformation of resources is no longer the principal means of using them. Atoms and molecules and their energies are the building blocks of our time. Nature's availability should be measured in these units, not in acres or tons."

of a bushel of grain, for instance—to rise. We mean by cost man-days plus capital resources to get a unit of output. But not only did unit cost fail to rise, it actually declined by more than half—whether measured in terms of labor-plus-capital costs or in labor cost alone. What about the hypothesis that scarcity increases with economic growth and time? In the period from 1870 to 1919, the unit cost of agricultural goods declined by a compounded annual rate of 0.4 percent, but in the 1919-1957 period it declined by 1.4 percent a year. Contrary to the natural resource scarcity hypothesis, our economic advance is accelerating.

What about minerals? These have been subject to depletion; demand has increased about 40 times over since 1870. The answer: Over the entire period, cost of a unit of minerals has fallen to a level only one-fifth as large. Again, the declines in unit costs (which mean an increase in productivity) were more rapid in the latter half of the period than in the earlier segment—a 1-plus percent yearly drop to World War I versus a 3-plus percent annual decline from 1919 to 1957.

The record in forestry, a small segment of the economy or of the extractive sector, *does* give support to the doctrine of natural resource scarcity. Unit costs of forestry products doubled, an average increase of about 1 percent annually in the 87-year period. Almost all of the increase occurred before World War I. There has been a more favorable cost record in the post-1920 period, with real costs approximately stable and a fairly constant output.

There have been major substitutions of metals, plastics, and masonry for lumber due to more favorable costs.

The scarcity doctrine receives no support from a view of the extractive industries as a whole. The labor-plus-capital input necessary to produce a unit of extractive goods output declined by two-thirds.

### Technological Cost Cutters

Why the declining trend in the real cost of extractive goods? Is the decline in cost general among commodities? Have some goods gone up in cost and others down? In agriculture there is a pronounced downward trend in unit costs for all crops, feed grains, oil crops (soybeans), sugar crops, cotton, hay and forage, fruits and nuts, vegetables, and tobacco but a less rapid decline in livestock and products, particularly meat animals. The same holds true for individual minerals. Each of the fuels has experienced a major decline in unit cost. Each of the metallic minerals examined has declined in unit cost, except lead and zinc which have had a level trend.

A pervasive and significant factor in declining costs of extractive products has been the substitution of minerals for land. For example, if the U.S. had to rely on work animals for its farm "horsepower," their feed alone would require 20 to 50 times as many acres of crop land as is cultivated today. If synthetic fibers from minerals and fuels were replaced by cotton, the additional land required would equal or exceed acreage now planted to cotton.

To what extent have imports been responsible for averting cost increases in extractive products? At the beginning of the test period, the U.S. was a net exporter but gradually shifted to being an importer by the 1930's. Since then, imports have ranged from 2.5 percent of consumption of extractive goods in 1937-1939 to about 4 percent in the 1951-1957 period. The bulk of agricultural imports are "exotic" crops not grown in this climate, like coffee and cocoa.

The foreign trade influence on minerals is quite different. Since World War II imports have increased to where they now account for about 10 percent of domestic minerals consumption. In certain commodities partial substitution of imports facilitated the decline in unit costs of domestic production by moderating demand pressures on our resources. This is true in petroleum, which accounts for the largest share of mineral imports, to the regret of domestic producers who are producing at far less than capacity in order to maintain prices. As for minerals like copper, lead, zinc, and bauxite, imports were significantly responsible for declining or level costs.

Technological change has been *the* dynamic factor in the declining cost trend for agricultural and mineral commodities. In addition to the substitution of mechanical power for animal and human effort, the discovery and introduction of improved breeds, fertilizers, weed killers, and other agricultural methods have fostered the long-term trend of declining costs. In forestry the use of the power saw and log-pulling tractor has augmented important technical advances in the development of substitutes for saw timber.

In minerals the advances are particularly striking. New domestic reserves of minerals have been found or have become economically accessible because of advances in geological knowledge and search techniques. Strip mining of coal has more than doubled daily output per worker. Long distance gas pipelines have opened markets for previously useless gas wells. Taconite pellets, concentrated to 60 or more percent iron content, are no less efficient than high-grade hematite ore in blast furnaces.

Yet knowledge advance and technological change have been lightly regarded in the natural resources "conventional wisdom." Implicitly, they are fleeting phenomena which might not persist, which might evaporate at any moment. Indeed, Alfred Marshall, the great neoclassical economist, believed diminishing returns to be a historical law, because improvements in production "must themselves gradually show a diminishing return."

This is not the case. Natural resource scarcity and diminishing returns through time are not a curse that society must bear. An examination of the historical record and an awareness of the multiplier effect of technological change argue against hoarding these resources. Of course, society has an obligation to future generations. But the natural environment is only part of what one generation passes on to another. Knowledge, technology, capital instruments, and economic institutions—these are more significant for economic welfare because they are, in fact, the determinants of real income per capita and economic growth. Higher production today, if it also means greater knowledge, research, and development, will serve the economic interest of future generations better than preservation of resources and lower production. In the United States, for example, the economic magnitude of the estate each generation passes on—the income per capita the next generation enjoys—has been approximately double that which it received, over the period for which data exist.

But if the U.S. no longer needs to be concerned about diminishing returns and natural resource scarcity, there is an even more important resources problem still facing this society. Have we learned how to protect the *quality* of life? Indeed, it might be said that diminishing qualitative, rather than quantitative, returns are really the central issue. Averting a deterioration in the quality of life may be more challenging than finding ways to circumvent increases in the economic scarcity of certain natural resources.

Preservation of natural beauty, urban agglomeration, waste disposal and pollution, changes in income distribution, water supply, land use—these are a few of the social problems related to natural resources and the quality of life. The modern natural resources problem is not one of facing up to diminishing returns, but rather one of social adjustment to a variety of effects of technological change and economic growth upon the nature-man relationship. If not solved, these social problems can undermine the quality of life. This should be our contemporary social concern with natural resources in this country, not the classical economics problem of scarcity and subsistence. Even in such nations as India the dilemma is not primarily obdurate natural resources. Rather, it is an inefficient ratio of population to productive capital and a culture not yet fully subjugated to the goals of economic growth. Man's relations to nature are not governed by uncontrollable natural forces. It is, rather, man's relations to man which in our time have become crucial for handling his relation to the natural environment.

FURTHER READING SUGGESTED BY THE AUTHOR:

*Natural Resources for U.S. Growth* by Hans H. Landsberg (Baltimore: Johns Hopkins Press, 1964).
*World Prospects for Natural Resources* by Joseph L. Fisher and Neal Potter (Baltimore: Johns Hopkins Press, 1964).
*Environmental Quality in a Growing Economy* edited by H. Jarrett (Baltimore: Johns Hopkins Press, 1966).

Harold J. Barnett, professor of economics at Washington University in St. Louis, has been with Resources for the Future, RAND Corporation, and several government agencies. His interest in natural resources began with concern for German synthetic fuels and rubber as targets in World War II and continued through his dissertation on atomic energy to his recent interest in environmental quality and the broadcast spectrum. This article was adapted from his book *Scarcity and Growth* (with Chandler Morse).

# IN SEARCH
# OF A SOLUTION

# Beyond Family Planning

What further proposals have been made to "solve" the population problem, and how are they to be appraised?

Bernard Berelson

This article rests on four propositions: (i) among the great problems on the world agenda is the population problem; (ii) that problem is most urgent in the developing countries, where rapid population growth retards social and economic development; (iii) there is a time penalty on the problem in the sense that, other things being equal, anything not done sooner may be harder to do later, due to increased numbers; and accordingly (iv) everything that can properly be done to lower population growth rates should be done, now. The question is, what is to be done? There is a certain agreement on the general objective (that is, on the desirability of lowering birth rates, though not on how far and how fast), but there is disagreement as to means.

The first response to too high growth rates deriving from too high birth rates is to introduce voluntary contraception on a mass basis, or try to. Why is family planning the first step taken on the road to population control? Probably because, from a broad political standpoint, it is the most acceptable one; since it is closely tied to maternal and child care it can be perceived as a health measure beyond dispute, and since it is voluntary it can be justified as a contribution to the effective personal freedom of individual couples. On both scores, it ties into accepted values and thus achieves political viability. Moreover, it is a gradual effort and an inexpensive one, both of which features contribute to its political acceptability.

How effective have family-planning programs been as a means toward population control? There is currently some controversy among qualified observers as to its efficacy (1), and this is not the place to review that issue. There is agreement, however, that the problem is of such magnitude and consequence that additional efforts are needed to

reach a "solution," however that is responsibly defined.

For the purpose of this article, then, let us assume that today's national family-planning programs, mainly based on voluntary contraception, are not "enough"—where "enough" is defined not necessarily as achieving zero growth in some extended present but simply as lowering birth rates quickly and substantially. "Enough" begs the question of the ultimate goal and only asks that a faster decline in population growth rates be brought about than is presently being achieved or in prospect—and, within the range of the possible, the faster the better (2, 3). Just to indicate roughly the order of magnitude, let us say that the proximate goal is the halving of the birth rate in the developing countries in the next decade or two—from, say, over 40 births per thousand per year to 20 to 25 (4). For obvious reasons, both emigration and increased death rates are ruled out of consideration.

What is to be done to bring that reduction about, beyond present programs of voluntary family planning? I address that question in two ways: first, by listing the programs or policies more or less responsibly suggested in recent years for achieving this end; second, by reviewing the issues raised by the suggested approaches.

## Proposals beyond Family Planning

Here is a listing of the several proposals, arranged in descriptive categories. The list includes both proposals for consideration and proposals for action.

A. *Extensions of voluntary fertility control.*

1) Institutionalization of maternal care in rural areas of developing countries: a feasibility study of what would

be required in order to bring some degree of modern medical or paramedical attention to every pregnant woman in the rural areas of five developing countries, with professional backup for difficult cases and with family-planning education and services a central component of the program, aimed particularly at women of low parity (5).

2) Liberalization of induced abortion (6; 7, p. 139; 8).

B. *Establishment of involuntary fertility control.*

1) Mass use of a "fertility control agent" by the government to regulate births at an acceptable level. The "fertility control agent," designed to lower fertility in the society to a level 5 to 75 percent below the present birth rate, as needed, would be a substance now unknown but believed to be available for field testing after 5 to 15 years of research work. It would be included in the water supply in urban areas and administered by "other methods" elsewhere (9). A related suggestion is the "addition of temporary sterilants to water supplies or staple food" (10).

2) "Marketable licenses to have children," given to women and perhaps men in "whatever number would ensure a reproduction rate of one" (say, 2.2 children per couple). For example, "the unit certificate might be the 'deci-child,' and accumulation of ten of these units, by purchase, inheritance or gift, would permit a woman in maturity to have one legal child" (11).

3) Temporary sterilization of all girls by means of time-capsule contraceptives, and of girls and women after each delivery, with reversibility allowed only upon governmental approval. Certificates of approval would be distributed according to national popular vote on desired population growth, and saleable on the open market (12).

4) Compulsory sterilization of men with three or more living children (13); a requirement of induced abortion for all illegitimate pregnancies (6).

C. *Intensified educational campaigns.*

1) Inclusion of educational materials on population in primary and secondary school systems (6, 14, 15).

2) Promotion of national satellite television systems for directly disseminating information on population and family planning and for indirectly pro-

The author is president of the Population Council, 245 Park Avenue, New York 10017. This article is adapted from a longer article that will be published in full in an early issue of *Studies in Family Planning*, issued by the Population Council. Copies of the longer version are available from the Council on request.

moting acceptance of modern attitudes and practices in general (7, p. 162; *16; 17*, especially pp. 13–14; *18*).

D. *Incentive programs*. As used here, the term *incentive programs* refers to payments, or their equivalent, made directly to couples who use contraceptives or to couples who do not have children for specified periods. It does *not* refer to payments to field workers, medical personnel, volunteers, and others, for securing acceptance of contraceptive practice.

1) Payment, or the equivalent (for example, the gift of a transistor radio), for accepting sterilization (6, *19–21*) or for the effective practice of contraception (*21–24*).

2) A bonus for child spacing or nonpregnancy (*25–28*); a savings certificate to couples for each 12-month period in which no child is born (*29*); a lottery scheme for preventing illegitimate births among teenagers in a small country (*30*); "responsibility prizes" for each 5 years of childless marriage or for vasectomy before the birth of a third child, and special lotteries, with tickets available to the childless (7, p. 138).

E. *Tax and welfare benefits and penalties*—that is, a system of social services that would discourage childbearing rather than encourage it, as present systems tend to do.

1) Withdrawal of maternity benefits, perhaps after the birth of *N* (3?) children (6, *21, 26*) or in cases where certain limiting conditions, such as adequate child spacing, knowledge of family planning, or attainment of a given level of income, have not been met (*31*, pp. 130–31).

2) Withdrawal of child or family allowances, perhaps after the birth of *N* children (6; *26; 31*, pp. 131–36).

3) Levy of tax on births after the *N*th child (*21; 26; 28*, p. 30).

4) Limitation of governmentally provided medical treatment, housing, scholarships, loans, subsidies, and so on, to families with fewer than *N* children (6, *26*).

5) Reversal of tax benefits, to favor the unmarried and the parents of fewer rather than more children (6; *7*, pp. 136–37; *21; 26; 31*, p. 137; *32*).

6) Provision by the state of *N* years of free schooling, at all levels, to each family, to be allocated among the children as desired (*33*).

7) Pensions for poor parents with fewer than *N* children, as social security for their old age (*21, 34, 35*).

F. *Shifts in social and economic institutions*—that is, broad changes in

fundamental institutional arrangements that could have the effect of lowering fertility.

1) Raising the minimum age at marriage, through legislation or through imposition of a substantial fee for marriage licenses (6, *32*); through direct payment of bonuses for delayed marriage (*25*); through payment of marriage benefits only to parents of brides over 21 years old (*31*, p. 130); through government loans for wedding ceremonies when the bride is over a given age, or with the interest rate inversely related to the bride's age (*36*); through a "governmental 'first marriage grant' . . . awarded each couple in which the age of both [sic] partners was 25 or more" (7, p. 138); or through establishment of a domestic "national service" program for all men for the appropriate 2-year period in order to develop social services, inculcate modern attitudes toward (among other matters) family planning and population control, and delay marriage (*37*).

2) Measures to promote or require the participation of women in the labor force (outside the home), in order to provide roles and interests for women that are alternative or supplementary to marriage (6, *32, 38*).

3) "Direct manipulation of family structure itself—planned efforts at deflecting the family's socializing function . . . or introducing nonfamilial distractions . . . into people's lives," specifically through employment of women outside the house (*39*); "selective restructuring of the family in relation to the rest of society" (6).

4) Promotion of "two types of marriage, one of them childless and readily dissolved, and the other licensed for children and designed to be stable"; marriages of the first type would have to constitute 20 to 40 percent of the total in order to allow free choice of family size for marriages of the second type (*16, 40*).

5) Encouragement of long-range social trends leading toward lower fertility—for example, "improved and universal general education, or new roads facilitating communication, or improved agricultural methods, or a new industry that would increase productivity, or other types of innovation that may break the 'cake of custom' and produce social foment" (*41*); improvement in the status of women (*42*).

6) Efforts to lower death rates even further, particularly infant and child death rates, in the belief that lower birth rates will follow (*43*).

G. *Political channels and organizations*.

1) U.S. insistence on "population control as the price of food aid," with highly selective assistance based thereon, and exertion of political pressures on governments or religious groups that impede "solution" of the population problem (7, pp. 161–66; *44*).

2) Reorganization of national and international agencies to deal with the population problem: within the United States, "coordination by a powerful governmental agency, a Federal Department of Population and Environment . . . with the power to take whatever steps are necessary to establish a reasonable population size" (7, p. 138; *45*); within India, creation of "a separate Ministry of Population Control" (*46*, p. 96); development of an "international specialized agency larger than WHO to operate programs for extending family limitation techniques to the world . . . charged with the responsibility of effecting the transfer to population equilibrium" (*16*).

3) Promotion of zero growth in population as the ultimate goal, and acceptance of this goal now in order to place intermediate goals of lowered fertility in proper context (6).

H. *Augmented research efforts*.

1) More research on social means for achieving necessary fertility goals (6).

2) Focused research on practical methods of sex determination (*47*).

3) Increased research directed toward improvement of the contraceptive technology (*48*).

## Proposals: Review of the Issues

Here are 29 proposals beyond family planning for dealing with the problem of undue population growth in the developing world. Naturally I cannot claim that these are all the proposals that have been made more or less responsibly toward that end, but my guess is that there are not many more and that these proposals are a reasonably good sample of the total list.

Since several of the proposals tend in the same direction, it seems appropriate to review them against the criteria that any such proposals might be required to meet. What are such criteria? There are at least six: (i) scientific, medical, and technological readiness; (ii) political viability; (iii) administrative feasibility; (iv) economic capability; (v) moral, ethical, and philosophical acceptability; and (vi) presumed effectiveness. In other words, the key questions are: Is the scientific, medical, technological base available or likely? Will governments approve? Can the proposal be administered? Can the society afford the proposal? Is it morally acceptable? And, finally, will it work?

*Scientific, medical, technological readiness.* Two questions are involved: (i) is the needed technology available? and (ii) are the medical or paramedical personnel needed in order to assure medical administration and safety available or readily trainable?

With regard to temporary contraception, sterilization, and abortion, not only is the needed technology available now, but it is being steadily improved and expanded. The intrauterine device (IUD) and the oral pill have been major contraceptive developments of the past decade, and several promising leads are now being followed up (*49*), though it cannot be said with much confidence that any of the efforts will produce measures suitable for mass use within the next few years (*50*). Improved technologies for sterilization, both male and female, are being worked on, and there has been a recent development in abortion technique, the so-called suction device.

However, neither Ehrlich's "temporary sterilants" nor Ketchel's "fertility control agent" (B-1) is now available or on the technological horizon, though that does not mean that the research task ought not to be pursued against a subsequent need, especially since any such substance could be administered to individuals on a voluntary basis as well as to the population as a whole on an involuntary basis. In the latter case, if administered through the water supply or a similar source, the substance would have to be medically safe and free of side effects for men and women, young and old, well and ill, physiologically normal and physiologically marginal, as well as for animals and perhaps plants. As some people have remarked, the proposal that such a substance be added to a water supply would face far greater difficulties of acceptance, simply on medical grounds, than the far milder proposals with regard to fluoridation to prevent tooth decay.

Though a substantial technology in fertility control does exist, that does not necessarily mean that the techniques can be applied where they are most needed; this is true partly because of limitations in the number of trained personnel. In general, the more the technology requires the services of medical or paramedical personnel (or, what is much the same, is perceived as requiring them), the more difficult it is to administer in the developing countries. In the case of sterilization and abortion, the medical requirement becomes more severe. For example, when the policy of compulsory vasectomy of men with three or more children was first being considered in India (see *13*), it was estimated that the policy would affect about 40 million males: "one thousand surgeons or parasurgeons each averaging 20 operations a day for five days a week would take eight years to cope with the existing candidates, and during this time of course a constant supply of new candidates would be coming along" (*51*)—at present birth rates, probably some 3.5 million a year. A program of large-scale abortion (provided such a program was legal and acceptable) might additionally require hospital beds, which are in particularly short supply in most developing countries. However, the newer abortion technique might not require hospitalization—theoretically, the abortion "camp" may be feasible, as the vasectomy "camp" was, though the problems are substantially greater.

In short, the technology is available for some but not for all current proposals, and the case is similar for properly trained personnel.

*Political viability.* The "population problem" has been increasingly recognized by national governments and international agencies over the past decade, and policies for dealing with it have been increasingly adopted: national family-planning programs in some 20 to 25 countries; positive resolutions and actions within the United Nations family; large programs of support by such developed countries as the United States and Sweden; the so-called World Leaders' Statement, in which 30 heads of governments endorsed efforts to limit population growth. There is no reason to think that the trend toward population limitation has run its course.

At the same time, the political picture is by no means unblemished. Some favorable policies are not strong enough to support a vigorous program, even one limited to family planning on health grounds; in national politics, "population control" can become a handy issue for a determined opposition; internal ethnic balances are sometimes delicately involved, with political ramifications; national size is often equated with national power, from the standpoint of international relations and regional military balances; the motives behind the support and encouragement of population control by the developed countries are sometimes perceived as neocolonialist or neoimperialist; and on the international front, as represented by the United Nations, there is still considerable reluctance based on both religious and political considerations. In short, ambivalence on the part of the elite and recognition of the issue as a political liability are not absent even in the countries that favor population limitation.

Any social policy adopted by government rests on some minimum consensus concerning goals and means. They need not be the ultimate goals or the final means; the socioeconomic plans of developing countries are typically 5-year plans, not 20- or 40- or 100-year plans. Indeed, the ultimate goal of population policy—that is, zero growth—need not be agreed upon or even considered by officials who *can* agree upon the immediate goal of lowering growth by a specified amount or by "as much as possible" within a period of years. And since there are always goals beyond goals, one does not even need to know what the ultimate goal is—only the direction in which it will be found (which is usually more readily agreed upon). Would insistence *now* on the acknowledgment of an *ultimate* goal of zero growth advance the effort or change its direction?

To start with, the proposal of compulsory controls in India in 1967 (B-4) precipitated "a storm of questions in Parliament" (*52*); the proposal was withdrawn, and the issue resulted in a high-level shift of personnel within the family-planning organization. No other country has seriously entertained the idea. Other considerations aside, in many countries political instability would make implementation virtually impossible.

Social measures designed to affect the birth rate indirectly—for example, tax benefits, social security arrangements, and so on—have been proposed from time to time. In India there have been several such proposals: for example, by the United Nations mission (*53*, chap. 11), by the Small Family Norm Committee (*26*), by the Central Family Planning Council (*54*), and in almost every issue of such publications as *Family Planning News, Centre Calling,* and *Planned Parenthood.*

As Samuel reports, with accompanying documentation (*21*), "the desirability of imposing a tax on births of fourth or higher order has been afloat for some time. However, time and again, the suggestion has been rejected by the Government of India." In some cases action has been taken either by the central government [for example, income tax "deductions for dependent children are given for the first and second child only" (53, p. 87)] or by certain states ["Maharashtra and Uttar Pradesh have decided to grant educational concessions and benefits only to those children whose parents restrict the size of their families" (55)]. Indicative of political sensitivity is the fact that an order withdrawing maternity leave for nonindustrial women employees with three or more living children—at best a tiny number of educated women—was revoked before it went into effect (56). There is a special political problem in many countries, in that economic constraints on fertility often turn out in practice to be selective on class, racial, or ethnic grounds, and thus exacerbate political tensions. Moreover, the promotion of female participation in the labor force runs up against the political problem that such employment would be competitive with men in situations of already high male unemployment and underemployment.

Whether programs for eliminating population growth are or are not politically acceptable appears to depend largely upon whether they are perceived as positive or negative; where "positive" means that they are seen as promoting not only population limitation but other social benefits as well, and where "negative" means that they are seen as limited to population control. For example, family planning programs, as noted above, are often rationalized as contributing to both maternal and child health and to the effective freedom of the individual family; a pension for the elderly would have social welfare benefits as well as indirect impact upon family size, in countries where a large family has been the traditional "social security system"; contraceptive programs in Latin America are promoted by the medical community as a medical and humanitarian answer not to the population problem but to the extensive illegal and dangerous practice of abortion. On the other hand, imposing tax liabilities or withdrawing benefits after the birth of the $N$th child, not to mention involuntary measures, can be attacked as punitive means whose only purpose is that of limiting population.

It would thus require great political courage, joined to very firm demographic convictions, for a national leader to move toward an unpopular and severe prescription designed to cure his country's population ills. Indeed, it is difficult to envisage such a political move in an open society where a political opposition could present a counter view and perhaps prevail.

The governmental decisions about measures to be taken to deal with undue population growth must be made mainly by the countries directly involved; after all, it is their people and their nation whose prospects are most centrally affected. But in an interconnected world, with peace and human welfare at issue, others are properly concerned, for reasons both of self-interest and of humanitarianism—other governments from the developed world, the international community, private groups. What of the political considerations in this connection?

A recommendation (G-1) that the United States exert strong political pressures to effect population control in developing countries seems more likely to generate political opposition abroad than acceptance. It is conceivable that such measures might be adopted here, but it is hardly conceivable that they would be agreed to by the proposed recipients. Such a policy seems likely to boomerang against its own objective, quite aside from ethical or political considerations.

The proposal (G-2) to create an international superagency seems more likely of success, but is not without its difficulties. The World Health Organization, UNICEF, and UNESCO have moved some distance toward family planning, if not population control, but only slowly and in the face of considerable political restraint on the international front (57). A new international agency would find the road easier only if its efforts were restricted to the convinced countries. Certainly the international organizations now concerned with this problem would not be expected to abdicate in favor of a new agency. If it could be brought into being and given a strong charter for action, then, almost by definition, the international political climate would be such as to favor action by the present agencies, and then efficiency and not political acceptability would be the issue.

*Administrative feasibility.* Given technical availability and political acceptability, what can actually be done? This is where several "good ideas" run into difficulties in the developing world, in the translation of a theoretical idea into a practical program.

It is difficult to estimate the administrative feasibility of several of the proposals listed above, if for no other reason than that the proponents do not put forward the necessary organizational plans or details. How are "fertility control agents" or "sterilants" to be administered on an involuntary mass basis in the absence of a central water supply or a food-processing system? How are men with three or more children to be reliably identified in a peasant society and impelled to undergo sterilization against their will; and what is to be done if they decline, or if a fourth child is born? What is to be done with parents who evade the compulsory programs, or with the children born as a result of this evasion? How can an incentive system be honestly run in the absence of an organized network of offices positioned and staffed to carry out the regulatory activity? How can a system of social benefits and penalties, including incentives to postpone or forego marriage, be made to work in the absence of such a network?

These questions are meant only to suggest the kinds of difficulties that must be taken into account if proposals are to be translated into programs. It would seem desirable that every responsibly made proposal address itself to such administrative problems. Some proposals do move in that direction. The feasibility in administration, personnel, and costs of the plan (A-1) to institutionalize maternal care in rural areas, with family planning attached, is currently under study in several developing countries.

The plan (C-1) to include population as a subject in the school curriculum has been carried forward as far as the preparation of educational materials, and in a few cases beyond that (58). The plans for incentive programs sometimes come down to only the theoretical proposition that people will do anything for money (in this case refrain from having children), but in some cases the permissible payment is proposed on the basis of an economic analysis, and in a few cases an administrative means is also proposed (59). The plan for governmental wedding loans scaled to the bride's age recognizes that a birth-registration system might be needed to control against misreporting of age (6).

Thus the *why* of population control is easy, the *what* is not very hard, but the *how* is difficult. We may know that the extension of popular education or an increase in the number of women in the labor force or a later age at marriage would all contribute to population control in a significant way. But there remains the administrative question of how to bring those developments about. In short, several proposals assume workability of a complicated scheme in a country that cannot now collect its own vital statistics in a reliable manner. Moreover, there is a limit to how much administrative burden the typical developing country can carry: it cannot manage many large-scale developmental efforts at a time, either within the field of population or overall. After all, population is not the only effort; agriculture, industry, education, health, communications, the military—all are important claimants. And, within the field of population, a country that finds it difficult to organize and run a family-planning program will find that harder when other programs are added. So, difficult administrative choices must be made.

*Economic capability.* From the standpoint of economic capability there are two questions: (i) is the program worthwhile when measured against the criterion of economic return, and (ii) if worthwhile, can it be afforded from present budgets?

Most of the proposals probably pass the second screen. If a fertility-control agent suitable for mass administration becomes available and politically and administratively acceptable, such a program would probably not be prohibitively expensive; incorporation of population materials into the school curriculum is not unduly expensive; imposing of taxes or withdrawing of benefits or increasing fees for marriage licenses might even return a net gain after administrative cost.

But a few proposals are costly in absolute if not relative terms. For example, the institutionalization of maternal care (proposal A-1) might cost some $500 million for construction and $200 million for annual operation in India, or, respectively, $25 million and $10 million in a country with population of 25 million (5) (although recent estimates are substantially lower). The plan for a "youth corps" in India would cost upward of $450 million a year if the participants were paid only $50 annually. The plan for payment of pensions to elderly fathers without sons could cost from $400 million to $1 billion a year, plus administrative costs

(35). The satellite television system for India would cost $50 million for capital costs only, on a restricted project (17, p. 23), with at least another $200 million needed for receiving sets, broadcast terminals, and programming costs if national coverage were to be secured. All of these proposals are intended to have beneficial consequences beyond population control and hence can be justified on multiple grounds, but they are still expensive in absolute amounts.

The broad social programs of popular education, improved methods of agriculture, and increased industrialization (F-5) already absorb even larger sums, and they could no doubt utilize even more. Here the question is a different one. At present, in such countries as India, Pakistan, South Korea, and Turkey, the funds allocated to family-planning programs constitute less than 1 percent—in most cases, much less—of the total funds devoted to economic development. Would that tiny proportion make a greater contribution to population control, over some specified period, if given over to education or industrialization or road-building than it makes when utilized directly for family planning (60)? From what we now know, the answer is certainly "No."

Beyond family planning, the situation is still less clear. On the assumption that some level of incentive or benefit would have a demographic impact, what would the level have to be to cut the birth rate by, say, 20 percent? We simply do not know: the necessary experiments on administration and effectiveness have not been carried out. Let us review what has been proposed with respect to incentives. On the ground that incentives for vasectomy are better than incentives for contraception—since vasectomy is a one-time procedure and is likely to be more effective in preventing births—Pohlman (20) proposes for India a range of money benefits depending upon parity and degree of acceptance—from $7 to a father of four or more children if half the villagers in that category enter the program up to $40 to a father of three children if 75 percent enter. If the 50-percent criterion were met in both categories throughout India, the current plan would cost on the order of $260 million in incentives alone, apart from administrative costs. The decline in the birth rate would be slightly over a fourth, perhaps a third—roughly equivalent to $35 to $40 per prevented birth (61).

Simon proposes an incentive of half the per capita income "each year to each fertile woman who does not get pregnant" (23). Here a special popula-arises. In a typical developing population of 1000, about 25 to 30 percent of the married women of reproductive age give birth each year: a population of 1000 means from 145 to 165 such women, and a birth rate of, say, 40. Thus, the incentives paid to about three-fourths of the married women of reproductive age would have no effect on the birth rate, since these women would not be having a child that year in any case; thus the cost could be three to four times the amount "needed" for a desired result. Even if the incentive were fully effective and really did prevent a birth, a cut of ten points in the Indian birth rate would cost on the order of $250 million (or 5 million prevented births at $50 each). The cost would be substantially larger if the women (including the nonfecund or the semi-fecund) who would not have had a child that year in any case, could not be screened out effectively.

But these and other possibilities are only speculations: to date we simply do not know whether incentives will lower a birth rate, or, rather, we do not know how large the incentives would have to be in order to do so. These illustrations show only that an incentive program could be expensive. In any case, incentive systems would require a good amount of supervision and record-keeping; and, presumably, the higher the incentive (and hence the greater the chance of impact), the greater the risk of false reporting and the greater the need of supervision—which is not only expensive but difficult administratively.

*Moral, ethical, and philosophical acceptability.* Next, is the proposal not only politically acceptable but considered right and proper—by the target population, government officials, professional or intellectual elites, and the outside agencies committed to aid in its administration?

Coale states (3, 62), "One reason the policy of seeking to make voluntary fertility universal is appealing—whether adequate or not—is that it is a natural extension of traditional democratic values: of providing each individual with the information he needs to make wise choices, and allowing the greatest freedom for each to work out his own destiny. The underlying rationale is that if every individual knowledgeably pursues his self-interest, the social interest will best be served." But what if "stressing the right of parents to have the number of children they want . . . evades the basic question of population policy, which is how to give societies the number of children they need?" (6). The issue rests at the center of political philosophy: how best to reconcile individual and collective interests.

Today, most observers would acknowledge that having a child is theoretically a free choice of the individual couple. However, for many couples, particularly among the poor of the world, the choice is not effectively free in the sense that the individual couple does not have the information, services, and supplies needed to implement a free wish in this regard. Such couples are restrained by ignorance, not only of contraceptive practice but of the consequences of high fertility for themselves, their children, and their country; they are restrained by religious doctrine, even though they may not accept the doctrine; they are restrained legally, as in the case of people who would choose abortion if that course were open to them; they are restrained culturally, as in the case of women subject to a tradition that reserves for them only the childbearing and child-rearing roles. Hence effective freedom of choice in the matter of childbearing is by no means realized in the world today, as recent policy statements have remarked (63).

To what extent should a society be willing to compromise its ethical standards for the sake of solving a great social problem? Suppose a program for population control resulted in many more abortions in a society where abortion is morally repugnant and where, moreover, abortion by acceptable medical standards is widely unattainable; how much fertility decline would be "worth" the result? What of infanticide under the same conditions? How many innocent or unknowing men may be vasectomized for a fee (for themselves or for others who obtained their consent) before the practice calls for a moral restraint? How large an increase in the regulatory bureaucracy, or in systematic corruption through incentives, or in differential effect by social class to the disadvantage of the poor (64) is worth how much decrease in the birth rate? How much association of childbearing with monetary incentive is warranted before "bribing people not to have children" becomes contaminating, with adverse long-run ef-

fects on parental responsibility (65)? How much "immorality," locally defined as extramarital sex, outweighs the benefits of contraceptive practice (assuming that there is an association)? How much withholding of food aid is ethical, judged against degree of fertility decline? If it were possible to legislate a later age at marriage, would it be right to do so against the will of young women, in a society in which they have nothing else to do? In countries, like our own, where urbanization is a serious population problem, is it right to tell people *where* to live, or to impose heavy economic constraints that in effect "force" the desired migration? Is it right to withdraw educational benefits from children in "too large" families? Such withdrawal would not only be repressive from the standpoint of free education but in the long run would be unfortunate from the standpoint of fertility control. In the balance—and this is a question of great but neglected importance—what weight should be given the opportunities of future generations as against the ignorance, the prejudices, or the preferences of the present one?

Guidance on such ethical questions is needed. For further consideration, these propositions are put forward. (i) "An ideal policy would permit a maximum of individual freedom and diversity. It would not prescribe a precise number of children for each category of married couple, nor lay down a universal norm to which all couples should conform" (3). (ii) "An ideal program designed to affect the number of children people want would help promote other goals that are worth supporting on their own merits, or at least not conflict with such goals" (3).(iii) An ideal program would not burden the innocent in an attempt to penalize the guilty—for example, would not burden the Nth child by denying him a free education simply because he *was* the Nth child of irresponsible parents. (iv) An ideal program would not weigh heavily upon the already disadvantaged—for example, by withdrawing maternal or medical benefits or free education from large families, policies that would tend to further deprive the poor. (v) An ideal program would be comprehensible to those directly affected and hence subject to their response. (vi) An ideal program would respect present values concerning family and children, values which some people may not be willing to bargain away in a cost-benefit anal-

ysis. (vii) An ideal program would not rest upon the designation of population control as the final value justifying all others; "preoccupation with population growth should not serve to justify measures more dangerous or of higher social cost than population growth itself" (3).

*Presumed effectiveness.* If proposals are scientifically ready to be implemented, politically and morally acceptable, and administratively and financially feasible, to what extent will they actually work in bringing population growth under control? That is the final question.

To begin with, the compulsory measures would probably be quite effective in lowering fertility. Inevitably in such schemes, strongly motivated people are ingenious enough to find ways "to beat the system"; if such people were numerous enough the system could not be enforced except under conditions of severe political repression (66). Otherwise, if the scheme was workable, compulsion could have its effect.

What about the proposals for the extension of voluntary contraception? Institutionalizing maternal care in the rural areas, with family planning attached, does promise to be effective within, say, 5 to 10 years, particularly in its potential for reaching younger women and women of lower parity. The International Postpartum Program did have that effect in the urban areas (67), and presumably the impact would extend to the rural areas, though probably not to the same degree because of the somewhat greater sophistication and modernization of the cities.

A liberalized abortion system—again, if workable—could also be effective in preventing unwanted births, but it would probably have to be associated with a contraceptive effort; otherwise there might be too many abortions for the system, as well as for the individual woman (who might need three a year to remain without issue).

Free abortion in cases where contraception had failed would probably make for a decline in fertility, but how large a one would depend upon the quality of the contraceptive program. With modern contraception (the IUD and the pill) the failure rates are quite small, but women who only marginally tolerate these two methods could fall back on abortion. Free abortion has certainly lowered fertility in Japan and in certain countries of eastern Europe (68) and, where medically feasible, would do so elsewhere as well; as a colleague observes, in this field one should not underestimate the attraction of a certainty as compared to a probability.

The large question of the impact of the various incentive and benefit or liability plans (D and E) simply cannot be answered: we have too little experience to know much about the conditions under which financial factors will affect childbearing to any substantial degree. Perhaps everyone has his price for everything; if so, we do not know what would have to be paid, directly or indirectly, to make people decide not to bear children.

Such as it is, the evidence from the pro-natalist side on the effectiveness of incentives is not encouraging. All the countries of Europe have family allowance programs of one kind or another (69), most of them legislated in the 1930's and 1940's to raise the birth rate; collectively Europe has the lowest birth rate of any continent. The consensus among demographers appears to be that such programs cannot be shown to have effected an upward trend in the birth rate where tried.

As in the case of abortion for illegitimate pregnancies, several of the benefit or liability proposals would affect only a trivial fraction of people in much of the developing world. However, because the impact of incentive and benefit or liability plans is uncertain and may become important, we need to become better informed on the possibilities and limitations, and this information can come only from experimentation under realistic circumstances and at realistic levels of payment.

A higher age at marriage and a greater participation of women in the labor force are generally credited with effecting fertility declines. In a recent Indian conference on raising the age at marriage, the specialists seemed to differ only on the magnitude of the fertility decline that would result: a decline of 30 percent in the birth rate in a generation of 28 years if the minimum age of the woman at marriage were raised to 20 (70), or a decline of not more than 15 percent in 10 years (71). I say "seemed to differ" since these figures are not necessarily incompatible. In either case, the decline is a valuable one. But an increase in the age at marriage is not easy to achieve, and that must come before the fertility effect.

Similarly, an increase in the proportion of working women would have its demographic effect, but could probably come about only in conjunction with other broad social trends like education and industrialization, which themselves would powerfully affect fertility, just as a decline in fertility would assist importantly in bringing these trends about (72). Both compulsory education and restrictions on child labor would lower the economic value of children, hence tend to produce a decline in fertility. The question is, how are they to be brought about?

Finally, whether or not research would affect fertility trends depends of course upon its nature and outcome. Most observers believe that, under the typical conditions of the developing society, any improvement in contraceptive technology would lead toward the realization of present fertility goals and might help turn the spiral down. Indeed, several observers believe that this is the single most important desideratum, over the short run. Easy means of determining sex should have some effect upon the "need for sons" and thus cut family size to some extent. Research on the social-economic side would probably have to take effect through programs of the kinds discussed above.

The picture is not particularly encouraging. The measures that would work to sharply cut fertility are politically and morally unacceptable to the societies in question (as with coercion), and in any case unavailable; or they are difficult of attainment in any foreseeable future, as in the case of broad social trends or a shift in age at marriage. The measures that might possibly be tried in some settings, like some version of incentives or benefit or liability plans, give uncertain promise of results at the probable level of operation. Legalization of abortion, where the needed medical facilities are available, would almost certainly have a measurable effect, but acceptability is problematic.

## Conclusion

This review leaves us with some conclusions concerning proposals that go beyond family planning.

1) There is no easy way to achieve population control. If this review has indicated nothing else, it has shown how many obstacles stand in the way of a solution to the population problem. Table 1 shows, by way of recapitulation, how the various proposals seem to fit the several criteria (73). That is only one observer's judgment of the present situation, but, whatever appraisal is made of specific items, it would appear that the overall picture is mixed.

2) Family-planning programs do not compare unfavorably with other specific proposals, especially when one considers that any *actual* operating program is at a disadvantage when compared with any competitive *ideal* policy. Indeed, on this showing, if family-planning programs did not exist, they would have to be invented; it appears that they would be among the first proposals to be made and the first programs to be tried, given their generally acceptable characteristics.

In fact, when such proposals are made, it turns out that many of them call for *more* family planning, not less, but in a somewhat different form. In the present case, at least a third of the proposals listed above put forward, in effect, simply another approach to family planning, often accepting the existing motivation as to family size. In any case, family-planning programs are established, have some momentum, and, importantly, would be useful as the direct instrument through which other proposals would take effect. So, as a major critic (74) acknowledges (6), "there is no reason to abandon family-planning programs."

What is needed is the energetic and full implementation of present experience. Much more could be done on the informational side, on encouraging commercial distribution of contraceptives, on the use of paramedical personnel, on logistics and supply, on the training and supervision of field workers, on approaches to special groups of individuals, ranging from women after childbirth to young men drafted into the armed forces. If workers in this field did well what they know how to do, that in itself would in all likelihood make a measurable difference, competitive in magnitude with the probable effects of other specific proposals—not to mention the further impetus of an improved contraceptive technology.

3) Most of the proposed ideas are not new; they have been around for some time. So, if they are not being tried, it is not because they have not been known but because they have not been accepted—presumably, for reasons like those discussed above. In India, for example, several of the social measures being proposed have been, it would seem, under almost constant re-

view by one or another committee for the past 10 to 15 years. So it is not correct to imply that it is only new ideas that are needed; the ideas are there, but their political, economic, or administrative feasibility are problematic.

4) All of the proposers are dissatisfied to some degree with present family-planning efforts, but that does not mean that they agree with one another's schemes for doing better. Thus, Ohlin believes that "the demographic significance of such measures [maternity benefits and tax deductions for children] would be limited" (34). Ketchel eloquently opposes several "possible alternatives to fertility control agents" (9). Meier argues against the tax on children on both humanitarian and political grounds (16). The U.N. Advisory Mission to India comments (53, p. 87), "it is realised that no major demographic effects can be expected from measures of this kind [maternity benefits], particularly as only a small proportion of families are covered . . . but they could contribute, together with the family planning programme, to a general change in the social climate relating to childbearing." Earlier, in supporting a family-planning effort in India, Davis noted that "the reaction to the Sarda Act [the Child Marriage Restraint Act

of 1929] prohibiting female marriage [below age 14] shows the difficulty of trying to regulate the age of marriage by direct legislation" (75). Myrdal warns against cash payments to parents in this connection and supports social awards in kind to the children (76). Kirk believes that "it might prove to be the height of folly to undermine the existing family structure, which continues to be a crucial institution for stability and socialization in an increasingly mobile and revolutionary society" (77). Finally, Ehrlich is contemptuous of the professors whose "ideas of 'action' is to form a committee or to urge 'more research.' Both courses are actually substitutes for action" (7, p. 191).

5) In a rough way, there appears to be a progression in national efforts to deal with the problem of population control. The first step is the theoretical recognition that population growth may have something to do with the prospects for economic development. Then, typically, comes an expert mission from abroad to make a survey and report to the government, as has occurred in India, Pakistan, South Korea, Turkey, Iran, Tunisia, Morocco, and Kenya, among others. The first action program is in family planning, and most of the efforts are still at that level. Beyond that, it apparently takes (i) some degree

of discouragement about progress combined with (ii) some heightened awareness of the seriousness of the problem to move the effort forward. To date, those conditions have been most prominently present in India—and that is the country that has gone farthest in the use of incentives and in at least consideration of further steps along the lines mentioned above.

6) Proposals need to be specific— proposals both for action and for further research. It is perhaps too much to ask advocates to spell out all the administrative details of the way their plan is to operate in the face of obstacles and difficulties, or even to spell out how it is to get permission to operate; the situations, settings, opportunities, and personalities are too diverse for that. But it does seem proper to ask for the fullest possible specification of actual plans, under realistic conditions, in order to test out their feasibility and likely effectiveness. Similarly, advocates of further research ought to spell out not only what would be studied, and how, but also how the results might be applied in action programs to affect fertility. Social research is not always readily translated into action, especially into administrative action; and the thrust of research is toward refinement, subtlety, precision, and qualification,

Table 1. Illustrative appraisal of proposals, by criteria.

| Proposal | Scientific readiness | Political viability | Administrative feasibility | Economic capability | Ethical acceptability | Presumed effectiveness |
|---|---|---|---|---|---|---|
| A. Extension of voluntary fertility control | High | High on maternal care, moderate-to-low on abortion | Uncertain in near future | Maternal care too costly for local budget, abortion feasible | High for maternal care, low for abortion | Moderately high |
| B. Establishment of involuntary fertility control | Low | Low | Low | High | Low | High |
| C. Intensified educational campaigns | High | Moderate-to-high | High | Probably high | Generally high | Moderate |
| D. Incentive programs | High | Moderately low | Low | Low-to-moderate | Low-to-high | Uncertain |
| E. Tax and welfare benefits and penalties | High | Moderately low | Low | Low-to-moderate | Low-to-moderate | Uncertain |
| F. Shifts in social and economic institutions | High | Generally high, but low on some specifics | Low | Generally low | Generally high, but uneven | High, over long run |
| G. Political channels and organizations | High | Low | Low | Moderate | Moderately low | Uncertain |
| H. Augmented research efforts | Moderate | High | Moderate-to-high | High | High | Uncertain |
| Family-planning programs | Generally high, but could use improved technology | Moderate-to-high | Moderate-to-high | High | Generally high, but uneven, on religious grounds | Moderately high |

whereas the administrator must act in the large. Short of such specification, the field remains confronted with potentially good ideas, such as "raise the age at marriage" or "use incentives" or "substitute pension systems for male children," without being able to move very far toward implementation.

7) Just as there is no easy way, there is no single way. Since population control will at best be difficult, it follows that every acceptable step that promises some measure of impact should be taken. The most likely prospect is that population control, to the degree it is realized, will be the result of a combination of efforts—economic, legal, social, medical—each of which has some effect but not an immediately overwhelming one (78). Accordingly, it is incumbent upon workers in the professional fields concerned to look hard at various approaches, including family planning itself, in order to screen out what is potentially useful for application. In doing so, it may be the path of wisdom to move with the "natural" progression. Some important proposals seem reasonably likely of adoption—institutionalization of maternal care, population study in the schools, the TV satellite system for disseminating information, a better contraceptive technology, perhaps even liberalization of abortion laws in some settings—and we need to know not only how effective such efforts will be but, beyond them, how large a money incentive would have to be to effect a given amount of fertility control and how effective those indirect social measures are that are morally acceptable and capable of realization. It may be that some of these measures would be both feasible and effective—many observers 15 years ago thought that family-planning programs were neither —and a genuine effort needs to be made. The "heavy" measures—involuntary measures and political pressures —may be put aside for the time being, if not forever.

8) In the last analysis, what will be scientifically available, politically acceptable, administratively feasible, economically justifiable, and morally tolerated depends upon people's perceptions of consequences. If "the population problem" is considered relatively unimportant or only moderately important, that judgment will not support much investment of effort. If it is considered urgent, much more can and will

be done. The fact is that, despite the large forward strides taken in international recognition of the problem in the 1960's, there still does not exist an informed, firm, and constant conviction in high circles that this is a matter with truly great implications for human welfare (79). Such convictions must be based on sound knowledge. Here it would appear that the demographers and economists have not sufficiently made their case to the world elite—or that, if made, the case has not sufficiently commanded their attention and support. Population pressures are not sharply visible on a day-to-day or even year-to-year basis, nor, short of major famine, do they show themselves in dramatic events. Moreover, the warnings of demographers are often dismissed, albeit unfairly and wrongly, on the basis of past forecasts that were not borne out (80). After all, only a generation ago we were being warned about a decline in population in the West. Asking government leaders to take steps toward population control is asking them to take very substantial steps indeed—substantial for their people as well as for their own political careers— hence the case must be virtually incontrovertible. Accordingly, the scientific base must be carefully prepared (and perhaps with some sense of humility about the ease of predicting or urging great events, for the record is not without blemishes). Greater measures to meet the problem—measures which exclude social repression and needless limitation of human freedom—must rely on heightened awareness of what is at stake, on the part of leaders and masses alike.

What is beyond family planning? Even if most of the specific plans are not particularly new, that in itself does not mean that they are to be disregarded. The questions are: Which plans can be effected, given such criteria? How can they be implemented? What will be the outcome?

This article is an effort to promote the discourse across the professional fields concerned with this important issue. Given the recent stress on family-planning programs as the "means of choice" in dealing with the problem, it is natural and desirable that counterpositions be put forward and reviewed. But that does not in itself settle the critical questions. What can we do now to advance the matter? Beyond family planning, what?

### References and Notes

1. See, for example, K. Davis, *Science* **158**, 730 (1967); R. G. Potter, R. Freedman, L. P. Chow, *ibid.* **160**, 848 (1968); F. W. Notestein, "Population growth and its control," paper presented before the American Assembly on World Hunger, Fall 1968.
2. See, for example, the section on "Goals" in K. Davis, *Science* **158**, 730 (1967).
3. A. J. Coale, "Should the United States start a campaign for fewer births?," presidential address presented before the Population Association of America, 1968.
4. For current targets of some national family-planning programs, see B. Berelson, "National family planning programs: Where we stand," paper presented at the University of Michigan Sesquicentennial Celebration, November 1967; the paper concludes: "By and large, developing countries are now aiming at the birth rates of Western Europe 75 years ago or the United States 50 years ago."
5. H. C. Taylor, Jr., and B. Berelson, *Amer. J. Obstet. Gynecol.* **100**, 885 (1968).
6. K. Davis, *Science* **158**, 730 (1967).
7. P. R. Ehrlich, *The Population Bomb* (Ballantine, New York, 1968).
8. S. Chandrasekhar, *Population Rev.* **10**, 17 (1966).
9. M. M. Ketchel, *Perspect. Biol. Med.* **11**, 687 (1968); see also Ketchel's article in *Med. World News* (18 Oct. 1968), p. 66.
10. Ehrlich appears to dismiss the scheme as unworkable (7, p. 136), though two pages later he advocates "ample funds" to "promote intensive investigation of new techniques of birth control, possibly leading to the development of mass sterilizing agents such as were discussed above."
11. K. E. Boulding, *The Meaning of the Twentieth Century: The Great Transition* (Harper & Row, New York, 1964), pp. 135–36.
12. W. B. Shockley, in a lecture delivered at McMaster University, Hamilton, Ontario, December 1967.
13. S. Chandrasekhar, as reported in the New York *Times*, 24 July 1967. Just as the present article was being completed, Chandrasekhar proposed (*ibid.*, 21 Oct. 1968) "that every married couple in India deny themselves sexual intercourse for a year. . . . Abstinence for a year would do enormous good to the individual and the country." The reader may wish to consider this the 30th proposal and test it against the criteria that follow.
14. S. Wayland, in *Family Planning and Population Programs*, B. Berelson, R. K. Anderson, O. Harkavy, J. Maier, W. P. Mauldin, S. J. Segal, Eds. (Univ. of Chicago Press, Chicago, 1966), pp. 353–62; ———, in "Family Planning Programs: Administration, Evaluation," J. Ross and J. Friesen, Eds., in preparation; "Teaching Population Dynamics: An Instructional Unit for Secondary School Students" (Columbia University, New York, 1965); "Critical Stages in Reproduction: Instruction Materials in General Science and Biology" (Columbia University, New York, 1965). The two last-named publications are pamphlets prepared under Wayland's direction at Teachers College.
15. P. Visaria, *Economic Weekly* (8 Aug. 1964), p. 1343.
16. R. L. Meier and G. Meier, "New Directions: A Population Policy for the Future," unpublished manuscript.
17. *Preparatory Study of a Pilot Project in the Use of Satellite Communication for National Development Purposes in India* (UNESCO Expert Mission, 1968).
18. W. Schramm and L. Nelson, *Communication Satellite for Education and Development— The Case of India* (Stanford Research Institute, Stanford, Calif., 1968), pp. 63–66.
19. S. Chandrasekhar, as reported in the New York *Times*, 19 July 1967.
20. E. Pohlman (Central Family Planning Institute, India), "Incentives for 'Non-Maternity' Cannot 'Compete' with Incentives for Vasectomy," unpublished manuscript.
21. T. J. Samuel, *J. Family Welfare* **13**, 11 (1966).
22. J. Simon, "Money Incentives to Reduce Birth Rates in Low-Income Countries: A Proposal to Determine the Effect Experimentally," unpublished manuscript; "The Role of Bonuses

and Persuasive Propaganda in the Reduction of Birth Rates," unpublished manuscript.
23. ———, "Family Planning Prospects in Less-Developed Countries, and a Cost-Benefit Analysis of Various Alternatives," unpublished manuscript.
24. S. Enke, *Population Rev.* **4**, 47 (1960).
25. M. Young, "The Behavioral Sciences and Family Planning Programs: Report on a Conference," *Studies in Family Planning*, No. 23 (1967), p. 10.
26. D. Bhatia, "Government of India Small Family Norm Committee Questionnaire," *Indian J. Med. Educ.* **6**, 189 (1967). As the title indicates, this is not a proposal but a questionnaire soliciting opinions on various ideas put forward to promote "the small family norm."
27. S. Enke, "The Gains to India from Population Control," *Rev. Econ. Statist.* **42**, 179, 180 (1960).
27a. J. W. Leasure, *Milbank Mem. Fund Quart.* **45**, 417 (1967).
28. J. J. Spengler, "Agricultural development is not enough," paper presented before the Conference on World Population Problems, Indiana University, May 1967.
29. M. C. Balfour, "A Scheme for Rewarding Successful Family Planners," *Population Council Mem.* (1962).
30. W. P. Mauldin, "Prevention of Illegitimate Births: A Bonus Scheme," *Population Council Mem.* (1967).
31. R. M. Titmuss and B. Abel-Smith, *Social Policies and Population Growth in Mauritius* (Methuen, London, 1960).
32. A. S. David, *National Development, Population and Family Planning in Nepal* (1968), pp. 53–54.
33. J. Fawcett, personal communication.
34. G. Ohlin, *Population Control and Economic Development* (Development Centre of the Organisation for Economic Co-operation and Development, New York, 1967), p. 104.
35. W. P. Davison, personal communication. Davison suggests a good pension (perhaps $400 a year) for men aged 60, married for at least 20 years, with no sons.
36. K. Davis, personal communication.
37. B. Berelson and A. Etzioni, brief formulations, 1962 and 1967, respectively.
38. P. M. Hauser, in "The Behavioral Sciences and Family Planning Programs: Report on a Conference," *Studies in Family Planning*, No. 23 (1967), p. 9.
39. J. Blake, in *Public Health and Population Change: Current Research Issues*, M. C. Sheps and J. C. Ridley, Eds. (Univ. of Pittsburgh Press, Pittsburgh, 1965), p. 62.
40. For the initial formulation of the proposal, see R. L. Meier, *Modern Science and the Human Fertility Problem* (Wiley, New York, 1959), chap. 7.
41. P. M. Hauser, *Demography* **4**, 412 (1967).
42. "Family Planning and the Status of Women: Interim Report of the Secretary-General" (United Nations Economic and Social Council, Commission on the Status of Women, New York, 1968), especially p. 17 ff.
43. R. Revelle, quoted by M. Viorst, *Horizon* (summer 1968), p. 35; D. M. Heer and D. O. Smith, "Mortality level and desired family size," paper presented before the Population Association of America, April 1967.
44. Ehrlich makes the same point in *New Scientist* (14 Dec. 1967), p. 655: "Refuse all foreign aid to any country with an increasing population which we believe is not making a maximum effort to limit its population. . . . The United States should use its power and prestige to bring extreme diplomatic and/or economic pressure on any country or organization (the Roman Catholic Church?) impeding a solution to the world's most pressing problem."
45. In an earlier article Ehrlich calls for a "Federal Population Commission with a large budget for propaganda," presumably limited to the United States.
46. S. Chandrasekhar, in *Asia's Population Problems*, S. Chandrasekhar, Ed. (Allen & Unwin, New York, 1967), p. 96; Chandrasekhar cites a suggestion made in 1961 by Julian Huxley.
47. S. Polgar, in "The Behavioral Sciences and Family Planning Programs: Report on a Conference," *Studies in Family Planning*, No. 23 (1967), p. 10.
48. *The Growth of World Population* (National Academy of Sciences, Committee on Science and Public Policy, Washington, D.C., 1963), pp. 5, 28–36. This recommendation has of course been made on several occasions by several people. For an imaginative account of the impact of biological developments, see P. C. Berry, appendix to *The Next Thirty-Four Years: A Context for Speculation* (Hudson Institute, Croton-on-Hudson, New York, 1966).
49. See, for example, S. J. Segal, "Biological aspects of fertility regulation," paper presented at the University of Michigan Sesquicentennial Celebration, November 1967.
50. It is worth noting that such expectations are not particularly reliable. For example, in 1952–53 a Working Group on Fertility Control was organized by the Conservation Foundation to review the most promising "leads to physiologic control of fertility," based on a survey conducted by Paul S. Henshaw and Kingsley Davis. This group did identify a "lead" that became the oral contraceptive (then already under investigation) but did not mention the intrauterine device. It was searching specifically for better ways to control fertility because of the population problem in the developing world, and considered the contraceptive approach essential to that end: "It thus appears imperative that an attempt be made to bring down fertility in overpopulated regions without waiting for a remote, hoped-for transformation of the entire society. . . . It seems plausible that acceptable birth control techniques might be found, and that the application of science to developing such techniques for peasant regions might yield revolutionary results" [*The Physiological Approach to Fertility Control, Report of the Working Group on Fertility Control* (Conservation Foundation, New York, 1953)].
51. A. S. Parkes, *New Scientist* **35**, 186 (1967).
52. New York *Times* (17 Nov. 1967). The then Minister had earlier suggested a substantial bonus (100 rupees) for vasectomy, the funds to be taken from U.S. counterpart funds, "but both Governments are extremely sensitive in this area. Yet in a problem this crucial perhaps we need more action and less sensitivity" [S. Chandrasekhar (*46*)].
53. *Report on the Family Planning Programme in India* (United Nations Advisory Mission, New York, 1966).
54. *Implications of Raising the Female Age at Marriage in India* (Demographic Training and Research Centre, Chembur, India, 1968), p. 109; *Centre Calling* (May 1968), p. 4.
55. *Planned Parenthood* (Mar. 1968), p. 3.
56. *Ibid.* (Apr. 1968), p. 2.
57. For a review of this development see R. Symonds and M. Carder, *International Organisations and Population Control (1947–67)* (Institute of Development Studies, Univ. of Sussex, Brighton, England, 1968).
58. At present, population materials are being included in school programs in Pakistan, Iran, Taiwan, and elsewhere.
59. See, for example, Balfour (*29*), Mauldin (*30*), and Pohlman (*20*) and, for the economic analysis, Enke (*27*) and Simon (*22*).
60. For the negative answer, see Enke (*27*) and Simon (*22*). Data are from family-planning budgets and national development budgets contained in 5-year development plans.
61. E. Pohlman, "Incentives in birth planning," in preparation.
62. Coale, however, does point out that "it is clearly fallacious to accept as optimal a growth that continues until overcrowding makes additional births intolerably expensive."
63. See, for example, the World Leaders' Statement [*Studies in Family Planning*, No. 26 (1968)] and the Resolution of the International Conference on Human Rights on "Human Rights Aspects of Family Planning," adopted 12 May 1968, reported in *Population Newsletter*, No. 2 (issued by the Population Division, United Nations) (1968), p. 21 ff. Incidentally, the issue of population policy was apparently a live one in classical times, and resolved by the great philosophers in ways not fully consonant with modern views. Plato, in the *Republic* (Modern Library ediiton, pp. 412, 414), says, "the number of weddings is a matter which must be left to the discretion of the rulers, whose aim will be to preserve the average of population and to prevent the State from becoming either too large or too small"—to which end certain marriages have "strict orders to prevent any embryo which may come into being from seeing the light; and if any force a way to the birth, the parents must understand that the offspring of such a union cannot be maintained, and arrange accordingly." Aristotle, in *Politics* (Modern Library edition, p. 316) says, "on the ground of an excess in the number of children, if the established customs of the state forbid this (for in our state population has a limit), no child is to be exposed, but when couples have children in excess, let abortion be procured before sense and life have begun. . . ."
64. After noting that economic constraints have not been adopted in South Asia, though often proposed, Gunnar Myrdal continues: "The reason is not difficult to understand. Since having many children is a main cause of poverty, such measures would penalize the relatively poor and subsidize the relatively well off. Such a result would not only violate rules of equity but would be detrimental to the health of the poor families, and so of the growing generation" [*Asian Drama: An Inquiry into the Poverty of Nations* (Pantheon, New York, 1968), vol. 2, pp. 1502–03].
65. F. W. Notestein, in *Family Planning and Population Programs*, Berelson *et al.*, Eds. (Univ. of Chicago Press, Chicago, 1966), pp. 828–29: "There is a real danger that sanctions, for example through taxation, would affect adversely the welfare of the children. There is also danger that incentives through bonuses will put the whole matter of family planning in a grossly commercial light. It is quite possible that to poor and harassed people financial inducements will amount to coercion and not to an enlargement of their freedom of choice. Family planning must be, and must seem to be, an extension of personal and familial freedom of choice and thereby an enrichment of life, not coercion toward its restriction."
66. In this connection see the novel by A. Burgess, *The Wanting Seed* (Ballantine, New York, 1963). At the same time, Myrdal, a long-time observer of social affairs, remarks that "the South Asian countries . . . can, to begin with, have no other principle than that of voluntary parenthood. . . . State direction by compulsion in these personal matters is not effective. . ." [G. Myrdal, *Asian Drama: An Inquiry into the Poverty of Nations* (Pantheon, New York, 1968), p. 1501].
67. G. I. Zatuchni, "International Postpartum Family Planning Program: Report on the First Year," *Studies in Family Planning*, No. 22 (1967), p. 14 ff.
68. For example, the repeal of the free abortion law in Rumania resulted in an increase in the birth rate from 14 in the third quarter of 1966 to 38 in the third quarter of 1967. For an early report, see R. Pressat, *Population* **22**, 1116 (1967).
69. See *Social Security Programs Throughout the World, 1964* (U.S. Department of Health, Education, and Welfare, Washington, D.C., 1964).
70. S. N. Agarwala in *Implications of Raising the Female Age at Marriage in India* (Demographic Training and Research Centre, Chembur, India, 1968), p. 21.
71. V. C. Chidambaram, *ibid.*, p. 47.
72. Actually, recent research is calling into question some of the received wisdom on the prior need of such broad institutional factors for fertility decline. If further study supports the new findings, that could have important implications for present strategy in the developing countries. See A. J. Coale, in *Proc. U.N. World Population Conf.* (1965), vol. 2, pp. 205–09, and ———, "The decline of fertility in Europe from the French Revolution to World War II," paper presented at the University of Michigan Sesquicentennial Celebration, 1967.
73. As the roughest sort of summary of Table 1, if one assigns values from 5 for "high" to 1 for "low," the various proposals rank as follows: family-planning programs, 25; intensified educational campaigns, 25; augmented research efforts, 24; extension of voluntary fertility control, 20; shifts in social and economic institutions, 20; incentive programs, 14; tax and welfare benefits and

penalties, 14; political channels and organizations, 14; establishment of involuntary fertility control, 14.

74. Davis was a strong advocate of family planning in India, and quite optimistic about its prospects even in the pre-IUD or pre-pill era. See K. Davis, in *The Interrelations of Demographic, Economic, and Social Problems in Selected Underdeveloped Areas* (Milbank Memorial Fund, New York, 1954). Davis concludes (pp. 87–88): "Although India is already well-launched in the rapid-growth phase of the demographic transition, there is no inherent reason why she should long continue in this phase. She need not necessarily wait patiently while the forces of urbanization, class mobility, and industrial development gradually build up to the point where parents are forced to limit their offspring on their own initiative and without help, perhaps even in the face of official opposition. . . . Realistically appraising her situation, India has a chance to be the first country to achieve a major revolution in human life—the planned diffusion of fertility control in a peasant population prior to, and for the benefit of, the urban-industrial transition."

75. K. Davis, in *The Interrelations of Demographic, Economic, and Social Problems in Selected Underdeveloped Areas* (Milbank Memorial Fund, New York, 1954), p. 86.

76. G. Myrdal, *Asian Drama: An Inquiry into the Poverty of Nations* (Pantheon, New York, 1968), p. 1503.

77. D. Kirk, "Population research in relation to population policy and national family planning programs," paper presented before the American Sociological Association, August 1968.

78. It begins to appear that the prospects for fertility control may be improving over the decades. Kirk, after reviewing several factors that "favor a much more rapid [demographic] transition than occurred in the West"—changed climate of opinion, religious doctrine, decline of infant mortality, modernization, fertility differentials, grass-roots concern, and improved contraceptive technology—shows, in a remarkable tabulation, that the later a country began the reduction of its birth rate from 35 to 20 births per thousand, the shorter the time it took to achieve this reduction: from 73 years (average) for the period 1831–60, for example, to 21 years after 1951; the trend has been consistently downward for over a century [D. Kirk, "Natality in the developing countries: recent trends and prospects," paper presented at the University of Michigan Sesquicentennial Celebration, 1967].

79. Nor, often, does such a conviction exist among the general public. For example, in midsummer of 1968 a national sample of adults was asked in a Gallup poll, "What do you think is the most important problem facing this country today?" Less than 1 percent mentioned population growth (Gallup release, 3 Aug. 1968, and personal communication).

80. For an old but enlightening review, see H. Dorn, *J. Amer. Statist. Ass.* **45**, 311 (1950).

# The Case for
# Compulsory Birth Control

*Edgar Chasteen*

Complete freedom is anarchy. If freedom may be thought of as the right to swing one's fist, then freedom stops where someone's nose begins. This crude but picturesque analogy serves to illustrate both the relative nature of freedom and its relationship to the population explosion. The more people there are, the less freedom there is.

Over the past 100 years, Western medicine has practically eliminated smallpox, diphtheria, scarlet fever, polio, and other mass killers. Almost all children are now inoculated against disease—in effect, life is imposed upon many who, if natural selection were allowed to operate, would not survive childhood. And when old age comes, every medical technique available is marshaled to maintain life beyond the point at which death would "naturally" occur.

The technology of death control has developed over the past century because government and medicine have deemed it good that man should live long. Governments have supported and rewarded research designed to control death, and medicine has responded as Merlin might have to King Arthur. So preoccupied with death control have government, medicine, and the biological sciences become that critics label this trinity the Health Syndicate. Over the years, its awesome efficiency has been exceeded only by the public adulation and reward heaped upon its practitioners. By contrast, those concerned with birth control have been restricted by the law and lampooned by the press.

As the technology of death control was perfected, a philosophy concerning its use was also developed. That philosophy held that it was the duty of government to ensure that all its citizens shared in these medical miracles. This was accomplished in a simple, straightforward manner—death control was made compulsory. Thus, we are not allowed to choose whether we shall be

Edgar Chasteen teaches sociology at William Jewell College, and is a board member of Zero Population Growth, Inc., the only population organization in the country to endorse compulsory birth control.

Reprinted by permission of the author from *Mademoiselle,* January 1970, pp. 142–143.

inoculated against disease; for our own and our community's well-being, we are forced to protect ourselves against epidemic and accident. Neither may we choose to die so long as the doctor or a drug can prolong life. Few people, however, see compulsory death control as an abridgment of their freedom because most want to live as long as possible. Fewer still have had the foresight or the courage to point out that we cannot forever practice compulsory death control without also practicing compulsory birth control.

We live in a finite world. Whatever the number of people it is capable of supporting, there is a limit. We do know that our world is doing a pretty poor job of supporting its present population of around 3½ billion. How long can we expect to continue to double world population every 35 years? To what end? In what ways will we be better off with 7 billion people than with 3½ billion? What possible advantages are there in even minimal population growth? Scores of disadvantages come readily to mind, but not a single benefit. The stork is not the bird of paradise.

Since man first appeared on the earth, his number has multiplied to its present level of 3½ billion. At the present rate of growth, this number will quadruple in less than 80 years. Each day now adds 325,000 babies to the world's population; 2,279,000 each week; over 118 million every year.

The number of *hungry* people in the world today is greater than the total number of people in 1900. The continents of Africa, Asia, and South America are losing the race with illiteracy, food scarcity, and political instability. With a population in excess of 200 million, America does not need any more people. Already we have too few jobs, schools, hospitals, and homes. The countryside is being gobbled up at the rate of 40 acres per mile of freeway, and still the journey to work takes longer than it did 100 years ago. The Northeastern Seaboard has become a vast and confusing megalopolis with up to 100,000 people per square mile. So contaminated is the air of Los Angeles that a sudden inversion of wind pattern could choke the life out of hundreds of people. Such a horror has stricken London twice in the past 20 years.

So desperate is the situation that an increasing number of usually placid demographers, biologists, and nutritionists have joined with conservationists and pollution critics to plead for immediate and drastic action. Georg Borgstrom's *The Hungry Planet,* Paul Ehrlich's *The Population Bomb,* Paul and William Paddock's *Famine—1975,* and Lincoln and Alice Day's *Too Many Americans* are but four recent expressions of the climate of crisis rapidly eroding the optimism of the technocrats so dominant over the past two decades.

Just as we have laws compelling death control, so we must have laws requiring birth control—the purpose being to ensure a zero rate of population increase. We must come to see that it is the duty of the government to protect women against pregnancy as it protects them against job discrimination and smallpox, and for the same reason—the public good. No longer can we tolerate the doctrinaire position that the number of children a couple has is a strictly private decision carrying no social consequences. There is ample precedent for legislation limiting family size; for example, the law which limits a married person to only one spouse. But if we are to understand the function of law as a regulator of human conduct, we must first recall man's history.

The history of civilization is the process of translating absolute rights into conditioned privileges. Roman fathers 2,000 years ago had the power of life and death over their children. If they so chose, they could leave a child on a hillside to be stolen by animals or killed by the elements. Likewise, Chinese fathers had the right to trade female children for some needed household item. Up to the turn of this century, American parents had the right to put children to work rather than send them to school.

But all this has now changed. Laws have been passed which severely restrict the right of parents over their own children. Compulsory-school-attendance laws, health laws, delinquency laws, housing laws—all have translated parental *rights* into *privileges*. The next logical extension of this process is to make it a privilege to have children. Such laws would serve not only to defuse the population bomb, but also to protect first-born children against too prolific reproduction by their parents. Recent studies have shown that the most crucial factor associated with the economic status of a family is its size; the larger the family, the more likely it is to be poverty-stricken. The chances of a child's acquiring an education, a healthy body, adequate shelter, and a decent job decline as the number of his brother and sisters increases.

Some future historian will look back on the 20th century and write that in the year 19___, laws were passed which struck down forever that anachronistic practice to which we had too long adhered—the right to have as many children as one wanted. That "want," after all, is socially created and may be socially redefined. No one is born wanting a certain number of children, any more than one wants at birth to speak English or to eat with a fork. The desire to give birth to one, four, seven, or 15 children is thus exposed for what it is—an accident—conditioned by the time and place of our own birth. That future historian will consider us as uncivilized for having permitted unregulated births as we do the Romans and Chinese for their "irresponsible" behavior.

Some will object to compulsory birth control, contending that it smacks of Big Brother and *1984*. On the contrary, it would seem that such Orwellian conditions are inevitable *without* a policy of compulsory birth control. For the quality of human life is irreversibly lowered as the numbers of Homo sapiens incessantly mount. A once-virgin globe has been stripped of its beauty, contaminated beyond redemption. Wildlife has been thoughtlessly slaughtered as man has inadvertently and ominously altered his ecological environment.

Some people argue that education can solve the population problem. But even a superficial analysis shows that education cannot solve even the education problem; laws are necessary to correct deficiencies in the educational process itself. It seems naïve, then, to rely on education to persuade individual parents not to have too many children.

Even though attempts have been made to educate smokers to the dangers of cigarettes, more people are now smoking than in 1964 when the Surgeon General's report linking cigarettes to cancer was issued. Drivers continue to sit on their seat belts despite the educational campaign by the National Safety Council, which urges us to "buckle up for safety." If such superficial behavior has not responded to education, can we expect more from our efforts to educate for "responsible parenthood"?

The argument of some religious authorities that compulsion in the face of conviction constitutes unjustified interference is less than convincing. Such reasoning was not sustained when members of the Church of God refused to pay income taxes because to do so would imply recognition of a power other than God. Neither was it upheld when the Mormons of the last century argued that plural marriages were part of their religion. The Amish have been forced to send their children to school beyond the eighth grade, and the Christian Scientist is compelled to accept medical attention for a critically ill child.

The completely effective and reversible contraceptive necessary for a policy of compulsory birth control is not yet available. Medical science is experimenting, however, with a shot and a time capsule that would inhibit fertility indefinitely. Within a few years, such contraceptives will be as available and as pleasant as the sugar-cube polio vaccine. This will make it possible to inoculate all males and females against fertility as they reach puberty. After marriage, this process could be reversed by another shot or pill designed to restore fertility temporarily.

If we can rid ourselves of outmoded values concerning laissez-faire parenthood and establish sensible and compulsory limits to family size, we shall eliminate a host of problems not otherwise soluble, and we shall expand the freedom "to be" which, after all, makes us human. If we cannot, then we must quit our practice of compulsory death control and let nature re-establish its own balance of births and deaths.

# Prognosis for the Development of New Chemical Birth-Control Agents

Parochial attitudes in technologically advanced nations make prospects increasingly dismal.

Carl Djerassi

The very rapid rate of increase in the world's population, notably in the developing countries, has become a matter of worldwide concern. Fifteen years ago this was virtually a taboo subject, whereas the term *population explosion* has now become a household phrase. Symptomatic of the international concern with this problem and its enormous economic, political, and human implications is the fact that the very first report by the Committee on Science and Public Policy of the Na-

The author is professor of chemistry at Stanford University, Stanford, California, and president of Syntex Research, Palo Alto, California. This article is adapted from a paper presented 22 October 1969 at the 19th Pugwash Conference on Science and World Affairs, in Sochi, U.S.S.R.

tional Academy of Sciences dealt with the population problem (*1*). A veritable flood of articles and books has appeared on this subject in recent years, and the general consensus is that effective family planning must play a key role in the solution of this world problem.

At first glance, the prognosis for improved family-planning methods appears promising. During the past 10 years a major breakthrough in birth-control techniques has been achieved: the development of orally administered contraceptive agents (*2, 3*) of virtually 100 percent effectiveness, and greatly increased use of improved intrauterine devices (IUD) (*4*). Both approaches lend themselves much more readily

than conventional earlier methods (for example, the diaphragm, the condom, and so on) to broad-scale family planning in developing countries, and it is not surprising, therefore, that the well-publicized large-scale programs in such diverse countries as Chile, Egypt, South Korea, and Taiwan are based virtually exclusively on steroid oral contraceptive agents (*5*) and IUD's. Abortion is another effective means of population control, as demonstrated during the past 20 years on a country wide basis in Japan and eastern Europe, but the general tendency in research has been to concentrate on improved chemical agents for birth control, the dramatic effectiveness of the steroid oral contraceptive agents having provided the main impetus. Thus, considerable effort is being expended on overcoming one of the major drawbacks of these chemical agents—the necessity of taking a pill daily or with short interruptions—by developing "once-a-month" pills, or sustained-action formulations (Silastic implants, pellets, and so on) effective for many months or conceivably even years. Philanthropic organizations such as the Ford Foundation and the Population Council have been dedicating increasing amounts of money to the support of such research, and, during the past year, the National Institute of Child Health and Human Development of the U.S. Public Health Service has organized a Center for Population Research whose annual multimillion-dollar budget will be devoted to "the development of a variety of new methods of fertility regulation."

When we consider that such research has become not only respectable but also very fashionable, that ample financial resources are being mobilized by government, industrial, and philanthropic sources, and that the urgency and magnitude of the world's population explosion is widely recognized, then the prospects for the development of new or improved chemical contraceptive agents appear rosy indeed. My purpose in this article is to demonstrate that one factor, which has generally been overlooked and which is of rather recent origin, makes the prognosis for the introduction of new agents a progressively more dismal one. The Pugwash Conference, with its wide representation from developed and developing countries, appears to be a particularly suitable arena for airing this sensitive problem, especially since the topic "problems of population growth" has been put on the agenda of the 19th Conference in the context of "modern science and developing countries." As I intend to demonstrate in what follows, it is precisely this juxtaposition of "modern science and developing countries" which is creating an increasingly inhibiting atmosphere in the area of practical birth-control research if we equate "modern science" with "scientifically advanced nations."

While many of my comments also apply to newer work on improved IUD's, notably those containing metal or other chemical ingredients, I restrict my presentation to the development of newer *chemical* contraceptive agents (6), since this is a research field in which I have been personally involved, directly or indirectly, for nearly 20 years (7). All of the currently used orally or parenterally administered contraceptive agents are steroids, but it is reasonable to assume that clinically effective nonsteroidal organic chemicals (especially in the area of abortifacients) will also be developed. Irrespective of their chemical structure, there are at least six special or even unique factors that must be taken into consideration.

1) *Scientific complexity.* To judge from past experience, the development of an orally effective or parenterally administered sustained-action contraceptive from the chemical laboratory to final clinical use is one of the most complex sequences in medicinal research. Chemical investigations on steroids are performed in comparatively

few laboratories (most of them large drug firms), and the large-scale synthesis of steroids is one of the most difficult of industrial chemical operations. The biological screening of potential candidates requires a very high level of sophistication, since the reproductive processes of the female and male are so complicated and involve so many endocrine as well as target organs. Examination for possible toxicity has to be of a long-term nature [the most recent U.S. Food and Drug Administration (FDA) requirements for animal tests establishing safety for chemical (6) contraceptives require testing for 10 years in monkeys], and not only must clinical trials be performed with large numbers of human subjects for long periods but they must also be accompanied by batteries of chemical laboratory tests in order to evaluate the effect of such contraceptive agents on many physiological parameters. The obvious conclusion is that such research, especially if it is of a pioneering nature leading to development of new contraceptive agents or approaches, can and will be done only by scientists from highly developed, scientifically advanced countries. Therefore, the fact that virtually all such work has so far been performed in North America and Europe is not surprising. In other words, the research and development work is being performed in those countries in which the population increase is the lowest, in which conventional birth-control measures have already been used for a long time, and—most importantly—in which it is possible to dispense with new birth-control measures without concomitant disastrous economic consequences.

2) *Time scale.* By definition, if a contraceptive agent is to be used for family planning rather than as an adjunct to occasional sexual intercourse (for which, incidentally, "post-coital pills" are currently under investigation), it will be employed by an individual for long periods, frequently over many years. The statement is frequently made, notably in the lay press, that agents such as the female oral contraceptive pills will be taken by a woman for periods exceeding 20 years and that nothing is known about possible side effects resulting from such prolonged usage. While it is perfectly true that experiments on several thousand women would have to be conducted for 20 years in order to yield an unambiguous answer to such a question, our accu-

mulated experience during the past 10 years shows that, given a receptive climate for the development of new agents, very few women would in fact remain on the same contraceptive pill for even 10 years. Nevertheless, every responsible investigator will grant that unusual caution must be exercised in the toxicological and clinical evaluation of such agents, and that statistically meaningful experiments on large numbers of women for reasonably long periods must be conducted before such drugs are released to the general public. In a recent private conference in our laboratory with several experts in biology and clinical medicine from the United States and Europe, it was concluded that more than 8 years would be required to satisfy all current U.S. FDA requirements for introduction of a new agent to the public—once the chemical and initial biological work had been completed. These initial studies are by no means trivial and would themselves entail 1 or more years; thus a new contraceptive agent, in order to be introduced in 1977 as an effective means of population control, must already, in 1969, have passed through the chemical and biological laboratories of its discoverer. The demographic implications of this statement are rather shocking for a developing country that may still be waiting for the ideal contraceptive agent (instead of using existing ones) while its population doubles every 20 years, as is now the case in many areas of the world.

The apparent need for new contraceptive methods is exemplified by the following quotation from an editorial in the *New York Times* (6 July 1969) on the world's population proliferation:

Although recent advances in contraceptive technology—notably the pill and the loop—have made possible dramatic reductions in the birth rate in a few small countries, efforts at population control have been disappointing so far in most of the developing world. Many demographers believe that if significant reductions in population growth are to be achieved there must be a technological breakthrough in contraception similar to that in food production.

This desire for new contraceptive agents seems to stem from the observation that, in large-scale studies in developing countries, the 2-year dropout figure with IUD's or with the steroid oral contraceptives exceeds 50 percent. Personally, I am not convinced that any better results can be obtained with any method which requires a conscious act

Table 1. Risk of death with various contraceptive methods. [From *Int. Planned Parenthood Fed. Med. Bull.* **2**, No. 4 (1968)]

| Method | Pregnancies (No.) | Women aged 20–34 years ($10^6$ users per year) | | Women aged 35–44 years ($10^6$ users per year) | |
|---|---|---|---|---|---|
| | | Deaths due to pregnancy | Deaths due to method | Deaths due to pregnancy | Deaths due to method |
| IUD | 30,000 | 7 | Not known | 17 | Not known |
| Oral contraceptives | 5,000 | 1 | 13 | 3 | 34 |
| Diaphragm | 120,000 | 27 | 0 | 69 | 0 |
| Safe period | 240,000 | 55 | 0 | 135 | 0 |
| Pregnancy | 1,000,000 | 228 | | 576 | |

of conception control. For the populations of these developing countries it will be necessary to develop a procedure which produces, by a single administration of a birth-control agent, indefinite (but reversible) sterility, which could then be overcome temporarily by administration of a second, "fertility-producing" drug. The general state of the adult human population under these circumstances would be one of infertility which could be changed only by a conscious act, rather than the reverse state of affairs existing now. In the light of my subsequent remarks about the increasingly negative climate and conditions for clinical testing of new contraceptive agents, it seems exceedingly improbable that such a new approach can be brought to practical fruition in this century.

The *New York Times* editorial statement that "there must be a technological breakthrough in contraception similar to that in food production" must be viewed against this realistic background. Such remarks are frequently made in scientific as well as lay circles, but they are superficial. Improvement in food production (notably the recent dramatic results in wheat and rice production) is a technological matter which does not affect the palatability, acceptability, or biological properties of the food. A more appropriate analogy with respect to new contraception technology would be one between recently achieved improvements in food technology and improved chemical methods of manufacturing contraceptive pills, which would lower their price but would hardly affect population growth. Conversely, an appropriate counterpart in the food technology field to the required technological breakthrough in contraception would be the development of a completely new food (for instance, a synthetic food), whose acceptability to different populations would first have to be established, and whose mode of administration (for example, in pill form) would be quite

novel. If solution of the world's food problems depended on such a basic technological development, then the prospects for solving them in this century would be rather dismal.

3) *Side effects and healthy population.* Items 1 and 2 are basically logistical ones, and we can now turn to some of the more sensitive issues emanating from the fact that the contraceptive approaches to be utilized in the underdeveloped parts of the world are in fact being discovered and developed in the most advanced nations. We are faced with the ironic situation that, in these advanced nations, in which sales of tobacco and alcohol are not restricted in spite of the serious "side effects" of these agents, new candidates for contraceptive agents must meet more rigorous standards than most other drugs. One of the reasons is the assumption that the use of contraceptive agents involves healthy individuals and that only absolutely minimum side effects can, and should, be tolerated. Such a position is illogical on several grounds. First, our society does not take such a position with much more dangerous agents such as alcohol and tobacco, in spite of the fact that no socially redeeming effects (for example, birth control) are associated with their use. Second, there really are no drugs that have no side effects; even aspirin has known gastric effects and causes occasional deaths (8). Third and most relevant to our topic is the fact that pregnancy itself, which the contraceptive agents prevent, is a condition (some women might even call it an illness) that is accompanied by side effects ranging from nausea to death (see Table 1). My thesis is that we cannot afford the luxury of such rigorous standards, which are probably unrealizable (it seems unlikely that a drug lacking side effects in a few individuals can ever be developed) and unrealistic (requirements of 10 to 20 years' clinical experience with human subjects prior to general use have

been proposed by some circles, though not yet by government regulatory agencies), unless we are prepared to accept the reality that no new chemical birth-control agent that meets these standards will ever be developed.

4) *International role of the Food and Drug Administration.* The protocols for, and the conduct of, clinical trials in the United States have to be submitted to the FDA, which can disapprove them. This is the agency which subsequently approves or disapproves a drug for marketing. Except for export of drugs, its mandate ends with the geographical boundaries of this country. Yet in actual fact its dominant role is now noted over most of the world (especially in Europe) and even recognized by the FDA itself through the establishment in 1966 of an Office of International Affairs (9). Irrespective of the reasons, a drug that is formally disapproved in the United States has little chance to be marketed in Europe, and in the field of the steroid oral contraceptives the FDA has a *de facto* veto power in most European countries. The consequences of this situation are particularly serious in the field of birth control.

The FDA is a government regulatory body which is subject to tremendous political, journalistic, and legislative pressures. In a way, it is remarkable that the FDA has managed to maintain a considerable amount of independence even though many of the pressures exerted upon it have nothing to do with scientific facts. As stated above, the FDA's policies and standards for final approval of new contraceptive agents affect the possibility of even conducting initial clinical trials in the United States, and even abroad. For understandable reasons, FDA personnel have no incentive for expediting approval of new drugs, because their primary mandate is to protect the public from harm and fraud, rather than to stimulate medical advances. Consequently, the more novel the drug or mode of administration, the more extensive the data the agency requires for approval. The expense involved in conducting drug trials and in obtaining FDA approval in the United States generally runs now to millions of dollars and thus leads to the inevitable, albeit unfortunate, result that only very large commercial organizations have the financial and technical resources needed for carrying a new drug all the way to final, clinical use by the public. Expeditious FDA approval of a new drug, were it possible, would be looked upon by the press and the public today as kowtowing to a profit-hungry enterprise. And there have been unsavory examples that encourage caution. Unfortunately, this atmosphere has a particularly devastating effect on the development of new contraceptive agents.

These drugs, it should be noted, are really the first medicinal agents to be administered for very long periods to essentially healthy individuals, and neither the FDA nor the medical community has as yet solved satisfactorily the problem of what the standards should be in evaluating a drug used in such a population group for such purposes. This question must be answered eventually, because the trend in modern medicinal research is toward preventive medication, and in many conditions of aging and deterioration—for instance in atherosclerosis—the ideal preventive will have to be given to "healthy" individuals many years in advance of the actual occurrence of the disease.

Approval by the FDA (or occasionally by some European equivalent) is a virtual *sine qua non* before any contraceptive agent is accepted for wide use in one of the developing countries that have no significant governmental drug-control agencies, and the standards and designs of the clinical and even biological experiments are adapted to the American milieu. This situation occasionally has very unfortunate consequences in the birth-control field. Let me cite three examples, all very different.

The first illustrates the fact that epidemiological factors tend to be ignored, since drug approval is sought within the context of the American, or Western European, population. Thus, in Egypt—a country in which most of the government-supported birth-control programs are based on oral contraceptives—there seems to be an abnormally high incidence of liver involvement (*10*) after the use of steroid oral contraceptives; this, on further reflection, is not too surprising in view of the prevalence of *Bilharzia* infection in that country. In Iran, galactorrhea as a consequence of administration of the oral contraceptive (*10*) has been reported relatively frequently, whereas such a complication is seen very rarely in Europe or the United States. Under the present circumstances, such epidemiological factors will be studied only after a drug has passed the 10-year screen of FDA approval, which, of course, is much too late.

A second example illustrates the combined effect of general legal restrictions and FDA requirements. For perfectly understandable reasons, the FDA requires evidence that new drugs do not have teratogenic effects. While some tentative conclusions can be derived from animal experiments, the ultimate answer must come from human experience. Even the layman will recognize that agents affecting the ovum or sperm may present risks in that regard, and that it would be highly desirable therefore if, in the event the contraceptive agent being tested failed to prevent pregnancy, the pregnancy could be terminated through abortion and the fetus examined. In the United States and many other countries, such a procedure is legally impossible, and, as a result, initial clinical experiments with really novel "once-a-month" pills, which require access to potential abortion, cannot be conducted in the United States. The consequences of conducting such clinical work abroad in countries where it is permitted are considered below.

The third example illustrates what is potentially the most dangerous consequence, one arising from the fact that there exists no independent scientific body to which FDA scientific decisions can be appealed. Under certain circumstances, the FDA may wish to appoint an ad hoc advisory body of experts, whose decisions are not binding on the FDA, but there exists no independent group to whom the experimenter can appeal if he (rather than the FDA) wishes to do so. The need for such national and international appeal bodies is great in the field of birth-control agents, for the following reason. The single biggest bottleneck in fertility-control research is the lack of a satisfactory test animal, other than man, for evaluating efficacy and safety. Despite this lack, the FDA has recently imposed very special requirements for animal testing of female contraceptive agents (requirements quite distinct from those for other drugs)—one of them being the stipulation that toxicity studies with very high daily doses be made in dogs for 7 years and in monkeys for 10 years before large-scale clinical trials are permitted (*11*). The motivation, on political and even humane grounds, is understandable, but the scientific rationale for selecting these animals, notably the dog (whose semi-annual heat cycle and notorious sensitivity to female sex hormones hardly allow meaningful extrapolation to the human female with her monthly menstrual cycle), is highly debatable. Thus the World Health Organization Scientific Group (*3*) reached the following conclusion about animal studies with steroid contraceptives:

The extrapolation to women of data derived from dose and duration studies in experimental animals is of questionable validity and may be misleading, particularly when it is impossible to assess the comparability of dosages and lifespans. In the light of these considerations, the interpretation of such data is extremely difficult. *There is no evidence to justify recent emphasis on the presumed advantages of observations in subhuman primates and in canines* [italics mine].

In spite of this scientific uncertainty, requirements that long-term tests be made in dogs have, to my knowledge, resulted in the recent discontinuance of at least two clinical trials of promising compounds. Even more serious is the fact that, as a consequence, this experience with FDA's practical power to determine scientific protocol has led one of the largest of American drug companies (which does not market any contraceptive agent) to discontinue virtually all research on contraceptive agents chemically related to female steroids. This self-imposed restriction may not be regretted by competitive drug firms, but it is certainly unfortunate as far as general scientific advances in population control are concerned, because this company's research organization is internationally recognized as being among those at the very top. There is little doubt that if the present climate concerning clinical testing of contraceptive agents had existed 15 years ago, none of the steroid oral contraceptives now being used would ever have been developed.

My prediction is that, as the FDA-imposed requirements for clinical testing of contraceptive agents become more and more complicated, increase costs enormously, and are not appealable (except through the courts) to an independent body, new companies will not enter the field, and existing ones with a very heavy commercial stake in the field will do less research (most of it of the "me-too" variety because of the somewhat lower risks of failure to secure official approval), and the resulting vacuum will not be filled by anybody else. Under these circumstances, the newly organized NIH Center for Population Research may well stimulate interesting basic research in reproductive physiology, but this will hardly result in development of a practical birth-control agent before the next 3 billion human beings are added to the world's population.

A partial solution to this problem—one that could be easily implemented in the United States—would be the appointment by the National Academy of Sciences of a permanent body of independent experts to whom questionable scientific decisions of the FDA with respect to animal and clinical testing could be appealed, and whose conclusions would be binding on the FDA.

5) *Foreign clinical experimentation.* Irrespective of the justification for prohibition, once clinical trials with a drug have been prohibited in the United States, it is difficult to resume them elsewhere. As a result—and this is particularly true of contraceptive agents because of the additional testing requirements imposed by both the United States and Great Britain as compared with requirements in the testing of other drugs—more and more of the preliminary clinical trials, following the initial chemical and biological studies, are performed abroad, frequently in one of the developing countries. Regardless of the caliber of such work, it takes little imagination to predict what kind of major issue can develop from such a state of affairs, in which preliminary trials on human beings, under the auspices of technically advanced countries, are performed first in developing countries.

6) *Implications for population control in developing countries.* Regardless of the site of initial clinical experimentation, there is no doubt that, on moral and political grounds alone, a new chemical contraceptive agent to be used on a massive scale in a developing country must also be approved and used on a wide scale in the country of its origin (the United States or a European country). For all practical purposes this means that, in most instances, it must have passed scrutiny by the FDA or one of its European counterparts (for example, the Dunlop Committee in Great Britain), with all of its advantageous protective safeguards but, also, unfavorable bureaucratic delays. The moral and political justification for such a stand is fairly obvious. The advanced countries are not only the ones from which new contraceptive agents emanate technically; they are also the ones that supply motivation and even pressure, coupled with financial and technical assistance, to the developing countries for the introduction of family-planning programs in

which such contraceptive agents are used. These advanced countries are placed in a virtually untenable position when they propose the use of agents and procedures which they, themselves, are not prepared to use on their own populations (*12*). On a smaller scale, this is the objection to conducting initial clinical trials abroad.

It should be remembered that, even under ideal circumstances, the motivation of technologically advanced countries (generally countries of white population) preaching the family-planning gospel to the developing countries (frequently of nonwhite population) is highly suspect. Even within the United States, some of the economically deprived black inhabitants of our urban ghettos attribute genocidal motives to family-planning programs in their areas.

With these factors in mind, it must be realized that any position taken in the United States or Europe on presently used or potentially interesting future contraceptive agents has repercussions which extend far beyond the borders of these countries, and has worldwide consequences as far as population control is concerned. Thus, in the United States, the more recent reports on an apparent relationship between the use of certain oral contraceptive steroids and thromboembolism leading to deaths in a very small number of individuals appears in the press under headlines like "Pill Kills," with implied or specifically stated criticism of the fact that their use in the United States continues to be permitted. Even if one accepted all these deaths as an established consequence (*13*) of the use of steroid contraceptive agents, the data in Table 1 demonstrate that the number of deaths is still far fewer than those associated with pregnancy. Indeed, even if the number of associated deaths were ten times as great, a strong logical case could still be made for the continued use of these steroids as lifesaving agents.

Of particular relevance is the observation that a statistically meaningful causal relationship (*13*) between thromboembolism and steroid contraceptive agents could be suggested only after extensive use by several hundred thousand women, since the incidence is in any event so very low. It is probably quite impractical to anticipate or even demonstrate the occurrence of other side effects of such low incidence in clinical trials (as compared to actual clinical practice), because the scope of such an experimental project in terms

of number of subjects as well as duration of experiment would simply be too vast and would make it exceedingly difficult to bring to practical fruition any really novel chemical approach to contraception, be it in the female or the male. If major advances in fertility control are to occur, we must realize—and so must the regulatory agencies of the technically advanced countries—that some risks should be willingly undertaken in promoting and facilitating widespread clinical trial and reasonably prompt practical use of such new agents, risks commensurate with scientific caution, but caution unencumbered by bureaucratic inertia. Otherwise, with every passing year, the accumulated burden and penalties associated with a bulging world population become more severe.

## Conclusion

In a thought-provoking article on the population problem, Berelson stated (*14*) that "what will be scientifically available, politically acceptable, administratively feasible, economically justifiable, and morally tolerated depends upon people's perceptions of consequences." Within the narrow scope of the present article—namely, the prognosis for the development of new chemical birth-control agents—no degree of politically acceptable, administratively feasible, and economically justifiable motivation on the part of the developing countries will lead to new advances in contraception unless the technically advanced countries, foremost of which is the United States, recognize that their virtual scientific monopoly in the field of reproductive physiology imposes upon them a moral and logical obligation to take a global rather than a parochial view of novel contraceptive approaches. The pivotal role for future developments anywhere in the world rests to a considerable extent on government agencies such as the U.S. Food and Drug Administration, whose legal mandate is the protection of the national, rather than the international, population within the confines of national rather than global problems. Such a parochial view may perhaps be tolerated in research dealing with specific diseases, but its consequences will be disastrous when applied to a problem like the world's population growth.

Indeed, it is not fair to place the entire onus for satisfactory scientific designs of clinical protocols, scientific evaluation of clinical data, permission for eventual use by the general public, and continuous subsequent monitoring of the drug (in the present case, the contraceptive agent) on one agency, which can hardly fulfill all these partially competing functions in an objective manner. As far as the prospects for the development of better birth-control agents are concerned, the Achilles heel seems to be the presently unassailable ultimate authority of government regulatory agencies to pass judgment on scientific matters. The more questionable the scientific fact is, the more questionable this single scientific authority becomes. In view of the extraordinary scientific complexity and the many unanswered scientific questions in the field of human reproductive physiology, which cannot await leisurely answers because of the enormity of the problem of population growth, the ultimate authority on such scientific matters (especially during the experimental preclinical and clinical phases) should rest on independent bodies of experts to whose scientific judgment the governmental regulatory agencies as well as the investigator are prepared to bow. Since the appointment of membership to such "final courts of scientific appeal" is such a delicate matter, my recommendation is that the national responsibility in the United States be delegated to the National Academy of Sciences, and that the international responsibility be delegated to the World Health Organization. In fact, the World Health Organization already has such groups (3, 4) consisting of experts from developed and developing countries. All that is needed is to bestow on them the necessary authority.

### References and Notes

1. *The Growth of World Population* (National Acad. of Sciences, Washington, D.C., 1963).
2. C. Djerassi, *Science* **151**, 1055 (1966).
3. "Hormonal Steroids in Contraception," *World Health Organ. Tech. Rep. Ser. No. 386* (1968) (report of a WHO scientific group).
4. "Basic and Clinical Aspects of Intra-uterine Devices," *World Health Organ. Tech. Rep. Ser. Nos. 332* and *397* (1966; 1968) (report of a WHO scientific group).
5. The cost of the agents themselves is no longer a critical factor, since, in such large-scale government-sponsored projects, it has already reached the level of 10 cents per woman per month.
6. For the purposes of this article, the conventional foam tablets, jellies, and the like are not considered within the definition of "chemical contraceptive agents."
7. My association with this field has been through Syntex Corporation, a commercial organization of which I am a director and president of the research division, rather than in my capacity as professor of chemistry at Stanford University. This connection may raise some question, perhaps reasonably, as to the objectivity of my remarks. However, this has also given me a kind of practical experience that is not readily available to anyone who has not been directly involved in the commercial development of pharmaceuticals for wide public use. I would also add that my own strong feelings about the importance of finding practical solutions to the world population problem have been a primary incentive in my work and in my efforts to bring my views to public attention. Therefore, I hope that any criticism will be directed at the content, rather than the source, of this article.
8. See, for instance, J. J. Bonica and G. D. Allen, in *Drugs of Choice, 1966–1967*, W. Modell, Ed. (Mosby, St. Louis, 1966), pp. 199–232; "National Clearinghouse for Poison Control Center Bulletin," *U.S. Dep. Health, Educ. Welf. Annu. Rep.* (Government Printing Office, Washington, D.C., 1968).
9. K. E. Taylor and C. O. Miller, *FDA Pap.* (1968), p. 27.
10. E Diczfalusy, Karolinska Institute, Stockholm, personal communication.
11. E. I. Goldenthal, *FDA Pap.* (1968), p. 13.
12. In retrospect, it is interesting for me to recall a series of lectures that I presented in Sweden in September 1962 under the auspices of the Swedish Chemical Society, dealing with the development of steroidal oral contraceptives. Sweden had at that time not yet approved oral contraceptive steroids for domestic use, yet, as part of its impressive and intelligent foreign assistance program involving population control measures, it was already promoting with great vigor the use of such contraceptive agents in certain Asian countries. In my lectures I emphasized the moral and logical objections to such a position.
13. The medical community seems by no means to be unanimous on this question; see L. E. Moses, *J. Amer. Med. Ass.* **208**, 694 (1969) and references cited therein.
14. B. Berelson, *Science* **163**, 533 (1969).

# Population Problem:
# In Search of a Solution

The time has come to face the population problem
forthrightly and with major emphasis on motivation.

Joseph J. Spengler

*There's little we can do about er-
roneous teachings, but do the taxpayers
have to subsidize them?*—NICHOLAS
VON HOFFMAN

*Misgivings are to be silenced. Re-
wards will come later.* I Ching: The
Book of Changes

No problem commands more attention in the world of discourse than the
population problem. The solution consists in halting population growth
promptly. Yet man's efforts to accomplish this are remindful of the efforts
of an acrobat who bounds up and down
on a trampoline in the vain hope that
eventually a rebound will carry him up
to the top of the Empire State Building.
Why has a solution not been forthcoming? The answer is very simple.
Forgotten is the fact that positive re-
pressants will halt population growth in
a pressure-ridden world if preventive
measures are not taken in time to preserve this world's potential for comfort.
No society really wills a solution. A
solution will nowhere be found until
it is willed, Panglossian voices are
stilled, and whatever needs to be done
is done.

## The Problem

The population problem flows from
the finiteness of the world in which man
is multiplying. Excesses may assume
two forms. No more growth may be
indicated because a country's existing
stock of population may be large
enough. Or the rate of flow of additions to it may be too large even
though the stock is of less than opti-

The author is professor of economics at Duke
University, Durham, North Carolina 27706.

mum size. Growth of components of
man's average standard of life is limited by the growth of elements entering
into each component, above all by
those elements whose supply increases
least rapidly. Of these elements, the
food supply is only one, and not always
as critical as Malthus assumed 171 years
ago. Man's mobility is very much
greater, however, with the result that
consciousness of density is correspondingly greater.

Even Malthus's fears may at last be
irremediably confirmed. Within little
more than a century the world's population may have grown abreast of the
world's food supply of that time, even
if the latter should grow eightfold and
near to the attainable maximum. So
great an increase in the world food supply, while feasible under one-world conditions, is unlikely in a hostility-ridden
divided world; it presupposes a doubling
of world acreage under cultivation and
a quadrupling of average yield per
acre. A population octuples in just over
105 years, if it grows 2 percent per
year; in about 140 years, if it grows
1.5 percent per year.

The rate of population growth has
accelerated over the past three centuries. Of most concern is the acceleration in the present century. By the
1950's the world rate of population
growth was about 3⅓ times the 0.53
percent per year experienced in 1900–
10. The rate is expected to be slightly
higher in 1960–90; thereafter it may
decline slightly.

The rate of population growth has
progressed differently in the underdeveloped than in the developed world.
In 1900–10 the annual rate in the developed world was 0.87 percent, nearly
2½ times the 0.36 percent experienced

in the underdeveloped world. By the
close of this century the rate in the
underdeveloped world will be double
that in the developed world. The latter,
usually responsive to the impact of war
or economic depression, is expected to
approximate 1 percent in 1960–2000,
a rate about one-seventh above the
1900–10 level. Meanwhile, in the underdeveloped world, the annual rate,
only 0.36 percent per year in 1900–10,
is expected to average slightly over 2
percent (1).

It is not surprising, therefore, that
population threatens to overtake the
food supply as well as other slowly
growing components of the budget of
life. Suppose the current world food
supply is increased eightfold; even then,
should world population continue to
grow at a rate falling within the range
of rates projected by the United Nations Secretariat to the year 2000—1.5
to 2.2 percent—it also would octuple
by the latter part of the next century or
soon thereafter.

Population would continue to grow
for some time even after the *true rate*
of increase had descended to zero, because its age composition must become
transformed into that associated with
the fertility and mortality patterns
destined to produce balance between
births and deaths. In the United States,
for example, an increase of 30 to 50
percent might still take place after net
reproduction had settled to unity (2).
Higher percentages might be found in
some countries.

The dangers of population growth
are not confined to the underdeveloped
world. In the United States, for example, what Washington rhetors promised would be a "Great Society," could
become a "Eudaemonically Puny Society." The population of the continental
United States will number 300 million
or more by the close of this century.
Should the American population continue to grow about 1 percent per
year, it would number one billion early
in the 21st century. Of these, 80 to 90
percent would be situated in cities,
many of them elements of crowded and
continuous "metropolitan" areas. Land
of *all* sorts would be down to 2 acres
(0.81 hectare) or less per person. Much
of it would not be very accessible, and
little of it would be suited to supply
the amenities of finite nature, demand
for which is rising with the rapid
growth of *discretionary* time and income per capita.

## Social Response

The degree to which population growth is controlled, given a stable mortality pattern, depends upon the means of control available and the degree of pressure members of a population are under to employ these means. Up to now, few administrators or scholars have given much attention to the pressure or motivational aspect of population growth; among the exceptions are Stephen Enke and Leonard Bower (3). Moralists, of course, have always indulged in what journalists call "jawbone control," urging the fecund either to reproduce, or to refrain from reproduction, for the good of state, cult, or private situation. Some technologists and publicists for money-hungry Mission Controls put forward as solutions for many of man's problems (among them the control and feeding of his numbers) the complicated gadgetry and superb organization which has put men on the moon. Septuagenarian ecclesiastical celibates, on the contrary, are still content to rule effective solutions off limits.

It is true, of course, that the population problem is of relatively recent vintage. The need to regulate fertility hardly existed before the 19th century, so high was mortality. In the Middle Ages, and perhaps at other times, young people were often advised not to marry until they could support children in keeping with their own station in life. Voluntary and involuntary celibacy also served to curb fertility in Western Europe more than in Asia. In the 19th century, long before modern methods of control had been developed, general fertility was quite effectively regulated, in Ireland by deferment of marriage and nonmarriage, and in France by these and available contraceptive methods. One may say, therefore, that in these countries the General Will to regulate numbers was strong, well fortified by the universe of rewards and penalties operative in each country. In other Western countries fertility passed under partial control, greater in amount than had obtained earlier, but less than was to be found in Ireland and France. Outside the sphere of Western European civilization, however, fertility changed very little because it was counterbalanced, as a rule, by unchanging high mortality.

The need for greater population control was not considered acute until the present century, particularly after the 1930's, when the decline in mortality accelerated in various underdeveloped countries. With little or no decline in fertility, the decline in mortality more than tripled the annual rate of population growth between the first and the sixth decade of the present century. Meanwhile, the increment of population discharged into a finite world each decade rose from about 90 million in 1900–10 to about 482 million in 1950–60; it may approximate 942 million by the 1990's.

The recognition of the acute need to control numbers, together with the necessity of providing families with a means of limiting the number of children to three or four or less, stimulated research on the improvement of contraceptive methods. Intrauterine devices and the contraceptive pill were added to the methods in use, and some of the latter were improved. Even more satisfactory means are in the offing.

While effective research has been done on contraceptive means, little has been done on the motivation to make use of these means. Man seemingly has acted upon Samuel Johnson's dictum, "How small . . . that part which laws or kings can cause or cure." Advocates of birth control (4) have counted on individual incentive and on private "conscience," oblivious of the fact that free rein is thus allowed to men without "conscience" whose number may be legion. Little account is taken of the fact that man lives in a universe of penalties and rewards and tends to pursue courses of action free of penalty and productive of reward. Even less account is taken of the fact, stressed by Hardin (5) and economists generally, that the birth of a child gives release to a stream of external effects, some adverse and costly, which are incident upon others than the parents. Indeed, in many countries, among them the United States, this incidence is accentuated by legislation and administrative practice. Hence much of the cost of producing children is shifted to others than the parents, with the result that reproduction is stimulated. Furthermore, in sanctionless "free-ride" societies such as our own, efforts to shift even more of the cost from responsible parents to others are quite powerful, supported as they are by ideology, strong organization, and an imperfect understanding of cost-shifting by its victims.

## Failure?

In view of what has been said, it is unlikely that population growth will be halted, either in the developed or in the underdeveloped world. Optimistic reports come from those engaged in pressing for fertility control, though they have little effect, in view of the magnitude of the problem. One senses an ex parte aura about these reports. Nor does one find strong grounds for optimism in the fine reports of the Population Council or in recent world reviews of the state and extent of contraceptive practice (6).

There is little evidence of a General Will in any country to regulate numbers effectively. In no developed country has the so-called right to parenthood been transformed into a privilege to be earned before it may be exercised. In no developed country has effective response been made to the fact that poverty is associated with excessive family size. In no underdeveloped country has a government undertaken, or been allowed to undertake, a really effective fertility-control policy.

Failure is writ large in *Population Bulletin No. 7* of the United Nations, issued in 1965. The countries of the world, it was found, fell into two categories: the developed, with gross reproduction rates below 2 and averaging about 1.4; and the underdeveloped, with gross reproduction rates above 2 and averaging 2.6 or more. Around 1960 crude birth rates averaged 22 per 1000 inhabitants in the developed world and 41 to 42 per 1000 in the underdeveloped world. The world as a whole, with a crude birth rate of 35 to 36 per 1000, produced 105 to 110 million births, close to four-fifths of which took place in the underdeveloped world. Three decades from now, only about one-fourth of the world's population will live in the present developed world; in 1960, as in 1900, about one-third lived there.

The muted conclusion of the United Nations Secretariat is quite pessimistic. "The launching of new countries upon the transition from high to low fertility seems to have been temporarily halted; with a few possible exceptions, there is little sign of decided downward trends having begun in the remaining countries of high fertility" (7). Moreover, in some countries when fertility has declined, the decline has been at least partly offset by a decline in mortality much as happened in 19th- and early 20th-century Europe. Of course, the impact of further declines in mortality is small after expectation of life at birth moves into the 70's.

## Stabilization Proposals

Population growth can be halted, but it will not be halted until a General Will to halt it develops and becomes effectively institutionalized and supported by adequate sanctions. It is preferable, of course, that institutionalization assume the form of controlling mechanisms which are economic and fairly automatic in character and as free as possible of cumbersome administrative intervention.

A clear-cut target needs to be established. This would consist in, for example, an average number of living children per family sufficient to replace a stable population, given the prevailing mortality pattern and the population's marital composition. This average in most countries would fall within a range of from just over two to somewhat over three children per married couple. This average would aggregate into an annual number of births sufficient, in the longer run, to balance the number of deaths. In the shorter run, as noted earlier, births would continue to exceed deaths until the stable age composition associated with a zero rate of growth had been achieved. Of primary importance, however, is not statistical nicety but the establishment of a target number of births and living children, to be followed by such modification of the universe of rewards and penalties as proves necessary to assure realization of this target.

A distinction needs to be made between the number of births $R$ required to replace a population and the excess $E$ when the total number of births $T > R$ (or whatever is the number of births needed to assure the target rate of population growth). The cost of births $R$ may be viewed as the overhead cost of replacing a population and therefore properly chargeable, at least in part, to the total community. It need not and should not be charged to the community entirely or even in major part, however, because the utility or satisfaction which parents expect to derive from their children is so great that they will bear much if not all of the cost of producing them. Halting population growth may then be crudely said to consist of preventing $E$ through re-ducing $T$ to $R$—mainly by raising the cost of $E$ to a level high enough to discourage births in excess of $R$ when population replacement is the objective. The births included under $E$ may be described as *demerit wants*, a penalizable category of wants that may, as Louis Gasper suggests in another connection, be treated as counterparts to *merit wants*, a normative category of wants whose satisfaction the state is likely to finance (*8*).

The halting process is somewhat more complicated, of course, than has been suggested. Reduction of fertility to a replacement level gradually produces a change in a population's age composition, and this in turn modifies the number of births until they move into long-run balance with deaths. Of major importance from an economic point of view, besides the slowing down of the rate of population growth, is the increase in the relative number of persons of productive age. For purposes of illustration consider the transformation of a stable female population described by Coale (*9*) and characterized initially by an expectation of life at birth of 70 years and a gross reproduction rate of 2.25, as in some underdeveloped countries. We should then have an annual growth rate of about 2.64 percent, with a population of which 3.05 percent would be aged 70 or more years, and 48.83 percent would be aged less than 20. Suppose now that the gross reproduction rate declines to 1.25 and the population again assumes stable form with a growth rate of about 0.55 percent. The percentage of the population aged 70 years or more rises to 8.13 while that of persons under 20 declines to 31.77. The percentage of the population of working age—20 to 69—rises from 48.12 to 60.1, signifying an increase in average potential productivity of about 25 percent and a decline of about 39 percent in the ratio of persons of dependent age to those of working age.

Roughly similar changes would take place in the male population component, corresponding to those of the female component, and together they would constitute the total population. Male life expectancy is lower than female life expectancy and male age composition differs slightly from female age composition (*9*).

Of primary concern here are the potential economic benefits associated with the decline in fertility. These are the increase in the ratio of persons of productive age to the total population, the decline in the ratio of dependents to persons of productive age, and the virtual disappearance of increase in population pressure occasioned by population growth.

The transformation described, together with its beneficial effects, does not come about automatically, although it has been approximated in part in the developed world as a result of the long-run decline in natality. Even given general availability of cheap and effective means of contraception—a condition not present in perhaps two-thirds of the world—achievement and maintenance of the requisite gross reproduction rate would not result. There exists no socioeconomic mechanism adequate to bring this result about automatically, much as the price mechanism brings about balance between supply and demand. The existing universe of rewards and penalties is not currently constituted to eventuate in $R$ births and no more. Nor is there disposition to alter the incidence of carrot and stick suchwise as to improve the net impact of current rewards and penalties. Indeed, this universe is being made more rather than less favorable to reproduction in many countries, among them the United States, with the result that forces making for poverty and deprivation are accentuated.

In the past, as noted earlier, reliance has been placed almost entirely upon "private conscience" despite the fact that the reproductive behavior of a considerable fraction of any population is little influenced by conscience. Herein lies the inadequacy of planned parenthood programs, admirable as they are and pathbreaking as they have been. There is need in addition for suitable motivation for the carrot and the stick.

Motivation to reproduction assumes a variety of forms, several of which are overriding except in marginal cases. Control of fertility may therefore be achieved through replacing these motives in part by functionally equivalent motives which do not result in reproduction. This may be done suchwise as merely to reduce average family size from current levels to levels compatible with stabilization of the population if that is the objective.

It is highly desirable, of course, that children not be penalized by policies intended to discourage reproduction. Such a policy could in effect penalize both innocent children and society insofar as it denied children their due share of opportunity to develop their potentials. A case in point might be recourse to the imposition of taxes upon low-income parents with excessive numbers of children. As a result, means for the rearing and training of these children might be unduly reduced by such a tax.

Of the diverse motives for reproduction several have always been dominant. One is the expectation of filial affection throughout life and especially in old age. This need cannot, as a rule, be met adequately through collective arrangements designed to replace the services of children; but it can be met nicely so long as there are one or two children. The other and probably more important motive for reproduction in most countries is the parents' expectation of economic support in their old age at the hands of their children. This motive may not, of course, be so powerful any longer in advanced countries with pension and social security systems. It exists even there, however, since pecuniary provision for support in retirement years, even when well-planned, is apt to be eroded by modern governments which sometimes prove more inclined to unproductive expenditure (armament races, space and other potlatch, and war) and savings-eroding inflation than to maintenance of the purchasing power of retirement income.

A first step to the effective control of fertility in underdeveloped countries is the gradual introduction of a social security system for those over 65 years of age, for instance. Given this arrangement, potential parents will be less inclined to have a family in excess of replacement size in order to be reasonably assured of support in old age. For this system to work, however, its benefits must be limited to those with no more then $x$ children when the value of $x$ is in the neighborhood of the replacement number of births (some of which will be multiple) under existing mortality conditions. The system would need to be financed through something like proportional income taxation and to yield correspondingly variable retirement income. The system would have to be introduced gradually and initially limited to families with $x$ or fewer children and susceptible of further increase. The social cost of this system would fall quite short of the cost of reproducing and rearing the additional children who would have been born had the system not existed, in part because support of the aged is an overhead societal cost, much of which will be borne by society in any event.

It is essential to the success of this program that those under the social security system expect to be decidedly better off in their old age than they otherwise would have been. This requirement is easily met, however, as was indicated above in "Stabilization Proposals." Not only will the decline in natality release a large amount of resources formerly absorbed by population growth, but also the decline in the relative number of young persons of unproductive age is only partially offset by increase in the relative number of persons aged over 69, with the result that potential output per capita is significantly increased. For these reasons, together with the fact that savings per older person will be higher absolutely and in relation to his preretirement income, the situation of those under the social security program will be decidedly better than it otherwise would have been.

Under this social security system the deterrent to excessive reproduction in underdeveloped countries adopting it is the threat to families of not sharing in retirement benefits upon reaching age 65 if the number of living children should be excessive. This system can be made part of the fertility-regulating institutional structure of underdeveloped countries, most of which are without retirement systems. Such a system might also be grafted onto social security systems current in advanced countries.

This conditional social security arrangement may need to be supplemented or replaced in countries where it cannot be made effective. Such additional arrangement must meet three needs: (i) make potential parents aware at marriage of the probable aggregate cost of caring properly for two or three children; (ii) help assure adequate material support for children subsequently born to these parents; (iii) provide these parents with incentive not to exceed what is for them the target number of children. At the time of marriage a couple might be required to pay into a combination insurance and interest-bearing fund, designed to support surviving children in the event of the household-head's death, and otherwise to supplement the support of the couple's children in their more expensive teens. Should a couple remain childless or have fewer than the target number of children, all or some of the cumulating proceeds would be restored. Some time—say 20 years—after the birth of a couple's first child, they would be awarded a bonus if they had

not produced more than the target number of children. The bonus would amount to a partial reward for a couple's contribution to the collective cost of population replacement. The arrangement described may be modified to increase the number of births if it should fall below the replacement level, or below some other desired level, as may happen in the United States.

The joint incentive flowing from the prospect of a share in both retirement benefits under the social security system and the insurance-bonus arrangement should be sufficient to induce most families not to exceed the target number of live children. Moreover, should this joint incentive not prove powerful enough, it might be strengthened by increasing the financial advantages associated with compliance. Recourse to physical sanction (for example, sterilization) should not, therefore, prove necessary, even if social approval of its use were given with respect to physically or mentally submarginal individuals.

In what has gone before, no provision has been made for varying the distribution of the stipulated aggregate number of births and children among the families composing a population. Such a provision becomes necessary, however, in proportion as a society accepts the principle that parenthood is not a right but a *privilege* to be reserved to those financially and morally capable of meeting the responsibilities of parenthood. A considerable number of any nation's population is physically, mentally, or otherwise unfit to assume and support these responsibilities. This is especially true of modern urban societies, into whose economies very few submarginal persons are economically absorbable under modern governmental, trade-union, and related constraints. At the same time a considerable number of families are willing and able to rear four or five children. Hence arrangements need to be made for the distribution of responsibility for the aggregate desired number of births and children. While state agencies might accomplish such distribution, it would be preferable to use deferred incentives of the sort already described, and thus allow the incidence of costs and returns to govern interfamily distribution of births and children.

Compliance with postredistribution quotas or targets might be assured through adaptation of the social security and insurance fund arrangements described earlier. This would maximize the degree of freedom of choice compatible with realization of the target. Participation in retirement benefits would be limited to those who did not exceed their reduced or enlarged quotas. Right to receipt of a bonus would be contingent upon an insuree's not exceeding his postdistribution quota. Required payment into the insurance fund would vary directly and proportionately with the number of children in the insuree's postdistribution quota. An arrangement of this sort would be preferable to the state's licensing the right to have one or more children and then distributing the licenses in some manner. This arrangement would call for sanctions against violation in much greater measure than the arrangements proposed above.

## Conclusion

A dilemma arising from a conflict of freedoms confronts the inhabitants of most countries. In any one country, there is little advantage and much disadvantage to be had either from any population growth (most of Europe, Asia, parts of Africa, and the Western Hemisphere), or from a population growth at a rate, for instance, in excess of 0.5 to 1.0 percent. Growth at an excessive rate arises largely either from ignorance of effective means of birth control, or from current arrangements which permit much of the cost of excessive population growth to be shunted from parents with excessive numbers of children to nondiscretionary members of society, or from both—in sum, *from unrestricted freedom to procreate.* Exercise of this freedom thus conflicts with a variety of freedoms of the remainder of the population.

Solution of the population problem consists in reconciling exercise of this freedom to procreate with exercise of other freedoms—in equilibrating the two in such a way as to prevent continuation of disadvantageous population growth. Thus, the underlying problem is not novel, although the form which it assumes is novel. New also is the fact that continuation of undesirable population growth gives rise to irremediable evils, whereas continuation of most other disequilibria among freedoms gives rise mainly to evils which are

remediable. Cushioning of excessive population growth does, of course, reduce its *visible* costs, but at the expense of *less visible* resources—use which might otherwise contribute to the increase of average material income, leisure, access to amenities, and so on.

Reconciliation of the freedoms in conflict may be accomplished through administrative measures based on appropriate legislation and decrees. This approach is not to be recommended, however, except as a last resort. It is cumbersome. It could become another "brick" in an emerging police state. It generates antigovernmental response from persons affected, since they tend to believe themselves to be arbitrarily deprived of options from among which they should be free to choose. It violates the rule that, since a great deal of government necessarily consists either of administrative or police action, or both, additions should not be made to a government's total administrative and police load when alternative measures, especially economic measures, may be used to accomplish particular collective purposes. Avoidable administrative measures are particularly undesirable in present-day states, whether developed or underdeveloped, because competent bureaucrats are in very short supply and governments already undertake a great deal of activity which they are quite unfit to conduct efficiently.

It is extremely desirable that population growth be halted in most countries and slowed down in others. As yet, however, there exists no General Will to bring about these objectives. Furthermore, even if a General Will should develop, it might be weakened if recourse were left entirely to administrative and police measures. It is essential to reorient the composition of the universe of penalities and rewards in such a way as to induce men to replace in part the freedom to reproduce by other freedoms. Two arrangements have been outlined that are jointly utilizable and compatible with retention of a high degree of freedom of choice. They have not been described in detail, since detail would necessarily vary with country and situation.

The two arrangements proposed— arrangements which are susceptible of considerable improvement—entail as little interference as possible with individual freedom of choice. Emphasis is

placed upon the composition of the options available and to which individuals respond. The advantage of the proposed arrangements consists in the fact that payment for compliance is deferred until noncompliance is no longer possible. The incentive to limit family size appropriately thus is continually present so long as the wife is of reproductive age. Payment need not be repeated as under programs designed to encourage use of intrauterine devices. The ultimate payment can be made large enough, however, to encourage strong efforts at compliance. Furthermore, compliance in most instances is compatible with a family's having two or three children and therefore enjoying the utilities and advantages associated with having these children.

The arrangements proposed are designed to reduce the functional importance of more than two children in most instances. The weaknesses in these arrangements are three. First, among those whose discount of the future is very high, future monetary rewards may offer only limited incentive in the present when decisions respecting reproduction must be made. Second, confidence in the governmental apparatus of the state may be limited. It may be feared that when rewards come due 20 to 45 years hence, the state will refuse to pay or pay in full. A combination of this fear with a high discount rate could, therefore, greatly reduce the capacity of the joint incentives to diminish fertility. Finally, the arrangements cannot succeed unless the means to control family size are widely available and very cheap in relation to the incomes of the masses.

### References and Notes

1. M. Macura, in *World Population–The View Ahead*, R. N. Farmer, J. D. Long, G. J. Stolnitz, Eds. (Bureau of Business Research, Indiana Univ., Bloomington, 1968), p. 27.
2. T. Frejka, *Population Stud.* 22, 379 (1968).
3. S. Enke, *Science* 164, 798 (1969); L. Bower, *Demography* 5 (1), 422 (1968).
4. K. Davis, *Science* 158, 730 (1967).
5. G. Hardin, *ibid.* 162, 1243 (1968).
6. *Family Planning and Population Programs*, International Conference on Family Planning Programs, edited by planning committee, B. Berelson, chairman (Univ. of Chicago Press, Chicago, 1966); *Demography* 5 (2), whole issue (1968) (this is a special issue devoted to the progress and problems of fertility control throughout the world).
7. *Population Bulletin of the United Nations, No. 7* (1965), pp. 1, 135, 150, and 151.
8. R. A. Musgrave, *The Theory of Public Finance* (McGraw-Hill, New York, 1959), p. 13.
9. A. J. Coale and P. G. Demeny, *Regional Model Life Tables and Stable Populations* (Princeton Univ. Press, Princeton, N.J., 1966), pp. 114 and 210.

# Population Policy for Americans: Is the Government Being Misled?

Population limitation by means of federally aided birth-control programs for the poor is questioned.

Judith Blake

Pressure on the federal government for "action" to limit population growth in the United States has intensified greatly during the past 10 years, and at present such action is virtually unchallenged as an official national goal. Given the goal, the question of means becomes crucial. Here I first evaluate the particular means being advocated and pursued in public policy, then I present alternative ways of possibly achieving the goal.

The prevailing view as to the best means is remarkably unanimous and abundantly documented. It is set forth in the 17 volumes of congressional hearings so far published on the "population crisis" (1); in "The Growth of U.S. Population," a report by the Committee on Population of the National Academy of Sciences (2); in a statement made by an officer of the Ford Foundation who was asked by the Department of Health, Education, and Welfare to make suggestions (3); and, finally, in the "Report of the President's Committee on Population and Family Planning," which was officially released this past January (4). The essential recommendation throughout is that the government should give highest priority to ghetto-oriented family-planning programs designed to "deliver" birth-control services to the poor and uneducated, among whom, it is claimed, there are at least 5 million women who are "in need" of such federally sponsored birth-control assistance.

By what logic have the proponents of control moved from a concern with population growth to a recommendation favoring highest priority for poverty-oriented birth-control programs?

The author is chairman of the Department of Demography, University of California, Berkeley.

First, they have assumed that fertility is the only component of population growth worthy of government attention. Second, they have taken it for granted that, to reduce fertility, one sponsors birth-control programs ("family planning"). Just why they have made this assumption is not clear, but its logical implication is that population growth is due to births that couples would have preferred to avoid. Furthermore, the reasoning confuses couple control over births with societal control over them (5). Third, the proponents of the new policy have seized on the poor and uneducated as the "target" group for birth-control action because they see this group as the only remaining target for a program of voluntary family planning. The rest of the population is handling its family planning pretty well on its own: over 95 percent of fecund U.S. couples already either use birth-control methods or intend to do so. The poor, on the other hand—at least those who are fecund—have larger families than the advantaged; they not only use birth-control methods less but they use them less effectively. The family-planning movement's notion of "responsible parenthood" carries the implication that family size should be directly, not inversely, related to social and economic advantage, and the poor are seen as constituting the residual slack to be taken up by the movement's efforts. Why are the poor not conforming to the dictates of responsible parenthood? Given the movement's basic assumptions, there are only two answers: the poor are irresponsible, or they have not had the opportunity. Since present-day leaders would abhor labeling the poor irresponsible, they have chosen to blame lack of opportunity as the cause. Opportunity has been lacking, in their eyes, either because the poor have not been "educated" in family planning or because they have not been "reached" by family-planning services. In either case, as they see it, the poor have been deprived of their "rights" (2, p. 22; 6). This deprivation has allegedly been due to the prudery and hypocrisy of the affluent, who have overtly tabooed discussion of birth control and dissemination of birth-control materials while, themselves, covertly enjoying the benefits of family planning (7).

So much for the logic underlying recent proposals for controlling population growth in the United States. But what is the evidence on which this argument is based? On what empirical grounds is the government being asked to embark on a high-priority program of providing contraceptive services to the poor? Moreover, what, if any, are some of the important public issues that the suggested policy raises—what are its social and political side effects? And, finally, is such a policy, even if appropriate for the poor and even if relatively unencumbered by public disapproval, relevant to the problem of population growth in America? If demographic curtailment is really the objective, must alternative policies be considered and possibly given highest priority?

Turning to the alleged need for government-sponsored birth-control services, one may ask whether birth control has in fact been a tabooed topic among the middle and upper classes, so that the less advantaged could be said to have suffered "deprivation" and consequently now to require government help. One may then question whether there is a mandate from the poor for the type of federally sponsored service that is now being urged, and whether as many as 5 million women are "in need" of such family-planning assistance.

## Has Birth Control Been a Tabooed Topic?

The notion that the American public has only recently become willing to tolerate open discussion of birth control has been assiduously cultivated by congressmen and others concerned with government policy on population. For example, Senator Tydings credited Senators Gruening and Clark and President Johnson with having almost single-handedly changed American public attitudes toward birth control. In 1966 he read the following statement into the 28 February *Congressional Record* (8).

The time is ripe for positive action. Ten years ago, even five years ago, this was a politically delicate subject. Today the Nation has awakened to the need for Government action.

This change in public attitude has come about through the efforts of men who had the courage to brook the tides of public opinion. Senator Clark is such a man. Senator Gruening is such a man. So is President Johnson. Because of their leadership it is no longer necessary for an elected official to speak with trepidation on this subject.

A year later, Senator Tydings reduced his estimate of the time required for the shift in public opinion to "3 or 4 years" (9, p. 12; 10). Senator Gruening maintained (11) that the "ninety-eight distinguished men and women" who testified at the public hearing on S. 1676 were "pioneers" whose "names comprise an important honor roll which historically bears an analogy to other famous lists: the signers of the Declaration of Independence, those who ratified the Constitution of the United States and others whose names were appended to and made possible some of the great turning points in history." Reasoning from the continued existence of old, and typically unenforced, laws concerning birth control (together with President Eisenhower's famous anti-birth-control statement), Stycos, in a recent article (12), stated:

The public reaction to family planning in the United States has varied between disgust and silent resignation to a necessary evil. At best it was viewed as so delicate and risky that it was a matter of "individual conscience." As such, it was a matter so totally private, so sacred (or profane), that no external agents, and certainly not the state, should have anything to do with it.

Does the evidence support such impressionistic claims? How did the general public regard government sponsorship of birth control long before it became a subject of congressional hearings, a National Academy report, and a Presidential Committee report? Fortunately, a question on this topic appeared in no less than 13 national polls and surveys conducted between 1937 and 1966. As part of a larger project concerned with public knowledge and opinions about demographic topics, I have gathered together the original data cards from these polls, prepared them

Table 1. Percentages of white U.S. men and women between the ages of 21 and 44 who, in various national polls and surveys made between 1937 and 1964*, expressed the opinion that birth-control information should be made available to individuals who desired it.

| Year | Men | | Women | |
|------|-----|-----|-------|-----|
| | % | N | % | N |
| 1937 | 66 | 1038 | 70 | 734 |
| 1938 | 67 | 1111 | 72 | 548 |
| 1939 | 74 | 1101 | 73 | 630 |
| 1940 | 72 | 1127 | 75 | 618 |
| 1943 | 67 | 628 | 73 | 866 |
| 1945 | 64 | 714 | 70 | 879 |
| 1947 | 76 | 353 | 75 | 405 |
| 1959 | 78 | 301 | 79 | 394 |
| 1961 | 82 | 336 | 81 | 394 |
| 1962 | 85 | 288 | 80 | 381 |
| 1963 | 78 | 323 | 79 | 373 |
| 1964 | 89 | 324 | 86 | 410 |

* The questions asked of respondents concerning birth control were as follows. In 1937: Do you favor the birth control movement? In 1938, 1939, 1940, 1943, 1945, and 1947: Would you like to see a government agency (or "government health clinics") furnish birth-control information to married people who want it? In 1959, 1961, 1962, and 1963: In some places in the United States it is not legal to supply birth-control information. How do you feel about this—do you think birth-control information should be available to anyone who wants it, or not? In 1964: Do you think birth-control information should be available to anyone who wants it, or not?

for computer processing, and analyzed the results. The data are all from Gallup polls and are all from national samples of the white, adult population. Here I concentrate on adults under 45—that is, on adults in the childbearing age group.

The data of Table 1 contradict the notion that Americans have only recently ceased to regard birth control as a tabooed topic. As far back as 30 years ago, almost three-quarters of the women questioned in these surveys actively approved having the *government* make birth-control information available to the married. By the early 1960's, 80 percent or more of women approved overcoming legal barriers and allowing "anyone who wants it" to have birth-control information. The figures for men are similar. The question asked in 1964—the one question in recent years that did not mention illegality—brought 86 percent of the women and 89 percent of the men into the category of those who approved availability of birth-control information for "anyone who wants it." Furthermore, in judging the level of disapproval, one should bear in mind that the remainder of the respondents, in all of these years, includes from 7 to 15 percent who claim that they have "no opinion" on the subject, not that they "disapprove."

An important difference of opinion corresponds to a difference in religious affiliation. Among non-Catholics (including those who have "no religion" and do not attend church) approval has been considerably higher than it has been among Catholics. Among non-Catholic women, over 80 percent approved as early as 1939, and among non-Catholic men the percentages were approximately the same. The 1964 poll showed that 90 percent of each sex approved. Among Catholics, in recent years about 60 percent have approved, and, in 1964, the question that mentioned neither the government nor legality brought opinions of approval from 77 percent of the women and 83 percent of the men.

Clearly, if birth-control information has in fact been unavailable to the poor, the cause has not been a generalized and pervasive attitude of prudery on the part of the American public. Although public officials may have misjudged American opinion (and may have mistakenly assumed that the Catholic Church "spoke for" a majority of Americans, or even for a majority of Catholics), most Americans of an age to be having children did not regard birth control as a subject that should be under a blanket of secrecy and, as far back as the 1930's, evinced a marked willingness to have their government make such information widely available. It seems unlikely, therefore, that poorer sectors of our population were "cut off" from birth-control knowledge primarily because informal channels of communication (the channels through which most people learn about birth control) were blocked by an upper- and middle-class conspiracy of silence.

What has happened, however, is that pressure groups for family planning, like the Catholic hierarchy they have been opposing, have been acting as self-designated spokesmen for "public opinion." By developing a cause as righteous as that of the Catholics (the "rights" of the poor as against the "rights" of a religious group), the family planners have used the American way of influencing official opinion. Now public officials appear to believe that publicly supported birth-control services are what the poor have always wanted and needed, just as, in the past, official opinion acceded to the notion that such services would have been "offensive" to certain groups. Nonetheless, the question remains of whether

Table 2. Mean number of children considered ideal by non-Catholic women, according to education and economic status, for selected years between 1943 and 1968.

| Date | Age range | Level of education* | | | Income or economic status† | | | | Total respondents | |
|------|-----------|------|------|------|---|---|---|---|---|---|
| | | College | High school | Grade school | 1 | 2 | 3 | 4 | $\bar{X}$ | N |
| 1943 | 20–34 | 2.8 | 2.6 | 2.6 | 2.9 | 2.7 | 2.7 | 2.5 | 2.7 | 1893 |
| 1952 | 21 + | 3.3 | 3.1 | 3.6 | | 3.3 | 3.3 | 3.3 | 3.3 | 723 |
| 1955‡ | 18–39 | 3.1 | 3.2 | 3.7 | 3.2 | 3.1 | 3.2 | 3.5 | 3.3 | 1905 |
| 1955§ | 18–39 | 3.3 | 3.4 | 3.9 | 3.4 | 3.3 | 3.4 | 3.7 | 3.4 | 1905 |
| 1957 | 21 + | 3.4 | 3.2 | 3.6 | | 3.3 | 3.2 | 3.5 | 3.3 | 448 |
| 1959 | 21 + | 3.5 | 3.4 | 3.9 | | 3.5 | 3.5 | 3.6 | 3.5 | 472 |
| 1960‡ | 18–39 | 3.1 | 3.2 | 3.5 | 3.1 | 3.2 | 3.3 | 3.2 | 3.2 | 1728 |
| 1960§ | 18–39 | 3.2 | 3.4 | 3.6 | 3.2 | 3.3 | 3.5 | 3.4 | 3.4 | 1728 |
| 1963 | 21 + | 3.2 | 3.4 | 3.5 | 3.3 | 3.3 | 3.5 | 3.5 | 3.4 | 483 |
| 1966 | 21 + | 3.1 | 3.3 | 3.7 | 3.2 | 3.2 | 3.4 | 3.7 | 3.3 | 374 |
| 1967 | 21 + | 3.1 | 3.3 | 3.4 | 3.3 | 3.2 | 3.1 | 3.4 | 3.3 | 488 |
| 1968 | 21 + | 3.2 | 3.3 | 3.7 | 3.2 | 3.0 | 3.4 | 3.6 | 3.3 | 539 |

* Level of education is measured by the highest grade completed. † Levels 1 to 4 for economic status range in order from "high" to "low." ‡ Minimum ideal (results from coding range answers to the lowest figure). § Maximum ideal (results from coding range answers to the highest figure).

or not publicly supported services are actually appropriate to the attitudes and objectives of the poor and uneducated in matters of reproduction. Is the government responding to a mandate from the poor or to an ill-concealed mandate from the well-to-do? If there is no mandate from the poor, the provision of birth-control services may prove a convenience for certain women but is likely to have little effect on the reproductive performance of the poor in general. Let us look at the evidence.

## Is There a Mandate from the Poor?

The notion that the poor have larger families than the affluent only because they have less access to birth-control information implies that the poor *desire* families as small as, or smaller than, those of the well-to-do. The poor are simply unable to realize this desire, the argument goes, because of lack of access to birth-control information. The National Academy of Sciences Committee on Population stated the argument very well (2, p. 10).

The available evidence indicates that low-income families do not want more children than do families with higher incomes, but they have more because they do not have the information or the resources to plan their families effectively according to their own desires.

The committee, however, presents none of the "available evidence" that "low-income families do not want more children than do families with higher incomes." Actually, my data supply evidence that runs counter to the statement quoted above, both with respect

to the desired or ideal number of children and with respect to attitudes toward birth control.

I shall begin with the preferred size of family. A number of national polls, conducted over some 25 years, provide data concerning opinions on ideal family size. In addition, I include tabulations of data from two national surveys on fertility (the "Growth of American Families Studies"), conducted in 1955 and 1960 (13, 14). My detailed analyses of the results of these polls and surveys are given elsewhere (15) and are only briefly summarized here. Table 2 gives mean values for the family size considered ideal by white, non-Catholic women, according to education and economic status.

The data lend little support to the hypothesis that the poor desire families as small as those desired by the middle and upper classes. Within both the educational and the economic categories, those on the lower rungs not only have larger families than those on the higher rungs (at least in the case of non-Catholics) but say they want larger families and consider them ideal. This differential has existed for as long as information on preferred family size in this country has been available, and it persists. It thus seems extremely hazardous to base a major governmental effort on the notion that, among individuals (white individuals, at least)' at the lower social levels, there is a widespread and deeply held desire for families as small as, or smaller than, those desired by the well-to-do. No major survey shows this to be the case.

Not only do persons of lower socioeconomic status prefer larger families

than the more affluent do, they also generally favor birth control less. Tables 3 and 4 show the percentages of white men and women who expressed approval of birth control in surveys made between 1937 and 1964, by educational level and economic status, respectively.

Looking at the educational differential (Table 3), one finds that, in general, the proportion of those who approve birth control drops precipitately between the college and grade school levels. As far back as the early 1940's, over 80 percent of women and 75 percent of men with some or more college education approved government action on birth control. By 1964, over 90 percent of both sexes approved. By contrast, only 60 percent of men and women with an elementary school education approved in the 1940's, and, despite a rise in approval, there is still a differential. When non-Catholics alone are considered, the educational difference is even more pronounced in many cases.

Turning to economic or income status (Table 4), one generally finds the same results. The high proportions (close to 100 percent) of women in the highest and next-to-highest economic brackets who, in recent years, have approved birth-control efforts is noteworthy, as is the fact that approximately 80 percent of women in these brackets approved such efforts as far back as the 1930's. On the other hand, men and women in lower income brackets have been slower to approve birth-control policies.

Despite the inverse relationship just described, I may have overemphasized the lesser approval of birth-control programs on the part of persons of lower economic and social status. After all, in recent years approval often has been high even among people at the lowest social levels. Among women with only a grade school education, the percentage of those favoring birth-control programs averaged 73 percent in polls taken between 1959 and 1964; among men at the lowest educational level, the corresponding average was 66 percent. Yet it is undeniably true that, throughout the period for which data are available, the people who needed birth-control information most, according to recent policy pronouncements, have been precisely the ones who were least in favor of a policy that would make it widely available.

The truth of this conclusion becomes more evident when we move to an analysis of a question asked on the

524

Table 3. Percentages of white U.S. men and women between the ages of 21 and 44 who, in various national polls taken between 1943 and 1964, expressed the opinion that birth-control information should be made available to individuals who desired it. The percentages are given by level of education*; the numbers in parentheses are total numbers of respondents in each category.

| Year | Men | | | Women | | |
|------|---------|----------------|-----------------|---------|----------------|-----------------|
| | College | High school | Grade school | College | High school | Grade school |
| 1943 | 75 (184) | 68 (284) | 56 (157) | 82 (216) | 74 (442) | 60 (207) |
| 1945 | 74 (202) | 62 (360) | 58 (140) | 83 (216) | 68 (434) | 56 (207) |
| 1947 | 91 (84) | 72 (199) | 67 (66) | 81 (89) | 74 (228) | 72( 81) |
| 1959 | 88 (89) | 76 (163) | 65 (49) | 91 (55) | 79 (279) | 68 (41) |
| 1961 | 88 (102) | 81 (188) | 67 (46) | 84 (81) | 81 (265) | 78 (50) |
| 1962 | 91 (93) | 85 (171) | 61 (23) | 84 (79) | 82 (258) | 66 (44) |
| 1963 | 86 (105) | 79 (178) | 53 (40) | 81 (80) | 78 (251) | 81 (42) |
| 1964 | 92 (107) | 88 (188) | 83 (29) | 94 (79) | 86 (293) | 74 (38) |

* The level of education is measured by the last grade completed.

1966 Gallup poll: Do you think birth-control pills should be made available free to all women on relief who are of childbearing age? This question presents the public with the specific issue that is the focus of current policy—namely, birth control especially for the poor. A summary of the replies to this question is given in Table 5, together with average percentages of people who, in the five surveys made between 1959 and 1964, replied that they approved birth control generally.

It is clear that the overall level of approval drops when specific reference to a poverty-oriented birth-control policy is introduced. The decline is from an average of approximately 80 percent for each sex during the period 1959–64 to 65 percent for men and 71 percent for women in 1966. Of most significance, however, is the fact that the largest proportionate drop in approval occurs among members of the "target" groups themselves—the poor and uneducated. In particular, there is a remarkable drop in approval among men at this socioeconomic level. There is a 42-percent decline in approval among men who have had only a grade school education and a 29-percent drop among those with a high school education. Among the college-educated men the drop in approval is only 6 percent. The results, by income, parallel those by education: there is a 47-percent drop for men in the lowest income group but only a 9-percent drop for those in the highest income bracket. Even if the tabulations are restricted to non-Catholics (data that are not presented here), the results are essentially the same.

If the ghetto-oriented birth-control policy urged on the federal government meets with limited public enthusiasm, how does the public view extension of that policy to teen-age girls? This question is of some importance because a notable aspect of the pressure for government-sponsored family-planning programs is advocacy of making birth-control information and materials available at the high school level.

The Committee on Population of the National Academy of Sciences urges early education in "family planning" in order to prevent illegitimacy (2, p. 13).

. . . government statistics show that the mothers of approximately 41 per cent of the 245,000 babies born illegitimately in the United States every year are women 19 years of age or younger. Thus a large proportion of all illegitimate children are progeny of teen-age mothers. To reduce the number of such children born to teen-age mothers, high-school education in family planning is essential.

Katherine B. Oettinger, Deputy Secretary for Family Planning of the Department of Health, Education, and Welfare, importunes us not to "demand the eligibility card of a first pregnancy before we admit vulnerable girls to family planning services" (16). The Harkavy report states (3, p. 29):

Eligibility requirements should be liberal with respect to marital status. Such services should be made available to the unmarried as well as the married. . . . Eligibility requirements should be liberal with respect to the age of unmarried women seeking help. This will undoubtedly pose some problems, but they may not be insurmountable. Some publically supported programs are already facing them (for example, in Baltimore).

Representative Scheuer from New York has berated the federal government for not "bringing family planning into the schools." He has cited the "desperate need for family planning by unmarried 14-, 15-, and 16-year-old girls in school [which] is so transparently evident that it almost boggles the imagination to realize that nothing has been done. Virtually no leadership has come from the federal government" (9, p. 18).

Obviously there is little recognition in these statements that such a policy

Table 4. Percentages of white U.S. men and women between the ages of 21 and 44 who, in various national polls taken between 1937 and 1964, expressed the opinion that birth-control information should be made available to individuals who desired it. The percentages are given by economic status (levels 1–4*); the numbers in parentheses are total numbers of respondents in each category.

| Year | Men | | | | Women | | | |
|------|-----------|-----------|-----------|-----------|-----------|-----------|-----------|-----------|
| | 1 | 2 | 3 | 4 | 1 | 2 | 3 | 4 |
| 1937 | 78 (112) | 70 (406) | 61 (520) | | 67 (69) | 78 (293) | 64 (372) | |
| 1938 | 65 (125) | 74 (453) | 62 (521) | | 80 (51) | 73 (232) | 70 (259) | |
| 1939 | 78 (116) | 75 (432) | 73 (553) | | 71 (68) | 77 (260) | 71 (302) | |
| 1940 | 79 (131) | 75 (443) | 68 (553) | | 80 (49) | 78 (258) | 71 (311) | |
| 1943 | 76 (80) | 72 (219) | 62 (330) | | 80 (90) | 79 (272) | 68 (500) | |
| 1945 | 73 (67) | 66 (286) | 62 (352) | | 83 (75) | 77 (264) | 64 (531) | |
| 1947 | 86 (42) | 77 (123) | 72 (188) | | 92 (38) | 71 (119) | 73 (237) | |
| 1959 | 83 (101) | 76 (120) | 73 (79) | | 83 (139) | 82 (152) | 72 (95) | |
| 1961 | 93 (42) | 85 (80) | 87 (103) | 69 (111) | 88 (41) | 80 (97) | 80 (76) | 81 (138) |
| 1962 | 82 (45) | 89 (71) | 86 (94) | 80 (74) | 82 (51) | 80 (75) | 84 (110) | 77 (140) |
| 1963 | 88 (60) | 84 (79) | 76 (96) | 61 (97) | 87 (67) | 79 (107) | 79 (98) | 75 (100) |
| 1964 | 90 (67) | 87 (26) | 93 (82) | 85 (79) | 96 (90) | 90 (87) | 85 (104) | 78 (120) |

* Levels 1 to 4 for the years 1961–64 range from income of $10,000 and over down to incomes under $5000. Prior to 1961, levels 1 to 3 represent "upper," "middle," and "lower" income brackets.

Table 5. Percentages of white U.S. men and women between the ages of 21 and 44 who, in a 1966 poll, expressed approval of free distribution of birth-control pills for women on relief, and average percentages of individuals in this age group who, in polls taken between 1959 and 1964, expressed approval of birth control. Percentages approving and numbers of individuals interviewed are given as totals and also by education and economic status of the respondents.

| Item | Men | | | Women | | |
|------|-----|-----|-----|-----|-----|-----|
| | 1966 | | 1959–64 | 1966 | | 1959–64 |
| | % | N | (av. %) | % | N | (av. %) |
| Total | 65 | 264 | 82 | 71 | 385 | 81 |
| Education | | | | | | |
| College | 82 | 98 | 87 | 75 | 197 | 87 |
| High school | 58 | 142 | 82 | 70 | 392 | 81 |
| Grade school | 38 | 24 | 66 | 59 | 32 | 73 |
| Economic status | | | | | | |
| 1 | 79 | 80 | 89 | 70 | 110 | 87 |
| 2 | 69 | 75 | 84 | 76 | 99 | 82 |
| 3 | 59 | 65 | 83 | 70 | 91 | 80 |
| 4 | 39 | 41 | 74 | 67 | 76 | 78 |

might engender a negative public response. Yet such a possibility cannot be discounted. The results of the 1966 question "Do you think they [the pills] should be made available to teen-age girls?" suggest that a policy of pill distribution to female adolescents may be viewed by the public as involving more complex issues than the mere democratization of "medical" services. These results, tabulated by social level, are shown in Table 6.

It may be seen that, in general, a proposal for distribution of pills to teen-age girls meets with very little approval. There is more disapproval among women than among men. Even among women under the age of 30, only 17 percent approve; among men in this age group, 29 percent approve. At no age does feminine approval reach 20 percent, and in most cases it is below 15 percent. Furthermore, restriction of the results to non-Catholics does not raise the percentages of those who approve the policy. Most noteworthy is the socioeconomic gradient among men. Whereas 32 percent of college-educated men approve distribution of pills to young girls, only 13 percent of men with a grade school education do. Thirty-three percent of men in the highest income bracket approve, but only 13 percent in the lowest bracket do.

Clearly, the extension of "family planning" to poor, unmarried teen-agers is not regarded simply as "health care." Individuals may approve, in a general way, a wider availability of birth-control information without approving federal expenditure to facilitate a high level of sexual activity by teen-age girls. One suspects that explicit recognition and implied approval of such activity still comes hard to our

population, and that it comes hardest to the group most involved in the problems of illegitimacy and premarital conception—namely, the poor and uneducated themselves. The extreme disapproval of a policy of pill distribution to teen-age girls that is found in lower-class groups (particularly among lower-class men) suggests that a double standard of sexual behavior is operative in these groups—a standard that does not allow open toleration of the idea that the ordinary teen-age girl requires the pill, or that a part of her junior high school and high school education should include instruction in its use.

### Can "Five Million Women" Be Wrong?

The most widely publicized argument favoring federal birth-control programs, and apparently the one that elected officials find most persuasive, is the claim that there are approximately "five million" poor women "in need" of publicly subsidized birth-control help (17). I list below some of the principal assumptions upon which this estimate is based—all of which introduce serious upward biases into the evidence.

1) It is claimed that women at the poverty and near-poverty levels desire families of 3.0 children. While this may be true of nonwhite wives at this economic level, it is not true, as we have seen, of white women, who comprise a major share of the "target" group and who, on the average, desire a number of children closer to 4 (especially if Catholics are included, as they are in the "five million").

2) It is assumed by the estimators that 82 percent of all poor women aged 15 to 44 are at risk of conception (that is, exposed sexually), in spite of the

fact that only 45 percent of poor women in this age group are married and living with their husbands. In arriving at the figure of 82 percent, the estimators assumed that all women in the "married" category (including those who were separated from their husbands and those whose husbands were absent) were sexually exposed regularly, and that half of the women in the "non-married" category—that is, single, widowed, and divorced women—were exposed regularly. Information is scarce concerning the sexual behavior of widows and divorced women, but Kinsey's data on premarital coitus leads one to believe that the assumption of 50 percent for single women may be high. Among the women with a grade school education in Kinsey's sample, 38 percent had had coitus at some time between the ages of 16 and 20, and 26 percent, at some time between the ages of 21 and 25. Moreover, as Kinsey emphasizes, these encounters were characteristically sporadic (18).

3) The proportion of sterile women among the poor is assumed to be 13 percent, although the Scripps 1960 "Growth of American Families Study" showed the proportion among white women of grade school education to be 22 percent (14, p. 159).

4) No allowance is made for less-than-normal fecundity, although the Scripps 1960 study (14, p. 159) had indicated that, among women of grade school education, an additional 10 percent (over and above the 22 percent) were subnormal in their ability to reproduce.

5) It is taken for granted by the estimators that no Catholic women would object, on religious grounds, to the use of modern methods, and no allowance is made for objection by non-Catholics, on religious or other grounds. In other words, it is assumed that all women "want" the service. Yet, in response to a question concerning the desirability of limiting or spacing pregnancies, 29 percent of the wives with grade school education who were interviewed in the Scripps 1960 study said they were "against" such limitation or spacing (14, p. 177). Among the Catholic wives with grade school education, the proportion "against" was 48 percent, although half of these objectors were "for" the rhythm method. Similar objections among the disadvantaged have been revealed by many polls over a long period.

6) Perhaps most important, the estimate of 5 million women "wanting"

and "in need of" birth-control information includes not only objectors but women who are already practicing birth control. Hence, in addition to all the other biases, the estimate represents a blanket decision by the estimators that the women require medical attention regarding birth control—particularly that they need the pill and the coil. In the words of the Harkavy report (*2*, attachment A, p. 19):

This may be considered a high estimate of the number of women who need to have family planning services made available to them in public clinics, because some of the couples among the poor and near poor are able to exercise satisfactory control over their fertility. However, even these couples do not have the same access as the non-poor to the more effective and acceptable methods of contraception, particularly the pill and the loop. So, simply in order to equalize the access of the poor and the near-poor to modern methods of contraception under medical supervision, it is appropriate to try to make contraceptive services available to all who may need and want them.

Yet the 1960 Scripps study found that, among fecund women of grade school education, 79 percent used contraceptives (*14*, p. 159). The 21 percent who did not included young women who were building families and said they wanted to get pregnant, as well as Catholics who objected to birth control on religious grounds. As for the methods that women currently are using, it seems gratuitous for the federal government to decide that only medically supervised methods—the pill and the coil—are suitable for lower-income couples, and that a mammoth "service" program is therefore required. In fact, the implications of such a decision border on the fantastic—the implications that we should substitute scarce medical and paramedical attention for all contraceptive methods now being used by poor couples.

In sum, the argument supporting a "need" for nationwide, publicly sustained birth-control programs does not stand up under empirical scrutiny. Most fecund lower-class couples now use birth-control methods when they want to prevent pregnancy; in the case of those who do not, the blame cannot simply be laid at the door of the affluent who have kept the subject of birth control under wraps, or of a government that has withheld services. As we have seen, opinion on birth control has been, and is, less favorable among the poor and the less well educated than among the well-to-do. In addition, the poor desire larger families.

Table 6. Percentages of white U.S. men and women who, in a 1966 poll, expressed approval of making birth-control pills available to teen-age girls. Percentages approving and numbers of individuals interviewed are given by age group, by education, and by economic status.

| Item | All religions | | | | Non-Catholics | | | |
|---|---|---|---|---|---|---|---|---|
| | Men | | Women | | Men | | Women | |
| | % | N | % | N | % | N | % | N |
| **Age** | | | | | | | | |
| Under 30 | 29 | 86 | 17 | 149 | 34 | 65 | 19 | 102 |
| 30–44 | 19 | 172 | 8 | 238 | 20 | 133 | 7 | 169 |
| **Education** | | | | | | | | |
| College | 32 | 98 | 15 | 100 | 36 | 75 | 13 | 71 |
| High school | 18 | 142 | 9 | 264 | 19 | 110 | 9 | 180 |
| Grade school | 13 | 24 | 11 | 35 | 6 | 17 | 14 | 28 |
| **Economic status** | | | | | | | | |
| 1 | 33 | 80 | 11 | 113 | 35 | 58 | 11 | 75 |
| 2 | 20 | 75 | 13 | 105 | 24 | 58 | 14 | 72 |
| 3 | 19 | 65 | 7 | 94 | 18 | 50 | 5 | 64 |
| 4 | 13 | 41 | 16 | 82 | 15 | 33 | 14 | 66 |

Although it may be argued that, at the public welfare level, birth control has, until recently, been taboo because of the "Catholic vote," most individuals at all social levels have learned about birth control *informally* and without medical attention. Furthermore, the most popular birth-control device, the condom, has long been as available as aspirin or cigarettes, and certainly has been used by men of all social classes. When one bears in mind the fact that the poor have no difficulty in gaining access to illegal narcotics (despite their obvious "unavailability"), and that the affluent had drastically reduced their fertility before present-day contraceptive methods were available, one must recognize and take into account a motivational component in nonuse and inefficient use of contraceptives. Indeed, were relative lack of demand on the part of the poor not a principal factor, it would be difficult to explain why such an important "market" for birth-control materials—legal or illegal—would have escaped the attention of enterprising businessmen or bootleggers. In any event, any estimate based on the assumption that all poor women in the reproductive group "want" birth-control information and materials and that virtually all "need" publicly supported services that will provide them—including women with impaired fecundity, women who have sexual intercourse rarely or not at all, women who object on religious grounds, and women who are already using birth-control methods —would seem to be seriously misleading as a guide for our government in its efforts to control population growth.

Moreover, the proposal for government sponsorship takes no account of the possible advantages of alternative means of reaching that part of the "market" that may not be optimally served at present. For example, competitive pricing, better marketing, and a program of advertising could make it possible for many groups in the population who are now being counted as "targets" for government efforts to purchase contraceptives of various kinds. When one bears in mind the fact that an important reason for nonuse or lack of access to contraceptives may be some sort of conflict situation (between husband and wife, adolescent child and parent, and so on), it becomes apparent that the impersonal and responsive marketplace is a far better agency for effecting smooth social change than is a far-flung national bureaucracy loaded with well-meaning but often blundering "health workers." The government could doubtless play an initial stimulating and facilitating role in relation to private industry, without duplicating, on a welfare basis, functions that might be more efficiently handled in the marketplace.

## Would the Policy Have Side Effects?

The possible inadvisability of having the government become a direct purveyor of birth-control materials to poverty groups becomes more clear when we consider some of the risks involved in such a course of action.

Even if the goal of reducing family size were completely and widely accepted by the poorer and less well educated sectors of the population, we should not assume that the general public would necessarily view a policy concerned with the means and practice of birth control (in any social group) as it views ordinary medical care—that is, as being morally neutral and obviously "desirable." Birth control is related to sexual behavior, and, in all viable societies, sexual behavior is regulated by social institutions. It is thus an oversimplification to think that people will be unmindful of what are, for them at least, the moral implications of changes in the conditions under which sexual intercourse is possible, permissible, or likely. An issue such as distribution of pills to teen-age girls runs a collision course with norms about premarital relations for young girls—norms that, in turn, relate to the saliency of marriage and motherhood as a woman's principal career and to the consequent need for socially created restrictions on free sexual access if an important inducement to marriage is not to be lost. Only if viable careers alternative to marriage existed for women would the lessening of controls over sexual behavior outside of marriage be unrelated to women's lifetime opportunities, for such opportunities would be independent of the marriage market and, a fortiori, independent of sexual bargaining. But such independence clearly does not exist. Hence, when the government is told that it will be resolving a "medical" problem if it makes birth-control pills available to teen-agers, it is being misled into becoming the protagonist in a sociologically based conflict between short-run feminine impulses and long-run feminine interests—a conflict that is expressed both in relations between parents and children and in relations between the sexes. This sociological conflict far transcends the "medical" issue of whether or not birth-control services should be made widely available.

Actually, the issue of sexual morality is only one among many potentially explosive aspects of direct federal involvement in family-planning programs for the poor. Others come readily to mind, such as the possibility that the pill and other physiological methods could have long-run, serious side effects, or that racial organizations could seize on the existence of these programs as a prime example of "genocide." Eager promoters of the suggested programs tend to brush such problems aside as trivial, but the problems, like the issue of sexual morality, cannot be wished away, for they are quite patently there (9, p. 62). There *are* risks involved in all drug-taking, and it is recognized that many of the specific ones involved in long-term ingestion of the pill may not be discovered for many years. No one today can say that these are

less than, equal to, or greater than the normal risks of pregnancy and childbirth. Equally, a class-directed birth-control program, whatever its intent, is open to charges of genocide that are difficult to refute. Such a program cannot fail to appear to single out the disadvantaged as the "goat," all the while implying that the very considerable "planned" fertility of most Americans inexplicably requires no government attention at all.

## Population Policy for Americans

It seems clear that the suggested policy of poverty-oriented birth-control programs does not make sense as a welfare measure. It is also true that, as an inhibitor of population growth, it is inconsequential and trivial. It does not touch the principal cause of such growth in the United States—namely, the reproductive behavior of the majority of Americans who, under present conditions, want families of more than three children and thereby generate a growth rate far in excess of that required for population stability. Indeed, for most Americans the "family planning" approach, concentrating as it does on the distribution of contraceptive materials and services, is irrelevant, because they already know about efficient contraception and are already "planning" their families. It is thus apparent that any policy designed to influence reproductive behavior must not only concern itself with all fecund Americans (rather than just the poor) but must, as well, relate to family-size goals (rather than just to contraceptive means). In addition, such a policy cannot be limited to matters affecting contraception (or even to matters affecting gestation and parturition, such as abortion), but must, additionally, take into account influences on the formation and dissolution of heterosexual unions (19).

What kinds of reproductive policies can be pursued in an effort to reduce long-term population growth? The most important step toward developing such new policies is to recognize and understand the existing ones, for we already have influential and coercive policies regarding reproductive behavior. Furthermore, these existing policies relate not merely to proscriptions (legal or informal) regarding certain means of birth control (like abortion) but also to a definition of reproduction as a primary societal end and to an organiza-

tion of social roles that draws most of the population into reproductive unions.

The existence of such pronatalist policies becomes apparent when we recall that, among human beings, population replacement would not occur at all were it not for the complex social organization and system of incentives that encourage mating, pregnancy, and the care, support, and rearing of children. These institutional mechanisms are the pronatalist "policies" evolved unconsciously over millennia to give societies a fertility sufficient to offset high mortality. The formation and implementation of antinatalist policies must be based, therefore, on an analysis and modification of the existing pronatalist policies. It follows, as well, that antinatalist policies will not necessarily involve the introduction of coercive measures. In fact, just the opposite is the case. Many of these new policies will entail a *lifting* of pressures to reproduce, rather than an *imposition* of pressures not to do so. In order to understand this point let us consider briefly our present-day pronatalism.

It is convenient to start with the family, because pronatalism finds its most obvious expression in this social institution. The pronatalism of the family has many manifestations, but among the most influential and universal are two: the standardization of both the male and the female sexual roles in terms of reproductive functions, obligations, and activities, and the standardization of the occupational role of women—half of the population—in terms of child-bearing, child-rearing, and complementary activities. These two "policies" insure that just about everyone will be propelled into reproductive unions, and that half of the population will enter such unions as a "career"—a life's work. Each of the two "policies" is worth considering.

With regard to sex roles, it is generally recognized that potential human variability is greater than is normally permitted *within* each sex category. Existing societies have tended to suppress and extinguish such variability and to standardize sexual roles in ways that imply that all "normal" persons will attain the status of parents. This coercion takes many forms, including one-sided indoctrination in schools, legal barriers and penalties for deviation, and the threats of loneliness, ostracism, and ridicule that are implied in the unavailability of alternatives. Individuals who—by temperament, health, or constitution—do not fit the ideal sex-role pattern are nonetheless coerced into attempting to achieve it, and many of them do achieve it, at least to the extent of having demographic impact by becoming parents.

Therefore, a policy that sought out the ways in which coercion regarding sex roles is at present manifesting itself could find numerous avenues for relieving the coercion and for allowing life styles different from marriage and parenthood to find free and legitimatized expression. Such a policy would have an effect on the content of expectations regarding sex roles as presented and enforced in schools, on laws concerning sexual activity between consenting adults, on taxation with respect to marital status and number of children, on residential building policies, and on just about every facet of existence that is now organized so as exclusively to favor and reward a pattern of sex roles based on marriage and parenthood.

As for the occupational roles of women, existing pressures still attempt to make the reproductive and occupational roles coterminus for all women who elect to marry and have children. This rigid structuring of the wife-mother position builds into the entire motivational pattern of women's lives a tendency to want at least a moderate-size family. To understand this point one must recognize that the desired number of children relates not simply to the wish for a family of a particular size but relates as well to a need for more than one or two children if one is going to enjoy "family life" over a significant portion of one's lifetime. This need is increased rather than lessened by improved life expectancy. Insofar as women focus their energies and emotions on their families, one cannot expect that they will be satisfied to play their only important role for a diminishing fraction of their lives, or that they will readily regard make-work and dead-end jobs as a substitute for "mothering." The notion that most women will "see the error of their ways" and decide to have two-child families is naive, since few healthy and energetic women will be so misguided as to deprive themselves of most of the rewards society has to offer them and choose a situation that allows them neither a life's work outside the home nor one within it. Those who do deprive themselves in this fashion are, in effect, taking the brunt of the still existing maladjustment between the roles of women and the reproductive needs of society. In a society oriented around achievement and accomplishment, such women are exceptionally vulnerable to depression, frustration, and a sense of futility, because they are being blocked from a sense of fulfillment both at home and abroad.

In sum, the problem of inhibiting population growth in the United States cannot be dealt with in terms of "family-planning needs" because this country is well beyond the point of "needing" birth control methods. Indeed, even the poor seem not to be a last outpost for family-planning attention. If we wish to limit our growth, such a desire implies basic changes in the social organization of reproduction that will make nonmarriage, childlessness, and small (two-child) families far more prevalent than they are now. A new policy, to achieve such ends, can take advantage of the antinatalist tendencies that our present institutions have suppressed. This will involve the lifting of penalties for antinatalist behavior rather than the "creation" of new ways of life. This behavior already exists among us as part of our covert and deviant culture, on the one hand, and our elite and artistic culture, on the other. Such antinatalist tendencies have also found expression in feminism, which has been stifled in the United States by means of systematic legal, educational, and social pressures concerned with women's "obligations" to create and care for children. A fertility-control policy that does not take into account the need to alter the present structure of reproduction in these and other ways merely trivializes the problem of population control and misleads those who have the power to guide our country toward completing the vital revolution.

### References and Notes

1. *Hearings on S. 1676, U.S. Senate Subcommittee on Foreign Aid Expenditures* (the 1965 and 1966 Hearings each comprise seven volumes; the 1967–1968 Hearings, to date, comprise three volumes) (Government Printing Office, Washington, D.C.).
2. "The Growth of U.S. Population," *Nat. Acad. Sci.–Nat. Res. Council Pub.* 1279 (1965).
3. O. Harkavy, F. S. Jaffe, S. S. Wishik, "Implementing DHEW Policy on Family Planning and Population" (mimeographed, 1967; available from the Ford Foundation, New York).
4. "Report of the President's Committee on Population and Family Planning: The Transition from Concern to Action" (Government Printing Office, Washington, D.C., 1968).
5. K. Davis, *Science* 158, 730 (1967); J. Blake, in *Public Health and Population Change*, M. C. Sheps and J. C. Ridley, Eds. (Univ. of Pittsburgh Press, Pittsburgh, Pa., 1965).
6. In the words of the Committee on Population, "The freedom to limit family size to the number of children wanted when they are wanted is, in our view, a basic human right . . . most Americans of higher income and better education exercise this right as a matter of course, but . . . many of the poor and uneducated are in fact deprived of the right."
7. W. J. Cohen, *Family Planning: One Aspect of Freedom to Choose* (Government Printing Office, Washington, D.C., 1966), p. 2. Cohen, former Secretary of Health, Education, and Welfare, says: "Until a few years ago, family planning and population problems were considered 'hush-hush' subjects. Public discussion was curtailed not only in polite society, but in the legislative and executive branches of the government as well."
8. *Hearings on S. 2993, U.S. Senate Subcommittee on Employment, Manpower, and Poverty*, 89th Congress, Second Session, May 10 (Government Printing Office, Washington, D.C., 1966), p. 31.
9. *Hearings on S. 1676, U.S. Senate Subcommittee on Foreign Aid Expenditures*, 90th Congress, First Session, November 2 (Government Printing Office, Washington, D.C., 1967), pt. 1.
10. Senator Tydings (D–Md.) said at the Hearings on S. 1676 (see 9): "As recently as 3 or 4 years ago, the idea that Federal, State or local governments should make available family planning information and services to families who could not otherwise afford them was extremely controversial. But in a brief period of time there has been a substantial shift of opinion among the moral leadership of our country, brought about in large measure by the vigorous efforts of the distinguished Senator from Alaska, Ernest Gruening, the chairman of this subcommittee."
11. E. Gruening, "What the Federal Government is now Doing in the Field of Population Control and What is Needed," speech presented before the U.S. Senate, 3 May 1967.
12. J. M. Stycos, in *World Population and U.S. Government Policy and Programs*, F. T. Brayer, Ed. (Georgetown Univ. Press, Washington, D.C., 1968).
13. R. Freedman, P. K. Whelpton, A. A. Campbell, *Family Planning, Sterility and Population Growth* (McGraw-Hill, New York, 1959).
14. P. K. Whelpton, A. A. Campbell, J. E. Patterson, *Fertility and Family Planning in the United States* (Princeton Univ. Press, Princeton, N.J., 1966).
15. J. Blake, *Demography* 3, 154 (1966); *Population Studies* 20, 27 (1966); *ibid.* 21, 159 (1967); *ibid.*, p. 185; *ibid.* 22, 5 (1968).
16. *Family Planner* 2, 3 (1968).
17. The estimate (by Arthur A. Campbell) under discussion here may be found in the Harkavy report (see 3, attachment A, pp. 4–19). Another estimate has been circulated by the Planned Parenthood Federation in a brochure entitled *Five Million Women* (Planned Parenthood, New York).
18. A. C. Kinsey, W. B. Pomeroy, C. E. Martin, P. B. Gebhard, *Sexual Behavior in the Human Female* (Saunders, Philadelphia, 1953), pp. 291 and 337.
19. K. Davis and J. Blake, *Econ. Develop. Cult. Change* 4, 211 (1956).
20. I make grateful acknowledgment to the Ford Foundation for support of the research presented in this article and to the National Institutes of Health (general research support grant 1501-TR-544104) for assistance to Statistical Services, School of Public Health, University of California, Berkeley. I am also indebted to Kingsley Davis, whose critical comments and helpful suggestions have greatly advanced my thinking. The Roper Center and the Gallup Poll kindly supplied me with polling data.

# Prospects for Reducing Natality in the Underdeveloped World

## By Dudley Kirk

ABSTRACT: The prospects for reductions in birth rates in the less industrialized countries are improving owing to the increasingly favorable climate of opinion relating to birth control, the invention of better contraceptives, and the adoption of national family planning programs. Some twenty-three countries, including over half the population in the developing countries, now have such programs. These are too new to have had a measurable effect on the birth rate in most countries. Nevertheless, the birth rate is already falling in a few of the economically more progressive countries in East Asia such as Taiwan, Korea, and Singapore. These reductions in the birth rate may be expected to deepen and spread, accelerated by national family programs operating within the context of rapid socioeconomic change. In two decades the solutions to the world population problem may well be in sight, though not yet fully achieved. But these changes will not occur fast enough to forestall massive population growth and continuing critical problems of population at least through the next decade.

---

*Dudley Kirk, Ph.D., New York City, is Demographic Director of The Population Council, New York. He served with the United States Department of State, 1947–1954, in various capacities, including demographer, sociological adviser, chief planning officer in the Office of Intelligence Research, and chief of the Division of Research for Near East, South Asia, and Africa. He is coauthor of The Future Population of Europe and the Soviet Union (1944), author of Europe's Population: The Interwar Years (1946), and coauthor of Principles of Political Geography (1957). He has taught sociology at Princeton University and was a member of the staff of the Office of Population Research there.*

Reprinted by permission of the author and the publisher from *Annals of the American Academy of Political and Social Science* 369:48–60, January 1967.

TWO-THIRDS of the world's people live in its "developing" or less industrialized countries.[1] The populations of these countries are growing at an accelerating pace in the so-called "population explosion," thanks to welcome gains in reducing mortality.

The present imbalance between birth and death rates in the developing world is generally recognized. Current rates of population growth cannot continue for any long historical period. Already the growth rate in many developing countries exceeds 3 per cent per year, a rate at which numbers double in twenty-three years and increase twenty-fold in the course of a century. From the mathematics of compound interest, it is clear that in the not too distant future, birth rates must come down or death rates must go up.

Of more immediate concern is the fact that the present and emerging rates of population growth seriously handicap socioeconomic advance in many of the developing countries. In some it has created food shortages and even the threat of famine. A lower rate of growth (that is, a lower birth rate) would facilitate their development.

With continuing decline in death rates throughout the world, the modal European birth rates of some seventeen or eighteen births per thousand population would seem to be a reasonable target for the world as a whole by the end of the century. This is what has been achieved in Japan, and this is probably a factor in the spectacular economic success of that country. As in Europe and Japan today, such birth rates would still leave a margin of population growth.

Birth rates in the developing areas still average 40 to 45 per 1,000 population. To bring these rates down to a reasonable balance of natality and mor-

[1] Africa, Asia excluding Japan and the Soviet Union, and Latin America excluding Argentina and Uruguay.

tality (that is, the European level) involves a drop of some 25 points, or more than 50 per cent from the current level. With a present population of 2.3 billion in the underdeveloped world, such a reduction implies the prevention of well over 50 million births per annum at this time. These are the dimensions of the problem of reducing natality in the underdeveloped world.

Fortunately, there are grounds for optimism that birth rates can be brought down in time to avert a rise in death rates, barring some catastrophe such as nuclear war. The prospect for reductions in the birth rate in the less industrialized countries has never been more hopeful than it is today.

(1) Foremost perhaps is the rapid change in climate of opinion regarding family planning. To appreciate the significance of this change it is important to note that the European demographic transition occurred in an atmosphere of overt and covert institutional hostility toward birth control. The European population learned to limit family size, but the process was gradual and stemmed from private decisions made *in spite of* restrictive legislation, religious opposition (Protestant as well as Catholic), and public denunciation of birth control practices in what was generally a "conspiracy of silence" on sexual matters and human reproduction. The prevailing middle-class morality prevented free public discussion, and public authorities harassed militant fringe groups that advocated birth control. With the growing understanding of the impact of high rates of population growth on economic development, the hitherto restrictive atmosphere is rapidly yielding to a climate of public approval and sponsorship of family planning programs which can be expected to accelerate the adoption of contraceptive practice.

(2) In the developing world, except

for Latin America, religious doctrine does not oppose family planning. Religions other than the Catholic and the Orthodox do not have clear doctrinal positions that ban the use of contraceptives, and their views on abortion are often more permissive; for example, the Moslem doctrine forbids abortion after the quickening, but it is far less clear on earlier abortions. This is not to suggest that religion does not play a part in natality differentials in the developing countries; it does, but not in the sense of formal opposition to family planning.

(3) New methods of contraception, derived by intensive research, now offer a wider choice of methods and already include some that seem applicable in poor and peasant cultures. The two major new developments are the oral contraceptives and the intra-uterine devices (IUD's). Even better methods are on the way.

In the Western experience, the decline in the birth rate resulted from later age at marriage; from male methods of contraception, especially *coitus interruptus* and the condom; and from the female method of abortion. These are still much the most common methods of family limitation in the world. The "conventional" chemical and mechanical methods have probably not been of major importance in controlling Western fertility, and seem unsuited to the peoples of the developing world. Continued research will almost certainly produce even more effective, simple, inexpensive, and safe methods, unrelated to the sex act. Not to be overlooked are better techniques of abortion and the general availability and acceptance of abortion in many countries.

(4) The rapid decline of the death rate in today's developing countries is itself an important factor in changing motivations in favor of family limitation. With more children surviving, the pressure of larger families, especially in the context of growing aspirations for the children, is more quickly evident. The change from low to moderate and even high survival rates within a single generation has an impact on parents and grandparents that favors considerably more rapid acceptance of family planning than occurred in the West, where slowly declining death rates were followed by a gradual decline in births.

(5) The traditional view that birth rates and population growth are a "given" not amenable to deliberate social and governmental influence is no longer tenable. Today it is increasingly appreciated among all cultures and strata of people that, within nature's limits, man can control his destiny over births as well as deaths. Numerous surveys in many developing countries on knowledge, attitudes, and practice (the so-called KAP surveys) have shown that the general public, rural as well as urban, is interested in controlling family size. Very few now think it necessary to have as many children "as God wills." On the contrary, almost everywhere there is a substantial "market" for contraceptive knowledge, materials, and services, provided these are made available in a form appropriate to local conditions.

(6) A final point concerns the relationship between population growth and economic progress. Despite impressive aggregate economic gain in many developing countries in recent years (of the order of 4 per cent to 6 per cent per year on growth of real gross domestic product),[2] per capita gains have often been trivial and even negative. In the matter of food and agricultural production, world output since 1958 has grown at about the same rate as world population, but only because the developed world has compensated for deficiencies in per

[2] United Nations, *Statistical Yearbook, 1965*. Tables 183, 184.

capita output in the developing countries.[3] Although primarily agricultural, the developing countries, with over two-thirds of the world's people, account for less than 45 per cent of the world's agricultural output.[4]

## Population Policies

Confronted with these realities and the failure of their economic development plans to materialize in per capita terms, responsible leaders in developing countries are increasingly concerned with the handicaps of rapid population growth to social and economic progress. Their growing realization that people want and presumably will use available contraceptive information and services has precipitated and reinforced a novel view: that governments can and should do something about high rates of population growth.

The pressures for the adoption of policy are more than a quinquennial affair related to drawing up five-year economic development plans. They are experienced daily in many forms: shrinking plots of land as numerous children inherit their parents' holdings, as in India; in the formidable task of providing schooling for a child population that exceeds 40 per cent of the total population; in crowded urban slums, as rural people migrate to cities to seek escape from the poverty of the countryside; in large numbers of unemployed and many more underemployed; and in growing resort to induced abortion, as in Latin America, where one-fourth of the beds of the major maternity hospitals are occupied by women with complications arising out of illegal abortions.

In response to these and similar forces, population policy has become an accepted part of development programs. By now more than half the people in the developing world live under governments that favor family planning.[5]

### Asia

A review of government family planning programs appropriately begins with Asia. In numbers it is the principal home of mankind; it has the most visible population problems; the four largest countries in the developing world are on that continent; and it is the region where national family planning programs under governmental auspices began.

### India, Nepal, and Pakistan

The first country to adopt a national policy to control population growth was India. The beginnings, in the mid-1950's, were modest. Major bottlenecks were lack of an administrative structure to reach India's enormous rural population, and acute shortages of medical personnel, especially of women doctors. Except for financial subsidies, authority rests with the individual states. Organization in the Ministry of Health has moved slowly, and the government has been slow to adopt the newer methods of contraception. Nevertheless, the program has gained momentum as indicated by the data on expenditures in Table 1.

TABLE 1—India's Family Planning Expenditures, 1951–1971

| Five Year Plan | Expenditures (Millions of Rupees) |
|---|---|
| First (1951–1956) | 1.5 |
| Second (1956–1961) | 21.6 |
| Third (1961–1966) | 261.0 |
| Fourth (1966–1971)—Allocation | 950.0 |

Annual expenditures have risen from 13.8 million rupees in 1961–1962 to 60.5

[3] *Ibid.*, Table 6.
[4] *Ibid.*, Table 4.

[5] For official statements of governmental policy on population, see The Population Council, *Studies in Family Planning*, No. 16 (New York: Population Council, in press).

in 1964–1965 and to an estimated 120 in 1965–66.[6] The last two represent per capita expenditures of about two and four cents. The Fourth Plan allocation implies an annual expenditure of $25.4 million or about five cents per person. Food shortages have made India's efforts more urgent. Symbolic of this is the change in name from Ministry of Health to Ministry of Health and Family Planning.

The Indian program has relied chiefly on clinics, which numbered 15,808 in July 1965. Although rhythm and conventional mechanical and chemical methods were first offered, IUD's were introduced in 1965, with one million inserted by mid-1966. Since 1963 over 100,000 male and female sterilizations have been performed per year in "sterilization camps" temporarily set up for this purpose. The cumulative total of sterilizations is soon expected to exceed one million. Oral contraceptives have not yet been approved for general use in India.

Impressive as these recent achievements are, they have not had any measurable influence on the Indian birth rate, except perhaps in the largest Indian cities, where family planning seems to be spreading in the population (but probably as much through private as through government services). The object of the program is to reduce the annual birth rate from over 40 to 25 per thousand population "as soon as possible." Targets rise annually to 1971 when it is hoped to have 19.7 million IUD users, 4.5 million sterilizations, and 4.7 million condom users.[7] Success in this magnitude is indeed necessary for a major impact on the Indian birth rate. India is a country of almost 500 million

people, with some 100 million women in the reproductive ages and some 20 million births annually.

Interested in these developments in India, **Nepal** incorporated a family planning program in its Third Plan, 1965–1970, but it has yet to be implemented.

**Pakistan** formulated a population control program in the late 1950's which was allocated 30.5 million rupees in the Second Five Year Plan (1960–1965). The objective is to supply family planning services through the existing health services in hospitals, dispensaries and rural clinics for voluntary participation of couples in limiting family size and spacing of children.

These efforts encountered many of the problems noted in India. In the first four years only 9.4 million rupees[8] of the budgeted expenditures of 24.7 million were actually used.[9] The problems related more to administration and organization than lack of funds. The plan for reaching 1.2 million women as contraceptive users and the targets for distribution of contraceptives, specifically condoms and foam tablets, were met only at the level of 17 per cent and 15 per cent, respectively.[10]

In July 1965 the Family Planning Directorate was upgraded to one of the most ambitious in the world today. Its five-year budget of 300 million rupees represents an average annual budget of about 12 cents per person. A major innovation is to be the insertion of IUD's by midwives, under medical supervision. These midwives will receive incentive payments for referrals and insertions. By 1970 no less than 50,000 village midwives are to be recruited and given a five-week training course.[11]

[6] B. L. Raina, "India," in Bernard Berelson *et al.* (eds.), *Family Planning and Population Programs: A Review of World Developments* (Chicago: University of Chicago Press, 1966).
[7] *Ibid.*, p. 119.

[8] One Pakistan rupee equals 21 cents.
[9] E. Adil, "Pakistan," in Berelson *et al., op. cit.*, p. 127.
[10] *Ibid.*, p. 128.
[11] Government of Pakistan, *Family Planning Scheme for Pakistan during the Third Five Year Plan Period, 1965–1970*, pp. 3, 10.

## Korea and Taiwan

More immediate success has been achieved in two smaller Asian countries, South Korea and Taiwan. South Korea's Supreme Council for National Reconstruction adopted a national family planning policy in 1961 as an integral part of the development plan. The targets were more specific than in most countries as regards training, use of contraceptives and effects on the rate of growth. By April 1965 some 2,200 full-time field workers had been recruited and trained, one for each 2,500 women in the childbearing ages.[12] Main reliance of the program is now on the IUD. Insertions were 112,000 in 1964, and 233,000 in 1965,[13] against targets of 100,000 and 200,000, respectively. The latter is estimated to be about 15 per cent of the target women, that is, those exposed to the risk of unwanted pregnancy. IUD's and conventional contraceptives are being manufactured in Korea.

The official objective is to reduce the rate of population growth from a current estimate of 2.9 per cent per year to 1.8 per cent in 1971. The Economic Planning Board estimates that by 1980 full implementation of the family planning program will bring down the rate of growth to 1.16 per cent compared to 3.15 without a reduction in the birth rates. The difference in growth rates will mean a per capita income 36 per cent higher in 1980 that would be the case in the absence of a fertility decline.

These ambitious objectives would sound unrealistic were it not for the fact that the government program is clearly "swimming with the tide" of social change. Attitude surveys show an overwhelming approval of family planning in the Korean population and a rapid increase in contraception and abortion,[14] the latter perhaps because of Japanese influence. Though not yet approved by the government, a bill is currently before the Korean Assembly to legalize induced abortion.

In the absence of accurate vital statistics, it is difficult to measure year-to-year changes in the birth rate. An indirect measure, ratios of children under five to women in the childbearing ages, does strongly suggest a recent rapid decline in the birth rate, especially in 1965. Although this decline was already in process, the greater rate of decline in 1965 might reflect the effects of the government program in 1964, when it first reached mass proportions.

Taiwan does not have an official population policy, but family planning services are now provided throughout the island by the Provincial Department of Health. Impetus for the island-wide program stemmed from the mass action research program in the city of Taichung [15] (in which it was first established that the IUD would be widely accepted in a mass campaign) and from experimental projects begun in 1959 under the euphemistically-called "Prepregnancy Health Program." This term paid tribute to the sensitivities of the United States Agency for International Development (AID), which was providing indirect assistance to the health services. The expanded action program for the island as a whole was initiated in 1964, and in 1965 the program effectively

---

[12] Government of Korea, *Korea, Summary of First Five-Year Economic Plan, 1962–1966.*

[13] Ministry of Health and Social Welfare, Government of Korea, *Monthly Report on IUD Insertions* (mimeographed).

[14] According to a survey made in 1964, one out of three pregnancies among married women in Seoul is terminated by induced abortion. See S. B. Hong, *Induced Abortion in Seoul, Korea* (Seoul: Dong-A Publishing Company, 1966), p. 78.

[15] This is fully described in Bernard Berelson and Ronald Freedman, "A Study in Fertility Control," *Scientific American,* 210 [5] (May 1964), pp. 3–11.

54     THE ANNALS OF THE AMERICAN ACADEMY

achieved the target of inserting 100,000 IUD's.[16]

The principal feature of the Taiwan plan is insertion of 600,000 IUD's within five years.[17] Were there no removals or expulsions this would mean a loop for one-third of the married women of childbearing age, including those marrying in the interim. Since a substantial percentage of the IUD's are not retained, the net effect will probably be less. Oral contraceptives are being introduced on an experimental basis to provide an alternative method for women who cannot or do not wish to use the IUD.

In contrast with most developing countries Taiwan has excellent vital statistics and other methods of evaluating program success. It can be seen on the basis of the information in Table 2 that the birth rate in Taiwan has been falling precipitously.

TABLE 2—TAIWAN: CRUDE BIRTH RATE

| YEAR | RATE |
| --- | --- |
| 1959 | 41.2 |
| 1960 | 39.5 |
| 1961 | 38.3 |
| 1962 | 37.4 |
| 1963 | 36.3 |
| 1964 | 34.5 |
| 1965 | 32.7 |

Source: United Nations, Demographic Year-book, 1965, Table 12.

The government program could not have initiated this decline, but the especially large drop in 1964 and 1965 is to be noted. Rising age at marriage, an increase of about two months per year, is known to be a factor. In addition to its direct effects, the government program may operate indirectly to stimulate greater interest in family planning

[16] Government of Taiwan, Family Planning in Taiwan, Republic of China, 1965–1966 (1966), p. iii.

[17] Government of Taiwan, Taiwan, Ten Year Health Program, 1966–1975.

and in induced abortion. Since abortions are illegal, their number is not known. The real tests of the effectiveness of the government program still lie in the future.

*Southeast Asia*

In Hong Kong, Singapore, and Malaysia, family planning programs were initiated under private auspices and with government subsidies. The private Family Planning Associations in these areas have been among the most successful in the world. In Singapore the government took over the private family planning services in January 1966. These services may well have been a factor in the rapid decline of the birth rate in Singapore from 45.4 per 1000 in 1952 to 29.9 in 1965, although rising age at marriage and changes in age structure were important elements.

Malaysia incorporated a family planning policy in its First Malaysia Plan 1966–1970, adopted in 1965. Voluntary organizations, government departments, and mass communications are to be used for education in and promotion of family planning. The birth rate in Malaysia has been declining, especially among the population of Chinese ancestry. While the role of the private Family Planning Association may have been important in popularizing birth control, its direct services were numerically insufficient to have affected the birth rate.

In Ceylon, the government's national family planning program is being introduced by stages into different sections of the country, first in the Colombo area.[18] Ceylon is a kind of Ireland of Asia—its high age at marriage has led to a lower birth rate than in neighboring India. Swedish technical assistance supports the Ceylon program.

[18] Government of Ceylon, Provisional Scheme for a Nationwide Family Planning Programme in Ceylon, 1966–1976.

**Thailand** does not have a population policy, but pilot projects in family planning have been strikingly successful, and family planning is now being introduced as an integral part of health services in major hospitals and in the health units of the northeastern region.

### Mainland China

Government interest in family planning in **Mainland China** goes back to 1956 and 1957 when a birth control campaign was initiated by the government and services were provided in government health clinics. In 1958 a change of policy slowed the campaign to very low gear, but by 1962 renewed governmental interest became evident. In January of that year import regulations were revised to admit contraceptives duty-free. The government advocated later age at marriage. Japanese doctors visiting China in 1964 and 1965 reported that family planning was being advocated as part of maternal and child health programs and that all methods of contraception, including sterilization and abortion, were available. Oral contraceptives and IUD's manufactured in China were apparently becoming increasingly popular.

According to Premier Chou:

Our present target is to reduce population growth to below 2 per cent; for the future we aim at an even lower rate. . . . However, I do not believe it will be possible to equal the Japanese rate (of about one per cent) as early as 1970. . . . We do believe in planned parenthood, but it is not easy to introduce all at once in China. . . . The first thing is to encourage late marriages.[19]

Many of the 17 million Communist party members and 25 million Young Communists have received birth control instruction, and they, in turn, are expected to become models and teachers. One son and one daughter are now considered an ideal family size.[20]

Far too little is known about the Chinese program, but it may well be the most important national program in the world, if for no other reason than the tremendous numbers involved. The Chinese population may now be as high as 800 million, equal to about one-fourth of the human race.

### Middle East and Africa

Four countries in the Middle East and North Africa have adopted national family planning programs. In the **United Arab Republic (UAR)** the government's interest goes back to 1953, when a National Population Commission was established and a few clinics were opened. Government policy dates from the May 1962 draft of the National Charter, in which President Nasser declared:

Population increase constitutes the most dangerous obstacle that faces the Egyptian people in their drive towards raising the standard of production. . . . Attempts at family planning deserve the most sincere efforts supported by modern scientific methods.[21]

However, a substantial program was not initiated until February 1966, when the government launched a widespread campaign using oral contraceptives.

In **Tunisia** an experimental program to develop a practical family planning service with IUD's was started in 1964. The success of this experiment led to a national campaign with a goal of 120,000 IUD's.[22] An unusually interesting feature of the Tunisian program has been

[19] As reported by Edgar Snow in *The New York Times,* February 3, 1964.

[20] *The Sunday Times* (London), January 23, 1966.

[21] UAR, Information Department, *The Charter* (draft presented by President Nasser on May 21, 1962), p. 53.

[22] A. Daly, "Tunisia," in Berelson *et al., op. cit.,* p. 160.

the use of Destour party members as a major source of information and publicity. The program may have been set back by President Bourguiba's speech on Woman's Day, August 12, 1966, against celibacy and in favor of a young vigorous population.

In April 1965 Turkey repealed an old law against contraception and provided the legal framework and financial basis for a nationwide family planning program.[23] Full-time family planning personnel are to be trained and added to the Health Ministry, and supplies are to be offered free or at cost. Interesting features of the Turkish program are plans for an informational campaign on birth control in the armed forces (to provide a "ripple" effect when the conscripts return to civilian life) and incorporation of demographic and biological aspects of population into the school curriculum.

**Morocco** decided in 1966 to adopt a national family program to be introduced by stages through the public health clinics in the various parts of the country. A national sample survey of attitudes on family planning has been started by the government.

Although **Algeria** has no population policy or program, Dr. Ahmed Taleb, Minister of National Education, stated on the opening of the school year (fall 1966):

. . . we have to fight an extremely high birth rate. If nothing is done to stop this growth rate through birth control, the problem of educating all the Algerian children will remain unsolved.[24]

### Tropical Africa

Although no formal population policies have yet been adopted by countries in Africa south of the Sahara, consider-

able interest was expressed in population matters at the First African Population Conference held at the University of Ibadan, Nigeria, in January 1966.[25]

**Kenya**'s 1966–1970 Development Plan includes "measures to promote family planning education" through the establishment of a Family Planning Council and by providing services in government hospitals and health centers. In **Mauritius** the 1966 budget provides funds for family planning services.

### Latin America

Latin America has the most rapid rate of population growth of any major region of the world. This has not generally been a matter of much public concern, partly because of the traditional position of the Catholic Church and partly because Latin-American countries have a historical image of themselves as underpopulated.

Two forces are rapidly changing this disinterest. One is the growing recognition that high growth rates are obstacles to achieving planning goals. In many countries population is growing faster than food supply; the difficulties in providing public education, health services, and other facilities are formidable; and the intrusive problem of unemployment and underemployment has serious political as well as economic implications as people flock into the cities. A second element is the growing concern, especially in the medical profession, over the problem of induced abortion. The possibility of family planning appears to be gaining favorable attention both among responsible leaders, and among large segments of the population, according to sample attitude surveys in eight Latin-American capitals (coordinated by the United Nations Latin-

[23] T. Metiner, "Turkey," in Berelson *et al.,* *op. cit.,* p. 136.

[24] Translation from *La Presse,* Tunis, Tunisia, 30 September 1966.

[25] Proceedings to be published in 1967. Also see J. C. Caldwell, "Africa," in Berelson *et al., op. cit.*

American Demographic Center in Santiago, Chile).[26]

Latin-American countries may be less likely to adopt formal population policies than other parts of the underdeveloped world owing to the influence of the Church. However, natality regulation has been approved for the public health service in Chile, and several major birth control projects using public health facilities exist in Santiago. In Honduras the Minister of Health recently announced that family planning is to be an integral part of preventive medical services. In Jamaica a Family Planning Unit has been established within the Ministry of Health with administrative costs provided by AID. In Colombia the private Association of Medical Faculties has established a Population Division, which has organized a nationwide program for training health officers in family planning. In October 1966 AID authorized the use of counterpart funds to finance this program. In Peru a government-sponsored population studies center was established to "formulate programs of action with which to face the problems of population and socioeconomic development." Barbados has had an official policy favoring family planning since 1954, expressed chiefly by subsidy of the private Family Planning Association.

EVALUATION OF FAMILY PLANNING
PROGRAMS

Most government family planning programs are very new, and it would be unfair to expect major results so soon. Their very existence in so short a time is in itself remarkable. Operating through the existing health network, generally under the Health Ministry, most programs are still largely clinic-oriented despite the common experience that other means may be more effective. Problems of organization; administration; production, distribution and supply of contraceptives; and shortage of skilled personnel are more serious than the question of finance.

Partly because of their newness, the programs have tended to place great emphasis on the magic of the new contraceptive methods. They all have shied away from abortion, which has been a major factor in reducing birth rates in large populations as in Japan, the Soviet Union, and eastern Europe. The present female-oriented programs minimize the role of male participation, which, if not for presently recommended methods, is nevertheless important for information and motivation. Few of the programs have thus far made use of mass communication, and Ministries of Information and Education have yet to be effectively involved.

National programs may be evaluated at different levels: in-service statistics, as, for example, success in reaching targets in number of clinics, patients, contraceptive users, and the like; more broadly in their effects on knowledge, attitudes, and practices of the general population (measured by the so-called KAP students); and, for the present purpose, the effects on the birth rate, the ultimate test of a population control program.

Since very few of the countries of the underdeveloped world have sufficiently accurate vital statistics to measure year-to-year changes in the birth rate, other means must be sought. Censuses can be used to measure natality changes, but these occur too infrequently for the purpose at hand. In the absence of official data, sample registration and periodic sample population surveys are conducted to provide data for measuring year-to-year changes. These have come

[26] C. A. Miro and F. Rath, "Preliminary Findings of Comparative Fertility Surveys in Three Latin-American Cities," *Milbank Memorial Fund Quarterly*, Vol. XLIII, No. 4 (October 1965), Part 2, pp. 36–68.

to be known as Population Growth Estimate (PGE) Studies. Experimental projects of this type are going forward in Pakistan, Turkey, and Thailand.

As programs accelerate, the deficiency in accurate vital data will become increasingly important. In-service data can give good measures of the scope of the programs and their success in achieving targets. However, the number of contraceptive "users," as measured by accepters, can be very deceptive, since failure of the method and, even more important, failure of couples to use methods as required, can significantly reduce "use-effectiveness." This is true of IUD's as well as other effective methods such as oral contraceptives and condoms. Many women do not retain the IUD's or have them removed. In the national program in Taiwan 62 per cent of the women still had the IUD in place at the end of twelve months, 52 per cent at the end of eighteen months. Experience elsewhere has been better, up to 80 per cent retention at the end of a year. In all methods there is substantial shrinkage between ideal use and actual effectiveness in preventing pregnancy.

It should also be noted that family planning programs are most likely to succeed rapidly in countries of greatest socioeconomic advance, where realization of the smaller family ideal has already made some progress. The success of a program in countries like Korea and Taiwan chiefly reflects rapid progress in other ways. In such countries mass acceptance of government services is not an equivalent gain in family planning practice, since many of the couples concerned were already practicing family planning (perhaps by less effective methods or abortion) or would have done so regardless of a government program. In these countries the government program may accelerate a trend already in existence. Indeed, in some countries,

the influence of the program on couples to use private sources of supply, methods not requiring supplies, and abortion may well surpass the effect of the direct services offered. Yet this indirect effect is least susceptible to measurement.

## SUMMARY AND CONCLUSIONS

By now at least twenty-three nations in the underdeveloped world have explicit official population policies. One is struck by the recency and rapidity with which these programs have come into being. In some instances there is policy, but little if any program; in others, program, but no policy. In most cases neither policy nor program has yet had much opportunity to produce a measurable effect on the national birth rate. Even in those countries with most marked successes, such as Korea and Taiwan, the reduction of the birth rate so far is surely much more the result of general social change than of public policy.

The newness and frailties of family planning programs reflect the tentative approach of governments to their population problems. Thus far, they have involved very small material investments in relation both to economic development plans and to potential economic gains. Some have argued that the "normal" tendency of the birth rate to decline in the course of socioeconomic development will bring about a resolution of present population problems. Government family planning programs now seem to be part of this "normal" development.

With knowledge rapidly becoming available for individual couples to exercise voluntary control over births, fortified by governmental approval and assistance in supplies and medical services, it is quite possible that family planning may progress more rapidly than some other forms of socioeconomic advance. Several non-European areas of different cultures and relatively low per capita incomes (notably Taiwan, Korea, Singapore, and Hong Kong; Soviet Asia and the western provinces of Turkey; and Argentina and Uruguay) already give clear evidence of reductions in birth rates. Given the favorable attitudes found in the KAP surveys, family planning may be easier to implement than major advances in education or the economy, which require large structural and institutional changes in the society as a whole.

The most rapid progress will come in East Asia where the normal demographic transition is already well advanced. While the evidence is scant, family planning may also move ahead rapidly in Mainland China despite its low level of socioeconomic development. The Communist regime has done much to disrupt the ancient pattern of Chinese family life, which, in any case, based on the experience of Chinese outside Mainland China, is less a barrier to the small family norm than had been supposed.

In India, many cultural practices restrain freedom of sexual expression. Widespread acceptance of sterilization (vasectomy), while not yet sufficient to affect the birth rate, is, nevertheless, surprising evidence of a greater concern for family size among men than might have been supposed. Although ten years old, the Indian family planning program has reached significant proportions only in the last year or so. If present trends continue, both in the national program and in independent individual initiative in contraceptive practice, one may expect a sufficient escalation of family planning to produce a decline in the birth rate. That it will achieve the goal of a birth rate of only 25 per 1,000 population by 1971 seems doubtful, but I venture to predict a perceptible drop from the present level of over 40. At the same time, however, the death rate will probably have dropped below 15 so that to reach the target growth rate of one per cent will require still further reductions in the birth rate.

In Moslem society, family planning is making headway among the upper classes and among populations closest to European influence, as in Albania, Turkey, and the Central Asia Republics of the Soviet Union. Several Moslem countries have population policies (Turkey, Tunisia, the United Arab Republic, Morocco), but other things being equal, family planning is likely to gain slower popular acceptance among Moslems than among most other cultural groups.[27]

As measured by most indices of socioeconomic advance, tropical Africa would not seem ready for widespread family planning practice. Nevertheless, Africans gladly seize on cultural innovation, and a surprising interest has already been shown. One can scarcely expect any measurable effect on the birth rate in a tropical African country in ten years; but in twenty years I would expect this to have occurred.

In Latin America, urban-rural fertility differentials are not so large as in other parts of the world, partly because of the heavy immigration into the urban shanty towns of rural people who have yet to become integrated into urban life. Nevertheless, studies reveal widespread interest in family planning (at least in the large capital cities), and abortion has become very common. A shift in the position of the Catholic Church toward permissive policies, if not outright acceptance of family planning, will accelerate what is already a major social trend.

In several, perhaps most, Latin-American countries I would anticipate a measurable reduction in their very high birth rates within the next ten years.

[27] D. Kirk, "Factors affecting Moslem Natality," in Berelson, et al., op. cit.

Within twenty years, growth rates should be markedly reduced despite a continuing decline in mortality. Present fertility plus the inertia of age structure, however, will probably double the population of Latin America by the end of the century.

The picture that emerges is a range in birth rates of 20 to 25 per 1,000 population within a decade in the most progressive parts of East and Southeast Asia, and possibly within two decades in India and Mainland China if those countries avoid war, disaster, and social chaos. By that time, one can expect important reductions in the birth rate in all of the larger developing countries in Asia, in the Middle East and North Africa, and in Latin America. Taking the underdeveloped world as a whole, within two decades I expect to see the solution well in sight, though not yet fully achieved.

These conclusions imply great efforts and accomplishments in the face of cultural resistance and inertia. The achievements will not be easily won, nor will they forestall the massive population growth that, in the absence of catastrophe, will be with us at least through the 1970's. The critical problem of world population growth will remain, though in the longer run there is now real hope for its solution.

# Abortion—or Compulsory Pregnancy?

GARRETT HARDIN*

*The problem of abortion is usually seen as one of justifying a particular surgical operation on the assumption that great social loss is incurred by it. This approach leads to intractable administrative problems: rape is in principle impossible to prove, the paternity of a child is always in doubt, the probability of defective embryos is generally low, and the socioeconomic predicament of the supplicant has little power to move the men who sit in judgment. These difficulties vanish when one substitutes for the problem of permissive abortion the inverse problem of compulsory pregnancy. The latter is a special case of compulsory servitude, which the Western world has agreed, in principle, has no valid justification. Unfortunately, state legislatures are now in a process of setting up systems for the management of compulsory pregnancy. The experience of Scandinavia indicates that women do not accept bureaucratic management of their unwanted pregnancies; therefore we can confidently predict that the reform bills now going through our legislatures will have little effect on the practice of illegal abortion. Only the abolition of compulsory pregnancy will solve the erroneously conceived "abortion problem."*

THE year 1967 produced the first fissures in the dam that had prevented all change in the abortion-prohibition laws of the United States for three-quarters of a century. Two states adopted laws that allowed abortion in the "hardship cases" of rape, incest, and probability of a deformed child. A third approved the first two "indications," but not the last. All three took some note of the mental health of the pregnant woman, in varying language; how this language will be translated into practice remains to be seen. In almost two dozen other states, attempts to modify the laws were made but foundered at various stages in the legislative process. It is quite evident that the issue will continue to be a live one for many years to come.

The legislative turmoil was preceded and accompanied by a fast-growing popular literature. The word "abortion" has ceased to be a dirty word—which is a cultural advance. However, the *word* was so long under taboo that the ability to think about the *fact* seems to have suffered a sort of logical atrophy from disuse. Popular articles, regardless of their conclusions, tend to be over-emotional and to take a moralistic rather than an operational view of the matter. Nits are picked, hairs split. It is quite clear that many of the authors are not at all clear what question they are attacking.

It is axiomatic in science that progress hinges on asking the right question. Surprisingly, once the right question is asked the answer seems almost to tumble forth. That is a retrospective view; in prospect, it takes genuine (and mysterious) insight to see correctly into the brambles created by previous, ill-chosen verbalizations.

* *Garrett Hardin, Ph.D., is Professor of Biology, University of California, Santa Barbara.*

The abortion problem is, I think, a particularly neat example of a problem in which most of the difficulties are actually created by asking the wrong question. I submit further that once the right question is asked the whole untidy mess miraculously dissolves, leaving in its place a very simple public policy recommendation.

## RAPE AS A JUSTIFICATION

The wrong question, the one almost invariably asked, is this: "How can we justify an abortion?" This assumes that there are weighty public reasons for encouraging pregnancies, or that abortions, per se, somehow threaten public peace. A direct examination of the legitimacy of these assumptions will be made later. For the present, let us pursue the question as asked and see what a morass it leads to.

Almost all the present legislative attempts take as their model a bill proposed by the American Law Institute which emphasizes three justifications for legal abortion: rape, incest, and the probability of a defective child. Whatever else may be said about this bill, it is clear that it affects only the periphery of the social problem. The Arden House Conference Committee[1] estimated the number of illegal abortions in the United States to be between 200,000 and 1,200,000 per year. A California legislator, Anthony C. Beilenson,[2] has estimated that the American Law Institute bill (which he favors) would legalize not more than four percent of the presently illegal abortions. Obviously, the "problem" of illegal abortion will be scarcely affected by the passage of the laws so far proposed in the United States.

[1] Mary Steichen Calderone (ed.), *Abortion in the United States*, New York: Hoeber-Harper, 1958, p. 178.

[2] Anthony C. Beilenson, "Abortion and Common Sense," *Per/Se*, 1 (1966), p. 24.

Reprinted by permission of the author and the publisher from *Journal of Marriage and the Family* 30:246–251, May 1968.

I have calculated[3] that the number of rape-induced pregnancies in the United States is about 800 per year. The number is not large, but for the woman raped the total number is irrelevant. What matters to her is that she be relieved of her unwanted burden. But a law which puts the burden of proof on her compels her to risk a second harrowing experience. How can she *prove* to the district attorney that she was raped? He could really know whether or not she gave consent only if he could get inside her mind; this he cannot do. Here is the philosopher's "egocentric predicament" that none of us can escape. In an effort to help the district attorney sustain the illusion that he can escape this predicament, a talented woman may put on a dramatic performance, with copious tears and other signs of anguish. But what if the raped woman is not an actress? What if her temperament is stoic? In its operation, the law will act against the interests of calm, undramatic women. Is that what we want? It is safe to say also that district attorneys will hear less favorably the pleas of poor women, the general assumption of middle-class agents being that the poor are less responsible in sex anyway.[4] Is it to the interest of society that the poor bear more children, whether rape-engendered or not?

A wryly amusing difficulty has been raised with respect to rape. Suppose the woman is married and having regular intercourse with her husband. Suppose that following a rape by an unknown intruder she finds herself pregnant. Is she legally entitled to an abortion? How does she know whose child she is carrying anyway? If it is her husband's child, abortion is illegal. If she carries it to term, and if blood tests then exclude the husband as the father, as they would in a fraction of the cases, is the woman then entitled to a *delayed* abortion? But this is ridiculous: this is infanticide, which no one is proposing. Such is the bramble bush into which we are led by a *reluctant* consent for abortion in cases of rape.

### How Probable Must Deformity Be?

The majority of the public support abortion in cases of a suspected deformity of the child[5] just as they do in cases of rape. Again, however, if the burden of proof rests on the one who requests the operation, we encounter difficulties in administration. Between 80,000 and 160,000 defective children are born every year in the United States. The number stated depends on two important issues: (a) how severe a defect must be before it is counted as such and (b) whether or not one counts as birth defects those defects that are not *detected* until later. (Deafness and various other defects produced by fetal rubella may not be detected until a year or so after birth.) However many defective infants there may be, what is the prospect of detecting them before birth?

The sad answer is: the prospects are poor. A small percentage can be picked up by microscopic examination of tissues of the fetus. But "amniocentesis"—the form of biopsy required to procure such tissues—is itself somewhat dangerous to both mother and fetus; most abnormalities will not be detectable by a microscopic examination of the fetal cells; and 96 to 98 percent of all fetuses are normal anyway. All these considerations are a contra-indication of routine amniocentesis.

When experience indicates that the probability of a deformed fetus is above the "background level" of 2 to 4 percent, is abortion justified? At what level? 10 percent? 50? 80? Or only at 100 percent? Suppose a particular medical history indicates a probability of 20 percent that the baby will be defective. If we routinely abort such cases, it is undeniable that four normal fetuses will be destroyed for every one abnormal. Those who assume that a fetus is an object of high value are appalled at this "wastage." Not uncommonly they ask, "Why not wait until the baby is born and then suffocate those that are deformed?" Such a question is unquestionably rhetoric and sardonic; if serious, it implies that infanticide has no more emotional meaning to a woman than abortion, an assumption that is surely contrary to fact.

### Should the Father Have Rights?

Men who are willing to see abortion-prohibition laws relaxed somewhat, but not completely, frequently raise a question about the "rights" of the father. Should we allow a woman to make a unilateral decision for an abortion? Should not her husband have a say in the matter? (After all, he contributed just as many chromosomes to the fetus as she.)

I do not know what weight to give this objection. I have encountered it repeatedly in the discussion section following a public meeting. It is clear that some men are disturbed at finding themselves powerless in such a situation and want the law to give them some power of decision.

Yet powerless men are—and it is nature that

---

[3] Garrett Hardin, "Semantic Aspects of Abortion," *ETC.*, 24 (1967), p. 263.

[4] Lee Rainwater, *And the Poor Get Children*, Chicago: Quadrangle Books, 1960, p. ix and chap. 1.

[5] Alice S. Rossi, "Abortion Laws and Their Victims," *Trans-action*, 3 (September-October, 1966), p. 7.

has made them so. If we give the father a right of veto in abortion decisions, the wife has a very simple reply to her husband: "I'm sorry, dear, I wasn't going to tell you this, but you've forced my hand. This is not your child." With such a statement she could always deny her husband's right to decide.

Why husbands should demand power in such matters is a fit subject for depth analysis. In the absence of such, perhaps the best thing we can say to men who are "hung up" on this issue is this: "Do you really want to live for another eight months with a woman whom you are compelling to be pregnant against her will?"

Or, in terms of public policy, do we want to pass laws which give men the right to compel their wives to be pregnant? Psychologically, such compulsion is akin to rape. Is it in the public interest to encourage rape?

### "Socio-Economic"—an Anemic Phrase

The question "How can we justify an abortion?" proves least efficient in solving the real problems of this world when we try to evaluate what are usually called "socio-economic indications." The hardship cases—rape, incest, probability of a deformed child—have been amply publicized, and as a result the majority of the public accepts them as valid indicators; but hardship cases constitute only a few percent of the need. By contrast, if a woman has more children than she feels she can handle, or if her children are coming too close together, there is little public sympathy for her plight. A poll[5] conducted by the National Opinion Research Center in December, 1965, showed that only 15 percent of the respondents replied "Yes" to this question: "Please tell me whether or not you think it should be possible for a pregnant woman to obtain a legal abortion if she is married and does not want any more children." Yet this indication, which received the lowest rate of approval, accounts for the vast majority of instances in which women want—and illegally get—relief from unwanted pregnancy.

There is a marked discrepancy between the magnitude of the need and the degree of public sympathy. Part of the reason for this discrepancy is attributable to the emotional impact of the words used to describe the need. "Rape," "incest," "deformed child"—these words are rich in emotional connotations. "Socio-economic indications" is a pale bit of jargon, suggesting at best that the abortion is wanted because the woman lives by culpably materialistic standards. "Socio-economic indications" tugs at no one's heartstrings; the hyphenated abomination hides the human reality to which it obliquely refers.

To show the sort of human problem to which this label may be attached, let me quote a letter I received from one woman. (The story is unique, but it is one of a large class of similar true stories.)

I had an illegal abortion 2½ years ago. I left my church because of the guilt I felt. I had six children when my husband left me to live with another woman. We weren't divorced and I went to work to help support them. When he would come to visit the children he would sometimes stay after they were asleep. I became pregnant. When I told my husband, and asked him to please come back, he informed me that the woman he was living with was five months pregnant and ill, and that he couldn't leave her—not at that time anyway.

I got the name of a doctor in San Francisco from a Dr. friend who was visiting here from there. This Dr. (Ob. and Gyn.) had a good legitimate practice in the main part of the city and was a kindly, compassionate man who believes as you do, that it is better for everyone not to bring an unwanted child into the world.

It was over before I knew it. I thought I was just having an examination at the time. He even tried to make me not feel guilty by telling me that the long automobile trip had already started a spontaneous abortion. He charged me $25. That was on Fri. and on Mon. I was back at work. I never suffered any ill from it.

The other woman's child died shortly after birth and six months later my husband asked if he could come back. We don't have a perfect marriage but my children have a father. My being able to work has helped us out of a deep financial debt. I shall always remember the sympathy I received from that Dr. and wish there were more like him with the courage to do what they believe is right.

Her operation was illegal, and would be illegal under most of the "reform" legislation now being proposed, if interpreted strictly. Fortunately some physicians are willing to indulge in more liberal interpretations, but they make these interpretations not on medical grounds, in the strict sense, but on social and economic grounds. Understandably, many physicians are unwilling to venture so far from the secure base of pure physical medicine. As one Catholic physician put it:

Can the patient afford to have another child? Will the older children have sufficient educational opportunities if their parents have another child? Aren't two, three or four children enough? I am afraid such statements are frequently made in the discussion of a proposed therapeutic abortion. [But] we should be doctors of medicine, not socio-economic prophets.[6]

[6] Calderone (ed.), *op. cit.*, p. 103.

To this a non-Catholic physician added: "I sometimes wish I were an obstetrician in a Catholic hospital so that I would not have to make any of these decisions. The only position to take in which I would have no misgivings is to do no interruptions at all."[7]

## WHO WANTS COMPULSORY PREGNANCY?

The question "How can we justify an abortion?" plainly leads to great difficulties. It is operationally unmanageable: it leads to inconsistencies in practice and inequities by any moral standard. All these can be completely avoided if we ask the right question, namely: *"How can we justify compulsory pregnancy?"*

By casting the problem in this form, we call attention to its relationship to the slavery issue. Somewhat more than a century ago men in the Western world asked the question: "How can we justify compulsory servitude?" and came up with the answer: *"By no means whatever."* Is the answer any different to the related question: "How can we justify compulsory pregnancy?" Certainly pregnancy is a form of servitude; if continued to term it results in parenthood, which is also a kind of servitude, to be continued for the best years of a woman's life. It is difficult to see how it can be argued that this kind of servitude will be more productive of social good if it is compulsory rather than voluntary. A study[8] made of Swedish children born when their mothers were refused the abortions they had requested showed that unwanted children, as compared with their controls, as they grew up were more often picked up for drunkenness, or antisocial or criminal behavior; they received less education; they received more psychiatric care; and they were more often exempted from military service by reason of defect. Moreover, the females in the group married earlier and had children earlier, thus no doubt tending to create a vicious circle of poorly tended children who in their turn would produce more poorly tended children. How then does society gain by increasing the number of unwanted children? No one has volunteered an answer to this question.

Of course if there were a shortage of children, then society might say that it needs all the children it can get—unwanted or not. But I am unaware of any recent rumors of a shortage of children.

## ALTERNATIVES: TRUE AND FALSE

The end result of an abortion—the elimination of an unwanted fetus—is surely good. But is the act itself somehow damaging? For several generations it was widely believed that abortion was intrinsically dangerous, either physically or psychologically. It is now very clear that the widespread belief is quite unjustified. The evidence for this statement is found in a bulky literature which has been summarized in Lawrence Lader's *Abortion*[9] and the collection of essays brought together by Alan Guttmacher.[10]

In tackling questions of this sort, it is imperative that we identify correctly the alternatives facing us. (All moral and practical problems involve a comparison of alternative actions.) Many of the arguments of the prohibitionists implicitly assume that the alternatives facing the woman are these:

*abortion————no abortion*

This is false. A person can never do nothing. The pregnant woman is going to do something, whether she wishes to or not. (She cannot roll time backward and live her life over.)

People often ask: "Isn't contraception better than abortion?" Implied by this question are these alternatives:

*abortion————contraception*

But these are not the alternatives that face the woman who asks to be aborted. She *is* pregnant. She cannot roll time backward and use contraception more successfully than she did before. Contraceptives are never foolproof anyway. It is commonly accepted that the failure rate of our best contraceptive, the "pill," is around one percent, i.e., one failure per hundred woman-years of use. I have earlier shown[11] that this failure rate produces about a quarter of a million unwanted pregnancies a year in the United States. Abortion is not so much an alternative to contraception as it is a subsidiary method of birth control, to be used when the primary method fails—as it often does.

The woman *is* pregnant: this is the base level at which the moral decision begins. If she is pregnant against her will, does it matter to society whether or not she was careless or unskillful in her use of contraception? In any case, she is threatening society with an unwanted child, for which society will pay dearly. The real alternatives facing the woman (and society) are clearly these:

[7] *Ibid.*, p. 123.
[8] Hans Forssman and Inga Thuwe, "One Hundred and Twenty Children Born after Application for Therapeutic Abortion Refused," *Acta Psychiatrica Scandinavica*, 42 (1966), p. 71.

[9] Lawrence Lader, *Abortion*, Indianapolis: Bobbs-Merrill, 1966.
[10] Alan F. Guttmacher (ed.), *The Case for Legalized Abortion*, Berkeley, California: Diablo Press, 1967.
[11] Garrett Hardin, "A Scientist's Case for Abortion," *Redbook* (May 1967), p. 62.

*abortion————compulsory pregnancy*
When we recognize that these are the real, operational alternatives, the false problems created by pseudo-alternatives vanish.

### Is Potential Value Valuable?

Only one weighty objection to abortion remains to be discussed, and this is the question of "loss." When a fetus is destroyed, has something valuable been destroyed? The fetus has the potentiality of becoming a human being. A human being is valuable. Therefore is not the fetus of equal value? This question must be answered.

It can be answered, but not briefly. What does the embryo receive from its parents that might be of value? There are only three possibilities: substance, energy, and information. As for the substance in the fertilized egg, it is not remarkable: merely the sort of thing one might find in any piece of meat, human or animal, and there is very little of it—only one and a half micrograms, which is about a half of a billionth of an ounce. The energy content of this tiny amount of material is likewise negligible. As the zygote develops into an embryo, both its substance and its energy content increase (at the expense of the mother); but this is not a very important matter—even an adult, viewed from this standpoint, is only a hundred and fifty pounds of meat!

Clearly, the humanly significant thing that is contributed to the zygote by the parents is the information that "tells" the fertilized egg how to develop into a human being. This information is in the form of a chemical tape called "DNA," a double set of two chemical supermolecules each of which has about three billion "spots" that can be coded with any one of four different possibilities, symbolized by *A, T, G,* and C. (For comparison, the Morse code offers three possibilities in coding: dot, dash, and space.) It is the particular sequence of these four chemical possibilities in the DNA that directs the zygote in its development into a human being. The DNA constitutes the information needed to produce a valuable human being. The question is: is this information precious? I have argued elsewhere[12] that it is not:

Consider the case of a man who is about to begin to build a $50,000 house. As he stands on the site looking at the blueprints a practical joker comes along and sets fire to the blueprints. The question is: can the owner go to the law and collect $50,000 for his

[12] Garrett Hardin, "Blueprints, DNA, and Abortion: A Scientific and Ethical Analysis," *Medical Opinion and Review,* 3:2 (1967), p. 74.

lost blueprints? The answer is obvious: since another set of blueprints can be produced for the cost of only a few dollars, that is all they are worth. (A court might award a bit more for the loss of the owner's time, but that is a minor matter.) The moral: *a non-unique copy of information that specifies a valuable structure is itself almost valueless.*

This principle is precisely applicable to the moral problem of abortion. The zygote, which contains the complete specification of a valuable human being, is not a human being, and is almost valueless. . . . The early stages of an individual fetus have had very little human effort invested in them; they are of very little worth. The loss occasioned by an abortion is independent of whether the abortion is spontaneous or induced. (Just as the loss incurred by the burning of a set of blueprints is independent of whether the causal agent was lightning or an arsonist.)

A set of blueprints is not a house; the DNA of a zygote is not a human being. The analogy is singularly exact, though there are two respects in which it is deficient. These respects are interesting rather than important. First, we have the remarkable fact that the blueprints of the zygote are constantly replicated and incorporated in every cell of the human body. This is interesting, but it has no moral significance. There is no moral obligation to conserve DNA—if there were, no man would be allowed to brush his teeth and gums, for in this brutal operation hundreds of sets of DNA are destroyed daily.

The other anomaly of the human information problem is connected with the fact that the information that is destroyed in an aborted embryo *is* unique (unlike the house blueprints). But it is unique in a way that is without moral significance. A favorite argument of abortion-prohibitionists is this: "What if Beethoven's mother had had an abortion?" The question moves us; but when we think it over we realize we can just as relevantly ask: "What if Hitler's mother had had an abortion?" Each conceptus is unique, but not in any way that has a moral consequence. The *expected* potential value of each aborted child is exactly that of the average child born. It is meaningless to say that humanity loses when a *particular* child is not born, or is not conceived. A human female, at birth, has about 30,000 eggs in her ovaries. If she bears only 3 children in her lifetime, is there any meaningful sense in which we can say that mankind has suffered a loss in those other 29,997 fruitless eggs? (Yet one of them might have been a super-Beethoven!)

People who worry about the moral danger of abortion do so because they think of the fetus as a human being, hence equate feticide with murder. Whether the fetus is or is not a human being is a matter of definition, not fact; and we can define any way we wish. In terms of the human problem involved, it would be unwise to define the fetus as human (hence tactically unwise ever to refer to the fetus as an "unborn child"). Analysis based on the deepest insights of molecular biology indicates the wisdom of sharply distinguishing the information for a valuable structure from the completed structure itself. It is interesting, and gratifying, to note that this modern insight is completely congruent with common law governing the disposal of dead fetuses. Abortion-prohibitionists generally insist that abortion is murder, and that an embryo is a person; but no state or nation, so far as I know, requires the dead fetus to be treated like a dead person. Although all of the states in the United States severely limit what can be done with a dead human body, no cognizance is taken of dead fetuses up to about five months' prenatal life. The early fetus may, with impunity, be flushed down the toilet or thrown out with the garbage—which shows that we never have regarded it as a human being. Scientific analysis confirms what we have always known.

## The Management of Compulsory Pregnancy

What is the future of compulsory pregnancy? The immediate future is not hopeful. Far too many medical people misconceive the real problem. One physician has written:

Might not a practical, workable solution to this most difficult problem be found by setting up, in every hospital, an abortion committee comprising a specialist in obstetrics and gynecology, a psychiatrist, and a clergyman or priest? The patient and her husband—if any—would meet with these men who would do all in their power to persuade the woman not to undergo the abortion. (I have found that the promise of a postpartum sterilization will frequently enable even married women with all the children they can care for to accept this one more, final pregnancy.) If, however, the committee members fail to change the woman's mind, they can make it very clear that they disapprove of the abortion, but prefer that it be safely done in a hospital rather than bungled in a basement somewhere.[13]

[13] H. Curtis Wood, Jr., "Letter to the Editor," *Medical Opinion and Review*, 3:11 (1967), p. 19.

What this author has in mind is plainly not a system of legalizing abortion but a system of managing compulsory pregnancy. It is this philosophy which governs pregnancies in the Scandinavian countries,[14] where the experience of a full generation of women has shown that women do not want their pregnancies to be managed by the state. Illegal abortions have remained at a high level in these countries, and recent years have seen the development of a considerable female tourist trade to Poland, where abortions are easy to obtain. Unfortunately, American legislatures are now proposing to follow the provably unworkable system of Scandinavia.

The drift down this erroneous path is not wholly innocent. Abortion-prohibitionists are showing signs of recognizing "legalization" along Scandinavian lines as one more roadblock that can be thrown in the way of the abolition of compulsory pregnancy. To cite an example: on February 9, 1916,* the *Courier*, a publication of the Winona, Minnesota Diocese, urged that Catholics support a reform law based on the American Law Institute model, because the passage of such a law would "take a lot of steam out of the abortion advocate's argument" and would "defeat a creeping abortionism of disastrous importance."[15]

Wherever a Scandinavian or American Law Institute type of bill is passed, it is probable that cautious legislators will then urge a moratorium for several years while the results of the new law are being assessed (though they are easily predictable from the Scandinavian experience). As Lord Morley once said: "Small reforms are the worst enemies of great reforms." Because of the backwardness of education in these matters, caused by the long taboo under which the subject of abortion labored, it seems highly likely that our present system of compulsory pregnancy will continue substantially without change until the true nature of the alternatives facing us is more widely recognized.

[14] David T. Smith (ed.), *Abortion and the Law*, Cleveland: Western Reserve University, 1967. p. 179.
[15] Anonymous, *Association for the Study of Abortion Newsletter*, 2:3 (1967), p. 6.

* 1966